THE COLD WAR
IN RETROSPECT

THE COLD WAR IN RETROSPECT

The Formative Years

■

ROGER S. WHITCOMB

Foreword by Anatoly Dobrynin

Westport, Connecticut
London

Library of Congress Cataloging-in-Publication Data

Whitcomb, Roger S., 1939–
    The Cold War in retrospect : the formative years / Roger S.
Whitcomb ; foreword by Anatoly Dobrynin.
        p.   cm.
    Includes bibliographical references and index.
    ISBN 0–275–96253–9 (alk. paper)
    1. United States—Foreign relations—Soviet Union.   2. Soviet
Union—Foreign relations—United States.   3. United States—Foreign
relations—1945–1989.   4. Cold War.   I. Title.
E183.8.S65W477   1998
327.73047—dc21   97–43943

British Library Cataloguing in Publication Data is available.

Library of Congress Catalog Card Number: 97–43943
ISBN: 0–275–96253–9

First published in 1998

Praeger Publishers, 88 Post Road West, Westport, CT 06881
An imprint of Greenwood Publishing Group, Inc.

Printed in the United States of America

The paper used in this book complies with the
Permanent Paper Standard issued by the National
Information Standards Organization (Z39.48–1984).

10 9 8 7 6 5 4 3 2 1

For Roberta

Contents

Foreword

The Soviet-American Cold War confrontation was not inevitable. As we move away from the long struggle that marked the relationship between our two countries during the last half of the twentieth century, historians are continuing to reassess the causes, nature, and conduct of that conflict. A crucial factor in this ongoing reassessment is the opening up of the archives of the former Soviet Union, as well as new materials becoming available in the West. Political scientists and historians on both sides have become more nuanced in their interpretations of the policies pursued by the decision-makers in Moscow and Washington. As a result, we are beginning to develop a more sophisticated view of the conflict.

Among other things, these developments are putting into question the long-standing dominant view in the West that the Soviet Union was primarily responsible for the Cold War and that the United States was simply responding to intransigence, if not conspiratorial thinking, in Moscow. It is in this sense that Professor Whitcomb, in *The Cold War in Retrospect: The Formative Years,* makes a valuable contribution to a clearer understanding of the conduct of both Russia's and America's decision-makers during the Second World War and the years immediately thereafter.

Whitcomb is one of a new group of analysts who have begun to synthesize the wealth of material now available on the Cold War, and to generate broad-based generalizations. His analysis of America's historic cultural tradition as an important conditioning factor in its approach to the outside world is especially useful. In particular, he rightly points out that it was that tradition which heavily influenced the development of his country's so-called containment rationale toward the Soviet Union—an approach which he characterizes as misguided, based on a misreading of both Russian intentions and capabilities.

The central thesis of his book is a valid one, namely, that the impasse was a product of mutual antagonisms, originating in misperceptions, misunder-standings and mistrust of one another's motives, In this sense, America was no less culpable than Soviet Russia for the tensions and conflicts that marked their relationship. As Whitcomb explores with great insight and clarity, the conduct of top-level decision-makers in the Roosevelt, Truman, and Eisenhower administrations contributed significantly to the conflict.

Americans have long preferred to ignore or belittle Russia's very real geopolitical concerns, especially our long-standing national interests grounded in the need for territorial security. The current debate on the future role of NATO in Europe is a case in point. This is not to suggest, of course, that America's leadership deliberately set out to frustrate and antagonize Soviet Russia in the postwar era. My many years in Washington would certainly confirm the view that America's leaders were honorable men who nevertheless inevitably approached their relations with others influenced by their own personal backgrounds, the realities of domestic politics, as well as that of American history.

The tragedy of the Cold War is that it took place in a world peopled not so much with "good guys" and "bad guys," but with flesh-and-blood human beings who were products of their generations and times. Hopefully, we have learned something from this experience, and will apply it constructively for the benefit of our children and grandchildren in the years to come.

Anatoly Dobrynin
Soviet Ambassador to the United States, 1962–1986

Preface

This book contains an analysis of and critical commentary on the general approach of American foreign policy toward Soviet Russia during the formative years of the Cold War. In a larger sense it is fundamentally a critique of the historical tradition of foreign affairs that conditioned that approach. The point of view reflected in these pages stems from a belief by this writer that America did not handle itself very well during the initial two decades of its post-World War II leadership role. Put in another way, it is we ourselves who must bear a major share of the responsibility for the endless litany of conflicts, crises, and military confrontations that came to mark the record of our foreign relations after 1945.

A key to an understanding of America's inability to exert a more positive impact on the world during this period is to be found in the substance of its foreign affairs tradition. That tradition, for all its strengths and virtues, possessed at least two flaws that served our people poorly in approaching the world during and after World War II. First, it led the country to entertain persistent misperceptions of the realities of the international milieu in which it had to operate. That these misperceptions occurred at all should not be surprising insofar as her conduct flowed from an image structure that reflected a peculiar parochial outlook not always consonant with reality elsewhere. Second, there was a certain incompatability between many of the nation's most cherished values—for example, its commitments to self-determination and democracy—and the habits of action that Americans exhibited in their relationships with others.

Americans were just not psychologically prepared during and after that conflict to assume the burdens of world responsibility. It seems as if history itself decided to play some sort of monstrous joke on us. At the very moment when the nation stepped squarely onto the world stage, the nature of that arena underwent a rather drastic change. The very makeup of the international system became something remote from its former reality, as the bipolar era came to pass.

Predictably, America, rushing backward into the future, sought to adapt the older classical diplomatic and political approaches, with which it had always been uncomfortable and with which it never really had had much experience, to meet its new international challenges. But the older order had passed and, consequently, Americans had to try to internalize, simultaneously and in a hurry, those tested qualities of traditional diplomatic wisdom that were still valuable, such as the need for moderation and flexibility in dealing with others, and those thorny new techniques of statecraft that virtually no one knew, such as the proper rationale for foreign aid, the role of propaganda, and the conduct of the new warfare.

In addition, the suddenness with which America assumed world leadership added difficulty to a situation already challenging enough. In less than ten years after the initial decisions of 1946–1947, America acquired over forty allies; indeed, the main outlines of the alliance structure were worked out in the mere three years between the proclamation of the Truman Doctrine in March, 1947 and the outbreak of the Korean War in June, 1950. Surely no other state in modern history ever acquired such awesome political and military power so ill-prepared by its history and with so little time to prepare itself.

America's approach to dealing with a difficult and paranoid Soviet Russia reflected these hard realities most pointedly. Toward the end of World War II America found itself in a virtually unique position in world history. Blessed with unparalleled material resources and human energies, the country was faced with an international situation that afforded it ample opportunity to translate these advantages into benefits not only for its own people but for the rest of mankind. But the American people were not able, as it turned out, to effect the sort of humane and constructive relationship with the rest of the world that one would have hoped.

In the last months of the war, America moved ahead confidently with plans to ensure that its citizens would have a more stable and amenable environment in which to prosper—a belief predicated in large part on an effective application of the principles of the Atlantic Charter, institutionalized in the structure of the new United Nations Organization. Within three years, these hopes lay floundering under the weight of an alarming, rapidly intensifying conflict with Soviet Russia. The Russian-American Cold War confrontation had dawned and would soon metamorphose into a struggle played out on many stages, plunging innumerable peoples into miasmas of death and destruction in a process that would last for some forty years.

A consensus quickly developed in this country concerning the root cause of this state of affairs: the perceived threat of Russian-inspired "communist" aggression and subversion. America's foreign policies were improvised in the late 1940s and early 1950s by people who were convinced that the one real danger to universal peace and tranquility was constituted by a world-wide communist conspiracy. It was to this threat—believed to have been maintained, in one fashion or another, at a constant threshold of danger—that much of

America's foreign policy after 1945 was directed.

Throughout the Cold War era, America's basic orientation remained constant. Insofar as Soviet Russia and its friends were responsible for the continuing threat of general war, for the constant exacerbation of international tensions, for the failure of the United Nations to keep the peace, America's vigilance had to be kept at a high level so that its necessarily extensive involvement in world affairs could be successfully carried forward. Only in this fashion would the fundamental values of the American people have a realistic chance of survival in an ever-dangerous international system.

Such was the predominant image of the world held by the overwhelming majority of America's decision-making elite throughout the Cold War era. How accurate was this vision? Was this approach to dealing with the Russians at bottom a realistic one, or was it in some sense an ill-advised posture that itself contributed to the very conditions of conflict that America was ostensibly trying to avoid?

It is a central thesis of this book that the monolithic nature of the Cold War confrontation that developed between the two giants was not inevitable. Rather, the impasse was a product of mutual antagonisms, originating in misperceptions, misunderstandings, and mistrust of one another's motives. In other words, the Russian–American colloquy was stimulated largely by mutual misperceptions stemming from their own peculiar historical experiences. In this sense, America was no less culpable than Soviet Russia for the tensions and conflicts that marked their relationship. Indeed, America's policies toward Soviet Russia during this period amounted to what may be called a "Hamletian" response to reality—a definable and definitive policy syndrome originating in the country's great disillusionment with Russia's conduct during and after the war. This theme is developed to the fullest in the belief that America's misconceptions and mistakes of this seminal period remain to a great degree misunderstood and unrenounced today.

THE COLD WAR
IN RETROSPECT

Introduction: America Meets Russia, 1941–1961: A Case Study

The widespread and destructive confrontation between America and Soviet Russia after 1944 would come to represent the centerpiece of interstate relations for the last half of the twentieth century. Perhaps only the Anglo-French competition of the eighteenth and nineteenth centuries rivals it in modern history. Historic conflicts of this sort,[1] profoundly destabilizing as this one surely was, tend to divide those who perceive such struggles as elemental, even inevitable, from those, such as this writer, who prefer to address their shorter-term causations and the possibilities that may have been missed for their avoidance.

Some fifty years have passed since scholars began to examine seriously the dimensions of this imbroglio. Despite an immense volume of literature, the debate over the causes of the conflict between the two giants remains one of the most contentious of modern times. If anything, scholars disagree in their assessments of causation and culpability today even more than when the examination began. Over four decades of scholarship have certainly generated no consensus.[2] The actual day-to-day record of the history of the interactions between the two states is fairly clear; but beyond an increasingly more accurate accounting of those events, the quest for meaning has often led observers into a twilight zone of confusion where the real motivations behind the policies are reduced to conjecture or simply assumed. Then, too, the absence of certainty has sometimes served to spur on those with axes to grind to hold fast to established intellectual preferences. As Ernest May reminds us, it is not unusual for debates of this sort to be framed in terms of preferred visions or frames of reference. "Within limits, interpretations that seem directly contradictory can all be true."[3]

In America two views of the Cold war once dominated the discussion. The traditional or orthodox approach blamed the Russians for the outbreak of the Cold War, Soviet Russia being portrayed as relentlessly expanionist and ideologically motivated. According to this view, American officials wanted to get along with the Russians but slowly came to realize that accommodation was impossible because of the Kremlin's drive for world domination. As the Cold War unfolded, a second view came to the fore—a "revisionist" interpretation that sought to explicate Russian policies as more conservative and reactive in character, while viewing America's actions as frequently provocative, needlessly confrontational, and even imperialistic. Since the early 1970s these contrasting explanations of American behavior have become blurred by a proliferation of studies emphasizing a variety of newer but divergent perspectives. Taking on such labels as "post-revisionist," "neo-realist," "corporatist," and "world system" orientations, these more recent points of departure have significantly added to the storehouse of our knowledge by concentrating more systematically on additional variables that may well have contributed to the conduct of the two superstates. Although a consensus on the roots of American Cold War policies does not exist, this new generation of scholarship has greatly enriched our knowledge of a wide range of issues by focusing more carefully on geopolitics, social structures, institutional arrangements, and the functioning of the American economy within the international economic order.

As a result, historians and political scientists have become more nuanced in their interpretations of developments in the Kremlin. Early views that Soviet Russia had a clear blueprint for world domination have been discredited. In place of the older interpretations attributing the sources of Russian conduct almost solely to Marxist-Leninist desires for world revolution or merely to the dynamics of a totalitarian society, more recent studies have highlighted such factors as Russian history and geography, traditional Russian expansionism, bureaucratic differences within the Russian decision-making elite, and baseline security requirements arising from Soviet Russia's unique geopolitical position.[4]

Revisionist historians have certainly been invaluable in forcing a rethinking of previous stereotyped interpretations, most especially the notion that Soviet Russia was solely or even largely responsible for the confrontation. The extent, however, to which some of these critics have gone in characterizing premeditated American actions as the major cause is simplistic.[5] One factor often overlooked in many of their studies is the decentralized nature of the American policy-making process. There has also been a tendency to ignore the fact that conflicts may develop over issues and interests that are not clearly thought through in advance or that may arise through imperceptible, incremental commitments, bureaucratic momentum, and mutual misperception.[6]

So, too, those who have emphasized the former Soviet Union's Marxist-Leninist pretensions as the major factor in the conflict long downplayed a variety of other inputs into the Soviet Russian decision-making process. The interplay of the personal predispositions of Russia's leadership, their not infrequent habit of employing "national themes" in factional party infighting, Communist Party elite perceptions or anticipation of effective mobilizing symbols in order to maintain and/or enhance personal positions and viewpoints, not to mention real stimuli in the outside world, may all be seen to have been important variables in its policy formation after 1917.[7]

Perhaps most crucially of all, there is the overwhelming importance of cultural tradition, born of actual experience, that inevitably conditioned the approaches of each country toward the other and toward the rest of the world. The main contention of the revisionist reinterpretation remains valid, namely, that America bears a heavy burden of responsibility for both the onset and continuation of the Cold War. It does not necessarily follow from this, however, that America's foreign policy-makers engaged in some sort of conspiracy to thwart legitimate Russian interests. What now needs to be done in Western scholarship on this question is to fit the available evidence into a more rigorous framework that takes into account the full range of factors that contributed to this impasse.[8]

American archival materials for this period are plentiful, but there still remains a dearth of Russian documents, and for this reason it has been difficult to discern with a high degree of confidence the motives and goals of Soviet Russia during these years. Even though that country's records are now becoming more widely available, we are still very far away from a definitive account of its foreign policies. It is encouraging to note that greater access for Western scholars to the archives of the Soviet era is now an ongoing reality—a situation that is permitting a fuller understanding of the motives of the Kremlin's decision makers over a seventy-four-year period. What follows is intended as a contribution to this end.

In the four chapters that constitute this book, an attempt is made to more clearly elucidate the root causes of and factors which came to characterize the Russian-American Cold War relationship. In considering the record of these years, America's longer-range tradition of foreign affairs, as previously analyzed and synthesized by the author in his *An Uncertain Tradition: The American Approach to Foreign Affairs* (1998), is applied to an in depth review of the substance of that relationship. Viewed in this manner, the record reveals an overriding pattern of persistence and continuity, with contradictory consequences for the American people and the world.

In retrospect, it is apparent that Soviet Russia's behavior during and after World War II confused America's decision makers, for the vast disparity betwen Russian "imperialist" action, limited to a precise region of the globe, and Russian revolutionary rhetoric clouded over for the American mind the essential factors of motivation and real intent underlying Soviet Russia's actions. Ultimately, the traditions of America's foreign affairs proved to be a major liability as its leaders sought to address the challenges posed by the Russian state.

The author's main point of departure here is that the so-called "containment rationale," which represented the centerpiece of America's approach to Soviet Russia after 1945, was a misguided approach based on a misreading of both Russian intentions and capabilities. Indeed, the main character of Russian policies throughout the post-1945 period was misinterpreted by Washington. America's image of the Russian state in the years after 1945 being restrained from occupying every piece of real estate not actually under the domination of the Red Army, solely out of fear of military resistance, is an oversimplification of the complex motives that actually guided the policies of a regime which by both ideology and historical experience was always acutely sensitive to the political and psychosocial conditions of geopolitical life and of national survival.

NOTES

1. Not so destabilizing according to John Lewis Gaddis, *The Long Peace: Inquiries into the History of the Cold War* (New York: Oxford University Press, 1987). See also his article, "Hanging Tough Paid Off," *Bulletin of the Atomic Scientists* (January/February 1989): 21–45. For an excellent study that effectively challenges the "long peace" thesis, see Michael Brecher and Jonathan Wilkenfeld, *Crisis, Conflict and Instability* (Oxford: Pergamon Press, 1989).

2. Witness the recent outpouring of monographs, articles, and books on the subject, reflecting new information stemming from the opening up of the Russian and East European archives, and the spate of commentaries regarding these new findings. Some have concluded that these newly-available sources refute the revisionist attempt to downplay ideology as the primary wellspring of Soviet Russia's conduct of the Cold War. See, for example, Douglas J. MacDonald, "Communist Bloc Expansion in the Early Cold War: Challenging Realism, Refuting Revisionism," *International Security* (Winter 1995-1996): 152–188; John Lewis Gaddis, "The Tragedy of Cold War History," *Foreign Affairs* (January/February 1994): 142–154; and Steven Merrit Miner, "Revelations, Secrets, Gossip and Lies," *New York Times Book Review*, May 14, 1995: 19–21.

A useful summary of early opinions is Norman A. Graebner, "Cold War Origins and the Continuing Debate: A Review of the Literature," *Journal of Conflict Resolution* (March 1969): 123–132. An excellent more recent summary of the full range of viewpoints at various times in the post-1945 era may be found in Michael H. Hunt, "The Long Crisis in U.S. Diplomatic History," *Diplomacy* (Winter 1992): 41–58.

3. Ernest R. May, ed., *American Cold War Strategy: Interpreting NSC 68* (Boston: St. Martin's Press, 1993), p. 90.

4. Russian archival materials and memoirs, for example, underscore the brutality of Joseph Stalin but nonetheless also suggest that he was opportunistic and pragmatic in his foreign policy, seeking to further Russian power but keenly attuned to constraints and risks.

5. See, for example, Gabriel Kolko, *The Politics of War: The World and United States Foreign Policy, 1943–1945* (New York: Random House, 1968), who argued that America's support for reactionaries and conservatives in Eastern Europe constituted a deliberate attempt to frustrate Soviet Russia's legitimate security goals.

6. For a still useful commentary on fallacies contained in models of Soviet behavior see Harvey Fireside, "Analyzing Soviet Affairs: Methods and Myths," *Problems of Communism* (May-June 1972): 77–79.

7. A cybernetic or organismic explanation of a state's foreign policies

presupposes a reactive propensity on the part of those who act in the name of the state that external events have an impact on attitudes and produce structural adaptation, and that attitudinal divergence and political conflict are persistent attributes of the political process even within rigidly hierarchical command systems. An early important effort emphasizing Western policies as an explanation for Soviet Russia's moves was the pioneering work of Marshall Shulman, *Stalin's Foreign Policy Reappraised* (Cambridge, Mass.: Harvard University Press, 1963). An even more profoundly reactive explanation can be found in William Gamson and Andre Modigliani, *Untangling the Cold War* (Boston: Little, Brown, 1971).

On the question of historic Cold War American views of Soviet Russia's foreign policy, see Herbert S. Dinerstein, *Intervention Against Communism* (Baltimore: Johns Hopkins University Press, 1967); William Zimmerman, "Elite Perspectives and the Explanation of Soviet Foreign Policy," *Journal of International Affairs* (1970): 84–98; William Welch, *American Images of Soviet Foreign Policy* (New Haven, Conn.: Yale University Press, 1970); William Welch and Jan F. Triska, "Soviet Foreign Policy Studies and Foreign Policy Models," *World Politics* (July 1971): 704–717; and William Zimmerman, "Soviet Foreign Policy Goals in the 1970s," *Survey* (Spring 1973): 188–198.

8. Trail blazing works in this context include Ole Holsti, "The Belief System and National Images: A Case Study," *Journal of Conflict Resolution* (September 1962): 245–271; Graham Allison, *Essence of Decision: Explaining the Cuban Missile Crisis* (Boston: Little, Brown,1976); and Robert Jervis, *Perception and Misperception in International Politics* (Princeton, N. J.: Princeton University Press, 1976). More recent initiatives designed to facilitate a broader appraisal include the 1990–1991 sessions of the so-called "Working Group on the Cold War," supported by the Institute for Policy Studies; a conference on "Rethinking the Cold War" convened at the University of Wisconsin in 1991–1992; and, commencing in 1991, "The Program on the International History of the Cold War," an archives-oriented, ongoing series of studies based at the Woodrow Wilson International Center for Scholars.

1

The Troubled Partnership: The Bear and Eagle in World War II

"A relationship with Russia will not get very far unless we give up our peculiar habit of regarding moral excellence as a prerequisite for wartime collaboration."[1]

—William Henry Chamberlin

On the eve of World War II a basic decision was made by the American government (in the face of a deeply divided citizenry) that isolationism could no longer represent a meaningful strategic foreign policy orientation. By deciding to play an active role in world affairs, it was now imperative that the Roosevelt administration put in place an acceptable rationale for formulating, prioritizing, and implementing policy goals and objectives. A key element in all of this was the necessity of analyzing as objectively as possible the major realities of the international situation. As it turned out, America was not able to do so always, everywhere, in a realistic manner. During the course of the war its lack of experience in European affairs, combined with the largely unrealistic legacies of its foreign affairs tradition, came in time to confound her decision makers' best intentions, in the process contributing to the great impasse with Soviet Russia that came to be called the Cold War.

That Soviet Russia and America should have come to such a disruptive and bitter confrontation reflected at the same time the great contradictions and even pathologies inherent in their respective traditions of foreign affairs—traditions that would contribute in great measure to the myriad misperceptions and misunderstandings of one another's attitudes, motives, and policies as the war proceeded. There would be numerous occasions during that conflict when opportunities for tension reduction and trust-building would be frittered away, paving the way for the disastrous policies that would follow later.

INTRODUCTION

The point of view reflected in this chapter proceeds from a number of assumptions—beliefs which the documentary record appears to confirm. The future Russian-American cold war conflict did not originate in a milieu of ignorance and naive images in Washington about Soviet Russia during the war. The available literature clearly indicates that the Roosevelt administration understood, albeit imperfectly, Moscow's desire, articulated with great frequency throughout the war, to regain and solidify some sort of territorial security in Eastern Europe. There was certainly no American attempt to create a sphere of influence in Eastern Europe in order to frustrate the realization of Russian interests in that region. Neither was American foreign policy toward Eastern Europe from 1941 to 1945 spurred by the same sort of balance-of-power considerations that later led to the promulgation of the Truman Doctrine, the Marshall Plan, or the North Atlantic Treaty. Nor are there any reliable data to confirm that American foreign policy during the war was determined to contain Bolshevism or, for that matter, leftist movements in general.

Finally, the gestation of this conflict cannot be attributed, as some have argued, to a group of high-level policymakers in America, from both the public and private sectors, conspiring to carve out economic markets for American business interests in Eastern Europe. Bona fide and verifiable evidence for this sort of conspiracy theory does not exist. Prior to 1939, America never sought to prevent the establishment of Russian hegemony in Eastern Europe, and it had articulated no seminal economic interests of its own in this part of the world. There is, however, ample evidence that by the end of the war many officials in the Roosevelt and Truman administrations had come around to the view that America's future prosperity would require an open world marketplace in the postwar era if the country was to avoid another depression.

In other words, a general mindset in regard to what would be necessary to enhance and preserve America's economic well-being had evolved within the Roosevelt administration during the war—a situation that would serve to condition the country's approach to Soviet Russia after the war was over. Thus, it was not until the Second World War, when Russian and American policies were joined specifically over Eastern Europe, that the stage was set for the all-out confrontation that was to follow. It is crucial to emphasize at the outset, however, that the Cold War imbroglio which ensued was neither planned nor calculated, *either in Washington or Moscow*, and was therefore all the more avoidable.[2] It is in this sense that the ensuing Russian American conflict bears the signature of genuine tragedy, as the internal contradictions of both America's and Russia's foreign affairs traditions impelled them forward toward misperception, misunderstanding, and confrontation.

AMERICAN ATTITUDES TOWARD RUSSIA BEFORE 1941

There is a strange sense of paradox about the relations between Russia and America during the eighteenth and nineteenth centuries. Few states had less in common than these two countries during those years.[3] The two peoples saw little of each other and their systems of government were radically different. Yet, when the two countries did encounter one another, it was often with great intensity and emotion. Prior to the beginning of the twentieth century, those interactions typically took place on the North American continent, conflict occurring over Russian settlements in Alaska and along the California coast. But the Russians invariably retreated in the face of America's posturing expansionists, even agreeing after the American Civil War to withdraw from North America altogether. It is therefore rather fruitless to tie in any direct way the antagonisms of the post-1945 years to the experiences of those earlier times. Indeed, some of the frenzy of the Cold War era may be attributable to the unfamiliarity of each state with the values, habits, assumptions, and interests of the other.[4]

Yet, dissension on ideological grounds had frequently manifested itself. In human terms, Russia often impinged on the American psyche as a specter of cruelty and repression—"the prisonhouse of nations." In the nineteenth century this perception focused on the minority peoples incorporated into the Russian empire during its centuries of expansion. The tsarist system was regarded with the same sort of ideological aversion as the Marxist-Leninist regime would be later—Alexander I and Nicholas I being disliked as much as Stalin. And the feeling was mutual, the Russian autocracy at that time distrusting Britain and America as the home of liberal ideas which, if spread abroad, would lead to revolution and disorder.

The Romanovs' suppression of the Poles in 1830 and their intervention in Hungary in 1848 created an uproar in America. Later, persecuted Russians would be included in America's lexicon of "tired and poor." After 1881 for example, we reacted very negatively to the repressive policies of Alexander III. Indeed, by 1913 some 300,000 Russian immigrants—mostly Jews, Catholics, and Lutherans—had come to America. The basic anti-government message of these immigrants did much to undermine the official pragmatic diplomatic relationship that marked nineteenth-century relations. Moreover, many of those who came to America were political activists, some militant—radical trade unionists, anarchists, and members of political sects like the Social Democratic Bund. Over time these activists came to be viewed with anxiety and even alarm by the established order in America—as threats to "our way of life."[5]

The first real clash, however, came over China at the turn of the century. During the last decade of the century, America had come to the view that an "open door" to trade with China's rich province of Manchuria was a prerequisite for its future prosperity. Russia, bent on dominating Manchuria, represented the most direct threat to that policy. In response to America's call for unimpeded access, the Romanovs sought to shut off to foreign businessmen with whom they could not compete successfully those markets over which the Russians had control. It was for that reason that we tended to tilt toward the British and Japanese during this period, and why Japan's attack on Russia in 1904 did not generate any particular cry of indignation in America, although Theodore Roosevelt did play the role of peacemaker. In fact, Roosevelt came away from those negotiations with a rather negative image of the Russians, who "are utterly insincere and treacherous; they have no conception of the truth . . . and no regard for others."[6] By 1914, when Russia allied itself with the British and French, relations between Washington and St. Petersburg could hardly be said to have been warm and friendly. Colonel Edward House, a close adviser of President Wilson, put it baldly when he said that "If the Allies win, it means the domination of Russia on the continent of Europe; and if Germany wins, it means the unspeakable tyranny of militarism for generations to come."[7]

The triumph of the Bolsheviks in Russia generated an intense reaction in America. It may well be, however, that the vehemence of our response to the Bolshevik revolution stemmed more from the stresses and conflicts in American society than with the behavior of the Bolsheviks themselves. The Russian Revolution caught America at a time of deeply unsettling social change, intensified by our involvement in the war. The country's social fabric was strained by class struggle, the stresses involved with assimilating millions of new immigrants, and the women's rights movement. It was inevitable that these realities would produce some volatile antigovernment behavior. The new brand of domestic "radicalism" that would emerge, marked as it was by sporadic anti-system violence, came to be viewed by many Americans as unwarranted and unacceptable. More to the point, these activities were seen by some as a projection of Marxism-Leninism from abroad. During the course of the war, this "imported" brand of radicalism would be largely discredited, and the state-sponsored persecution that came immediately thereafter was stimulated in part by the alleged association with Bolshevism by some of these groups. That is why the so-called Red Scare of 1919 was so intense, even hysterical.[8]

As for the official government reaction, as David McFadden points out,[9] American policy toward the Bolshevik regime remained for a long time in a state of flux, influenced by contradictory influences. This period of vacillation over what course to take regarding Russia sprang in part from the difficulty in obtaining accurate information as to what was happening in Russia and to an unwillingness by the Wilson administration to commit itself irrevocably to a particular line while the situation was in such a state of fluidity. Then, too, it reflected a conflict between those Americans who regarded the Bolshevik regime as the quintessence of evil and those who, for pragmatic political and economic reasons, as well as humanitarian sentiments, held that American interests in Russia required the normalization of relations.

Wilson's own attitude was a reflection in microcosm of the contradictions inherent in the traditional American approach to self-determination and radical revolutionary upheaval. In his January 1918 message to Congress in which he presented the historic Fourteen Points for a just and lasting peace in the world, point six referred specifically to Russia in which he demanded that she be given full opportunity to decide her own future without foreign interference. But with the Bolshevik government's signing of the Brest-Litovsk agreement in March, Wilson was prevailed upon by the Allies to participate in two armed interventions in the Russian civil war—interventions that began in the summer.

In European Russia, the Allies intervened ostensibly to prevent large stores of war goods from falling into German hands. Some 5,000 American troops were dispatched to Murmansk and Archangel and ended up, whatever the original motivation for their being there, defending the White Russians and dissident Bolsheviks against Leninist forces. The other intervention took place in Siberia, designed to frustrate alleged Japanese designs on that area. In the case of the Siberian invasion, the presense of Western forces, including some 9,000 American troops, tended to favor the reactionary anti-communist forces there. In both cases, American troops ended up fighting Bolshevik loyalists. The Bolshevik response was to organize the Red Army to defend the country and to institute a radical policy of "war communism" at home in order to weed out the forces of opposition to the regime.[10]

In October, Bolshevik Commissar for Foreign Affairs Georgi Chicherin addressed a long and bitter letter to Wilson, asking him how he could reconcile his Fourteen Points with America's action in Siberia. America, said Chicherin, had faced the "acid test" and failed.[11] Despite this situation, it was to America that the new Russian government turned after the November 1918 armistice with an offer to negotiate existing differences. In order to end the civil war and the foreign intervention, the Bolsheviks indicated a willingness to recognize the debts owed by Russia to the Allies, which had earlier been repudiated; to grant concessions for the exploitation of Russia's natural resources; and even to discuss the possible cession of territory. They also were ready to pledge noninterference in the internal affairs of other countries and to meet with all other political groups in Russia.[12]

The Allies never did ascertain the sincerity of these far-reaching Russian concessions. After much discussion at Versailles, it was agreed to hold a meeting of all Russian factions on some neutral territory, but the refusal of the other incipient "governments" on Russian territory to deal with the Bolsheviks torpedoed any such meeting. Wilson continued to hope for a solution to the Russian problem and, to that end, sent a personal representative, William C. Bullitt, on a secret mission to Moscow to find out more about the new government. Convinced that the Bolsheviks were here to stay, Bullitt sat down with the Bolshevik leaders and drafted an agreement between Russia and the Allies that reiterated much of Moscow's previous willingness to be reasonable in regard to debts and noninterference. In the course of these discussions, the Russians proposed that America take over all Allied claims against Russia. The Russians evidently believed that it would be advantageous for them to have only one creditor, hoping that Washington would offer better terms than its associates.

Bullitt returned to Versailles with the proposed settlement, but it was rejected by the American president who had by now become distracted with other things. No doubt, the recent victories of the anti-Bolshevik armies under Admiral Kolchak in Siberia contributed to the cold shoulder. Then, too, any rapprochement with the Bolshevik government at that time would have aroused strong opposition in America. Wilson also appeared impervious to any information about Russian events that contradicted his own vision for the future of a liberal democratic world. A welter of misinformation concerning Bolshevik conduct had filtered across the Atlantic. Meanwhile, the founding of the Third Communist International in March 1919, followed in September by the establishment of an affiliated Communist Party in America, seemed to confirm the world revolutionary aims of the Bolsheviks.[13]

The State Department did not help matters much by publishing that summer information on the activities of the Bolsheviks—an action that helped to fuel public apprehension.[14] By the summer of 1919 Wilson had abandoned his verbal policy of neutrality, stating that the Moscow regime was "the negation of everything that is American."[15] Thus, Wilson was one of the first in a long line of American leaders whose ideological blinkers insulated them from the realities of Russian affairs. In the end, Wilson refused to open diplomatic relations, declaring that Lenin's government "is based upon the negation of every principle of honor and good faith."[16] At the Versailles Peace Conference in 1919, the victorious Allies sought to isolate the Bolsheviks by creating a ring of buffer states around Russia—a policy that led a young American observer named Walter Lippmann to lament that the victors had created a military cordon sanitaire, when peace required a "sanitary Europe" capable of building a society based on social justice.[17]

This orientation would be the basic American approach to Russia for the next fourteen years as Russian-American relations did not exist in any productive sense until 1933.[18] The activities of the Comintern under Lenin and Stalin, the expressed opposition of the Bolsheviks not only to traditional American liberal institutions but also to American commercial interests abroad, plus the refusal of the Bolshevik government to recognize American claims and debts in Tsarist Russia, all combined to make American foreign policy until after the 1932 presidential election hostile to Soviet Russia. Washington's refusal to establish diplomatic relations with the Russian revolutionary regime symbolized this hostility. Diplomatic recognition, it was felt, was out of the question, despite the fact that most other states resumed ordinary relations with Moscow by the mid-1920s. Nonrecognition by America of international situations that are viewed as threatening to order, stability, and the preservation of the status quo was thus once again manifested.

Trade was a major factor responsible for a turnabout in American-Russian relations in 1933. At the same time, the rise of mutual enemies proved to be more powerful than their ideological differences. After 1933 both Stalin and Franklin Roosevelt were concerned about Japanese expansionism, and by the end of the decade with Hitler's actions in Europe. But Roosevelt's hopes that relations with Moscow would lead to the settlement of the American claims against Soviet Russia proved baseless, while Stalin's efforts to get Washington to work together with the European democracies and Russia to contain Hitler were fruitless. Continued mistrust and mutual unwillingness to employ military power against the Axis countries combined to make Russian-American relations until August 1939 distant and "correct" at best.

At the Eighteenth Congress of the ruling Communist Party of the Soviet Union (C.P.S.U.) in early 1939, Stalin declared that the West was really hoping to turn Hitler east toward the Russians. He would not let this happen, he said, even though the economic crisis in the capitalist world made inevitable another imperialist war. But this time, he added, Russia would not bail out the West.[19] American distrust was intensified greatly by the Russian German pact in 1939. Indeed, relations after the German-Russian assault on Poland hit rock bottom, and only the persistence of isolationism prevented the development in Washington of a sentiment similar to that in London and Paris for yet another intervention against the Russians. Soviet Russia's invasion of Finland in 1940 provoked an even more intense outrage.

Even considering the record of Western hostility toward Soviet Russia during the interwar period, the reaction to the Russian invasion of Finland was astonishing. Finland, it may be recalled, had had close ties with Nazi Germany and a strong anti-Russian orientation. Already at war with Germany, despite little fighting, the French and British came within an ace of declaring war on Soviet Russia. And the League of Nations, which had ignored previous aggressions by Italy, Japan, and Germany, then proceeded to expel the Russians—the only member of the League of Nations ever to be so treated. One does not have to accept the standard Russian interpretation of these events to understand how they could see in these actions proof that their fears were well founded.[20] Even the German invasion of Russia in June 1941 was not sufficient immediately to bring about a significant shift in American public opinion in favor of Russia.[21] It required, as it had in 1917, the coming of a world war and a mutual sense of overriding danger from common opponents to produce anything even close to genuine rapprochement between Washington and Moscow—not the best spirit to start a new partnership.

In retrospect, America's recognition of Soviet Russia in 1933 never really did dispel the legacy of suspicion that had characterized their relationship after 1917. The great purges of the late 1930s dissipated much of the respect that Soviet Russia had gained as a result of its economic advances, its support of collective security after its admission to the League of Nations, and the adoption of its new "democratic" constitution in 1936. The Russians' participation in the traumatic events of the months immediately preceding the outbreak of the World War II—the Molotov-Ribbentrop Pact, the division of Poland, the brutal invasion of Finland—all made Stalin look particularly venal. So, too, Moscow's decision to sign a nonaggression deal with the Japanese in April 1941 seemed to confirm the view held by many in the West that Stalin's Russia was little better than Hitler's Germany.

It is in the context of these events that America and Russia found themselves joined together in late 1941 in alliance against a common enemy—the one, despite its ideological baggage, well versed in great power politics, and the other inexperienced in such matters, ignorant of and hostile to the traditions of power politics, and most assuredly poorly equipped by the traditions of its past to deal effectively with the challenges before it. Such marriages are not made in heaven.

THE GROWING STORM

With the invasion of Soviet Russia by the Germans in June 1941, the whole tenor and attitude of America toward the Russians began to change—but not, however, without serious misgivings. While the State Department announced in the wake of the invasion that America would aid the Russians, it added that the principles and doctrines of "communistic dictatorship" were as intolerable and as alien to America's beliefs as those of the "Nazi dictatorship." With that in mind, Roosevelt sent Harry Hopkins to Moscow in July to seek to ascertain where the Russians now stood. Disagreeing with most existing assessments that Soviet Russia would not survive the Nazi onslaught, Hopkins offered an optimistic view of that beleagured country's prospects, and urged that Washington provide assistance.[22]

This was followed by a three-power conference in Moscow in late September to discuss reciprocal deliveries of war materials. Lend Lease, which had been authorized by the Congress in March, was extended to Soviet Russia in November with the amending of American neutrality laws to permit arming of merchant ships and to allow American shipping to carry cargoes to belligerent ports. With the framework now in place to provide massive assistance to the belleagured Russians, President Roosevelt on November 2 authorized shipments of up to $1 billion to Moscow, at no interest, debt payments to commence five years after the war was over.[23]

In the summer of 1941 the first critical event in the evolving Russian-American conflict over Eastern Europe took place—a situation that involved both the British and the Russians. During July rumors were rife in Washington that London and Moscow had engaged in secret negotiations concerning postwar territorial and political arrangements in that part of the world. These reports suggested that the Russians intended to support the reestablishment of independent Polish, Czech, and Yugoslav states at the end of the war and, to that end, sponsor the creation of so-called "national committees of liberation" to be composed of prisoners-of-war from those countries in Soviet Russia. In this way, it was argued, they might be able to obtain Russian hegemony in Eastern

Europe at the war's conclusion.[24]

In a similar vein, there were indications that the British government was seeking to conclude a surreptitious understanding with Yugoslavia—a train of events that smacked of the situation during the World War I when America's allies negotiated secret agreements to redivide Europe.[25] State Department officials were convinced that one of the reasons Woodrow Wilson had so much difficulty in getting a just peace enacted at Versailles was the belated discovery that the British and French had secretly worked out a series of agreements regarding the postwar world. They were determined to learn from Wilson's experience.[26]

The State Department accordingly prevailed upon Roosevelt to seek a statement from British Prime Minister Churchill that "no postwar peace commitments as to territories, populations, or economies had been given."[27] These same concerns prompted American officials to raise the question of postwar commitments during the shipboard meetings held in the Atlantic between Churchill and Roosevelt in August 1941. During this initial meeting with Churchill, FDR announced that he thought it would be a good idea if the two leaders drew up a joint declaration setting forth certain broad principles that could serve as a basis for common policy.[28] That declaration became known as the Atlantic Charter. Four of its clauses bear repeating:

No. 1 - Their countries seek no aggrandizement, territorial or other;

No. 2 - They desire to seek no territorial changes that do not accord with the freely expressed wishes of the peoples concerned;

No. 3 - They respect the right of all peoples to choose the form of government under which they will live; and they wish to see sovereign rights and self-government restored to those who have been forcibly deprived of them;

No. 8 - They believe that all nations of the world, for realistic as well as spiritual reasons, must come to the abandonment of the use of force.

Unfortunately, the manner in which the Atlantic Charter was adopted and the issues it avoided would prove to be a continuing and intensifying irritant in Russian American relations. For starters, the actual inception of these principles left something to be desired. Prior to the August meetings, for example, no exchange of views had occurred with respect to them. During the actual conversations, Roosevelt and Churchill spent almost no time discussing their substance or even the most appropriate language in which to couch their statement. Agreement occurred with little or no debate.[29]

Moreover, the Charter made no reference to any specific events in Eastern Europe that had initially provoked concern and contributed to the American urge to draft a statement of common principles. Rather, Roosevelt and the Department of State focused their attention on preventing the initiation of secret wartime agreements in general. The fact that these secret agreements involved Eastern Europe was apparently not of primary importance and did not produce a definition of any specific American goals or objectives in this part of the world at that time. On the contrary, the record seems to indicate that American officials, preoccupied with the need to avoid the mistakes of the World War I, seized upon these principles as a means to promote a generic postwar peace without reference to particular issues.

There also appeared to exist no specific concern regarding the implications of a commitment by the American government to ensure the right of all peoples to determine their own political arrangements and postwar frontiers. Nor is there any record that there was any discussion regarding the difficulties that might be involved in achieving their implementation including securing the ad-herence of other states to these principles.[30] Evidently no one argued, as the Lon-don Polish government-in-exile would later do, that the abstract character of the principles might render them inadequate to meet the actual conditions in Europe.[31] In short, the political and intellectual rationale behind the statement of these principles was not very well thought out. Nevertheless, these principles were soon generally accepted as the basis for postwar peace and would later guide America in its dealings with Soviet Russia over a variety of questions in Eastern Europe.

Thus, America's first tentative war aims were announced even before she was an active participant in the conflict. The message was clear: If America was to get involved in the war, it would have to be based on a highly idealistic set of principles, true to America's foreign policy tradition of antagonism toward power politics. In terms of national psychology, then, the Atlantic Charter was a clear statement both of America's anxieties about and disdain of traditional European diplomacy.

In September 1941, the other governments at war against Germany, including Soviet Russia, were prevailed upon to approve these principles, but not without Moscow taking careful note of the special situation in that country. "Considering that the practical application of these principles will necessarily adapt itself to the circumstances, need, and historical peculiarities of particular countries, the Soviet Government can state that a consistent application of these principles will secure the most energetic support on the part of the government and peoples of the Soviet Union."[32]

In December 1941, several days after Pearl Harbor, British Foreign Secretary Anthony Eden went to Moscow. The purpose of the trip was to explore the prospects for a political-military alliance with Russia. The British were concerned about the possibility that any potential unhappiness with British cooperation might lead the Russians to sign a separate peace with Germany.[33] During Eden's visit, Stalin made explicit his desire for a secret protocol defining working arrangements for the demarcation of future boundary lines in Eastern Europe, insisting upon international recognition of Russia's pre-June 22, 1941 frontier, its reincorporation of the Baltic states, and reacquisition of parts of Rumania. He also proposed but did not press for the establishment of the Curzon line as the frontier between Soviet Russia and Poland.[34] When Eden observed at one point in the meeting that Russia's desire for spheres of influence might violate the Atlantic Charter, Stalin asked whether the Charter was directed at Germany or Soviet Russia?[35]

The trip quickly aroused suspicions in Washington. The State Department contended that the proper way to allay Russian suspicions regarding British and American cooperation in the prosecution of the war was to continue military aid. The European Division of the State Department in particular was determined to uphold the principles of the Atlantic Charter and the unity of the military alliance against Germany by seeking the postponement of all secret treaties or territorial arrangements until after the war. The department argued that premature approval of postwar frontiers would weaken the anti-Axis coalition by introducing mutual suspicions among its members. They believed that abandonment of the principle of no territorial commitments would place the two Western governments in a difficult position to resist additional Russian demands which would almost certainly follow, thus encouraging Stalin to resort to similar tactics to further what they termed "more far-reaching demands."[36] There is no record as to what the division meant by these demands. The negotiations were ultimately broken off when Eden made it clear to Stalin that he did not think he could make any commitments in light of the American position—a response that certainly aroused suspicion in the Russian dictator.[37]

What is revealing in the available documentation is that State Department officials did not seem to view Russian territorial and political interests in Eastern Europe as issues to be considered in their own right. Rather they were committed to upholding the more general aims of the unity of the Allied military alliance, the integrity of the Atlantic Charter, and the right of self-determination for all. Their bias was one of proceeding from general principles, for example, no settlements until after the war, to particular cases. Consequently, from the beginning, they avoided addressing the specific merits of the Eastern European issues in and of themselves.

While these officials seemed to understand what Soviet Russia's goals and objectives were in Eastern Europe,[38] they avoided a specific definition of American interests or goals in that part of the world. Above all, they did not consider Russian demands in relation to what frontier lines Washington would prefer. There is no indication that they justified their statements that the territorial adjustments sought by Russia would make Moscow the dominant power in the region with any identification of the reasons why this would or would not be in the American national interest. Their assumption that discussions of specific territorial settlements might prove embarrassing and handicap proceedings at any postwar peace conference did not lead to a definition of exactly what aims Washington would have at such a conference.[39] The justification for American policy implied that we did indeed have interests in Eastern Europe, but these were not delineated.

In February 1942, the British government formally requested American approval of Russian territorial demands in Eastern Europe in order to ensure Moscow's cooperation for the remainder of the war and thereafter. Contending that a simple refusal would lead to a deterioration in relations with Soviet Russia, the British Foreign Office argued:

On the assumption that Germany is defeated, that German military strength is destroyed and that France remains for a considerable period at least a weak power, there will be no counterweight to Russia in Europe, and cooperation will be desirable:
   —Because she might otherwise be tempted to collaborate with Germany in view of historical tendency to, and economic urge for, these powers to work together;
   —In order that we may recreate some reasonable balance of power in Europe, destroyed by the collapse of France against the possibility of revived Germany;
   —In order that, militarily speaking, Germany should be encircled.[40]

Faced with American obduracy, the British proposed a compromise giving Soviet Russia assurances that the two countries would support a demand by Moscow to establish bases in territories contiguous to Russia. The Roosevelt administration's response was to insist that the resolution of these matters should wait until the end of the war.[41]

The British sought to counter the American position by maintaining that the enjoyment of self-government by the Baltic states had not been very successful between the wars, and that FDR was being unduly optimistic in supposing that some form of security in lieu of the reoccupation of the Baltic states would prove acceptable to Stalin. Churchill suggested that the principles of the Atlantic Charter ought not to be construed so as to deny to Russia the frontier occupied when Germany attacked in 1941.[42] Not until March 1944 would the American government accept Churchill's contention that Soviet Russia's incorporation of the Baltic states did not fall within the provisions of the Atlantic Charter,[43] but by then that admission had become weighed down with serious negative baggage.

Those in Washington responsible for defending American policy never seriously addressed these British arguments. FDR characterized the original British recommendations as "provincial."[44] The British rebuttals were neither accepted nor refuted: that Stalin's demands for security would not be satisfied simply by German disarmament; that supply of material to Soviet Russia would not be a sufficient indication of good faith; that Moscow signed the Atlantic Charter on the assumption that the principles became effective for them on the basis of their 1941 frontiers. Other British concerns were ignored: the possibility that Moscow might collaborate with Germany; that an early German defeat with an accompanying rise in Russian influence and prestige would increase pressure for the establishment of communist governments in Europe; the need to influence Russian policy while it was still in a fluid state; and the strategic and historical reasons for Russian domination of the Baltic states.[45]

By April 1942 the British government informed Washington it was ready to go it alone and sign a treaty with Stalin in which Britain would recognize the integrity of Russia's territories prior to June 1941.[46] In response, Roosevelt proposed to Stalin that he send Molotov to Washington for an exchange of views on military questions. "I have in mind a very important military proposal involving the utilization of our armed forces in a manner to relieve your critical Western Front," he said. While aiming to reinforce the Russian war effort, such military plans might also serve to distract Stalin from his territorial demands. Sherwood tells us that Harry Hopkins apparently indicated to Eden in London that this would take the heat off the Russian politically-motivated diplomatic requests.[47]

However, if the primary purpose of Roosevelt's invitation to Molotov was indeed to bargain military aid for the withdrawal of Russia's frontier demands, it was never consciously pursued. At no time did Roosevelt or any of his advisors discuss military plans in relation to Russian territorial demands, although the American ambassador to London, John G. Winant, was instructed to reiterate to Molotov the American opposition to boundary discussions until after the war.[48] Molotov then surprised the British by agreeing suddenly to sign a treaty that made no reference to territorial settlements, including the incorporation of the Baltic states into Soviet Russia. On May 26, 1942, the treaty was signed. Reasons for Molotov's seemingly abrupt change are unclear.[49]

Misunderstanding and friction in regard to the opening of a second front continued over the course of much of the next two years. Following Roosevelt's meeting with Molotov, he sent Hopkins to Moscow to follow up, leading in early June 1942, to a joint Russian-American communique pointing out that complete agreement was reached during the discussions concerning the urgent need to open a second front in Europe in 1942.[50] As the summer wore on, however, manpower deficiencies and other logistical problems made it increasingly clear that such a front was not yet feasible.[51] In August Churchill went to Moscow to give Stalin the bad news that the Western Allies would not be opening a second front in Europe during 1942. A North African landing was proposed instead. Periodically during the remaining months of 1942 and well into 1943, Stalin kept badgering his Western Allies as to the projected date for a second front, while Roosevelt and Churchill kept putting it off, all the while justifying their actions in terms of military exigencies and bureaucratic obstacles.

An attempt to get the Big Three together in early 1943 failed. Evidently, Stalin was not too enthused about such a meeting given the lack of progress on a second front in Europe, although he pleaded urgency of business back in Russia as the official reason for not attending. It would be left to Churchill and Roosevelt, meeting in Casablanca, Morocco, in January 1943 to deal with manifold problems confronting the anti-Axis coalition. The most important piece of business to come out of Casablanca was the announced policy of unconditional surrender regarding the Germans.

Unconditional surrender as a strategic approach to Nazi Germany made little sense, but it was understandable, given America's diplomatic inexperience in dealing with the outside world, her distaste for power politics, and her propensity for reasoning by analogy. For what was unconditional surrender but a way out of not having to deal with the complexities of the real world? Moreover, it was retrospective in that we needed to right the mistakes of World War I. As Germany had not yet been defeated on the battlefield, it was therefore imperative to ensure that she would not wriggle out of her self-made difficulties this time. Moreover, by demanding unconditional surrender from the Germans, Roosevelt could continue to postpone political settlements until after the war. Some of Roosevelt's military and diplomatic advisers tried to get him to modify his stand, but to no avail.[52]

In late 1943 Averell Harriman replaced William Standley as the American ambassador to Russia, while John Deane took over the military mission at the embassy. Their appointments flowed from Washington's growing recognition that closer strategic planning for the second front was necessary, and to solicit Russian support for the war against Japan. The primary purpose of the Harriman-Deane mission was to improve diplomatic and military relations. As such it would be able to ascertain more clearly how Russia was going to view its relations with her Western allies in the future.[53]

Standley had already come around to the point of view that the administration's general policy of acceding to Moscow's requests had only appeared to arouse suspicion of our motives in their minds, even being perceived as a sign of weakness on our part. It was not long before Harriman began to accept this view as both he and Deane, increasingly frustrated with their dealings with the Russians in Moscow, began to grow more critical of the Russians' behavior. Support for a quid pro quo policy was growing at the American mission. No doubt our difficulties in dealing with the Russians on relatively simple, routine matters had contributed to Standley, Harriman, and Deane increasingly wondering "what was going on?"[54]

The first meeting between Roosevelt, Churchill and Stalin came at Teheran in November-December 1943. If there was ever a moment when the Roosevelt Administration should have set out for the Russians whether any important American national interests were involved in Eastern Europe, this was the moment. And it cannot be said that Roosevelt was unaware of the developing tension. Early in November, Harriman presented Roosevelt with a blunt assessment of Stalin's determination to prevent the re-creation of a cordon sanitaire around Soviet Russia.[55] But the record indicates that the American president did not engage in a thorough review of America's options, let alone come up with some sort of clear-cut position.[56] The documentation suggests that Roosevelt, in the one in-depth, substantive discussion he had with Stalin on this issue, left the impression that Eastern Europe was important to America only as a factor to be taken into account in the upcoming presidential election.[57] Thus, because Roosevelt failed to articulate for the Russian leader any vital long-range American interests in the region, it is understandable how Stalin might have concluded that there weren't any.

Meanwhile, at the conference itself, Stalin, in response to Washington's expressed interest in getting assistance from Moscow in prosecuting the war in the Far East, laid out just what political compensation for such aid he would expect: the Kurile Islands and lower Sakhalin Island, leases at Port Arthur and Darien, control of the Chinese Eastern and South Manchurian railways, and recognition of the People's Republic of Outer Mongolia. There is no record that FDR responded to these points either at the conference or after his return to Washington.

In early February 1944, Roosevelt wrote Stalin, conjuring up the spirit of Teheran, and averred that there were indeed vital Russian security interests involved in Eastern Europe. He went on to suggest that Poland, for example, was more important to America as a symbolic issue of international cooperation than for any other reason.[58] The Polish question, to be sure, had become by this time the major problem in the evolving Russian-American relationship.

The Polish Question

Beginning in the summer of 1941, the exile London Polish government, composed of political leaders who had fled that country in the wake of the German-Russian attack in September 1939,[59] sought American support for the following goals: abrogation of the 1939 Nazi-Soviet agreement, postponement of territorial settlements during the war, creation of a Polish army inside Russia, and release of Polish political and military prisoners in that country.[60] At first, the Roosevelt administration merely reacted by informing Moscow in very general terms of an American interest in seeing the difficulties between the Poles and Russians resolved. In response to the London Polish government's initial wartime position on this matter, the State Department, interestingly, did not restate American disapproval of any territorial or political settlements created by military force.   Apparently they did not want to jeopardize Russian-American military cooperation and hoped to remain neutral in the dispute. Out of fear of provoking Russian accusations of foreign intervention in its internal affairs, Washington also refused requests to undertake initiatives to improve the conditions of Poles inside Russia at that time.[61]

In July 1941, a Polish-Russian agreement was signed, providing for restoration of diplomatic relations, military cooperation in the defeat of Germany, Russian recognition that the 1939 pact was no longer valid, and formation of a Polish army and relief activities on Russian soil. In December, an agreement was reached for the establishment of nineteen special local Polish relief delegations in Russian communities with large populations of Poles.

The London Polish government, however, became increasingly irritated by Moscow's interference in the formation of a Polish army inside Soviet Russia and in the conduct of relief activities among Poles exiled there. At the same time, the Russians objected to Polish initiatives to create postwar confederations in East Europe, accusing the Poles of attempting to build up a bloc of states hostile to Soviet Russia.[62] Unwittingly, a continuing American advocacy of a policy of postponement of all territorial and political settlements neither halted

Polish and Russian efforts to resolve their territorial/political disputes on their own terms, nor relieved the Roosevelt administration's need to react to the mounting conflict between the Russian and Polish governments.

In July 1942 the Russian government closed down these relief offices and arrested members of the delegations on charges of collecting information about Poles inside Russian prisons, of furnishing information on the conditions of life of Poles in Russia, and of circulating anti-Russian newspapers. The American response to these arrests was one of simply stating that we hoped things could be worked out.[63] Washington responded in a similar vein when the Russians announced in January 1943, following the Russian military triumph at Stalingrad, that it considered the 1939 pact line to be its western frontier and all Polish citizens east of this line to be automatically Russian nationals, while at the same time, the London Polish government demanded a return to the frontier established by the 1921 Treaty of Riga.[64]

Roosevelt's message to Polish Prime Minister Wladyslaw Sikorski, in response to his request for America to take up the Polish position, was at one and the same time another restatement that America supported an independent Poland after the war, but also a rejection of their request for a public statement that the Atlantic Charter principles would be implemented in the drawing of the Polish postwar frontier. This position was apparently an affirmation of the view of the American ambassador in Moscow at this time, William Standley, who argued that any initiative on our part would serve to worsen, not improve, Polish-Russian relations.[65]

In April 1943, the deterioration in relations between the Polish and Russian governments reached a new climax with the German announcement of the discovery near Katyn of a mass grave containing the bodies of over 8,000 Polish army officers allegedly executed by the Russians in 1940. In response, the London Polish government issued a public request to the International Red Cross to conduct an impartial investigation of the alleged massacre. Stalin immediately informed Washington and London that Soviet Russia would not tolerate this "fascist slander" perpetrated by the German and London Polish governments and therefore intended to interrupt relations with the London Poles.[66]

America's continued avoidance of any direct discussion of the Polish question had now begun to appear to Stalin that the Americans and London Poles were working together to frustrate Russia's bona fide frontier claims.[67] But that was a misreading of the American position. American opposition continued to be based on a desire to postpone consideration of all frontier disputes until the end of the war, and was not simply an unwillingness to become involved in this particular question in order to block Russian demands.

It is interesting to note that by the spring of 1943 Standley had begun to criticize the American approach. Noting that the specific reasons for the break had been differences over frontiers and the composition of the Polish government, Standley suggested that the solution of at least one of these questions was necessary to end the impasse. Instead of addressing the problem of Polish citizenship, which Moscow would be unwilling to discuss at this stage unless the frontier question was also considered, Standley proposed that Sikorski be persuaded to eliminate from his government those elements whose presence made harmony with the Russians impossible. Acknowledging the American reluctance to interfere in the internal affairs of another United Nations country under normal circumstances, Standley concluded that the present situation at that time was not normal.[68] Washington, however, demurred.

During 1944 Russia's demands for an acceptance of the Curzon Line frontier and its attacks against the London Poles mounted. In January, Molotov accused the Polish government of saying that the Treaty of Riga frontier was immutable and went on to state that Stanislaw Mikolajczyk, the new Polish prime minister, had not disassociated himself sufficiently from the previous government's positions.[69] At the same time the Russians stated that a "radical improvement of the composition of the Polish Government, one that would exclude the pro-fascist imperialist elements and include democratic elements . . . could provide a favorable basis both for the reestablishment of Soviet-Polish relations, and settlement of the frontier question."[70]

Moreover, they said, "The Soviet Government does not regard the 1939 frontiers as immutable. Corrections may be introduced in Poland's favor in the sense that districts where Poles are in the majority should go to Poland. The Soviet-Polish frontier should run approximately along the so-called Curzon Line . . . with the Western Ukraine and Western Byelorussia going to the Soviet Union. Poland's western frontiers must be extended to include the old Polish lands formerly seized by Germany."[71]

The issue reached the boiling point in March when, in response to a tough message from Churchill warning Stalin that he risked the future viability of the grand alliance by his truculence on Poland, Stalin lashed out at the British prime minister, rejecting the notion that Moscow was hostile to Poland, that it wanted to impose a territorial settlement on it, while reacting vehemently to putting off the Polish question until after the war.[72] By July, with Russian armies overrunning Poland, Stalin announced that Moscow was now ready to recognize a Committee of National Liberation, headquartered in Lublin, to be the centerpiece of any future Polish government.

But throughout the summer and early fall, Roosevelt was preoccupied with his campaign for reelection. At least in part due to this factor, American policy remained ambiguous and contradictory. In June, when Roosevelt met with London Polish government leaders in Washington, he ignored his earlier tacit acceptance of Moscow's territorial assertions at Teheran, rather promising moral support for Polish boundary aspirations.[73] After the November presidential elections, Roosevelt issued a strong statement on behalf of Polish self-determination, simultaneously reassuring Stalin that his attitude had not undergone any change.[74] American officials apparently never saw any real cost in continuing to promote Atlantic Charter principles while seeking to postpone formal American approval of Russian interests in Poland. We surely knew what was going on inside Poland, but did not seem concerned that events there might confront us with a *fait accompli*.[75]

Spheres of Influence and the Armistice Agreements

In order to put a stop to a seriously deteriorating situation, involving not only Poland but the other states of Eastern Europe, Churchill informed Roosevelt that he intended to go to Moscow in October 1944 with the express intention of trying to reach an understanding with Stalin in that region. The British had maintained since 1941 that it was impractical to assume that Great Britain and America could compel an ascendant Soviet Russia to buy into frontiers less than those of 1940. The British continued to argue that the best way to persuade Moscow to play ball would be to reach a wartime agreement that would tie Russia to the very western borders that Stalin had claimed after June 1941. It was this orientation that would prompt Churchill at the Moscow meeting to attempt to reach certain "understandings" with Stalin in regard to British and Russian interests in southeastern Europe.

This had been the general thrust of British foreign policy for some months. The British and Russians reached an agreement the previous May, for example, that allowed Britain a predominant voice in Greek affairs and Soviet Russia the major say in Rumanian affairs. The British initiative in regard to Greece and Rumania was prompted by the recognition that failure to act to obtain some sort of understanding with the Russians on the future demarcation of Eastern Europe might well lead to the growth of zones of influence dividing Europe into rival camps led respectively by Great Britain and Soviet Russia.[76] As the leading Mediterranean power, Britain was especially concerned lest Greece fall into unfriendly hands, thus endangering London's communication lifeline to the Middle East and beyond. A civil insurrection, mounted by an indigenous communist-led group and aimed at overthrowing the British-supported monarchy, was making headway, much to the consternation of London. In June, Roosevelt agreed to a "three months trial period" to see how this understanding would work, after which it would be reviewed by the Big Three—a decision that represented the first significant crack in the wartime American insistence on not dealing with such issues while the fighting was taking place.[77]

It was this evolving mindset that led Washington and London to acquiesce in the Rumanian (September 12, 1944) and Finnish (September 19, 1944) armistices that gave the Russians the decisive voice in each of those countries even before the cessation of hostilities with Germany—agreements that provided that, until the conclusion of a general peace, control over the terms of the armistice would be vested in an Allied Control Commission operating "under the general direction and orders of the Allied (Soviet) High Command, acting on behalf of the Allied Powers."[78] Thus, Moscow was given the right to oversee the execution of the armistices in the name of its Allies. The Russians, as the

British would shortly discover, were bound and determined to incorporate the same approach in the Bulgarian and Hungarian armistices.

But on the eve of the Moscow meeting, Roosevelt, evidently in some quandary in regard to these events, could not yet be persuaded that this approach generally was the most appropriate one. While Washington's official position was still that such wartime agreements would inevitably violate the principles of the Atlantic Charter and, ultimately encourage Russian adventurism, FDR, a few days before the session was to begin, sent a message to Stalin attempting to clarify American policy on questions of territorial boundary lines in Eastern Europe. At the same time, he suggested that the British leader and Stalin permit Ambassador Harriman to sit in on the meetings, acting as the President's observer but not empowered to make any commitments on behalf of Washington.[79]

The October 4 communication would represent a significant turning point in the very fluid relationship with Moscow. On the one hand, by insisting that Harriman be present, Roosevelt made it perfectly clear to Stalin that on the matter of any bilateral British-Russian "understandings" regarding territorial questions in the region, Churchill would not be speaking for America.[80] On the other hand, if Roosevelt had simply used the occasion to reiterate his opposition to any deals while the war was still in progress, it would have been one thing, but he instead informed Stalin that America would henceforth insist that we have an equal say with both Russia and Britain regarding decisions affecting the countries of the Balkans.[81] From Moscow's perspective, the American position did not square with the previously exhibited British-American approach in handling the Italian occupation.

During 1943-1944, as Italy was progressively liberated from fascist-Nazi control, Washington and London were able to effectively deny Russian involvement in the key commission that had been set up to control the occupation of that country—a commission that the Russians had demanded.[82] The American position in the Italian case was basically one that said he who presides over the liberation of a particular country should have the controlling voice in its occupation.[83] Such a position carried with it enormous potential implications, serving as it did as a model for future occupation policies. It should not be surprising that the Russians would later employ this precedent to bar the West from the Rumanian occupation commission.[84] Moreover, it created a framework within which the occupying state might easily be accused of playing games.[85]

To say that Stalin did not much care for Roosevelt's message is to understate the situation.[86] Albert Resis argues that Roosevelt's note to Stalin that day marks the beginning of the Cold War—at least with respect to southeastern Europe.[87] By refusing to accede to Moscow's insistence that it have a pre-eminent role in fashioning armistices with Hungary and Bulgaria, America now seemed to be saying that Soviet Russia would not be permitted to have a role in postwar settlements comparable to that of its own.

With all this as background for his trip to Moscow, Churchill, upon arriving in Moscow, refused to acquiesce in the Russian demand for unilateral control in Hungary and Bulgaria. He proposed an arrangement which, while acknowledging Russian hegemony in Bulgaria for the duration of the war, would nevertheless have the Control Commissions for those two countries operate after the war in "accordance to the instructions of the Governments of the United States, Soviet Union and United Kingdom." [88] In effect, the Western Allies were now seeking to change the the de facto rules of the game by insisting that they have a greater role in Bulgaria than they had obtained in Rumania and Finland and a greater role than the Russians had been permitted in the case of the Italian armistice the previous year.

During and immediately after the Anglo-Russian summit, Washington sought from afar to diminish Moscow's influence on the proposed Bulgarian Allied Control Commission. [89] But at the Moscow meeting Churchill had little choice but to defer to Stalin, in effect going it alone and concluding the famous "percentages agreement" with him—an understanding that, interestingly, would later come to reflect and delimit the actual zone of domination by Russian forces in Eastern Europe. On October 28 the Bulgarian armistice was signed in Moscow, even though Secretary of State Hull reserved America's right to reopen this matter. [90] The meeting was not without its share of drama in regard to other matters. Churchill, apparently with Roosevelt's knowledge, if not concurrence, assured Stalin that Russia was "justified" in having access to the Mediterranean after the war, particularly since Turkey had collaborated with Hitler. [91]

During the fall, the State Department began receiving urgent communications from its high-level people in Moscow concerning Moscow's apparent intentions. George Kennan, newly arrived in Moscow after a hiatus of seven years, telegraphed his superiors that "it is a matter of indifference to Moscow whether a given area is communistic or not. All things being equal, Moscow might prefer to see it communized, although even that is debatable. But the main thing is that it should be amenable to Moscow influence, and, if possible, to Moscow's authority." [92]

Meanwhile, Ambassador Harriman and General Deane warned in late 1944 that American lend-lease generosity was being interpreted by the Russians as a sign of weakness. [93] Their message fell on deaf ears as Roosevelt evidently felt that any reduction of aid or tightening of procedure on our part would hurt the military effort and might well impair postwar relations between the two countries. Another consideration in Roosevelt's mind was that he wanted Soviet Russia to enter the war against Japan when conditions in Europe became more favorable. Thus, while the British lend-lease program had been steadily reduced, Russian lend-lease continued to be given top priority. [94]

Another memorandum from Harriman to Washington warned that time was running out on reaching any kind of substantive agreement with the Russians. [95] The Russians were "realists," he said, and had by then elaborated a clear idea of what they wanted. It was time for America to do the same. We should, he said, lay out for the Russians just what our interests in Eastern Europe were, clarifying for the Kremlin our top priorities in the process. What was the response from Washington? Nothing more than a vaguely written rehash of previous orientations, including a call for self-determination everywhere, an open door for trade, free flow of information, and postponement of territorial questions until after the war—all the while Soviet Russia's armies were moving inexorably across the Eastern European landscape.[96]

Policy Toward Germany

Throughout the early phase of the war, the Roosevelt administration's approach to Germany mirrored the same sort of refusal to deal with current political realities that characterized the country's overall world view. To discuss what to do about Germany while the war was still in progress was felt to be premature at best, injurious at worst. The one overriding constant that did pervade administration thinking in the early days was the fear that the British and Russians might negotiate separate peaces with Berlin—a view, ironically, shared by Moscow and London as well.[97] This mutual anxiety would make it more difficult to deal with the inevitable conflicts that arose over what policies to pursue. What was worse, however, when the president did finally come to recognize the need to develop a postwar policy for a defeated Germany, it would prove to be stillborn due to pervasive conflict and confusion within the government over the appropriate approach to take.

The conflict centered on whether to pursue a policy of punishment or reconciliation with the defeated Germans in order to forestall a revival of militarism in that country. Proponents of a hard line toward Germany pointed to the Versailles Peace Treaty after World War I as being too lenient, in effect permitting the National Socialists to rise to power. Those advocating a more moderate policy likewise pointed to what they viewed as the unduly harsh, punitive measures of the Versailles agreement—one, they said, that led directly to the economic and social degeneration of that country, thus paving the way for Hitler.[98] The State Department, as the leading proponent of a moderate peace with Germany, argued against the use of reparations for punitive purposes. Any indiscriminate reparations, it was argued, might well destroy what was left of the German economy, thereby undermining attempts to inculcate democratic instituions. Then, too, such an approach might later necessitate a massive relief effort by America, burdening the taxpayers. Finally, the collapse of the German economy might jeopardize the economic recovery of Europe as a whole.[99]

This dichotomy arose out of the absence of grand strategy within the administration—a situation that reflected a continuing preoccupation with winning the war at the expense of postwar planning. The State Department, looking for guidance from the chief executive, did not find any from a president preoccupied with military exigencies and domestic politics. When the war's course made it impossible to ignore the question of what to do about a defeated postwar Germany, the internal divisions within the government precluded a coherent, concerted, and clear-cut posture. As a result, America's interactions with the Russians and British on this issue were full of confusion and misunderstanding—a situation that made division and acrimony over Germany virtually inevitable.

Add to this the fact that Roosevelt's own hopes for a postwar collaboration with Soviet Russia, based on his "Four Policemen" concept, would color his approach toward Germany. A get-tough approach was appealing because, much like unconditional surrender, this might well help to maintain good relations with the Russians. Germany would be a key test for those relations.[100] At the same time, the War Department, preoccupied with military operations, resolved to consult civilians regarding Germany as little as possible during that expected short period after the cessation of hostilities when they would be in de facto control—an attitude that would impact the eventual occupation policy.[101] All of this pointed up the need to have in place a clearly delineated, coordinated policy regarding Germany before Washington approached the Russians and British. As of the end of 1943, however, no such policy had been elaborated.

Meanwhile, a series of initiatives unfolded at lower levels during that year that would present opportunities for the Big Three to work out common approaches for the surrender and occupation of the defeated states. As it turned out, they were not able to take advantage of those opportunities. In October at the Moscow Foreign Ministers' Conference Eden suggested the creation of a tripartite European Advisory Commission (EAC), to be located in London, the purpose of which would be to handle negotiations with defeated enemies. As finally agreed to, the EAC was given the broad mandate to make "recommendations to the three Governments upon European questions connected with the termination of hostilities." In addition, it was specifically given an initial assignment of making detailed suggestions on "the terms of surrender to be imposed upon each of the European states with which any of the three Powers are at war, and upon the mechanism required to ensure the fulfillment of those terms."[102]

Washington, however, was only a reluctant supporter of this agreement from the beginning, instructing its representative on the commission, Ambassador Winant, to avoid discussing general political questions. Winant protested. "If we present the Russians only with *faits accomplis* on these subjects, as we were obliged to do in the case of Italy, we can only expect to learn of their actions and policies in Eastern Europe in a similar manner."[103] Winant's instructions reflected the administration's continuing reluctance to deal with postwar political matters before the end of the war. Thus, an opportunity to employ a potentially valuable forum for tripartite discussions on Germany was squandered.

At Teheran, the heads of states and their foreign ministers did not really resolve very much in regard to these questions. From the outset it was apparent that Stalin sought the harshest possible measures against Germany. When Roosevelt revived his plan for the dismemberment of Germany, it won Stalin's enthusiastic endorsement. No definitive solutions on Germany were reached at Teheran, the German question being referred to the EAC, but their talks did lead to a tentative endorsement of the partition principle.

During 1944 the EAC was able, despite contradictory instructions from Washington, to hammer out tripartite agreements on surrender terms and control machinery for Germany.[104] In addition, through its auspices the Allies were able to come to an agreement on the nature and scope of the postwar occupation zones to be administered by the victors. But all of this represented merely the framework, not the substance, of a common approach. Attempts to move beyond this to the content of policy would come to naught because American military authorities refused to buy into it. The War Department and the Joint Chiefs of Staff refused to permit civilian agencies to formulate long-range policy for Germany lest this adversely influence the abilitiy of the Army's military governors to do their jobs. But as John Gaddis points out, the military's ability to shape future policy by preventing anyone else from making policy could never have been possible if they had not had the tacit support of the White House. Roosevelt, desirous of preserving his freedom of initiative, did not want the EAC to be in a position of determining policy.[105] Given the president's proclivity for personal diplomacy, this decision would prove to be a major mistake.

Nowhere was this situation more clearly manifest than on the question of reparations. In June 1944 the State Department proposed an economic plan for Germany—an approach that was approved by a special interdepartmental committee in August.[106] The ensuing document reflected the department's proposed temperate treatment of Germany, one that would guarantee payment of reparations to Germany's victims but would also seek to integrate it into "the type of world economy envisaged by the Atlantic Charter." This would entail maintaining a decent standard of living for its people, and would preclude any indiscriminate destruction of the country's industrial capability.[107]

All of this would produce a violent outburst from the Treasury Department, led by Henry Morgenthau, who viewed the State Department's approach as virtually criminal. Only by converting Germany into a "pastoral" country could future wars in Europe be prevented, he said. He therefore proposed a plan that would severely punish the German people, calling for the complete dismantling of German industry and an emasculation of its productive infrastructure. At first Roosevelt bought into the idea, inclined as he was to favor harsh treatment of Germany. He took his Treasury Secretary to the Quebec Conference in September and was persuaded to initial an document calling for the conversion of Germany into an agricultural state.[108] Almost immediately, however, a backlash set in. The State Department, in particular, was opposed, and by early October, with the plan having been leaked to the press and in the face of considerable adverse public reaction, the President backtracked.[109]

Unfortunately, the influence of the Morgenthau approach would linger on, especially in regard to the War Department's approach to Germany's occupation.

As Allied forces liberated western Germany, and in the absence of clear instructions from Washington on what to do, American occupation authorities took the position that Germany was to be treated as a defeated, not a liberated country. The reason for this was the Army's desire to avoid being stuck with the the responsibility for reviving the German economy. What that meant in practice was that there would be no attempt to rehabilitate the German economy, and, in particular, no importation and/or distribution of relief supplies except where they were absolutely necessary to prevent disease and disorder.[110]

The State Department did mange to assert some measure of authority over German policy just as Roosevelt was preparing for his trip to the Crimea for his last summit conference with Churchill and Stalin. The Department's briefing papers on Germany, prepared for the president's use at Yalta, emphasized the importance of preventing each occupying state from asserting unilateral positions. Tripartite agreement on centralized administration would guarantee that the industrialized portions of Germany under Anglo-American control would receive food shipments from the predominately agricultural Russian zone. Efforts should be directed toward assimilating "a reformed, peaceful and economically non-aggressive Germany into a liberal system of world trade." And the Allies should be encouraged to reach agreements across the board *before the termination of hostilities* so as to "minimize the danger of new European rivalries."[111] How far the State Department had come!

The Yalta Conference

Roosevelt had one last opportunity, at the February 1945 Yalta Conference, to finally articulate a sensible policy for America—a policy that would at one and the same time be workable, realistic, and comprehensible to the Russians. Such was not the case. The documentary evidence indicates that Roosevelt took with him to the conference no demonstrably clear sense of American interests in that part of the world.[112]

It does appear that he had at least two points of view to consider in regard to Poland. One State Department official, John D. Hickerson, urged the president to recognize the hard fact that Eastern Europe would be a Russian sphere of influence after the war. Frank recognition of this reality, said Hickerson, and its clear communication to the Russians, might be traded for their support on other issues of more importance to America. The other point of view was that of Ambassador Harriman, who had urged that we define our vital security interests in the region and defend them vigorously. Judging by his conduct at Yalta, it appears that Roosevelt chose to ignore both views.[113]

President Roosevelt began discussion of the Polish problem at Yalta by accepting the Curzon Line as the eastern frontier of Poland.[114] Based on the battlefield situation at the time, what with Russian armies on the German border, there was not much else he could do. FDR did not hinge this acceptance on any other conditions. He proposed, but did not insist, that Stalin grant a concession to the Poles by leaving within postwar Poland the city and oil fields of Lwow. The Polish western frontier with Germany was not mentioned. He agreed with little debate to what had been Moscow's primary territorial demand in Poland since 1941. Instead, he concentrated on the political question, specifically the composition of the future Polish government, recommending that this principle be fostered through the creation of a new interim government representative of all five political parties and the holding of free elections.[115] In so doing, Roosevelt thus gave up previous American insistence upon postponement of all territorial settlements until after the war, thereby explicitly violating the Atlantic Charter principle on postwar territorial changes.

The areas of agreement and disagreement between the Allies should have been clear. The Polish eastern frontier question was settled. Each government approved, at least verbally, the others' principles. They espoused the same overall goals of creating a free, strong, and independent Poland which would maintain friendly relations with Soviet Russia. They further agreed upon the need to construct an interim Polish government representative of the country's various political parties prior to the holding of free elections.[116]

Serious disagreement did exist over the composition or control of that interim government. The Americans advocated a presidential committee, the Russians expansion of the Lublin government. When Moscow's opposition to the presidential committee idea threatened to prevent Allied approval of any Polish settlement, Roosevelt withdrew the American proposal. What might have been the specific means to ensure the establishment of a new democratic Polish interim government was dropped.[117]

Roosevelt was satisfied to achieve general Allied agreement on the formation of a democratic and representative Polish government through the holding of free elections after the war. Proposals to ensure the implementation of this overall goal—the establishment of a presidential council and Allied responsibility for verifying the holding of free elections—were withdrawn when they threatened to prevent any agreement on Poland. Roosevelt displayed no concern with the individual problems erupting in East Europe once the Allies had agreed on the overall principles for liberated Europe. He never pressed for a definition of the rights of American and British representatives on the Allied Control Commissions in Rumania, Bulgaria, and Hungary, despite the October 4, 1944 memo arguing for a prominent Western role in those countries. Stalin may very well have interpreted the vagueness and generality of the agreements at Yalta as American and British acceptance of Russian preeminence in Eastern Europe. FDR did succeed in getting Moscow to participate in the U.N. and to enter the war against Japan as a kind of a *quid pro quo* in return for Washington's settling for promises of free elections in Poland, and recognition of the Curzon line.

As for Germany, the Big Three had agreed to provide a holding operation in Germany by temporarily dividing it into four occupation zones: Russia to control the northeastern provinces between the Oder-Neisse and Elbe rivers,

Britain the northwest, and America the southern portion of the country. France would later be granted control of two Rhineland states carved out of the American sector. Each zone was to be administered individually by the respective military commanders of the occupying powers. As a group, these commanders constituted the Allied Control Council which, by means of the principle of unanimity, would be charged with the responsibility of laying the groundwork for eventual German unification. The Russians insisted on massive reparations from Germany, to be extracted from the remaining industrial complex. The figure of $20 billion initially proposed by Stalin was agreed to at Yalta as a starting point for future negotiation. Finally, they agreed that Poland should receive "substantial accessions of territory" from Germany to compensate for land taken by Russia.

Yalta was Roosevelt's last chance to effectuate a realistic policy for Eastern Europe. Near the end of the conference Stalin said that peace could be kept so long as he, Churchill, and Roosevelt lived. Within two months, FDR was dead. A new American president, surveying the Roosevelt legacy, would conclude that it was the Russians who had been deceitful and treacherous, and that it was now time to put them in their place.

Post-Yalta Developments, February–September 1945

Harry S Truman assumed the presidency with very little experience and preparation in foreign affairs. Saddled with the responsibility of carrying out his predecessor's policies, but coming into office at a time when a reassessment of Russian policies was already underway, Truman had to try to make sense of what was happening and to endeavor to reach an honorable peace. In all of this it was inevitable that his own personality and background would greatly influence his outlook.

Appalled by the sloppiness and disorder that had pervaded Roosevelt's approach to decision making, Truman was determined from the outset of his presidency to convey the impression of forthrightness, efficiency and decisiveness in his general approach to government.[118] This orientation would lead him early on to make several hasty decisions regarding the Russians—all on the basis of incomplete information regarding Russian conduct—a situation that made it appear he had already begun to repudiate Roosevelt's Russian policy. While there is some evidence to suggest that the new president did indeed do so,[119] the summary record points up the essentially ad hoc and incremental nature of Truman's evolving approach to international affairs—an approach which created more problems than it solved.

One of Truman's earliest direct contacts with the Russians may well have had more to do with this stylistic approach than with substance. From his first moments in the White House, Truman was bombarded by messages from a number of officials in the government all to the effect that the only effective way to deal with the Russians was to take an unyielding stand. Influential or well-placed advisors including Averrill Harriman, John Deane, Admiral William Leahy, Undersecretary of State Joseph Grew, and Secretary of the Navy James Forrestal would maintain a virtual drumbeat in this vein from his earliest moments in office. In this they were echoed by Churchill who had by this time become quite concerned about the viability of the postwar relationship with Moscow. What tied these individuals together was their common belief that we had made too many concessions to Stalin. Soviet Russia, they concluded, was nothing less than a bully.[120]

Less than two weeks after Roosevelt's death, Truman received a message from Ambassador Harriman advising him to get tough with the Russians lest America be faced with a "barbaric invasion of Europe." By this time Harriman had become more convinced than heretofore that ideology had replaced security as the chief determinant of Russian policy, especially in regard to the Yalta agreements on Poland. "Russian plans for establishing satellite states are a threat to the world and to us," he said. "The Soviet Union, once it has control of bordering areas, will attempt to penetrate the next adjacent countries."[121] Thus, Poland became from Truman's first days in office a kind of symbol of America's ability to work with Moscow. Informed by his advisors that the Russians were not living up to their commitments in regard to that country, as we had understood them, Truman used the occasion of Vyacheslav Molotov's visit to Washington in late April to tongue-lash the Russian foreign minister in what amounted to a veritable dressing down of that Russian official in the White House.

Nevertheless, there is no conclusive evidence to prove the notion that this early confrontation with Molotov was the opening gambit in a well planned long-range strategy for playing hard ball with the Russians. For getting tough would also require America to depart from certain historic traditions, most especially nonentanglement in Europe's affairs, and a long-standing fear of a large-scale peacetime military establishment—concerns that resonated deeply among "Middle American" politicians of Truman's era. In addition, other countervailing forces prevented him from pursuing a consistently tough anti-Russian policy during his first months in office. His promise to carry out Roosevelt's policies, the nature of public opinion, and, above all, his own willingness to compromise were all factors. But his abrasive personality may well have led the Russians to conclude that FDR's goals had been abandoned.[122]

Meanwhile, in that same month that the president upbraided Molotov, an open letter by a leading member of the French Communist Party, Jacques Duclos, to his American communist colleagues attacked American party members for collaborating with nonrevolutionary forces during the war. This letter had a number of repercussions in America, not the least of which was the recreation of the American Communist Party by name. Was this an opening salvo in a drive to revert to the revolutionary tactics of the prewar period?[123] Some administration officials thought so, attaching great significance to it, concluding that Moscow had now decided to resume its efforts to spread world revolution by whatever means available to it.[124]

Even more importantly, the Duclos letter, combined with the arrest in June of several people, including State Department officials, for having leaked sensitive documents to a newspaper, led some to conclude that espionage had been going on. In June, the State Department prepared a long report on international communism, taking note of developments in the French, Italian, and American parties, concluding that communism now posed a serious challenge to America, and recommending that decisive action against domestic subversion might actually improve relations with Moscow by demonstrating our internal resolve.[125] Meanwhile, Kennan warned from Moscow in July that the abolition of the Comintern had in no way weakened Moscow's control of the international communist movement.[126]

These events helped to spur a resurgence of congressional activism, especially within the moribund House of Representatives Committee on Un-American Activities. The apparent shift of tactics by the international communist movement provided zealous congressmen with an excuse to launch a series of investigations of "communists in government." By the fall, the hardening congressional attitude, reflective of an inevitable postwar effort to reinvigorate the legislative branch's role and authority in foreign affairs, was a major contributing factor in driving Truman and his top advisors toward a tougher Russian policy. The new congressional assertiveness was manifested very early in the new president's term over the issue of continuing lend-lease assistance to the Russians.

On May 11, confronted by overwhelming evidence that the Russians were using lend-lease aid to help underwrite their country's reconstruction, Truman ordered a drastic cutback in such aid to Soviet Russia just three days after the cessation of hostilities against Germany. Congress had already made it clear that Moscow's policies were not acceptable and would not be countenanced at the expense of the American taxpayer. The curtailment of lend-lease, however, was handled poorly (even ships in transit were ordered to turn around), giving the decision makers in the Kremlin the impression that we were attempting to gain political concessions in the forthcoming peace negotiations through economic pressure.[127] Truman, in his memoirs, denied any such intention of coercing the Russians, stating that he felt large-scale lend-lease to simply be no longer justifiable.[128] The undeniable fact, however, that lend-lease cutbacks in the Russian case were the most severe compared to the other recipients could not have failed to register with Moscow.[129]

At the same time, Truman ordered American troops withdrawn from the proposed Russian zone of Germany effective June 21, 1945. On May 4, 1945, three days before the German surrender, Churchill urged delay on withdrawal: "The Polish problem may be easier to settle when set in relation to the now numerous outstanding questions of the utmost gravity which require urgent settlement with the Russians."[130] In late May Truman sent Harry Hopkins to speak with Stalin in the Kremlin, evidently hoping that Hopkins could ascertain more clearly the dictator's thinking and perhaps even reach an understanding on outstanding issues. Indeed, it appeared that a deal was worked out. Stalin proposed that the Warsaw government form the basis of the future Provisional Government of National Unity, but that representatives from other Polish groups friendly to the Allies and the Russians could have four or five out of the eighteen to twenty ministries. Truman accepted.

On other issues, Stalin was also cooperative, reiterating his commitment to enter the war against Japan; agreeing to scrupulously observe the independence of China—indeed, expressing a willingness to participate in a joint effort to help unify China under Chiang Kai-shek's leadership—and averring that the Allied Control Council for Germany should begin its work as soon as possible. Finally, he acquiesced in the American position on voting in the Security Council, thus averting a breakdown at San Francisco. All of this now appeared to leave only Germany as the major issue to be addressed at the next meeting of the Allied heads of state to take place at Potsdam later that summer. But developments between April and July forced the Truman administration to reassess Roosevelt's approach to Germany.

German Developments. After Germany's surrender Russia undertook a number of unilateral initiatives in its occupation zone, including stripping their areas of heavy industry, railroad rolling stock, and the like, while turning over a large section to the Poles, producing almost immediately a major flow of German refugees into the Western zones. Moscow proceeded to interpret this to mean all the way to the Oder and western Neisse Rivers—much too far to the west as far as Washington and London were concerned.

Meanwhile, the American position on reparations, agreed to at Yalta, had begun to change. General Lucius Clay, the American zonal military governor, fearing bankruptcy, informed the Russian occupation commanders in May that no more reparations would be removed from the Western zones. While this situation was unfolding, Moscow's request for a sizeable loan to help them initiate their own reconstruction was given new consideration. All of this appeared to present a situation in which the administration might be able to promote a quid pro quo strategy, for example, using a loan to Russia as a device for extracting political concessions. This was precisely the position that Harriman and Deane had been promoting for several weeks—one where the new administration ought to look more closely at the relationship among reparations, lend-lease, and postwar reconstruction.[131] This change of outlook, however, required that a deal be worked out with the Russians on reparations, most especially how to control the flow of reparations to Moscow without provoking a reprisal from them.

As the leaders of the Big Three were preparing to gather at Potsdam for the last of the wartime summit conferences, a reasonably clear cut American position on Germany had crystallized—an orientation that called for de-militarization, denazification, and deindustrialization, but not to the point of causing economic collapse that might impair the prospects for postwar European recovery and thereby impose a heavy burden on the American taxpayers. During the weeks leading up to that conference, a series of communications among the parties proved to be inconclusive, with the Russians rejecting the Anglo-American position because of Washington's insistence that the Yalta reparations formula be substantially modified. American and Russian representatives, meeting in Moscow, failed to reach agreement on the reparations question, requiring that the issue be addressed at the Potsdam Conference. Thus the stage was set for some hard bargaining at Potsdam. Unfortunately, Truman's unilateral termination of lend-lease prior to his meeting with Stalin and Churchill at Potsdam removed one of the bargaining chips from the table. One can understand why that meeting was such a dismal occasion for the protection of important American interests when one remembers that it was held after America had sought to change the rules of the game and then came to the table with less than a full hand.

The Potsdam Agreements

The final wartime conference at Potsdam (July-August 1945) reached a decision to establish a Council of Foreign Ministers, which would include France (and China, when Asia questions were before it). The Council was to prepare the peace treaties and handle questions of common concern. It was decided that "for the time being, no central German Government" would be established, although Germany was to be treated by the occupying powers "as a single economic unit." Pending a peace settlement where "final delimitation of the western frontier of Poland" would be agreed upon, Poland was permitted temporarily to administer German East Prussia, Silesia, and large parts of Brandenburg and Pomerania. These territories, under Polish control at Stalin's insistence, were to run westward to the Oder-Western Neisse rather than to the Oder-Eastern Neisse line that Britain and America preferred. Thus the political map of Central Europe was in effect redrawn at Potsdam; what was on paper provisional became permanent in practice. It would not be for another quarter of a century that a legal device was worked out whereby the issue of Poland's western frontier was resolved.[132] The most controversial aspects of these agreements, apart from the area left to Germany proper, were the size and territory of the individual zones and the question of Western access to Berlin. To honor these commitments, American forces in Germany had to be withdrawn in 1945 from the proposed Russian zone by as much as 125 miles.

There did occur an agreement on reparations at Potsdam. The adamant position taken by Truman, plus hard bargaining by the American delegates led to the Russians giving in. The agreement specified that there would be a fixed amount of reparations, Soviet Russia to receive reparations from her own zone plus "industrial capital equipment" from the western zones based on a formula which provided the Russians with 25 percent of German capital equipment from the Western zones, in return for which we agreed to allow the Polish to "administer" the disputed Oder-Neisse area. Meanwhile, the Russians were given absolute discretion to do whatever they wanted within their own zone—a situation which they were quick to exploit by stripping away virtually every valuable item that they could find. Finally, France, already a member of the Allied Control Commission, was invited to join the Reparations Commission.

But the conferees also agreed to increase the authority of the zonal commanders at the expense of the Control Council. In so doing, Potsdam undermined the principle of a unified Germany which the advocates of rehabilitation had long sought. Molotov understood only too well what was happening: "Would not this mean that each country would have a free hand in their own zones and would act entirely independent of the others?"[133] But Truman, preoccupied with his immediate goal of minimizing American responsibilities in Europe, failed to see or chose to ignore the long-range implications of his own policy.

The Unfolding of Atomic Diplomacy

Formulation of American foreign policy on the control of atomic energy at this time took place in an atmosphere of uncertainty, confusion, and ignorance—an outlook that only served to exacerbate America's relationship with the Russians. Indeed, the manner in which Truman handled the issue of control of nuclear weapons was a particularly frustrating illustration of the confused state of policy making in Washington in the fall of 1945.

Roosevelt had decided by late 1944 not to share information about the bomb with the Russians, even though it was thought likely that they knew about the project. Very early in his administration, Truman came under great pressure from the scientific community and advisors like Secretary of War Henry Stimson and Assistant Secretary of State Dean Acheson to pubicly endorse international control of atomic energy. At the same time, in the belief that America's possession of the bomb would make the Russians easier to deal with, Truman was advised by some in the administration to employ it explicitly to that end.

By the summer of 1945 this approach, and the growing Russian-American confrontation over Eastern Europe, led Truman and the new Secretary of State, James F. Byrnes, to discuss trying to obtain political concessions from the Russians in return for turning the bomb over to an international agency. An increasing number of public statements from administration officials, pointing up the bomb's enormous power, which only America possessed, served to illuminate the growing view that the bomb did indeed have some useful bargaining capability. In particular, it was hoped that some sort of quid pro quo with Moscow might be possible in Poland, Rumania, and the Far East before America lost its monopoly of the bomb.[134]

At Potsdam, Truman scrupulously avoided employing America's possession of the bomb in any particularly provocative way in his discussions with the Russians. But there is little question that, upon being informed of the successful test of the bomb in the New Mexico desert, Truman believed that America would now be in the "driver's seat," and that this had effectively shifted the balance of power in favor of Washington. This view may well have caused Truman to move away from a direct confrontation with Stalin later in the fall.[135]

Stimson, almost alone among the new president's top-level advisors, urged caution in employing the bomb as a pressure tactic against the Russians, arguing, at the same time, that bilateral negotiations with Moscow should be employed to try to get an agreement in which each side would recognize one other's legitimate security sphere. On September 11, 1945, Stimson, about to retire from the War Department, prophesized in a note to the president, "that it would not be possible to use our possession of the atomic bomb as a direct lever to produce the change" desired inside Eastern Europe. If Russian-American negotiations continue with "this weapon rather ostentatiously on our hip, their suspicions and their distrust of our purposes and motives will increase." He again urged direct, bilateral talks with Stalin to formulate control of the bomb and to effectuate a general peace settlement.[136]

Brynes, however, came to the view that any public announcement concerning America's intentions in this matter should be delayed until after a general European peace settlement. But without consulting his Secretary of State, and while Byrnes was in London involved in a very difficult series of meetings with his Russian counterpart, Truman on October 3 publicly endorsed international control of atomic energy.[137] Meanwhile, no one consulted Congress, whose leaders, suspicious from the beginning of international control, came to believe the administration was about to give the bomb away.[138] By October 27, when the president gave his first major postwar speech on foreign policy, he had begun to back off from the full implications of his earlier message. On the advice of Byrnes, backed up by Forrestal and others, Truman began to rethink the wisdom of taking up this issue with the Russians before the peace treaties were concluded with the former German satellites.

The Evolving Situation in Eastern Europe

The spate of peace treaties which were negotiated following the war proved to be a major cause of ill feeling between America and Soviet Russia. In August, 1945 the State Department let it be known that it was determined to attain a position of equality with the Russians in Rumania.[139] In London the next month the Foreign Ministers' Conference broke down because of Molotov's objections to the presence of the French and Chinese foreign ministers. While there was no major blowup over Bulgaria, Rumania, Hungary, and Finland at the conference, Molotov protested when the West attempted to provide assistance to the Finns, reminding his Western colleagues of the part Finland played in the 900-day seige of Leningrad. What did cause a conflict in the peace negotiations were the Italian and Yugoslav claims to the city of Trieste. The Russians contended that the city should be given to Yugoslavia, but Washington's hostility toward Tito and his people prevented that from happening.[140]

The Russian approach to the countries of Eastern Europe was not a uniform one. In Rumania, which had been a German ally and whose troops had participated in the invasion of Soviet Russia in 1941, the Russians at first sought to dominate the country by installing a government in which the indigenous communist party was a minority. Less than a month after Yalta, however, Stalin promulgated a tough ultimatum demanding that the Rumanian Communist Party be given absolute power within a space of a few hours in order to "restore order," or else Russia would "not be responsible for the continuance of Rumania as an independent state."

On the other hand, the Russians permitted elections to be held in Hungary—elections that enabled a non communist-dominated political coalition to gain power. At the same time, they oversaw elections in Bulgaria that proved to be satisfactory to the British if not the Americans. The Russians also permitted elections to be conducted in their occupation zone in Austria—elections in which they suffered a major defeat. Finally, Moscow agreed to allow an independent non communist government to take over power in Finland, so long as that government would follow a foreign policy orientation friendly to Soviet Russia.

The Polish question, however, continued to fester. In a letter dated April 24, 1945 (not uncoincidentally the day after the Molotov-Truman confrontation in the White House), Stalin responded to Anglo-American concerns about Russia's actions in Poland by observing that "Poland borders on the Soviet Union, which cannot be said about Great Britain or the USA. . . . I do not know," he continued, "whether a genuinely representative Government has been established in Greece, or whether the Belgium Government is a genuinely democratic one. The Soviet Union was not consulted when those Governments were being formed, nor did it claim the right to interfere in those matters, because it realizes how important Belgium and Greece are to the security of Great Britain." The Russian leader went on to say that he could not "understand why in discussing Poland no attempt is made to consider the interests of the Soviet Union in terms of security as well."[141]

The Russians stuck to their guns on the question of the composition of the Provisional Government and continued to insist that Poland's borders be moved west to the Oder-Western Niesse rivers, well inside the eastern part of Germany. By the time of the Potsdam Conference in July, Washington had recognized the Russian-dominated Polish government as a fait accompli, about which there was little they could do in any event.

The real test would come in Germany. The problem for the Allied Control Council that arose almost immediately was how to forge a unanimous policy in the face of radically divergent views. Throughout 1945 the British and Americans advocated a policy designed to maintain the territorial integrity of Germany as a whole—a policy orientation that would, after a necessary destruction of her warmaking capacity, restore her industry to a self-supporting level. The

Russians and French preferred a politically divided, economically weakened Germany. By the end of 1945, the chances for a unified and self-reliant Germany were rapidly diminishing. The French simply refused to countenance any sort of central German administrative authority, while in the Russian zone Stalin systematically moved to emasculate the Prussian landlord class, nationalize what industry was left, and impose Communist-Party controls on the population.[142]

THE ROOSEVELT LEGACY

The record of Roosevelt's diplomacy toward Soviet Russia during the war is at many levels a bewildering one. The evidence indicates it was a policy that evolved in a highly incremental manner and not as a result of a deliberate and self-conscious series of choices. His problems in this respect were rooted both in his operational approach to making policy and as a reflection of America's tradition of foreign affairs. In this sense, Roosevelt personified in an almost tragic sense the sort of halfway house or twilight zone that by mid-century had come to mark the American approach to the world.

At the same time, steeped in America's more utopian and destructive foreign affairs orientations—most especially a distate for traditional diplomacy with its preoccupation with power politics, alliances, spheres of influences, and the like, as well as a preference for moralist pretensions—he nevertheless understood, at least at one level of his thinking, that the world out there was a brutish one, and that deals and compromises would be required to get on with America's international relations. And, yet, the strategic policy issues posed for America by World War II were not initially faced nor even completely understood. Only slowly did the nature of the real issues dawn on American policy makers. And, finally, when victory would be won, it was to be on terms that facilitated the continuation of grave tensions in the heart of Europe.

Roosevelt's approach during the war certainly mirrored this dichotomous outlook. Preoccupation with the past seriously clouded America's vision of the postwar world. Reasoning by analogy was certainly never far from the minds of Roosevelt and his chief advisors. The administration's commitment to unconditional surrender, self-determination, a revival of world trade, and international organization all grew out of a desire to avoid the kind of mistakes that, in the view of its highest level decision makers, paved the way for World War II. In like fashion, Roosevelt's desire to postpone political settlements until after the war grew out of his commitment to democratic self-determination. Violations of that principle, in his view, were what led to the war in the first place.

The strategy of postponement that characterized America's approach to dealing with the Russians in the early phase of the war also reflected domestic political realities. Bipartisan agreement on foreign policy during the first months of the war went no deeper than the perceived requirement of defeating the Axis powers. Roosevelt feared that any detailed negotiations of political settlements might well provoke internal controversy, distracting attention from the war effort, and, ultimately, putting into jeopardy the nation's willingness to assume postwar responsibilities. While Roosevelt was chronically prone to exagerate domestic opposition to his foreign policy, the fact of the matter is that for whatever reasons, he apparently believed it.

Consider in this vein the policy of unconditional surrender pursued toward the Germans. Unconditional surrender was certainly injurious, not so much because of its specific denial of the possibility of undercutting Hitler at home—although that may have been extremely important—but because of the mindset it betrayed. We marched into Germany in World War II with the winning of the war as an end in itself. We did not understand that war is essentially a continuation of policy by other means. In this sense, we acted much as we had after World War I, asserting a policy of ending the traditional international politics of power balancing with its associated alliances and spheres of influence. Perhaps the chief error made by Roosevelt is that he did not fully understand or believe in the type of logic associated with the concept of equilibrating national interests so central to an effective balance of power. We had not lost faith that conflicts of interest among states would yield to good intentions and good will.[143] And yet, as we have seen, even this approach was not without its contradictions.

Then, too, throughout the war FDR believed that preservation of big-power unity was the chief essential for avoiding future conflicts. His Four Policemen concept, epitomized by the American proposal for the veto in the Security Council of the new United Nations Organization, was clearly a frank recognition that great power cooperation for peace was an essential prerequisite for the postwar world. Russia's good will and cooperation would be crucial to that end. But this was an especially American utopian view of how best to provide for the necessary "orderly" framework of the new international system—one that rejected the classical balance of power approach. At Yalta, there existed a pronounced tension between these American hopes and international realities, between America's sense of world order and the British and Russian assumption of a world divided into spheres of influence. In the process, the Russians could not grasp the peculiar combination of utopianism, idealism and self-righteousness exhibited by the Americans in their approach to outsiders. Nor could Stalin and his associates comprehend our belief in the ultimate virtue of goodfaith bargaining, or our preoccupation with placating the electorate.

His own personal style of decision-making certainly was a contributing factor to his inability to deal effectively with foreign issues. According to Arthur Schlesinger Jr., Roosevelt's "favorite technique was to keep grants of authority incomplete, jurisdictions uncertain, charters overlapping. The result of this competitive theory of administration was often confusion and exasperation on the operating level."[144] FDR's divide-and-rule method of controlling the bureaucracy bequeathed at best an ambiguous legacy in foreign relations. Roosevelt created an enormous bureaucratic empire, including the foundations of

America's postwar defense and foreign affairs complex involving, as it did, the creation of the first comprehensive intelligence-gathering infrastructure, machinery for the granting of foreign aid, and the utilization of propaganda. But he also concentrated on military strategy to the detriment of rational political decision making about the future shape of Europe.

Roosevelt, according to Kennan, "had little or no understanding for a disciplined, hierarchical organization. He had a highly personal view of diplomacy, imported from his domestic political triumphs. His approach to foreign policy was basically histrionic, with the American political public as his audience. FSOs [foreign service officers] were of little use to him in this respect."[145] Schlesinger points out, for example, that FDR went to Casablanca, Teheran, and Yalta with few senior diplomatic advisors and frequently ignored his foreign office in making wartime policy decisions.[146]

We were certainly not unaware of Russia's "suspicious" attitudes toward our actions. Stalin and his colleagues made no secret of their belief that we were ready to sell them out at the first useful chance. They consistently delayed in responding to our requests for shuttle bombing facilities on Russian soil.[147] When we made airplanes available to them across the Pacific under lend-lease, they insisted on flying them from Alaska rather than have us fly them to Vladivostok.[148] And they expected us at the end to accept an armistice on the Western front that would permit the Nazis to continue their war with Russia.[149]

While Roosevelt and his advisors pursued a contradictory approach to Soviet Russia throughout the war, nothing in the record demonstrates that FDR held the view that America possessed any important economic interests in Eastern Europe. Nor were there any expressed demonstrable security interests in evidence. Rather, Roosevelt appeared to be a prisoner of his own Wilsonian rhetoric and a victim of a personal style bereft of experience in the world of realpolitik. At no time did the president attempt to relay to Stalin any concrete, vital interests indicating, for example, that eastern Europe be preserved for democratic, free enterprise arrangements. The suggestion that some sort of systematic review of American interests in Eastern Europe was ever undertaken seems unlikely.[150]

Surely if some sort of vital security interest had been felt to exist in that area, it would have been to the advantage of the administration to articulate it. While American policy makers regularly acknowledged to themselves that Soviet Russia would in fact play the dominant role in Eastern Europe after the war, the record indicates that they never defined what that would mean.[151] Nor did the prospects of indigenous communist party-state regimes in Europe arouse much concern in Washington during the war.[152] Roosevelt, of course, kept his own counsel on issues dealing with postwar strategy, partly to avoid disrupting the wartime alliance with possible areas of disagreement, but also because he was well aware of the Wilsonian, universalist propensities of his own people. He therefore struck an uneasy and contradictory balance between Wilsonian idealism and a new kind of realism, manifested in his cooperative balance of power approach (as seen in his plans for the United Nations) and a competitive balance of power approach toward keeping the postwar peace (the so-called Four Policemen concept).[153]

To be fair, implementation of a specific, well-worked-out East European policy would have been tough to bring off. For one thing, relying on his military advisors, Roosevelt believed Russia's involvement in the Asian theater of operations, including the utilization of Siberia for the final assault on Japan's home islands, to be essential.[154] This fact, however, should not have been permitted to get in the way of a forthright and defensible expression of America's Eastern Europe interests.

Roosevelt, of course, was always overly sensitive to the vagaries of public opinion. On the one hand, this led him to overemphasize the "Polish vote" in his discussions with Stalin.[155] On the other hand, FDR and his top advisors genuinely believed that any denigration of the ideals of the Atlantic Charter might very well precipitate pervasive disillusionment within an expectant public, already mobilized by Roosevelt himself and nurtured by a rather naive press, leading to a rejection of the new U.N. organization as part of a injurious reversion to isolationism.[156] As a result, according to John Gaddis, because Roosevelt's actual options were in reality very few, it is Stalin who should have been more flexible.[157]

In retrospect, however, it is rather questionable that the public was so fickle that FDR had no room for maneuver.[158] No serious student of the history of these years would argue that it would have been easy for Roosevelt to lower the public's perceptions, highly inflated as they were by the idealism of the Atlantic Charter and his own rhetoric. A review of FDR's public commentary on this subject suggests, however, that he may well have undervalued his abilities to manage public opinion.[159]

Surely Roosevelt could have done a better job in educating the public to accept a settlement based on a spheres-of-influence arrangement. The president had apparently come to recognize as early as 1943, for example, that democratic idealism would not suffice as the basis for a postwar settlement in Eastern Europe.[160] At Teheran, Stalin pointed out that Roosevelt might well want to engage in a considerable amount of public relations work to sensitize the public.[161] And from within the State Department Hickerson pleaded with Roosevelt to begin preparing the press, Congress, and the public to accept a Russian sphere of influence in Eastern Europe as unfortunate but inevitable.[162]

As for the conduct of the war itself, FDR consciously declined to reorient military strategy in accordance with his evolving postwar political objectives, such as they were. Several factors suggest themselves: he and his chief military advisors' perceptions of the limits of America's power; that this might endanger the prospects for Russia's help against Japan; and that the American people would never tolerate keeping its young men and women overseas after the war.[163] But Roosevelt's strategy for winning the war—maximum use of America's industrial power, at a minimum loss of American lives—precluded the use of military power unless the chances for success were optimal. Unfortunately, this undermined the effort of building trust with Soviet Russia. For Stalin and his colleagues, a blood sacrifice in the form of an early second front seemed to be the only legitimate test of Anglo-American intentions.[164]

Several questions beg answers: Why did America think that the demonstrated historical record in Eastern Europe no longer applied? And what was that record? The Balkans had always tended to be dominated by one or another of adjacent great power neighbors, and only when those powerful neighbors were too weak to exercise effective control did these states possess any substantive degree of freedom. With the disappearance of Austria-Hungary after 1918, the contest became one between Germany and Russia, and they ended up dividing up the region in 1939. With Germany now about to be defeated, how could a situation be established and maintained where Soviet Russia would not at the very least exercise predominant influence in the region? To expect that the Russians would suddenly voluntarily abdicate their traditional ambitions in Eastern Europe in the name of some abstract standards of democracy, freedom, and human rights was naive. Were the Russians likely to pursue a policy in Eastern Europe any more benign and humane than that of the historic American approach to Central America and the Caribbean?

The only hope for avoiding the monolithic confrontation that was to crystallize over the next three years was to situate the struggle over Eastern Europe on the plane of concrete, limited, demonstrable national interests. Only mutual recognition of the legitimacy of one another's vital security interests might have created the basis for a reasonable settlement. The record indicates that Stalin tried this approach throughout most of the war. It is also apparent that Roosevelt was never able to elucidate, let alone explain, what specific American interests were at stake in Eastern Europe. The president's general unreceptiveness to Moscow's legitimate goals coupled with his proclivity for the non-explanation of policy confused and antagonized the Russians, confirming in their own minds the essentially hostile nature of American policy.

In the end, a gap occurred between what Roosevelt believed the people would tolerate and what the Russians would countenance.[165] It turned out that Roosevelt was not able to bridge the gap between the idealism which he so assiduously fostered for public consumption and to which he at least in part subscribed, and a growing realization that the real world was rather different. It was this great contradiction—and one that was to continue to plague American foreign policy after his death—that proved to be the bane of FDR's diplomacy. Increasingly, as the war droned on, FDR was able to verbalize his utopian feelings of solidarity with the peoples of Eastern Europe only in terms of ideology (e.g., democratic ideals). In addressing the issue in this way, he helped pave the road to cold war. The problem was that in Joseph Stalin the president faced an opponent whose convictions were much more concrete and deeply-held than his own. But unlike Roosevelt, Stalin was prepared and willing to operationalize his convictions in more concrete terms, to bargain on that basis, and to live with the consequences as necessary.

RUSSIA'S CONDUCT

For Soviet Russia, World War II and its aftermath remained a major reference point for its policymakers until the final dissolution of the Soviet Union in 1991. Russian perceptions of threat were shaped as much by their historical experience as by an objective evaluation of the forces ranged against them. The events of that terrible conflict represented a watershed for the rest of the century. Hitler's attack on Soviet Russia provided the opportunity for the Russians to emerge on the world stage as one of the primary actors of the international system. Russia's experiences in world affairs from the Molotov-Ribbentrop Treaty in 1939, through the enormous shock of the German invasion in 1941, to the many frustrations associated with the Anglo-American relationship, were all learning experiences in a world of unremitting hard knocks, and they would serve to underwrite and reinforce the long train of cynical opportunism and power politics that would be hallmarks of Russian policy thereafter. As it turned out, Stalin's views of the basic values and interests of the Western democracies, the danger of capitalist encirclement, the inevitability of war among them, the nature and sources of imperialism, and the unlikelihood of genuine disarmament changed very little between 1939 and 1945. Why should they have?

The impressions created by the disaster of June 1941 reinforced the lessons of the 1914–1920 period. First, Germany was again the source of a mortal threat, resurgent and seemingly all-powerful within twenty years of a humiliating defeat. But there were also other countries eager to lend a hand in dismembering Russia, including Hungary and Rumania. Second, a secure homeland called for a very large military force. Experience dictated that such a force could never be large enough. Third, there was a need for strategic offense, even preemption, if necessary, to safeguard the socialist motherland. Fourth, there was the overwhelming importance of space—buffer zones.

Thus, Stalin's primary concern with trying to ensure Russian security from any future attack from the West is a continuously recurring leitmotif in the record of the communications of the Big Three during the war. Poland's future status, in this regard, was both a real and a symbolic issue. The positions that Stalin articulated regarding Poland eventually were replicated in some way or other in Rumania, Bulgaria, Hungary, and Czechoslovakia. Whether Stalin was in fact driven toward more overt control of Eastern Europe as a result of the attitudes of America and Britain toward the Polish question is still open to debate. What the documentary record does reveal is that the opposite was not the case, namely, that Stalin wanted absolute Russian control all along.

Many legitimate reasons existed for the Russians to doubt America's intentions. The Russians still harbored memories of America's involvement in the military intervention there at the end of World War I. They recalled vividly that America was the last major state in the West to extend diplomatic recognition to Soviet Russia. They remembered clearly our procrastination in entering the war against the fascists, our refusal to inform them of the atomic bomb project, the long delay in opening up a second front in the West, despite FDR's explicit promises to do so, and an apparent American propensity not to consult with them on wartime strategy to the same extent as we did with the British. Add to this an apparent willingness to support Nazi collaborators in American-occcupied countries, notably Italy, while at the same time pressuring Soviet Russia to allow free elections in areas vital to their national security interests, notably in Poland.[166] Then, again, the dichotomy in the American and British approaches must have been a difficult one for the Russians to grasp at times, only serving to confuse them and, ultimately, to encourage them to act unilaterally.

Thus, Russia's misgivings about American intentions flowed, at least in part, from a preoccupation with "encirclement" as evidenced by the historical record of perceived hostility.[167] Indeed, if you were a decision maker sitting in the Kremlin at the end of the war, the question of why America, after September 1939 acquiesced in the conquest of Eastern Europe by the Nazis with hardly a murmur but refused to acknowledge any preeminent Russian interest in the region thereafter might well have been pondered.

It does not follow, in taking note of all this, that ideology played the key role in the Soviet Union's conduct during the war. Stalin's overriding goal by the end of the war had become one essentially of system maintenance and the preservation of his own position.[168] In the process, Marxist-Leninism had become largely instrumental, employed to legitimize the bureaucracy's iron grip by defining in Manichean terms the foreign threat that served to underwrite the terrible sacrifices of the Stalinist system. As a wellspring for political guidance and inspiration it had long since been thoroughly subordinated to the prevailing elite's views of the country's national interests.[169] By 1945 ideology's only real significance was its mobilization potential—both at home and abroad.

Who can say that, in the absence of America's confused and contradictory policies, Stalin might have refrained from exercising the rigid and pervasive control over Eastern Europe as he later instituted? But it is well to remember that the socalled Iron Curtain did not fall all at once. It would take three years for it to "fall," and then only incrementally and ad hoc. As we shall see in the next chapter, despite all of this, there would still be time to fashion a workable relationship with Moscow. Even though a sphere-of-influence settlement would have undoubtedly entailed tensions, it would in all probability have been the sort of tensions that have traditionally characterized great state relations.

THE TRUMAN FACTOR

Roosevelt believed that America could not sustain large military commitments to keep the peace when the war ended. He was also aware that America alone could not prevent the Russians from holding onto the areas they had already occupied in Eastern Europe and were about to occupy in the Far East. He therefore aimed at balancing the power of Soviet Russia with that of the British in Europe and of China in the Far East, and planned to sell this idea to the American people through the United Nations. The U.N. could only work, however, if it reflected the modalities of power and national interest in the postwar world.[170] This, of course, was not to be. In inheriting FDR's contradictory policy of idealism and realism toward dealing with the Russians, Truman could not flee from making an effort to establish a modus vivendi with Russia. In doing so, he believed he was fulfilling the aims of his predecessor's wartime diplomacy.

Unfortunately, Truman's initial approach to dealing with the Russians only served to aggravate and inflame an already serious situation. Certainly, Truman's cutback in aid to Russia is understandable when the history of lend-lease during World War II is considered. The other European states had to prove their need for lend-lease equipment; the Russians had only to ask. This policy was developed in 1941 by Roosevelt because he knew that a two-front war would greatly reduce Germany's military capability in the West. And because Soviet Russia was pressed for military hardware, he believed that such a policy would prove expeditious with regard to red tape and the need to reduce the time lag. By 1944, as the Russians had taken the offensive on the eastern front, and their position was no longer so desperate, America came to realize that she was being taken advantage of. But the manner in which the decision to terminate was handled, both in its abruptness and in its isolation from a broader strategic vision, was unfortunate.

If any initial postwar consideration shaped Truman's strategy during the last weeks of the war and the very early postwar period, it was a desire to minimize our overseas political responsibilities after Germany's surrender. As summer merged into fall in 1945, and misunderstandings proliferated, American and Russian differences over Eastern Europe became enmeshed with a growing conflict over other issues, especially the situations in Italy, Greece, and Japan. Unfortunately, no one suggested that we might want to consider acceding to Russian concerns in Eastern Europe in return for a political quid pro quo on one or another of these other matters.[171]

As Lynn Davis and others have suggested, a more sensible American approach designed to head off a major conflict with Soviet Russia could have been for Washington to back off its opposition to the formation of minority governments in Poland, Rumania, and Bulgaria, to tone down its rhetoric in favor of the holding of free elections, while at the same time seeking to assure the Russians that we had no interest in jeopardizing their legitimate security interests in that part of the world. Soviet Russia just might have abjured its later policy of clamping down on the coalition governments in Hungary and Czechoslovakia. And the West then just might have been less inclined to interpret Russian actions as indicators of a worldwide messianic threat. In the process, resolution of the German, Italian and Japanese occupations might have been more easily brought off in a less threatening environment.

What we do know is what actually happened. With the growing conflict unfolding within many different contexts as 1945 drew to a close, America began to view Russian actions in Eastern Europe, not simply as isolated events, but as barometers of Moscow's general approach. Grave concerns about Russian intentions in Western Europe arose, as Russian tactics employed in Eastern Europe began to be held up as models for the achievement of world revolution. The tragic litany of Russian-American misperceptions and misunderstandings over Eastern Europe would ultimately sabotage their ability to cooperate anywhere else, as the enervating spectacle of the Cold War took shape.

NOTES

1. "Russia: An American Problem," *Atlantic Monthly*, February 1942, p. 148.

2. There is, of course, considerable disagreement in regard to just what motivated the American government during this period. The critical literature centering on the World War II era regarding the origins of the Cold War is extensive. Several groups of analysts emerged over time arguing one or another point of view. This writer falls within the so-called post-revisionist school of thought—a perspective that accepts the main contention of the revisionists that America must bear a heavy share of the responsibility for the onset and intensification of the Cold War but which denies that it was deliberately created by U.S. policy makers for either political or economic reasons.

For the critical analysis contained in these pages, the author is indebted to a number of groundbreaking and insightful works, although he may not necessarily agree with all of their viewpoints and/or conclusions. Among the more important of these writings are: Lynn Etheridge Davis,*The Cold War Begins: Soviet-American Conflict over Eastern Europe* (Princeton: Princeton University Press, 1974); Voytech Mastny, *Russia's Road to the Cold War: Diplomacy, Warfare and the Politics of Communism, 1941–1945* (New York: Columbia University Press, 1979); Martin F. Herz, *Beginnings of the Cold War* (New York: McGraw-Hill, 1966); Albert Resis, "The Stalin-Churchill Secret 'Percentages' Agreement on the Balkans, Moscow, October, 1944", *American Historical Review* (April, 1978): 368-387; Hugh B. Hammett, "America's Non-Policy in Eastern Europe and the Origins of the Cold War," *Survey* (Autumn 1973): 144-162; LaFeber, *America, Russia and the Cold War*; Diane Shaver Clemens, *Yalta* (New York: Oxford University Press, 1970); Robert Garson, "The Atlantic Alliance, Eastern Europe and the Origins of the Cold War," in *Contrast and Connection: Bicentennial Essays in Anglo-American History*, ed. H. C. Allen and Roger Thompson (New York: Macmillan, 1976), pp. 296–320; and William Taubman, *Stalin's American Policy: From Entente to Detente to Cold War* (New York: Norton, 1982).

See also Adam Ulam, *Expansion and Coexistence: Soviet Foreign Policy, 1917–1973*, 2d ed. (New York: Praeger, 1974); Michael Sherry, *Preparing for the Next War* (New Haven, Conn.: Yale University Press, 1977); Robert H. McNeil, "Roosevelt through Stalin's Spectacles," *International Journal of Politics* (Winter, 1963): 194–206; James E. McSherry, Stalin, *Hitler and Europe* (Cleveland, Ohio:

World Publishing Co., 1968), pp. 50-66; William O. McCagg, Jr., *Stalin Embattled, 1943–48* (Detroit, MI.: Wayne State University Press, 1978); James R. Hawkes, "Stalin's Diplomatic Offensive: The Politics of the Second Front, 1941–1943," Ph.D. dissertation, University of Illinois, 1966; Louis Fischer, *The Road to Yalta: Soviet Foreign Relations, 1941–1945* (New York: Harper & Row, 1972); and Voytech Mastny, "The Cassandra in the Foreign Commissariat: Maxim Litvinov and the Cold War," *Foreign Affairs* 54 (January, 1976): 366–376.

3. For an accounting of Russian-American relations up to the Bolshevik Revolution, see Max H. Laserson, *The American Impact on Russia: Diplomatic and Ideological, 1784-1917* (New York: Macmillan, 1950); Nikolai N. Balkhovitnikov, *The Beginnings of Russian-American Relations, 1775-1815*—translation of a work by a former leading Soviet expert in this field (Cambridge, Mass.: Harvard University Press, 1976); Benson L. Grayson, *Russian-American Relations in World War I* (New York: Unger, 1979); and Nina N. Bashkira, ed., *The U.S. and Russia: The Beginning of Relations, 1765-1815*—a volume in the joint U.S.-Soviet documentary publishing project (Washington, D.C.: Government Printing Office, 1980). Additional valuable sources concerning these years include Thomas A. Bailey, *America Faces Russia: Russian-American Relations from Early Times to Our Day* (Ithaca, N.Y.: Cornell University Press, 1950); William A. Williams, *American-Russian Relations, 1781-1947* (New York: Octagon, 1971); and John Lewis Gaddis, *Russia, the Soviet Union and the United States: An Interpretive History* (New York: Wiley, 1978).

4. George F. Kennan, *Memoirs, 1925-1950* (Boston: Little, Brown, 1957), makes this point.

5. On this concern, see Bailey, *America Faces Russia*, pp. 125–26. On the early Russia-phobia in America, see Jerzy Jan Lerski, *A Polish Chapter in Jacksonian America: The United States and the Polish Exiles of 1831* (Madison: University of Wisconsin Press, 1958).

6. Quoted in William Henry Harbaugh, *Power and Responsibility: The Life and Times of Theodore Roosevelt* (N.Y.: Macmillan, 1961), p. 277.

7. Quoted in Walter LaFeber, *America, Russia and the Cold War, 1945-84*, 7th ed., (N. Y.: Knopf, 1993), p. 4. It is well to point out that these oscillations of American opinion and policy toward Russia were influenced primarily by diplomats and private travelers. There was no academic study of Russia (including its language) in America until the twentieth century. Myths, skewed images, and a few horror stories were virtually the only basis for American assessments of Russia, until the Bolshevik Revolution came along to inject a new set of myths, biases, and horror stories that would only serve to confound normal discourse, making matters worse. An influential nineteenth-century illustration may be seen in the writings and activities of George Kennan (a distant relative of the later George F. Kennan), whose book *Siberia and the Exile System* (New York: 1882) helped arouse American indignation against Russian despotism and the persecution of the political opposition. Kennan's polemics also had an impact on the Tsarist system, helping to precipitate some political reforms. On this point, see Laserson, *The American Impact on Russia*, p. 311.

8. For descriptions of this period, see Foster Rhea Dulles, *The Road to Teheran* (Princeton, N. J.: Princeton University Press, 1945), Chapter 10, and Frederick L. Schuman, *American Policy Toward Russia Since 1917* (New York: Macmillan, 1928).

9. David W. McFadden, *Alternative Paths: Soviets and Americans, 1917-1920*
(New York: Oxford University Press, 1993). See, also, Harold J. Goldberg, ed.,
Documents on Soviet-American Relations, Vol. I, *Intervention, Famine Relief,
International Affairs, 1917-1933* (Gulf Breeze, Fla.: Academic International Press,
1993)—the first volume in a 12-volume set that will form a comprehensive
documentary survey of American-Russian relations after 1917.   Vol. I contains 180
documents of both American and Russian sources.

10. The actual reasons for the Allied presence has been a subject for controversy.
President Woodrow Wilson defended the intervention in terms of aiding a 50,000-
man Czechoslovak armed force, deserters from the Austrian army, who had been left
behind the Eastern Front after the withdrawal of Russia from the war.   The Czechs,
though isolated in Siberia, retained their discipline and *élan* and represented an
important organized military force in Russia during the chaotic civil war period. But
the Czechs had been joined by Russian anti-Bolshevik factions in the civil strife, and
therefore support for them inevitably pitted America against the new Bolshevik state.
On the conduct and role of the Czechs, see John F. N. Bradley, *The Czechoslovak
Legion in Russia, 1914–1920* (Boulder, Col.: Eastern Europe Monographs, 1991).
For broader assessments, see George F. Kennan, *Soviet-American Relations,
1917–1920: The Decision to Intervene* (Princeton, N.J.: Princeton University
Press, 1958); N. Gordon Levin, Jr., *Woodrow Wilson and World Politics: America's
Response to War and Revolution* (New York: Oxford University Press, 1968); also
Arno J. Mayer, *Politics and Diplomacy of Peacemaking: Containment and
Counterrevolution at Versailles, 1918–1919* (New York: Knopf, 1968); John F. N.
Bradley, *Allied Intervention in Russia* (Lanham, Md.: University Press of America,
1984); Teddy V. Uldricks, *Diplomacy and Ideology: The Origins of Soviet Foreign
Relations, 1917–1930* (Beverly Hills, Calif.: Sage, 1979); and Richard Goldhurst,
The Midnight War: The American Intervention in Russia, 1919–1920 (New York:
McGraw-Hill, 1978).
Michael Kettle, in *Churchill and the Archangel Fiasco, November, 1918–July,
1919*, Vol. 3, *Russia and the Allies, 1917–20* (New York: Routledge, 1992), argues
that Britain played a far greater role in Russia's civil war than is generally thought.
The third of a projected five-volume series, Kettle's book is a minute dissection of
Britain's Russia policy at this time.   Interestingly, he asserts that Churchill was
especially active in forcing the issue of increased British involvement in both the
military and economic side of the intervention.

11. In his note, Chicherin, pointing out numerous inconsistencies, noted that
there was no mention of freedom for the Philippines, India, or Ireland in the
message—a viewpoint reflecting the Bolsheviks' hatred for liberal democracy. See
Sovetsko-amerikanskie otnosheniia (Moscow: Narkomindel, 1934), pp. 28–33.

12.   I. V. Kliuchnikov and Andrei Sabanin, eds., *Mezhdunarodnaia politika
noveishego vremeni v dogovorakh, notakh i deklaratsiiakh* (Moscow: Narkomindel,
1925-28), II, pp. 91–92.

13. On the Bullitt mission, see *Foreign Relations of the United States (FRUS)*,
1919, Russia, pp. 85-89. See, also *Sovetsko-amerikanski otnosheniia*, pp. 37–39.

14. The Department of State, *Memorandum on Certain Aspects of the Bolshevik
Movement in Russia* (Washington, D.C.: Government Printing Office, 1919), pp.
367–93.

15. Quoted in Ray Stannard Baker and William E. Dodd, eds., *War and Peace:*

Presidential Messages, Addresses, and Public Papers (1917-1924) by Woodrow Wilson (New York: Wiley, 1927), II, p. 15.

16. Cited in Walter LaFeber, *The Origins of the Cold War, 1941-47: A Historical Problem with Interpretations and Documents* (New York: Wiley, 1971), p. 58.

17. See his article in the New Republic, March 22, 1919.

18. Although American business firms in the 1920s, in return for financial reward, did give considerable technical assistance to Soviet Russian economic development, and American food relief after World War I had saved millions of Russians from starvation. See in this regard Benson L. Grayson, ed., *The American Image of Russia, 1917–1977* (New York: Unger, 1979); Peter J. Filene, *Americans and the Soviet Experiment, 1917–1933* (Cambridge, Mass.: Harvard University Press, 1967); and Joan Hoff Wilson, *Ideology and Economics: U.S. Relations with the Soviet Union, 1918–1933* (St. Louis: University of Missouri Press, 1974).

19. Myron Rush, ed., *The International Situation and Soviet Foreign Policy: Key Reports by Soviets Leaders from the Revolution to the Present* (Columbus: Ohio State University Press, 1970), pp. 85–96.

20. See Schuman, *American Policy toward Russia*, pp. 370–407, for a discussion of the Winter War against Finland; also, Anatole G. Mazour, *Finland Between East and West* (New York: Van Nostrand, 1956), especially pp. 84–129.

21. No fewer than twenty percent of the American people still distrusted Soviet Russia after the June 1941 German invasion. Data on American attitudes at the time may be found in Hadley Cantril and Mildred Strunk, eds., *Public Opinion, 1935–46* (Princeton: Princeton University Press, 1951).

22. Hopkins concluded, after extensive discussions with Stalin and other high-level officials in the Russian capital, that Moscow was determined to hang tough with the Germans and that a workable alliance could be forged with them. On the impact of this trip on American thinking in regard to Russia, see Robert E. Sherwood, *Roosevelt and Hopkins: An Intimate History*, rev. ed. (New York, Macmillan, 1950), pp. 303–04.

23. The repayments were to take place over a ten-year period. On February 13, 1942, a second $1 billion was authorized. Finally, on June 11, 1942, a new agreement on mutual aid replaced the previous understandings based on the notes of November 1941 and February 1942. On the evolution of lend-lease aid to Soviet Russia, see Raymond H. Dawson, *The Decision to Aid Russia, 1941: Foreign Policy and Domestic Politics* (Chapel Hill: University of North Carolina Press, 1959).

24. See, for example, the comments of A.J. Drexel Biddle, Jr., U.S. Ambassador to the Polish Government in Exile, to the Secretary of State, July 6, 1941, *Records of the Department of State*, National Archives, Record Group 59, Decimal File 860C.01/575, hereafter cited as *Records of Department of State*, Decimal File.

25. *Records of Department of State*, Decimal File 740.00119, *European War* 1939/826.

26. In a memorandum to the Secretary of State, August 4, 1941, Assistant Secretary Adolph Berle stated: "At our suggestion the President sent a message to Winston Churchill indicating that he could not recognize any post-war commitments except as a part of a general final settlement in which, presumably, we would take part." *Records of Department of State*, Decimal File 740.00119 *European War* 1939/826.

27. FDR to Churchill, July 14, 1941, *FRUS, 1941*, I (Washington, D.C.: Government Printing Office, 1948), p. 342.

28. According to Sumner Welles, *Seven Decisions that Shaped History* (New York: Random House, 1950), p. 24, Roosevelt had earlier told him that the meeting with Churchill "should be utilized to hold out hope to the enslaved peoples of the world. The English-speaking democracies both stood for principles of freedom and justice. They should jointly bind themselves now to establish at the conclusion of the war a new world order based upon these principles."

29. On this point, see Davis, *The Cold War Begins*, Chapter 1.

30. Only the principles concerning free access to economic markets spurred any substantive discussion. See Meeting between Rooosvelt and Churchill, August 11, 1941, *FRUS, 1941*, I, pp. 361–363, and Memorandum of a Conversation, by Under Secretary Welles, August 11, 1941, *FRUS, 1941*, I, pp. 364–67.

31. Davis, *The Cold War Begins*, Chapter 2. See also John Lewis Gaddis, *The United States and the Origins of the Cold War, 1941–1947* (New York: Columbia University Press, 1972), Chapter 1.

32. Statement by I. M. Maisky, Soviet Russia's ambasador to Great Britain, in accepting the principles of the Atlantic Charter on behalf of his government. Report of *Proceedings*, Inter-Allied meeting held in London at St. James Palace on September 24, 1941 (London: H.M. Stationery Office, 1941), Cmd. 6315. According to Cordell Hull's *Memoirs*, (New York: Macmillan, 1948), Vol 2, p.1165, Maisky "indicated that his government felt it should have been consulted beforehand regarding the Atlantic Charter." As for Great Britain, Churchill declared that the Atlantic Charter would not apply to the British Empire, viewing the document as merely "an interim and partial statement of war aims designed to assure all countries of our righteous purpose." See speech to the House of Commons on September 9, 1941, *House of Commons Parliamentary Debates*, 5th Series, Vol. 374, Coll. 68–69.

33. See U.S. Ambassador to the United Kingdon John G. Winant to the Secretary of State, December 4, 1941, *FRUS, 1941*, I, pp. 192–193. See also Llewellyn Woodward, *British Foreign Policy in the Second World War*, Vol. II (London: Her Majesty's Stationery Office, 1971), pp. 220-221. Refer *FRUS, 1942*, III, pp. 532–552. Cf. Mastny, *Russia's Road to the Cold War*, Chapter 2.

34. The Curzon line derived from a decision of the principal Allied Powers who in December 1919 considered it necessary only to include ethnographically Polish regions in the territory of the new Polish state that was being re-created after World War I.

35. See Anthony Eden, *The Memoirs of Anthony Eden, Earl of Avon*, Vol. 2, *The Reckoning* (Boston: Little, Brown, 1965), pp. 334–345.

36. Memorandum from Secretary of State Hull to President Roosevelt, February 4, 1942, *FRUS, 1942*, III, pp. 505–12. This memorandum was the product of a study undertaken by the European Division of the State Department in January, 1942. See also Welles, *Seven Decisions that Shaped History*, p. 135, and Hull to Winant, December 5, 1941, *FRUS: 1941*, I, pp. 194–195.

37. A situation that greatly concerned the British foreign secretary. See Eden, *The Reckoning*, pp. 334–345; Mastny, *Russia's Road to the Cold War*, pp. 41–44.

38. See Memorandum from European Division, *FRUS, 1942*, III, pp. 507, 510, and 511.

39. As illustration, America's attitude at this time regarding Russia's rein-

corporation of the Baltic States was not justified in terms of specific American desires in Eastern Europe but, rather, in relation to the maintenance of the integrity of the Atlantic Charter principles.

40. Memorandum of a Conversation by Undersecretary Welles with British Ambassador Halifax, February 18, 1942, *FRUS, 1942*, III, pp. 514–519.

41. Memorandum from Undersecretary Welles to Roosevelt, February 20, 1942, *FRUS, 1942*, III, pp. 521–522.

42. Winston Churchill, *The Second World War, The Hinge of Fate* (Boston: Houghton Mifflin Co., 1950), p. 327.

43. See Memorandum prepared in the Division of European Affairs, March 24, 1944, *FRUS, 1944*, IV, pp. 840–841.

44. Memorandum of Conversation, February 20, 1942, *FRUS, 1942*, III, p. 521.

45. Memorandum of a Conversation by Undersecretary Welles with Lord Halifax, February 20, 1942, *FRUS, 1942*, III, p. 521–532, 552. See also Eden, *The Reckoning*, p. 370.

46. Memorandum of Conversation, Welles with Halifax, p. 523. See also Memorandum of Second Secretary of the U.S. Embassy in the Soviet Union, Llewellyn Thompson, to Secretary of State, March 26, 1942, *FRUS, 1942*, pp. 535–536.

47. Sherwood, *Roosevelt and Hopkins*, p. 526.

48. Opposing interpretations of FDR's action exist. Herbert Feis states, "[T]he Soviet government was to be lured away from one boon by a choicer one, away from its absorption in frontiers by the attraction of quick military relief." See his *Between War and Peace: The Potsdam Conference* (Princeton, N. J.: Princeton University Press, 1960), p. 61. Robert Divine, in *Roosevelt and World War II* (Baltimore: Johns Hopkins University Press, 1969), doubts that Roosevelt was ever concerned enough about Moscow's boundary claims to base his military strategy on such a consideration. "Instead, I believe that his premature offer of a second front stemmed from his desire to encourage Russia at a critical moment in the course of the war" (p. 85).

Robert Daniels, in *Russia: Roots of Confrontation* (Cambridge, Mass.: Harvard University Press, 1985), pp. 85–89, argues that FDR probably gave the second front pledge out of a desire to encourage Russia's military effort on the eastern front, not as a reward for abandoning territorial demands. Mastny, in *Russia's Road to the Cold War*, p. 71, offers a somewhat different explanation and analysis. Molotov journeyed to Washington expecting a military reward, all the more imperative to offset the painful setback the Red Army had recently suffered as a result of its abortive offensive at Kharkov. When he first met Roosevelt on May 30, the president did not volunteer any promise. Pressed by Molotov about the second front, he asked General George C. Marshall, the Army Chief of Staff also present in the room, whether it was fair to say that America was preparing the operation. Given an affirmative answer, Roosevelt went a step further and "authorizes Mr. Molotov to inform Mr. Stalin that we expect the formation of a second front this year."

Since Washington was planning a landing in North Africa later that year, the statement was technically correct. It was also rash and misleading. FDR made a further blunder by discarding the State Department's carefully-worded draft of the public communique and accepting instead one prepared by Molotov. Thus the world was informed that "in the course of the conversations full understanding was reached

with regard to the urgent tasks of creating a second front *in Europe* in 1942."
(Author's emphasis).

By way of contrast, Mark Stoler argues that an American concern with Russian expansion was evident from the outset. See his "The 'Second Front' and the American Fear of Soviet Expansion, 1941–1943," *Military Affairs* (October, 1975): 136–140. In any event, the Russians believed that a deal had been made. See Standley to Hull, July 22, 1942, *FRUS, 1942*, III, pp. 613–614.

49. Published studies of Russian foreign policy during this period fail to provide any clear reasons for Molotov's acceptance of the treaty. Eden concluded that Molotov probably became convinced he could not get his way over the frontiers issue and decided that more was to be gained in the military field by accepting Britain's terms, and going to Washington with the treaty signed, than by failing to agree. Washington, of course, interpreted Molotov's action as deference to American opposition. On this, see Ulam, *Expansion and Coexistence*, pp. 335-336. But Mastny, *Russia's Road to the Cold War*, p. 73, argues that Stalin had Molotov drop the insistence on territorial questions after receiving Roosevelt's message about American plans for a second front.

50. See communique, June 12, 1942, cited in *Correspondence between the Chairman of the Council of Ministers of the USSR and the Presidents of the USA and the Prime Ministers of Great Britain during the Great Patriotic War of 1941–1945*, Vol. 2, *Correspondence with Franklin D. Roosevelt and Harry Truman* (Moscow: Progress Publishers, 1957), p. 275, hereafter referred to as *Wartime Correspondence*.

51. For evidence that military reasons accounted for the delay in executing the second front, see Maurice Matloff and Edwin L. Snell, Strategic Planning for Coalition Warfare: 1941–1942. United States Army in World War II: (Washington, D.C.: The War Department, 1953), especially pp. 217–232, and 322–327.

52. John P. Glennon, "'This Time Germany Is a Defeated Nation,' The Doctrine of Unconditional Surrender and Some Unsuccessful Attempts to Alter It, 1943–1944," in Gerald N. Grob, ed., *Statesmen and Statescraft of the Modern West* (Barre, Mass.: Barre Publishing Co., 1967), pp. 109–151.

53. On the success of the mission, see John R. Deane, *The Strange Alliance: The Story of Our Efforts at Wartime Cooperation with Russia* (New York: Norton, 1947), pp. 47–48.

54. There is no question that the Russians were difficult to deal with. For starters there was the language problem. Then there were the very frustrating administrative practices of the Russian *nomenklatura*. Russian foreign policy under Stalin was essentially one in which his ideas predominated with periodic input from institutional groups like the military, and more frequent advice from transitory groups of close associates. Stalin had to be consulted on virtually everything. His decision making style was one of making all the decisions himself but having the Politburo formally register them. Informal discussions took place at night. Very few minutes were taken. Stalin's habit was to make arbitrary decisions; and when they were wrong, others would be blamed.   Government agencies kept few records but refused to admit it. Add to that the officially sanctioned suspicion of foreigners pursued by the party and state apparatus. But perhaps most difficult of all was the tendency of the top governmental people to shift back and forth from great cordiality to meanness and vindictiveness in their dealings with foreign representatives.

For three excellent expositions of these factors see Niels Erik Rosenfeldt,

Knowledge and Power: The Role of Stalin's Secret Chancellery in the Soviet System of Government (Copenhagen: Rosenkilde and Bagger, 1978); Joseph G. Whelen, *Soviet Diplomacy and Negotiating Behavior* (New York: Knopf, 1982); and Philip E. Mosely, "Some Techniques of Negotiation," in Raymond Dennett and Joseph E. Johnson, eds., *Negotiating with the Russians* (Boston: Little, Brown, 1951), pp. 271–303.

55. Harriman to Roosevelt, November 4, 1943, *FRUS, The Conferences at Cairo and Teheran, 1943* (Washington, D.C.: 1961), pp. 154–155.

56. *FRUS, The Conferences at Cairo and Teheran*, 1943, pp. 511–532.

57. Ibid., p. 594. Assuming that FDR was aware of his territorial concerns in Eastern Europe, Stalin may have concluded that in the absence of any specific comments to the contrary, the Americans could be persuaded to go along. On the importance of the Teheran Conference for subsequent misunderstandings among the Big Three, see Keith Sainsbury, *The Turning Point* (New York: Norton, 1985).

58. *FRUS, 1944*, III, pp. 1243–1245.

59. On September 30, 1939, a Polish government-in-exile was established in France and promptly recognized by France, Great Britain and, shortly thereafter, by America. With the defeat of France in the spring of 1940, that government, along with thousands of Polish troops then under arms in France, were evacuated to Britain. Thereafter known as the London Polish government, it maintained especially close relations with the British government while seeking American support for its claims against both the Germans and the Russians.

60. For a review of these requests, see *FRUS, 1942*, III, pp. 100–220.

61. See, for example, Undersecretary Welles to FDR, February 19, 1942, *FRUS, 1942*, III, pp. 107–108; Secretary of State Hull to U.S. Ambassador to the Soviet Union, Rear Admiral William H. Standley, May 19, 1942, *FRUS, 1942*, III, p. 146.

62. See Ambassador Biddle to the Secretary of State, February 20, 1942, *Records of the Department of State*, Decimal File 740.0011, *European War* 1939/20193.

63. Secretary of State Hull to Ambassador Stanley, September 14, 1942, *FRUS, 1942*, III, p. 187.

64. See American report on the Soviet note in Ambassador Biddle to the Secretary of State, January 28, 1943, *FRUS, 1943*, III, pp. 323–324. For a description and history of the various Polish-American borders proposed over the years, see U.S. Department of State, *Postwar Foreign Policy Preparation, 1939-1945* (Washington, D.C.: Government Printing Office, 1950), pp. 496–509.

65. Ambassador Standley to Secretary of State, March 9, 1943, *FRUS, 1943*, III, p. 346, and p. 320.

66. Marshall Stalin to President Roosevelt, April 21, 1943, *FRUS, 1943*, III, pp. 395–396.

67. See Mastny, *Russia's Road to the Cold War*, Chapter 3.

68. Ambassador Standley to Secretary of State, June 18, 1943, *FRUS, 1943*, III, pp. 432–434.

69. Sikorski, who had been both prime minister and commander-in-chief of the Polish armed forces, was killed in an airplane crash in July 1943. His successor, Stanislaw Mikolajczyk, proved to be an able and more moderate political leader—one who demonstrated a willingness and capacity to reach out to the Russians, seeking genuine compromise based on legitimate mutual interests.

70. *Wartime Correspondence*, Note 56, pp. 280–281.

71. *Wartime Correspondence*, Note 55, p. 280.

72. *Wartime Correspondence*, Note 180, pp.124–126.

73. For memoranda of the various discussions held among Prime Minister Mikolajczyk, FDR and State Department officials, see *FRUS, 1944*, III, pp. 1277–1289.

74. Roosevelt to Stalin, December 16, 1944, *FRUS,1944*, III, pp. 1345–1347.

75. On August 1 the underground Polish military forces in Warsaw rose against the Germans in expectation of freeing the city before the Red Army reached it. The Russians dallied while the Polish freedom fighters slowly ran out of supplies in the face of a determined German counteroffensive. Mikolajczyk bombarded Moscow, London, and Washington with messages pleading for relief. In a message to Churchill, Stalin declared that he had become "convinced that the Warsaw action represents a reckless and terrible adventure which is costing the population large sacrifices. . . . In the situation which has arisen the Soviet command has come to the conclusion that it must dissociate itself from the Warsaw adventure. . . ." Cited in Winston Churchill, *The Second World War: Triumph and Tragedy* (Boston: Houghton Mifflin, 1953), pp. 133–134. For the Russian role in this tragedy, see John Erickson, *The Road to Berlin* (London: Wiedenfeld & Nicholson, 1983), pp. 269 ff.

76. Memorandum Prepared in the British Foreign Office, April 17, 1944, *FRUS, 1944*, I, pp. 596–599.

77. *FRUS, 1944*, I, pp. 610–611. See also Hull, *Memoirs*, Vol. 2, pp. 1451–1458.

78. See Andrew Rothstein, ed., *Soviet Foreign Policy during the Patriotic War*, Vol. 2 (London: Oxford University Press, 1946), for the texts of the Rumanian and Finnish armistices, pp. 123–125, and 128–132 respectively.

79. See FDR to Stalin, Wartime Correspondence, October 5, 1944, in which the American president stated that "I prefer to regard your forthcoming talks with the P.M. as preliminary to a meeting of the three of us." On this point see also Herbert Feis, *Churchill, Roosevelt, Stalin: The War They Waged and the Peace They Sought* (Princeton, N. J.: Princeton University Press, 1957), pp. 453–460; Winston Churchill, *Closing the Ring* (Boston: Houghton Mifflin, 1951), pp. 226–243.

80. "I was somewhat puzzled by your message of October 5," Stalin wrote. "I had imaged that Mr. Churchill was coming to Moscow in keeping with an agreement reached with you at Quebec. It appears, however, that my supposition is at variance with reality." *Wartime Correspondence*, Stalin to FDR, October 8, 1944, No. 231.

81. On the advice of Charles Bohlen, Harry Hopkins persuaded Roosevelt to send Stalin a message that would serve notice that henceforth America would no longer pursue a passive policy toward southeastern Europe. The Russian military advances into the region served to change the equation for a growing number of the president's advisors. See Sherwood, *Roosevelt and Hopkins*, pp. 833–834, and Charles Bohlen, *Witness to History, 1929-1969* (New York: Norton, 1973), pp. 162–163.

82. On August 22, 1943, Stalin sent Roosevelt and Stalin a message pointing out that "[T]he Soviet government has not been kept informed of the Anglo-American negotiations with the Italians. . . . I think the time is ripe for us to set up a military-political commission . . . for consideration of problems related to negotiations with various governments falling away from Germany. To date it has been like this: The

USA and Britain reach agreement between themselves while the USSR is informed of the agreement between the two Powers as a third party looking passively on. I must say that this situation cannot be tolerated any longer. I propose setting up the commission and making Sicily its seat for the time being." *Wartime Correspondence*, No. 104, p. 77.

After some further jawboning, agreement was reached in early September on the military-political commission concept. After announcing the appointment of Andrei Vyshinsky as Russia's representative to the commission, Stalin pointed out to his Western colleagues that "[L]ater, taking into account the initial experience of the commission, we shall be able to specify its functions in respect of both Italy and other countries." *Wartime Correspondence*, September 12, 1943, No. 115, p. 86.

83. On March 18, 1944 Harriman sent a note to Molotov in which he informed the Russians how the process was going to work regarding the authority of the proposed Allied Control Commission in Italy. Harriman went on to describe what the rationale was to be, namely, that the administration of such territories falls to those countries doing the fighting there, while any other allies not directly involved in that theater may be invited in. Harriman also took the occasion to reprimand Moscow for contacting the Italians directly. Major responsibility for Italy, he said, still resides with the military administrator, in this case British General Harold Alexander. Archives of the Foreign Ministry of the USSR, *U.S. Embassy Notes and Letters to the Foreign Ministry*, U.S. Division Fund, Op. 128, File 154, Subfile 2, pp. 81–83.

84. When the American and British governments later asked for a share in determing occupation policies in Rumania, Vyshinsky denied the request and referred to Italy as a precedent. The Russian chairman of the Control Commission for Rumania also pointed out that since Washington and London had made the executive decisions in Italy in the name of the United Nations, he felt entitled to do the same in Rumania. For an accounting of these actions and reactions, see Feis, *Churchill, Roosevelt, and Stalin*, pp. 546–549.

85. In early March 1945 the Russians were informed that some high-level Germans had met in Switzerland with representatives of the Anglo-American forces in the Mediterranean theater, and that Russian representatives had not been invited. After a series of ascerbic communications, the Russians concluded on March 22 in a note to the British Foreign Office that the belligerents had come to Berne "to negotiate with representatives of the Anglo-American Command the capitulation of the German forces in North Italy" without Russian involvement. Roosevelt found himself hard-pressed to assuage Russian fears that there was a deal in the offing to move German forces to the eastern front. On this matter, see *War Correspondence*, No. 417, April 5, 1945, pp. 311–313. See also Notes 87 and 88 to same, pp. 397–398.

86. According to Churchill, Stalin was concerned because Roosevelt's message "seemed to demand too many rights for the United States leaving too little for the Soviet Union and Great Britain, who, after all, had a treaty of common assistance." Churchill, *Triumph and Tragedy* , pp. 190–191.

87. Resis, The Stalin-Churchill Secret 'Percentages' Agreement, p. 386.

88. For an account of that meeting, see Anglo-Russian Political Conversations at Moscow, October 9–October 17, 1944, deposited in the Public Record Office as Prem. 3434/4 9565, hereafter cited as *Anglo-Russian Political Conversations*, in this instance, p. 48. See also *FRUS, 1944*, III, p. 446. For Churchill's own accounting of

the meeting, see his *Triumph and Tragedy*, pp. 196–203.

89. Hull to Winant, Washington, October 21,1944, *FRUS, 1944*, III, pp. 469–470.

90. *Ibid.*

91. *Anglo-Russian Political Conversations*, p. 6. For a somewhat different perspective on all of this, see Paul D. Moyle, "A Policy of Percentages? British Policy and the Balkans After the Moscow Conference of October, 1944," *International History Review* (February 1987): 78–103.

92. Russia—Seven Years Later, September, 1944, *FRUS, 1944*, IV, pp. 908–909.

93. Harriman to Hopkins, September 10, 1944, *FRUS, 1944*, IV, p. 989.

94. Herring, "Lend-Lease to Russia and the Origins of the Cold War," p. 95.

95. Ambassador Harriman to the Secretary of State, September 20, 1944, *FRUS, 1944*, IV, pp. 988–998.

96. American Policy Toward Spheres of Influence, January, 1945, *FRUS, 1945*, pp. 103–106.

97. According to Vojtech Mastny, "Stalin and the Prospects of a Separate Peace in World War II," *American Historical Review* (December, 1972): 1365–1388, Stalin secretly considered a separate peace with Hitler as late as mid-1943.

98. For excellent reviews of these divergent viewpoints, see John L. Snell, *Wartime Origins of the East-West Dilemma Over Germany* (New Orleans: University of Louisiana Press, 1959), Chapter 1. See also Walter L. Dorn, "The Debate Over American Occupation Policy in Germany in 1944-45," *Political Science Quarterly* (December, 1957): 481–501.

99. U.S. Proposal with Regard to Questions of Reparations, October 1943, *FRUS, 1943*, I, pp. 740–741.

100. See, on this, Robert Murphy, *Diplomat Among Warriors* (Garden City, N.Y.: Doubleday, 1964).

101. See in this regard, Paul Y. Hammond, "Directives for the Occupation of Germany: The Washington Controversy," in Harold Stein, ed., *American Civil-Military Relations* (Birmingham: University of Alabama Press, 1963), pp. 311–464, and Hajo Holborn, *American Military Government: Its Organization and Policies* (Washington, D.C.: Government Printing Office, 1947).

102. *FRUS, 1943*, I, pp. 554–572, 605–608, 706–711. See also Philip E. Mosely, "The Occupation of Germany: New Light on How the Zones Were Drawn," *Foreign Affairs* (July, 1950): 580–604.

103. Winant to Hull, January 4 and 6, 1944, *FRUS, 1944*, I, pp. 1–3.

104. These agreements are printed in *FRUS, Yalta*, pp. 110–127.

105. See his *The United States and the Origins of the Cold War, 1941–1947* (New York: Columbia University Press, 1972), Chapter 3, esp. pp. 63–94. See also Roosevelt to Hull, October 20, 1944, *FRUS, Yalta*, p.158.

106. Hammond, "Directives for the Occupation of Germany," pp. 342–343.

107. "Germany: General Objectives of United States Economic Policy with Respect to Germany," Memorandum by the Executive Committee on Economic Foreign Policy, *FRUS, 1944*, I, pp. 278–287.

108. For the author's version of the Morgenthau Plan, see Henry Morgenthau, Jr., *Germany Is Our Problem* (New York: Norton, 1945).

109. Roosevelt to Hull, September 29, 1944, *FRUS, Yalta*, p. 155.

110. See Forrest C. Pogue, *The Supreme Command. United States Army in World War II: The European Theater of Operations* (Washington, D.C.: Government Printing Office, 1954), p. 356.

111. Yalta briefing book papers, "The Treatment of Germany," "Economic Policies Toward Germany," and "Reparation and Restitution Policy Toward Germany," *FRUS, Yalta*, pp. 178–193 and 194–197.

112. *FRUS, Conferences at Malta and Yalta, 1945* (Washington, D.C.: 1955), pp. 230–250.

113. *Ibid.*, pp. 93–96.   George Kennan, Minister-Counselor in the Moscow Embassy echoed Hickerson.   In a letter to Charles E. Bohlen during the Yalta Conference, Kennan wrote that   "I recognize that Russia's war effort has been masterful and effective and must, to a certain extent, find its reward at the expense of other peoples in eastern and central Europe. . . . Why could we not make a decent and definitive compromise with it—divide Europe frankly into spheres of influence—keep ourselves out of the Russian sphere and keep the Russians out of ours?" See Bohlen, *Witness to History*, p. 175.

114. *FRUS, Malta and Yalta*, pp. 230–250. Formal acceptance of the Curzon line as Poland's eastern boundary was evidently one of the very few concrete positions that his advisors had urged him to present.

115. *FRUS, Malta and Yalta*, pp. 935–938. On this point, see Clemens, *Yalta*, pp. 212–215.

116. *FRUS, Malta and Yalta*, pp. 939–942.

117. *Ibid*, pp. 667–677.

118. For commentary on Truman's style of decision making at the outset of his presidency, see Henry L. Stimson, *Diary*, April 18, 1945, Henry L. Stimson Papers, Yale University Library; and Dean Acheson, *Present at the Creation* (New York: Norton, 1969), p. 731. In his *Memoirs*, Vol. 1, *Year of Decisions* (Garden City, N.Y.: Doubleday, 1955), pp. 12–13, Truman listed Roosevelt's poor administrative methods as the one aspect of the latter's policy-making about which the Missourian had serious concerns.

119. The matter of whether Truman set out to reverse his predecesor's approach to dealing with Soviet Russia immediately upon becoming president remains a controversial issue.   Most of the older, more traditional treatments of this period—for example, Feis and McNeill—emphasize an essential continuity of policy.   More recent works offer a variety of perspectives, all stressing the notion that Truman, for one reason or another, very quickly chose to take another course. The classic critique is that of Diane Clemens   who, while critical of some of FDR's positions at Yalta, nevertheless argues that it was Harry Truman who abandoned the "sensible" agreements reached there.   See her "Second Thoughts and Conclusions," *Yalta*, pp. 267–291. See also in this vein LaFeber, *Russia, America and the Cold War*; Rexford Guy Tugwell, *Off Course: From Truman to Nixon* (New York: Praeger, 1971); and Athan Theoharis, *The Yalta Myths* (Columbia: University of Missouri Press, 1970).

120.   On the views of these people and other so-called "hardliners" at this time, see Daniel Yergin, *Shattered Peace: The Origins of the Cold War and the National Security State* (Boston: Houghton Mifflin, 1977), p. 4 and p. 85. See also A. J. P. Taylor, "End of the Grand Alliance," *History of the Second World War* (London: BPC Publishing Co., 1966), pp. 2700–2712.

There seems to be little question that the State Department's historic hostility toward Russia, muted by FDR's personal diplomacy, came to the fore after his death. The department had warned Roosevelt shortly before his stroke that European stability "depends on the maintenance of sound economic conditions and reasonable prosperity in all parts of the continent," going on to argue that if Stalin got away with building his own sphere in Europe, Churchill, de Gaulle, *et al* might try to rebuild their blocs as well. *FRUS, Conferences at Malta and Yalta*, pp. 235–236.

121. Harriman to Stettinius, April 24, 1945, *FRUS, 1945*, V, pp. 817–820.

122. One day after Truman's meeting with Molotov, Stalin sent the president the following message: "Such conditions must be recognized unusual when two governments—those of the United States and Great Britain—beforehand settle with the Polish question in which the Soviet Union is first of all and most of all interested and put the government of the USSR in an unbearable position trying to dictate to it their demands." Stalin to Truman, April 24, 1945, *FRUS, 1945*, V, p. 264.

123. While historians have disagreed as to what the Duclos letter really meant, the consensus among scholars now is that it did not represent some sort of carefully orchestrated attempt on Moscow's part to resurrect a military revolutionary line in regard to the West. See in this vein William Zimmerman, "Choices in the Postwar World: Containment and the Soviet Union," in Charles Gati, *Caging the Bear: Containment and the Cold War* (New York: Bobbs-Merrill, 1974), pp. 85–108, and Joseph Starobin, "Origins of the Cold War," *Foreign Affairs* (July, 1969): 275–288. For a contrary view, see Arthur Schlesinger, Jr., "Origins of the Cold War," *Foreign Affairs :* (October, 1967): 22–52.

124. Grew to Kennan, July 25, 1945, *FRUS, 1945*, V, pp. 872–873; Forrestal Diary, May 14 and June 30, 1945, Walter Millis, ed., *The Forrestal Diaries* (New York: Knopf, 1951), pp. 57–58.

125. Memorandum by Raymond E. Murphy, special assistant to the Director of European Affairs, Department of State, on "Possible Resurrection of Communist International, Resumption of Extreme Leftist Activities, Possible Effect on United States," June 2, 1945, *FRUS, Potsdam*, I, pp. 267–280.

126. Kennan to Byrnes, July 15, 1945, *FRUS, 1945*, V, pp. 866–867.

127. Reports kept coming in that large amounts were being wasted, that much of the equipment ordered was of the type which the Russian army could not use, and that industrial equipment for postwar reconstruction was ordered during the height of the war. Some of the items that the Russians had received were sold to Eastern Europe and the Middle East in order to boost Moscow's political influence. See Herring, "Lend-Lease to Russia and the Origins of the Cold War," pp. 106-108. Gar Alperovitz regards the lend-lease cutback as one of Truman's central provocations of the Russians. See his *Atomic Diplomacy: Hiroshima and Potsdam* (New York: Simon and Schuster, 1965), and *Cold War Essays* (Garden City, N. Y.: Doubleday, 1970).

128. *Year of Decisions*, pp. 226–231.

129. Stalin told Hopkins at the end of May that while Washington had every right to stop lend-lease aid to Russia, the abrupt manner in which it was done was "unfortunate and even brutal." Bohlen notes, Hopkins-Stalin conversation, May 27, 1945, quoted in Sherwood, *Roosevelt and Hopkins*, pp. 894–897.

130. Churchill to Truman, June 4, 1945, *FRUS, 1945*, III, pp. 231–232, 240–241.

131. The Russians in January 1945 had requested a $6 billion loan to aid in the

reconstruction of their country—a request that been put on hold over the ensuing months. Harriman had already concluded that Russia could regain its prewar level of capital investment by 1948. See *FRUS, 1945*, V, pp. 939, 967.

132. The formula used in the Treaty of Moscow in 1970 would be repeated in the Final Act of the Helsinki Conference in 1975.

133. Bohlen Minutes, Byrnes-Molotov conversation, July 27, 1945, *FRUS, Potsdam* II, p. 450.

134. See Martin J. Sherwin, "The Atomic Bomb and the Origins of the Cold War," *American Historical Review* (October, 1973), pp. 945–968.

135. It appears that neither side was entirely truthful with the other on the question of atomic energy. Stalin told Harriman that "Soviet scientists had been working on the problem but had not been able to solve it." Truman, *Year of Decisions*, p. 426. For Stalin's view of Truman's dissembling about the bomb, see *Khrushchev Remembers*, trans, and ed. Strobe Talbott (Boston: Little, Brown, 1970), p. 221.

136. Henry Stimson and McGeorge Bundy, *On Active Service in Peace and War* (N.Y.: Norton, 1948), pp. 638–650.

137. On Brynes' position, see Minutes of the Meeting of the Secretaries of State, War and Navy, October 10, 1945, *FRUS, 1945*, II, pp. 55–57.

138. See, in this regard, Roland Young, *Congressional Politics in the Second World War* (New York: Macmillan, 1956), pp.146–148, and H. Bradford Westerfield, *Foreign Policy and Party Politics: Pearl Harbor to Korea* (New Haven, Conn.: Yale University Press, 1955), pp. 184–190, 203–212.

139. "Memo for the Secretary," August 20, 1945, Lot File, Staff Officers' Summary, *Archives of the Department of State*, Record Group No. 59.

140. Shortly before the commencement of the London Conference, two American aircraft had been shot down over Yugoslavia and, not without some pressure from the Russians, the Yugoslavs reluctantly agreed to pay compensation to the families of the victims.

141. *Wartime Correspondence*, April 24, 1945, No. 439, p. 331.

142. For reports on Russian actions in Germany at this time, see Kennan to Stettinius, April 27 and May 14, 1945, *FRUS, 1945*, III, pp. 1200–1205.

143. His Secretary of State, Cordell Hull, epitomized this orientation. In November 1943, returning from the Foreign Ministers Conference in Moscow, Hull addressed a joint session of Congress. Once the U.N. went into effect, he said, "there would no longer be any need for spheres of influence, for alliances, for a balance of power, or any other of the special arrangements through which, in the unhappy past, the nations strove to safeguard their security or to promote their interest." *Congressional Record*, (Washington, D. C.: U.S. Government Printing Office), November 18, 1943, pp. 9678–9679.

144. Arthur M. Schlesinger, Jr., *The Coming of the New Deal* (Boston: Houghton Mifflin, 1958), p. 527.

145. John Franklin Campbell, "An Interview with George F. Kennan", *Foreign Service Journal* (August, 1970), p. 22.

146. Schlesinger, *The Coming of the New Deal*, p. 528.

147. See Maurice Matloff and Edwin L. Snell, *Strategic Planning for Coalition Warfare, 1943–44: The U. S. Army in World War II*. The War Department. (Washington, D. C.: U. S. Government Printing Office, 1959), pp. 498–500.

148. Deane, *The Strange Alliance*, esp. pp. 20–63, 107–125, and 182–201

149. See on this matter Mastny, *Russia's Road to the Cold War*, Chapter 7.

150. No documentary evidence exists for it.

151. See, in this regard, Hammett, "America's Non-Policy in Eastern Europe," pp. 158–159.

152. The tendency to ascribe revolutionary developments to the machinations of Moscow did not become a prominent component of American foreign policy until after the war.

153. See Yergin, *Shattered Peace*, pp. 45-68. For a succinct characterization of the Four Policemen concept, see Gaddis, *Strategies of Containment*, p. 10.

154. Useful analyzes of the American position may be found in Louis Morton, "Soviet Intervention in the War with Japan," *Foreign Affairs* (July, 1962): 653–657; Ernest R. May, "The U.S., the Soviet Union and the Far Eastern War, 1941-45," *Historical Review* (May, 1955): 153–163; and Matloff and Snell, *Strategic Planning for Coalition Warfare, 1943-44.*

155. See, for example, Bohlen notes, Roosevelt-Stalin conversation, December 1, 1943, *FRUS, Teheran*, pp. 594–595.

156. The uncritical descriptions of Russia that had become so prevalent in the mass media during the war reflected a desire on the part of many Americans to find complete ideological consistency in the war aims of the anti-Axis coalition. This would lead to a profound disillusionment and bitter recrimination later when it became apparent that this image was not the correct one.

157. See his Conclusion, *The United States and Origins of the Cold War*, pp. 353–361, See, in this vein, FDR's Press Conference, May 30, 1944, Samuel I. Rosenman, ed., *The Public Papers and Addresses of Franklin D. Roosevelt*, XIII, pp. 141 and 146, and Speech to Foreign Press Association, October 21, 1944, *ibid*, p. 350. See, also, Willard Range, *FDR's World Order* (Athens: University of Georgia Press, 1959), and Robert A. Divine, *Second Chance: The Triumph of Internationalism in America During World War II* (New York: Oxford University Press, 1967), esp. pp. 114–115.

158. A Fortune poll of March, 1944 pointed out that less than 20 percent of the respondents still held isolationist sentiments (even in the Middle West). An overwhelming majority expected America to participate in the new international organization. In the early autumn 1945 Elmo Roper conducted an extensive poll of public attitudes on Russia. Of the respondents, 42 percent still expected improved relations with the Russians in the future. On the question of whether Russia was a peace-loving nation, the public was almost equally divided. Most revealing was the response to the question: "Which one of these do you think is the most important reason behind Russia's interest in the countries along her borders?" The largest number, 29 percent, said it was because she wants to be able to count on them in case of attack; 26 percent said it was because she wants to spread communism; 16 percent said it was because she needs things they can produce; 9 per cent said it was because she wants to improve conditions for people in those countries; and 20 percent said they didn't know. In short, the public's attitude, even as late as September 1945 was reasonably friendly but realistic. Fortune Survey (March 1944), p. 94, and "U.S. Opinion on Russia," *Fortune*, XXXII (September 1945), pp. 233–243.

159. See Gabriel Almond, *The American People and Foreign Policy*, pp. 94–95, and Brewster Smith, "The Personal Setting of Public Opinion: A Study of Attitudes

toward Russia," *Public Opinion Quarterly* (Winter, 1947-48): 507-523, esp. pp. 514–15.

160. Gaddis, *The United States and the Origins of the Cold War*, p. 17.

161. *FRUS, Cairo and Teheran*, p. 594.

162. *FRUS, Malta and Yalta*, pp. 93–96. Gaddis points out, however, in *Strategies of Containment*, pp. 12–13, that it was not a question of what the president should or should not have done, but what he himself believed he could do. On the executive branch's ability to create public support for policies it believes to be in the national interest, see Bernard Cohen, *The Public's Impact on Foreign Policy* (New York: Praeger, 1973).

163. See William Emerson, "FDR (1941–1945)" in Ernest R. May, ed., *The Ultimate Decision: The President as Commander-in-Chief* (New York: Knopf, 1960), pp. 168–172.

164. See Kent Roberts Greenfield, *American Strategy in World War II: A Reconsideration* (Baltimore: Johns Hopkins University Press, 1963), Chapter 3, and Richard M Leighton and Robert W. Coakley, *Global Logistics and Strategy, 1940–1943: United States Army in World War II. The War Department* (Washington, D. C.: Government Printing Office, 1968).

165. See on this point Ralph B. Levering, *American Opinion and the Russian Alliance, 1939–1945* (Chapel Hill: University of North Carolina Press, 1976), pp. 204–207.

166. Gabriel Kolko, *The Politics of War: The World and United States Foreign Policy, 1943–45* (New York: Random House, 1968), pp. 37–39, argues that we deliberately excluded the Russians from any authority in Italy in order to block the rise of the left in that country as a counterweight to Soviet Russia. Be that as it may, the efforts of the Anglo-American military authorities to disarm resistance groups in liberated countries certainly were viewed by the Russians as provocative. While the record seems to indicate that we did it to restore political stability, and to maintain the integrity of communications behind the advancing armies, it was not very difficult to impart to these actions ulterior political motives.

167. See Kennan, "The U.S. and the Soviet Union, 1917-76," *Foreign Affairs* (July, 1976): 670–690.

168. This is the view taken by Daniels, *Russia*, pp. 223–233, and Mastny, *Russia's Road to the Cold War*, in which he attributes Russia's foreign policy during the war more to a subordination of policy objectives to the internal realities of the communist party state, and less to some sort of master plan to take over Europe.

169. Witness Stalin in 1944–1945 ordering the powerful French Communist Party to cooperate with the Western Allies rather than to seize power because he wanted Anglo-American acquiescence to his actions in Eastern Europe. He restrained them also because they were (in his eyes) dangerously overambitious. See in this regard Lafeber, America, Russia, and the Cold War, Chapter 1.

For background on this point of view, three articles in the December 1977 issue of *Slavic Review* are of particular interest: Philip Gillette, "Motivational-Ideational Analysis of Stalin's Foreign Policy," pp. 590–597; Robert Tucker, "The Emergence of Stalin's Foreign Policy," pp. 563–589; and Alexander Dallin, "Personality, Nationalism, and Commitment," pp. 598–613. More generally, consult Robert V. Daniels, *Russia: Roots of Confrontation* (Cambridge, Mass.: Harvard University Press, 1985); J. N. Westwood, *Endurance and Endeavor: Russian History,*

1812–1980 (New York: Oxford University Press, 1981); Teddy V. Uldricks, *Diplomacy and Ideology: The Origins of Soviet Foreign Relations, 1917–1930* (Beverly Hills, Calif.:   Sage, 1979); Gerald Freund, *Unholy Alliance: Russian-German Relations from the Treaty of Brest-Litovsk to the Treaty of Berlin* (New York: Norton, 1957); Helmut Gruber, *Soviet Russia Masters the Comintern: International Communism in the Era of Stalin's Ascendency* (Garden City, N. Y.:   Doubleday, 1974); Lionel Kochan, *The Struggle for Germany, 1914–1945* (New York: Knopf, 1967); and Jonathan Haslom, *The Soviet Union and the Struggle for Collective Security in Europe, 1933–1939* (New York: St. Martin's Press, 1984).

170.   In a memorandum sent to the State Department from Moscow, cited in Feis, *Churchill, Roosevelt, and Stalin*, p. 436, Kennan commented on the idea that a world organization would solve the problems left unsolved during the war: "An international organization for the preservation of peace and security cannot take the place of a well-conceived and realistic foreign policy . . . and we are being . . . negligent of the interests of our people if we allow plans for an international organization to be an excuse for failing to occupy ourselves seriously . . . with the sheer power relationships of the European peoples."

171.   America's actions at the San Francisco conference set a number of unfortunate precedents, including the demand to include Argentina, and the exemption of the Monroe Doctrine from Security Council jurisdiction.   All of this left others with the clear impression that while America sought one standard for the world as a whole, she reserved for herself the right to operate unilaterally in her own hemisphere. Yet, at the same time, the Americans used the conference as a vehicle to denounce the Russians for their apparent lack of willingness to bargain and compromise. Washington's actions in regard to Latin America led Time Magazine, in its May 14, 1945 issue, to comment that we were playing "a straight power game . . . as moral as Russia's game in Eastern Europe."

2

The Postwar Scene (1945–1953): Cold War Triumphant

> It is an undeniable privilege of every man to prove himself right in the thesis that the world is his enemy, for if he reiterates it frequently enough . . . he is bound eventually to be right.
> —George F. Kennan

America emerged from World War II the strongest state in the world. At least for a brief period of time, it was the only country with adequate capability to be fairly called a credible world power. Coming out of the war relatively unscathed, and, indeed, even having profited from the conflict in the sense that her economy had been finally emancipated from the iron grip of the Great Depression, America was now in a unique position to play a decisive and constructive role in helping to heal the wounds of that conflict. Moreover, by means of the Bretton Woods infrastructure that had been put in place, she was uniquely situated to assist the European states to get back on their feet, and to begin to play the role of mentor to the non-Western peoples of the world. As is so often the case in such matters, the results of her endeavors turned out to be bittersweet, to say the least.

War produces not only deadly guns and terrible bombs but also golden dreams and illusions. The greater the war, the more fantastic the illusions. In one recurring illusion each is the "last war;" in another, "swords" are turned into "plough-shares"; in a third, the world is made "safe for democracy." World War II produced perhaps the grandest illusions of all. Fought in the name of ridding mankind of the evils of messianic totalitarianism (which had represented, after all, a challenge to the established processes of peaceful intercourse), the great democracies of the West allied themselves with the Russian communist state in a grand coalition. Even as they engaged in the bitter struggle, efforts were made to erect the foundations of a "new" international order that would forever secure the general peace that had so tragically eluded mankind for so long. Yet within three years of the end of the war, the world witnessed the collapse of the wartime dream of a great-power concert perpetuating the informal diplomacy of the Big Three. How all of this came to pass remains one of the great controversies of twentieth-century historiography.

THE ROAD TO IMPASSE

From the conclusion of the war in Europe until the early days of 1946, President Truman and a majority of his advisors believed that the policies that created a viable partnership between Roosevelt and Stalin during the war had to be maintained. A belief existed that once Stalin's suspicions were allayed he would join in the task of rebuilding and creating a world based on the common-sense principles of consultation, cooperation, and a commitment to peace. But Soviet Russia's conduct during the summer served to raise alarm bells within the government. In June 1945, as we have noted, the State Department prepared a long report on international communism, taking note of developments in the French, Italian. and American parties, concluding that communism posed a serious challenge to America, and recommending that decisive action against domestic subversion might actually improve relations with Russia by demonstrating our internal resolve.[1] In July, George Kennan warned from Moscow that the abolition of the Comintern had in no way weakened Moscow's control over the international communist movement.[2] Navy Secretary James Forrestal took this very seriously—so seriously that he commissioned a report on the relationship between communism and Russian foreign policy—an assessment that would be circulated within the government by early 1946.[3]

The great turning point in the course of postwar Russian-American relations came during the period between September 1945 and the summer of 1947. By the fall of 1945 two schools of thought on how to handle Soviet Russia had crystallized within the administration. Each represented a divergent perception of Moscow's intentions. One group of policy makers held that the Russians still shared with Americans a common interest in world peace and security. Admitting that serious disagreements had broken out, they felt that these could be overcome if both sides showed a willingness to negotiate and compromise. While not condoning Russian behavior in Eastern Europe, they questioned whether the Kremlin could realistically be expected to show greater flexibility in that region while Washington continued to oppose Russian participation in the occupation of Japan and in the administration of the former Italian colonies in Africa. The other group had already virtually written off the possibility of settling the outstanding issues between them; further concessions, they said, would only whet Moscow's appetite. America and its Western European allies, they argued, should now begin pooling their resources and oppose Moscow's ambitions if world peace was to be preserved.[4] These two groups would wage a protracted struggle for the heart and soul of Harry S Truman. In the end, the hardliners would win.

Much of the confusion that surrounded the formation of American policy in the fall of 1945 stemmed from the fact that the president had not committed himself fully to either point of view. Nevertheless, the perception was now beginning to grow among increasing numbers of key decision makers in the administration that the Russians wanted considerably more influence and control in central and eastern Europe than Washington was prepared to give. At the same time, it was becoming quite apparent to the Russians that America would not acquiesce gracefully in de facto Russian hegemony in Eastern Europe.[5] These essentially refractory images soon led each side to undertake the crucial steps in policy implementation that would only serve to reinforce the latent apocalyptic visions held by each country of the other.

A major catalyst in moving President Truman toward a more hard line direction was the disastrous London meeting of the foreign ministers of the Big Three in September of that year. This was their first postwar high-level get-together, the primary purpose of the meeting being to create peace treaties for the former German satellites Finland, Hungary, Rumania, and Bulgaria. Russia's actions in Eastern Europe, especially in Rumania and Bulgaria, in stonewalling Western efforts to reach acceptable understandings in regard to the peace treaties, had created considerable irritation in Washington. Now that the war was over, the American position was that free elections should be held in these countries under the auspices of the Yalta Conference's Declaration on Liberated Europe. Moscow had seemed willing to cooperate regarding Finland, and perhaps Hungary, but their behavior in Rumania and Bulgaria seemed to belie their public commitment to democratic procedure.

State Department officials realized that Washington lacked the necessary leverage to influence events in Rumania and Bulgaria directly, but they hoped that by delaying signature of any peace treaties and withholding diplomatic recognition they could impel Russia to comply with the Yalta agreement. Such was not to be the case. Secretary Byrnes evidently went to London prepared to use America's exclusive possession of the atomic bomb as an implied threat to get the Russians to cooperate.[6] His hope that possession of the bomb would make the Russians more cooperative proved to be a chimera. Molotov employed the conference as a stage to launch a series of attacks on the American position, while at the same time seeking to obtain whatever advantage he could for his country. Russia, he argued, should be given a share of control of the former Italian colonies in Africa, while at the same time proposing that an allied control council be established for Japan. He accused Washington of supporting anti-Russian elements in Eastern Europe, while pointedly stating that until the West accepted Russian terms for peace treaties in Eastern Europe, Moscow would not accept the Anglo-American draft for Italy. But the real bombshell dropped by the Russians at the conference was the demand that France and China be excluded altogether from further discussion of the satellite peace treaties, a position which would take a considerable period of time to resolve.

The London Foreign Ministers Conference demonstrated rather conclusively that America's possession of the atomic monopoly made little difference in our dealings with the Russians. The attitude displayed by the Russians must be seen in the context of the events of August at Potsdam, for if Potsdam was Byrnes's conference, the London meeting was Molotov's. It was virtually a foregone conclusion that the Russians would be as difficult as possible. Indeed, British Foreign Minister Ernest Bevin told his Cabinet colleagues in early October that he "thought that many of the difficulties met with in the recent meeting of the Council of Ministers could be attributed to Russian resentment at having been excluded from this [atomic] development."[7]

While Byrnes had no intention of actually threatening use of the bomb to force concessions from the Russians, he had hoped to hold back an American commitment to the international control of atomic energy until Soviet Russia agreed to a European peace arrangement that Washington could accept.[8] Unfortunately, Truman's October 3, 1945 message to Congress, endorsing international control, while Brynes was still in London and long before any European peace agreements were in place, served to undercut Byrnes's bargaining strategy.

Warnings from the American embassy in Moscow prompted Truman in the fall of 1945 to send over an investigating team to check on Russian activities. The subsequent so-called Ethridge Report found the Russians guilty of manipulating the internal affairs of the East European countries under their occupation. To concede the Russians a sphere of influence in Eastern Europe, the report stated, would only be to invite its extension.[9] Meanwhile, American intelligence had determined by December, 1945 that Soviet Russia would consolidate its power in the occupied countries of Eastern Europe "in preparation for further expansion" and then endeavor to extend its influence on a global basis "by all means short of war."[10]

At the Moscow Foreign Ministers conference in December, however, a compromise was reached: the Russians would permit free elections and coalition governments in Eastern Europe in return for Western recognition, thus paving the way for a peace conference to draw up treaties with Italy, Romania, Bulgaria, Hungary, and Finland. They also agreed on the establishment of a Joint U.S.-Soviet Commission in Korea; on the desirability of withdrawal of Russian and American forces from China "at the earliest practicable moment," and to sponsor a resolution, at the first General Assembly of the UN in January, 1946, to set up a UN Atomic Energy Commission. In addition, Washington agreed to make concessions on the Japanese treaty. America would establish an "Allied Council" made up of representatives of America, the British Commonwealth, China, and Soviet Russia, which would consult with and advise General MacArthur on occupation measures. But this concession in no way was comparable to the Allied Control Council in Germany. MacArthur was obliged to take its advice only if, in his opinion, the situation warranted it. Thus, this agreement permitted each side to save face, while not in reality permitting the other side to impair the occupying state's ultimate authority. It was in consonance with directives of the Moscow conference that peace treaties for these countries were subsequently adopted the following summer.

The results of the Moscow conference were not well received in Washington. When the deals Secretary of State Byrnes made at the Russian capital became known, including his failure to get the Russians to withdraw from northern Iran, he came under attack from congressional Republicans and hardliners in the admini-stration. The president himself was not happy with the outcome of the discussions,[11] issuing a private rebuke to his Secretary of State—one from which Brynes never recovered politically. The reprimand is significant in that it contained a clear indication that the president had begun to change his mind about Soviet Russia—a transformation that was in step with a similar change in congressional opinion already well under way as 1945 drew to a close.

Negotiations on Germany. Meanwhile, progress on preparing for a German settlement was at a virtual standstill. The position taken by the Truman administration at the Potsdam Conference in the summer of 1945, and the one substantially agreed to by the Russians during the course of those deliberations, called for the reunification of Germany on terms which, while ensuring its freedom and independence, would provide maximum assurance that a united German state would never again become a pawn, partner, or prime mover in aggression against either its eastern or western neighbors. Moreover, the protocol explicitly provided that, as long as the occupation lasted, that country would be treated as a single economic unit. It would not be very long, however, before this eminently sensible view was abandoned by both sides, the four occupation zones of Germany in the process of becoming separate satrapies hermetically sealed off from one another, serving as pawns in a growing confrontation.

As it turned out, the chief opposition to treating Germany as an economic unit came initially from the French, not the Russians. At Yalta, the Big Three had agreed to give France an occupation zone and a seat on the Allied Control Council. This placed the French government in a position to veto implementation of whatever parts of the Potsdam protocol it did not like. The French during the summer and fall of 1945 proceeded to adopt in their zone of occupation obstructionist policies toward the efforts of the Big Three to reach a final solution of the German question. In particular, in order to enforce their demands for some sort of indemnity or territorial concession from Germany, the French proceeded to veto in the Allied Control Council almost every action that might have led to the treatment of Germany as a political or economic whole and thus lead to the reestablishment of a German state.[12] These tactics, among other things, contributed to the subsequent deterioration of the four-power coalition, emboldening the Russians to alter their original policy of merely insisting on carrying out the Potsdam contract to one of seeking to extract every advantage they could by acting in a most brutal manner within their own zone. Russia's actions within their zone beginning during this period and continuing into 1946 need to be assessed in this context.

Evidence recently made available from East German and Russian documents indicates that from the beginning Moscow was more often than not impelled by specific situations within their occupation zone, rather than by any preconceived ideological biases. Originally motivated by a desire to win support for the communist-dominated Socialist Unity Party by means of promoting middle-of-the-road economic policies, coalition-building, and pushing for unification, Soviet Russia ultimately came around, de facto, to a different approach—one impelled by the need for reparations and for uranium from East German mines, and influenced by the frequent outrageous conduct of the Russian occupation troops toward the German citizenry. Looting and mass rape within their zone soon undercut Moscow's attempts to mobilize support for the German communists. Norman Naimark, in pointing to these events, argues that the Russian occupation zone of Germany was "bolshevized" not so much "because there was a plan to do so, but because that was the only way they knew how to organize society." [13]

Washington Adrift. By the beginning of 1946 American policy appeared to be adrift, lacking any real focus, while contending viewpoints on how best to respond to Russian initiatives vied for influence. It was this sense of uncertainty as to what was really underlying Moscow's actions that led to a vacilating foreign policy at this time—a situation that prompted Joseph and Stewart Alsop in January to state in the Washington Post that "We Have No Russian Policy." Meanwhile, public opinion polls began to reflect a change in American attitudes toward the Russians. In September 1945, 54 percent said we could trust the Russians to cooperate with us in the postwar world. By November it was 44 percent; by the end of February 1946, 35 percent.[14] There was little question that Russia's assertive policies had now led to an increasingly disillusioned America. This in combination with Truman's fear of Republican gains in the 1946 congressional elections would lead him to the conclusion that the wartime policy was no longer feasible politically. What would happen over the course of the next few months would ultimately have a decisive impact on the state of Russian-American relations for the next two decades.

In February, news of a Canadian spy case broke with the announcement from Ottawa of the arrest of twenty-two individuals on charges of trying to steal information on the atomic bomb for the Russians. The spy case frightened some Americans because it seemed to indicate a connection between Russian espionage activities and the world communist movement. The case certainly played into the hands of those in the country who had been calling for a tougher line against Moscow.[15]

In that same month, Soviet Russia held its first election in eight years. The campaign speeches by the CPSU's candidates were permeated by expressed fears of the outside world. Candidate Molotov called on the Russian people to be watchful for "intrigues against international security," while Stalin, in his first public utterance in six months, declared that World War II was "the inevitable result of development of world economic and political forces on a basis of monopolistic capitalism." He made clear his view that the recent victory of Russian arms confirmed the need for party control, planned industrialization, and collectivization. He went on to tell his people that Soviet Russia would develop its own atomic capability and surpass the West, adding that there could be no long-term accommodation between the communist and capitalist world.[16] Apparently he did not realize how this apparent return to prewar orthodoxy could be misread by nervous Western leaders as a statement of the inevitability of war between the Russian state and the capitalist countries, not just among the capitalists themselves. Was this not, therefore, a threat to export revolution on the tips of Russian bayonets?

Stalin's "reelection" speech and that of former British prime minister Churchill the following month, set the tenor for the subsequent policy reappraisals. While Stalin spoke of the ultimate triumph of communism over capitalism,[17] Churchill, at Fulton, Missouri, warned of an impending extinction of freedom in areas dominated by Soviet Russia. While Churchill conceded that the Russians did not desire war, he charged that they wanted the fruits of war, and went on to call for a "fraternal association of the English-speaking peoples" operating under the principles of the U.N., (but not inside that organization), and with the support of atomic weaponry, to reorder the world. Truman was aware of the contents of the Churchill speech before it was delivered. The speech was at least in part designed as a "trial balloon" to sample public opnion and to test the theories and ideas that had been presented to him by his more hawkish advisers (Kennan, Acheson, Harriman, and others) over the previous several months.[18]

Stalin's reaction to the speech was reported by *Time Magazine* in its March 25, 1946 issue. Attributing to Churchill a Hitler-like theory of Anglo-Saxon racial superiority, he recalled the Allied intervention of 1918, and accused Churchill of issuing a call to war, pointing out that the speech made the loyalty of the states of Eastern Europe more important than ever. In return, Stalin promised them protection from Western imperialism.[19]

The real question seems to be Truman's own thinking at this time. There is some evidence to suggest that he did not buy into Churchill's position totally. Margaret Truman quotes a letter from the president to his mother, dated March 11, 1946, in which Truman indicated that he thought that the speech had done some good, but that he was not willing to completely endorse the Churchill position.[20] Moreover, the considerable Anglophobic reaction to the Fulton speech, particularly the idea that America should provide a sizeable loan to London, pointed up the need to educate the American people.

As the year 1946 unfolded, an orientation that would in time come to dominate the American approach toward Soviet Russia began to take shape, namely, the notion that for postwar peace to be ensured there had to be order and stability, not only in Europe, but around the globe. And for that to happen, there had to be, in the short term, economic reconstruction of the shattered economies left over from the war. Even more imperative, however, over the longer term, there ought to be in place an acceptable infrastructure that could provide the necessary framework for economic stability and development in the international system. That was the premise underlying the Bretton Woods initiatives at the end of the war—an arrangement designed by Washington, predicated on the dollar, and one that would serve, it was hopeed, as a vehicle for domestic economic health and vitality. One of the primary motivations for this new approach was the desire to prevent massive unemployment after the war. To that end, a policy aimed at raising living standards around the globe so as to reduce the likelihood of war would come to be emphasized.

As part of this approach, the administration evidently thought that the Russians could be made to play ball by means of a combination of carrots (an invitation to participate as a full partner in the new system and a sizeable postwar reconstruction loan) and sticks (hard bargaining on the terms of the loan, and delaying on the issue of control of atomic energy). It didn't work. Moscow's response to what it perceived to be a hardening of outlook in Washington and London included rejection of the $1 billion loan she had been trying to obtain for many months, refusal to join the World Bank and International Monetary Fund—thus stonewalling Washington's attempt to use the lure of the dollar to get the Russians to be more cooperative on Eastern Europe—the inauguration of a new five-year plan for economic reconstruction and development, and the beginning of an ideological campaign to blunt Western influences within the country.

Washington's reaction was to try to work out some sort of clear-cut and meaningful policy in response to what it now perceived as a real threat to world peace emanating from Moscow. The Russians—at the very least, it was felt—had demonstrated by their recent conduct that they were not genuinely interested in reaching mutually satisfactory agreements on the Polish and German questions. Moreover, the view now began to be entertained in Washington that it was perhaps Western weakness in Europe that was providing a highly tempting attraction for the Russians to play the devil's disciple in that part of the world. What, therefore, should be the proper American approach to the evidently changed circumstances in Europe?

The rationale for a new, tougher line was not long in coming. In his famous "long telegram" from his post in Moscow in late February, Kennan provided what appeared to be a compelling diagnosis of the intensifying conflict betwen the two countries. Written ostensibly as an analysis of that country's recent campaign rhetoric, the document sought to put Russian policies and attitudes in historical perspective. Russia, he said, was absolutely dedicated to the proposition that there could be no fundamental agreement with America, and that if Russian security was to be protected, Washington's power and influence would have to be severely weakened.[21] He warned that Russia was now continuing a centuries-old policy of expansion—one that sought to move

Russia's borders further to the West, pointing to a power vacuum that Russia was trying to fill, a situation that would be detrimental to the West because the world balance of power would surely tilt away from America and Western Europe. He also took it upon himself to argue against the assumption, carried over by most Americans from the war, that conciliatory gestures and agreements on specific conflict areas could assuage the Kremlin and preserve the peace. "Suspicion," he said, "is an integral part of [the] Soviet system, and will not yield entirely to any form of rational persuasion or assurance."[22] Kennan advocated no specific policies in the long telegram, but stressed the need to educate the American people as to the dangers we now faced.

The document took Washington by storm, receiving wide circulation at the highest levels of government, and providing seemingly compelling ammunition for those in the administration who were advocating getting tough with the Russians.[23] In March, events in Iran seemed to confirm the worst-case scenario, emboldening the hard liners to demand action. After a joint American-British-Russian occupation of Iran during the war in order to forestall German activity in the region, the Big Three had agreed to withdraw six months after the end of the conflict. By early 1946 most of the American and British forces had been pulled out, but the Russians stalled, demanding oil concessions on a par with those obtained by the British. This was followed by a Russian-sponsored revolt of the Azerbaijanian population of northern Iran, with the apparent intention of establishing a Russian sphere of influence in that portion of the country.

Truman decided to force the Russians' hand, taking the position that it was better to find out now rather than later what their real intentions were. The strategy adopted was, first, to take the issue before the U.N. in an attempt to embarrass the Russians in a public forum. Second, a strongly worded note was fired off to Moscow by Secretary of State Byrnes demanding that the Russians withdraw from the country. Moscow was listening. In late March, Soviet Russia announced it had entered an agreement with the Iranian government to leave by the end of May. American firmness, and its willingness to handle the confrontation with the Russians in a highly public manner, certainly appeared to have carried the day.[24]

The growing tension was also reflected in the popular press. In April 1946, *Time* printed a map showing Iran, Turkey, and Manchuria as "infected" with the "Communist contagion," with other nations exposed. The Republicans launched an attack on the Democrats for "appeasement" of the Russians and promised to make it an issue in the 1946 campaign. In a poll taken in March 1946, 70 percent of the public disapproved of Soviet Russia and 60 percent thought the American response was "too soft."[25]

In the late spring of 1946 Truman ordered a sweeping, top-secret study of the military preparedness in those nations that ringed Soviet Russia. The Joint Chiefs replied on July 27, 1946, with a hawkish appraisal of Russian intentions. This reinforced the hard liners who argued that America must contain Russian influence on a global scale, strengthen its ties with "naturally friendly peoples," seek bases around the world to protects its interests, and shore up the morale of nations under Russian pressure.[26]

Meanwhile, another crisis occurred in August when the Russians requested a revision of the Montreux Convention to allow for joint Turkish-Russian defense of the Dardanelles. American officials viewed this action as the culmination of a long effort by Moscow to establish naval bases in Turkey and thus be in a position to intimidate that country. If we did not react vigorously here, Moscow might very well come to dominate the entire region. The Turks were strongly urged to resist and, to back them up, units of the American fleet were dispatched to the eastern Mediterranean. In the face of these actions, the Russians dropped their demands, and a major confrontation was averted. The importance of this action showed that, in effect, containment had already begun and that Washington was ready to risk war if necessary to block further Russian expansion.[27]

The major arenas in which the deteriorating Russian-American relationship would be played out for the remainder of 1946 were in Germany and at the UN. The evolution of the American attitude toward the German question during the coming months reflected the changing orientation. The immediate issue was reparations, agreed on in principle at Yalta and Potsdam but never in specific amounts. While there is some evidence to indicate that there was considerable difference of opinion in the Russian Politburo over how to treat Germany,[28] the view prevailed that as much as possible should be removed from their occupation zone, with the result that the Americans and British, who were de facto underwriting most of the German economy, found themselves subsidizing reparations to Soviet Russia. Convinced that Germany was now the key to confronting Russian gamesmanship, London and Washington took steps by mid-1946 to halt the drain of reparations from the western zones and prepare for the creation of a viable German economy.

In February and March, Washington, alarmed by the French obstructionist attitude toward Germany and Stalin's stonewalling tactics, became convinced that the Russians were using the delay in implementing the Potsdam Agreement to solidify their position in eastern Germany. French opposition to German economic unity threatened not only to make the division of that country permanent but to place upon Washington the burden of supporting the food-deficient Western zones. As a result, a series of diplomatic initiatives were launched in the spring designed to smoke out Russian intentions in Germany. The most important of these overtures was a proposal on April 29 by Secretary Byrnes to the Council of Foreign Ministers calling for a four-power treaty guaranteeing the disarmament of Germany for the next twenty-five years. Four days after Brynes made his proposal, the American military commander in Germany, General Lucius Clay, announced the suspension of further reparations shipments from the American zone until the four occupying powers agreed to treat Germany as an economic unit. This, said Undersecretary of State Dean Acheson, would "put Soviet protestations of loyalty to Potsdam to [the] final test and fix blame for [the] breach of Potsdam on [the] Soviets in case they fail to meet this test."[29] Both the Russians and the French rejected it within two months.

It became quite apparent during the course of that year that President Truman and his key advisors were moving toward the view that if the Russians refused to cooperate on the German question, a united Germany could and should be created and incorporated into an anti-communist Western bloc of states. Secretary of State Byrnes's Stuttgart speech in September marked the initial public indication of an American change of attitude—a posture that led America by early 1947 to an abandonment of the basic concept of reconciliation inherent in the Potsdam Agreement. Secretary Byrnes set the tone for much of the subsequent American approach to Soviet Russia and Europe when he said at Stuttgart that "[T]he time has come when the zonal boundaries should be regarded as defining only the areas to be occupied for security purposes by the armed forces of the occupying powers and not as self-contained economic or political units." If Germany could not be treated as a single economic unit, he implied that the Western states should merge their own zones, further declaring that steps should be taken to form a provisional German government.[30] On December 2 the American and British governments signed an agreement to fuse the economies of their zones of occupation in Germany.

It was at this time that Truman directed his special counsel, Clark Clifford, to compile a comprehensive report on America's relations with Russia. The resulting document, prepared after consultations with high-level military personnel and intelligence people, echoed Kennan's analysis by stressing the influence of ideology on Moscow's foreign policy. "The key to an understanding of current Soviet foreign policy," the report stated, "is the realization that Soviet leaders adhere to the Marxian theory of ultimate destruction of capitalist states by communist states." Concessions to the Russians would only have the effect "of raising Soviet hopes and increasing Soviet demands. . . . Soviet leaders appear to be conducting their nation on a course of aggrandizement designed to lead to eventual world domination by the USSR," Clifford wrote. Arguing that "they strive to postpone the inevitable conflict in order to strengthen and prepare the Soviet Union for its clash with the western democracies," Clifford, in effect, anticipated most, if not all, of the vigorous anti-Russian steps that the Truman Administration would take over the next three years: the Truman Doctrine to aid nations threatened by communism, the Marshall Plan to restore economic stability in Europe, the revival of Germany as a Western partner, the North Atlantic Treaty Organization, the domestic loyalty program and the prosecution of the American communist leaders, and the pursuit of national security based on America's superiority in nuclear weapons—all as part of a new approach called containment.[31]

RUSSIA'S STRATEGIC CALCULUS AT THE END
OF THE WAR

The crucial question, of course, centers on just what Russia's strategic mindset was at this time. Stalin's reaction in late 1945 and throughout 1946 to Washington's apparent change of outlook (and that of the British as well), while mirroring a growing concern about their intentions, also reflected uncertainty and ambivalence. For Moscow to do an about face would require, afterall, that the Russians move some distance from their wartime posture.

It must be remembered that Russia's perceptions of the likely postwar threat environment once victory was achieved were largely colored by the pattern of Big Three relationships during the conflict. To a great degree, these conformed to the pattern of the interwar period. For example, it was believed that the disagreements and even hostility manifested between America and Britain might well prevent the two most important capitalist countries from turning on Soviet Russia once victory had been won. And, Churchill, at least, had demonstrated during the war that he was sensitive to Moscow's security concerns. Moreover, it appeared likely that the wartime alliance, formalized by means of permanent membership in the new United Nations Security Council, would last into the postwar period. All of this could well mean there was an increased likelihood of preventing new aggression or a new war, if not for ever, then at least for an extended time, the public rhetoric notwithstanding.[32]

In April-August, 1945, with the prospect of a grand bargaining at a forthcoming peace conference, the Russians seemed uncertain about how much of their domain they would be able to retain.[33] They had given no signs of being determined to keep a long-term military presence in Central Europe, instead seeking the broadest possible range of collaborators, and passing over a number of opportunities to install indigenous communists in power.[34] William Zimmerman, for example, argues that in the first two years after the end of the war, there is clear evidence that the continuation of the wartime "honeymoon" between the Russians and their Western allies was looked at quite favorably by Moscow.[35] The evidence indicates, he says, that "a reasonably accurate, relatively benign, rightist, and in some ways revisionist view of world politics . . . dominated the [immediate] post-war period." [36] The so-called "Varga controversy" served as a kind of lightning rod for this period.

In late 1946 a book written at the end of the war by Eugene Varga, a leading Russian economist, was published. The book concluded that "the capitalist countries' attitude toward the Soviet Union will not be what it was in pre-war times. The democratic forces in all countries will aspire to a policy of cooperation with the Soviet Union, toward joint struggle with the Soviet Union against the revival of fascism and aggression in any form."[37] As Varga had long been closely connected with Stalin, the prominent publicity given to his views at this time was certainly no accident.

This matter is instructive because it was played out in the broader context of the deteriorating relationship between Russia and the West. As it became clear that the wartime alliance would not endure, the "rightist" policies that Vargas's doctrinal formulations epitomized were abandoned and "left-oriented" figures in Russia and elsewhere came to the fore. After all, the alternative, more hard-line approach had always been there, as Stalin was usually very careful to hedge his bets.

Beginning in the winter of 1945–1946, the initial response—politically, economically, and culturally—was to move to seal Russia off from the world outside its sphere of control, and to go on the offensive wherever opportunities presented themselves. As early as late November 1945 the British charge d'affaires in Moscow noted that the Russians had come to view Anglo-American solidarity, backed by the atomic bomb, as a potential menace, capable of endangering the security of Soviet Russia. They seemed to feel, he said, that in such an atmosphere, they could make no concessions. "When they are really afraid, they stonewall, hide their true feelings, and go on the attack—a Russian tendency, exacerbated by Marxist-Leninist dogma."[38] Moscow's moves at this time in Greece, Persia, and the Middle East can best be understood in this light; so, too, for the first time since the war, the renewed propaganda against Britain's colonial policies in such places as India and Egypt, as well as the escalation of attacks against social-democracy in Britain itself.[39]

Ironically, it was not as if there were no indications that an appreciation of Russia's interests in Eastern Europe existed in Washington. There existed an important school of thought within the U.S. State Department that apparently understood the need for a balance of power and spheres of influence accommodation with the Russians, especially in Eastern Europe.[40] Consider Secretary Byrnes's public concession in 1945 that the "Soviet Union has a right to friendly governments along its borders."[41] And, then there was John Foster Dulles's written commentary in January 1946, that "the three great powers which at Moscow agreed upon the 'closest cooperation' about European questions have shifted to a practice of separate, regional responsibility," and, also, Under Secretary of State Acheson's mention of "a Monroe Doctrine for Eastern Europe."[42] What was Moscow to believe?

The Atomic Bomb Card

It was in this worsening atmosphere that the first halting steps at nuclear arms control were taken. In the last months of the war, Roosevelt had begun to work through in his own mind how America's probable breakthrough in atomic weapons could best be exploited. As Martin Sherwin points out, at an important meeting between FDR and Churchill at Hyde Park in September 1944, the two reached an understanding in regard to the bomb that would guide the relationship between atomic weapons and American diplomacy for the remainder of Roosevelt's presidency and well into the Truman Administration—an approach predicated on keeping the bomb as an Anglo-American monopoly, while at the same time making no attempt to draw in the Russians to explore the possibility of postwar cooperation in the field of nuclear energy.[43]

Faced with alternatives in regard to the bomb—either to use it to initiate a diplomatic effort to work out a system for its international control, or to hold it in reserve should efforts at cooperation with America's allies fail—Roosevelt favored the second approach. Seeking to control world peace by amassing overwhelming military power seems to have been been a core element of his postwar plans. Unfortunately, what was lost in all of this was an opportunity to gauge Russia's views on the international control of atomic energy during the war. Thus, beyond the apparent recognition of their importance, by the time of Rossevelt's death, the country had no clear-cut, well-worked-out policy to deal with these weapons.

Truman, therefore, inherited a set of military and diplomatic atomic energy policies that were at one and the same time possessive, vague, and ambiguous, to say the least. But it would not be long before the possibilities inherent in America's monopoly of the weapon would present themselves. In April Byrnes told Truman that the bomb "might well put us in a position to dictate our own terms at the end of the war."[44] Indeed, in the belief that America's possession of the bomb would make the Russians easier to deal with, Byrnes opposed even discussing the subject until after a general European peace settlement. Over the next several weeks discussions were held among Truman, Stimson, Byrnes, and others about how possession of the bomb could be employed to extract concessions from Moscow on Eastern Europe.[45] But Truman came under considerable pressure from the majority of the country's atomic scientists, a number of his other advisers, including Acheson (and Stimson), and the British and Canadian governments to develop a policy designed to provide for the control of atomic energy.

What to do? Discussions within the Administration went on throughout the summer and well into the fall. In early November, the president endorsed a set of proposals developed by Vannevar Bush, director of the Office of Scientific Research and Development, designed to avoid an atomic arms race that might lead to future war. The plan advocated a series of steps, to each of which Moscow would be invited to adhere. The first step involved inviting the Russians to join the Americans and British to create, under the direction of the UN General Assembly, an organization to disseminate scientific information on the subject. The second step would involve the creation of a UN inspection agency that would have the right to monitor any scientific laboratory in any country engaged in nuclear research. After the inspection system had been tested and perfected, all states would then agree to stockpile their weapons, committing themselves to use nuclear materials for peaceful purposes only. The inspection body would report any diversion of fissionable materials to the production of weapons. Until the full plan was operationalized, America would be allowed to continue to produce fissionable material capable of being put into bombs, but would agree not to produce the bombs themselves.

In the first months of 1946, the State Department proceeded to refine and develop this plan (the so-called Acheson-Lilienthal Plan)—one that would, hopefully, "have a good chance of being accepted, especially by Russia."[46] Unfortunately, the approach which the State Department finally presented departed from the original formulations by failing to make completion of one stage an absolute requirement for the implementation of the next. Moreover, by controlling a majority within the proposed control authority, Washington could oversee the development of the industrial uses of nuclear energy anywhere in the world, even *within* Soviet Russia. Bernard Baruch was then chosen by the President to present the plan to the UN General Assembly.[47] From the beginning Baruch had problems with it, especially the fact that the proposed international control agency would derive its authority from the Security Council—a situation which he feared might lead to any permanent member of the Council vetoing enforcement action.

When the plan was presented in June 1946, with the exemption of the proposed new Atomic Development Authority from the Security Council veto, it certainly was no surprise that the Russians attacked it as one designed to undermine big-power unity on the Council. Moreover, the inspection/verification requirement stipulated by the plan represented an unacceptable invasion of Russia's security. One did not have to be a soothsayer to figure out that the Russians would reject it on this basis. When the plan came up for consideration at the United Nations in September, this is precisely what happened, with Moscow countering with a proposal for the destruction of all atomic weapons, the cessation of their production, agreement by all not to use these weapons, this to be followed later by a disucssion of controls. Washington demurred. When the Russians offered to bargain, Baruch replied that they must accept the entire American plan or there would be no plan at all. And, so, no plan was agreed to. In the end, Stalin found it much easier to participate in an arms race with his enemies than to expose his police state to foreign penetration and oversight.

In retrospect, however, it is apparent that the matter was even more complicated than this. Baruch's intransigence was only part of the difficulty. The real problem was that America's leaders, by the summer of 1946, were simply no longer willing to trust the Russians. It may well have been that by the time Truman was prepared to offer international supervision of the A-bomb, they had already come to the view that America's nuclear monopoly might prove to be, more generally, a significant factor in promoting American interests while at the same time represent a significant deterrent to alleged Russian expansionism. And, at the United Nations, Russia's rejection of the Baruch plan led to successful American efforts in that body to prevent the Russians from merging the issue of international control and disarmament, thereby scoring a propaganda coup. It turned out that for America at this time the decided risk of a nuclear arms race was preferable to the adoption of a less than foolproof scheme for the international control of atomic energy.[48]

TOWARD A FULL-SCALE CONFRONTATION

The Truman Doctrine

By the beginning of 1947, the self-fulfilling prophecy entertained by both sides was well along toward turning out to be true. Relations between Soviet Russia and the West had been deteriorating for some time. By early 1947 the relationship between them was such that they could no longer regard one another as "Allies" in any real sense. Rather, it could now be best characterized by substantial and growing tension, mitigated by continuing negotiation. Each side had begun to regard the other in two different roles: as partners in the continuing negotiations over the future of Germany and Austria, and as intensifying adversaries in most every other subject area.

It had taken, afterall, almost two years after the end of the war to resolve the issues surrounding the peace treaties with Germany's allies Italy, Hungary, Rumania, and Bulgaria. Those negotiations had been frequently acrimonious and by their close, each side had more than ample reason to suspect the motives of the other. From Moscow's perspective, Western unwillingness to accept predominant Russian hegmony in the countries of Eastern Europe provoked suspicion. Why did the Western powers seem so intent on depriving Soviet Russia of the security beneifts it had earned by bearing the lion's share of the struggle against Germany? From Washington's perspective, Moscow's heavy-handed tactics to assert its predominance in the region aroused fears that Russia's ambitions were something more than simply a desire to have "friendly" relations with their neighbors. Yet, despite all of this, by the spring of 1947 there had been no decisive break in relations.

The reason for this was quite straightforward: the German question had yet to be resolved. The Council of Foreign Ministers meetings in Paris and New York in November and December 1946 certainly got nowhere. Ironically, the event that actually triggered America's psychological mobilization was one that Stalin did not initiate. In the summer of 1946, fighting broke out once again in Greece between the royalist government, restored to power by British influence, and a communist-dominated anti-government insurrection. The Greek communists were aided and abetted by Josep Broz Tito in Yugoslavia who, flush with his victory over the fasicsts, now sought to develop a Balkan federation dominated by Belgrade. Britain, unable to provide the kind of help necessary to shore up the government as a result of its severely weakened postwar economic position, threw in the towel, pleading with Washington to step into the breach.

The watershed event in this regard occurred on February 21,1947, when the British embassy in Washington delivered to the State Department a pair of notes concerning the role of Great Britain in Greece and Turkey. Essentially, these notes indicated that Britain would have to cut off military and economic aid to Greece in its ongoing struggle with the guerrilla forces, while at the same time terminate economic assistance to Turkey by March 31. Reports from the region indicated that the Greek government could last only a few weeks without continuing British support. If Greece fell, it was argued, it was only a matter of time before Turkey and Iran would feel the full brunt of Russian intimidation and would perhaps collapse. Control of the eastern Mediterranean, it was felt, was at stake as well as the long-term prospects for the stability of Italy and France. As those two countries had large, popular communist parties, the question was now whether they could survive if the Russians made significant inroads along Europe's southern flank.

The February note followed hard on the heels of British decisions to leave India and to refer the Palestine mandate to the UN These three decisions, taken against a background of a massive British industrial shutdown in the great winter freeze of January-February 1947 precipitated an atmosphere of crisis in Washington. A decision was made to step in and bail out the British. The result was the so-called Truman Doctrine—the name given to the program of economic and military assistance extended in 1947 (and later) to Turkey and Greece—which served the role of lending the first concrete substance to the concept of getting tough with the Russians being "worked out" in the offices of the Policy Planning Staff of the State Department.

But Congressional approval had to be secured and the American people won over if America was to be able to sustain anything. In order to gain broad public support from a public that was becoming more critical of Soviet Russia, but was opposed to an all-out confrontational policy, Truman decided to make his appeal as broad-based as possible, couching his approach in highly moralist terms. Before a joint session of Congress, the world was portrayed by Truman as divided into two kinds of human beings—communists and anti-communists. Those who opposed the doctrine, ipso facto had to be communists; conversely, because communists opposed the Doctrine so vociferously, it must be good. What is most revealing is the subsequent testimony by then-Undersecretary Acheson at congressional hearings on the aid package. In response to a senator who asked whether the aid program would force the Russians to sit down and settle some of our differences, Acheson replied that "I think it is a mistake to believe that you can, at any time, sit down with the Russians and solve questions. I do not think that is the way our problems are going to be worked out with the Russians. I think they will have to be worked out over a long period of time and by always indicating to the Russians that we are quite aware of what our own interests are and that we are quite firm about them and quite prepared to take necessary action. Then I think solutions will become possible."[49]

Although President Truman and the State Department attempted to draw the line as sharply as possible, the issues were nevertheless more complex than that. In fact, the appropriate American response was debated within the government. Kennan and Marshall were in favor of a limited, specific response to the crisis and warned of the demands that would emerge from any universal declaration of American intentions to fight communism. Marshall also thought Truman overstated his case in his appearance before Congress.[50]

A glance at the record also reveals that, outside the communist-party world, vigorous and biting criticisms were raised—criticisms that went to the heart of matters that would later greatly influence the course of the Cold War. For one thing, the doctrine drew opposition from a considerable number of officials from non-communist states, particularly from the British Labour Party and a majority of the British press, and from such distinguished observers of the American scene as Walter Lippmann, William L. Shirer, and Marquis Childs.[51] A Gallup public opinion poll on March 27, 1947, showed that 55 percent of the American people disapproved the Doctrine's bypassing of the United Nations.[52] Even Kennan expressed a strong dissent. "To say that he found objection to it is to put it mildly," wrote Joseph M. Jones, who played a major role in drafting the doctrine. "He objected strongly to the tone of the message and to the specific action proposed." Kennan apparently spoke to a number of people in the State Department, including Acheson, in an attempt to stop the plan, but "it was too late."[53]

In a prophetic manner, Lippmann warned of the danger of the policy of global containment which the doctrine presaged. Pointing out that America did not possess the military manpower to encircle Soviet Russia, Lippmann went on to say that the policy could be implemented only "indirectly," that is to say by recruiting, subsidizing, and supporting a heterogeneous array of satellites, clients, dependents, and puppets around the perimeter of the Russian state. He concluded that:

Frequently, they will act for their own reasons, and on their own judgments, presenting us with crises for which we are unready. The "unassailable barriers" erected around the perimeter of the Soviet Union will present us with an unending series of insoluble dilemmas. We shall have either to disown our puppets, which would be tantamount to appeasement and defeat and the loss of face, or must support them at an incalculable cost on an unintended, unforeseen and perhaps undesirable issue.[54]

Unmindful of these pitfalls—later to bear such names as Korea, Guatemala, Formosa, Laos, Cambodia, Vietnam, Lebanon, Cuba, Nicaragua, El Salvador, the Dominican Republic, and Grenada—Truman forged ahead with the bailout. Defining the world in terms of Our Way of Life, bypassing the United Nations, and taking an implacably hard line toward the Russians—all the while interpreting most attempts to alter the status quo by force as communist-inspired—the new American foreign policy orientation was bound to lead to unforeseen consequences.

The effects of this new attitude were soon forthcoming. For one thing, a good argument can be made that the ill-fated Moscow Conference of foreign ministers in March 1947—a conference held under the unfavorable auspices of the newly-declared Truman Doctrine—ended in failure, at least in part, for this reason.[55] Moreover, the declaration of a belligerent American global policy that accompanied the Doctrine contributed not only to the general inability of America and Soviet Russia to reach an understanding with regard to Germany but was a key factor in making Moscow unable to understand and appreciate the subsequent offer of Marshall Plan aid. The sequence of events involving the Moscow Conference of foreign ministers, the Truman Doctrine, and the inception of the Marshall Plan is of the utmost importance, and is well worth a more detailed account, especially in view of the oft-expressed American charge that it was the Russians who proved intractable at this time and who flagrantly rejected Marshall's offer of assistance out of pervasive hatred for America and the capitalist world.

The 1947 Moscow Foreign Ministers Conference. After the failure of the Paris-New York foreign ministers sessions, it was decided to meet next in Moscow. Indeed, the scheduled session in Moscow in March-April, 1947 would prove to be decisive. On March 10, 1947, the Moscow Conference opened negotiations on the major problems confronting the two great states. Unfortunately, each side came to that meeting with a different emphasis. For the West, the solution of the German question had become a matter of great economic significance. As Germany was felt to be the main engine of Western Europe's economy, so long as Germany remained divided, the economies of the other states of Western Europe would suffer. Indeed, the winter of 1946-47 was a particularly severe one for Western Europe, reeking havoc on all concerned. Increasingly violent strikes came to mark Europe's labor relations as their economies began to hemorrhage. Only increased economic aid from Washington or the reintegration of German resources into the European economy, it was felt, offered the possibility of stemming the bleeding.

For Soviet Russia, the German question also had economic importance, but one framed more in terms of reparations. And Moscow wanted these reparations partly in the form of payments from current German production so as to better facilitate their own reconstruction. Politically, in order to prevent a resurgence of German power, the Russians desired demilitarization, neutralization, and the creation of a political system in which the German communists would play an important role.

According to Walt W. Rostow, Director of the State Department's Policy Planning Staff in the Kennedy and Johnson administrations, the failure of this conference was the irreversible turning point in postwar relations with Soviet Russia. Wrote Rostow: "The United States went to the Moscow meetings prepared with a range of clear detailed negotiating positions in order to establish whether Soviet objectives were compatible with American interests on the questions of German unity, German disarmament, and the end of the Austrian occupation."[56]

Here then was the key postwar moment. Here, if at any time, the split was preventable. A concerted American effort to go all out in a spirit of compromise to reach an accord with the Russians might have led to a major breakthrough. But, alas, "the position taken by the Soviet negotiators was thoroughly

unambiguous: Stalin refused to move toward a definitive settlement in Europe."
Thus, defeated in their sincere efforts to prevent the tragic inception of the Cold
War, the American negotiators came home from Moscow "firm in the
conclusion that the United States should never again negotiate from a base of
weakness." John Foster Dulles, another member of the American delegation put
it this way: "The Moscow conference was, to those who were there, like a
streak of lightning that illuminated a dark and stormy scene. We saw as never
before the magnitude of the task of saving Europe for Western civilization."[57]
Reports of Europe's unfortunate economic condition, said Rostow, then
converged "with the conclusions about Stalin's attitude and intentions drawn
from the Moscow Conference [to] set the stage for the Marshall Plan."[58]

The Marshall Plan was conceived as a "counter-offensive" (Rostow's term)
to Moscow's moves in Eastern Europe and as a reaction to Stalin's decision,
registered at the Moscow Conference, to rebuff all gestures of compromise
looking toward settlement of the problems dividing Europe. In line with this
partisan conception, the Marshall Plan bypassed the United Nations Economic
Commission for Europe. Said Rostow:

[T]here was even in being an organization dedicated to European economic cooperation—the Economic Commission for Europe. . . . The ECE was, however, an
organization of the United Nations, with Soviet and Eastern European countries as
members. Its very existence posed a basic question. Should an effort be made to
embrace all of Europe in a new enterprise of reconstruction, or should the lesson of
the Moscow Conference be read as indicating that the only realistic alternative for the
West was to accept the split and to strengthen the area still outside Stalin's grasp?[59]

The decision was to accept the split and in effect to intensify it. Central to
the argument in placing the onus for this split on Soviet Russia was the
contention that at the Moscow Conference a serious and well-articulated
American gesture of compromise was met with intransigence. The American
response to this state of affairs, then, was merely to adopt a reactive Cold War
posture and launch a counter offensive. The difficulty with this version of
events is that it failed to take into account the fact that it was precisely two days
after the start of the conference that President Truman proclaimed the doctrine
bearing his name.

Howard K. Smith, the eminent American journalist who was an eyewitness
at the Conference, reported the blighting effect of the doctrine on the negotiations:

Still in the glow of the settlement on the satellite peace treaties in New York two
months before [the Russians]were determined to be charming, amiable hosts.
Vishinsky, the official welcomer, wrung the hand of John Foster Dulles before
photographers as though he were a visiting delegate to the League of Proletarian
Advocates and not a Wall Street Fascist Beast.

In the first days of the conference Soviet press reports on it were thorough and free from their customary acid asides on Western motives. Molotov proved uncommonly concilatory in the opening discussion on rules of procedure and yielded his own suggestions first to those of Marshall, then to those of Bevin.

The Russians undoubtedly assumed that all was well and that things would go according to prescription. They had learned the formula for procedure from the satellite negotiations and were prepared to follow it. . . . Right on top of the conference, two days after it opened, burst the bombshell of the Truman Doctrine. President Truman said, "nearly every nation must choose between" two worlds; it sounded like an ultimatum to the rest of Europe to be with us or to be counted against us. That wiped the smiles off the Russians' faces. While America prepared to move into Greece, Russia proceeded to button up Hungary, arresting democratic leaders to the accompaniment of angry diplomatic protests from the West.

. . . [T]he four men sat down in a world in turmoil and tried to carry on as though it all had nothing to do with their conference. It was impossible.[60]

Ultimately, the conference proved unable to bridge the gap between Western and Russian interests. The Western powers refused to grant Moscow the reparations they wanted, and without a deal on reparations, the Russians proved unwilling to compromise on the question of Germany's political structure. Nor would they agree to Western proposals on the formation of an interim unified economic policy for all the occupation zones.

The Marshall Plan

From this impasse Marshall returned to Washington with plans for strengthening the bargaining position of the West. Nowhere was the democratic West's vulnerability felt to be more evident than in the economic sphere. System-threatening economic and social problems now confronted the countries of Western Europe, leaving them susceptible to internal discord and subversion. They desperately needed a wide range of commodities if they were to survive. Most of these materials could only be obtained from America. Unfortunately, these countries did not have the dollars to buy these products. What could be done to resolve the problem?

Without the revival of German production there could be no resurrection of Europe's economy. The answer was the Marshall Plan. To that end, the targeting of German coal production, it was felt, offerred the best prospects for success. But such an approach as the top priority for the foreseeable future, with its implications for the future of German industry, was bound to be extremely controversial, since any rational approach to the problem was bound to find itself perilously close to the rocks on which the meetings of the Council of Foreign Ministers had heretofore foundered: Russia's policy on reparations, French policy on the separation of the Ruhr and the Rhineland from Germany, and British policy on the ownership of the German coal industry which stressed state as opposed to private control. The version ultimately adopted by Marshall offered a way to circumvent Allied restrictions on German development by tying Germans to a general European program, while at the same time providing large sums of money to France to assuage her concerns.[61] In May, Acheson stated that America had to commit itself to a policy of rebuilding Europe rather than one of relief,[62] as Washington quietly began developing an approach to aid Europe with a systematic program designed to replace the patchwork efforts that had resulted in some $6 billion pouring into the region since the end of the war.

But what countries to include within its proposed scope? In point of fact there existed a schism in the State Department with respect to the proper attitudes to adopt toward Eastern European and Russian participation in the projected Marshall Plan.[63] Partly as a result of this schism, no official decision was taken to exclude either the Russians or any of the Eastern European states under their influence. Special care, in fact, was taken to provide the plan with a rhetoric that did not betray the more partisan intentions reflected in its origin. Thus, in his famous June 5 Harvard University commencement speech announcing the initiative, Secretary Marshall could declare: "Our policy is directed not against any country or doctrine but against hunger, poverty, desperation and chaos."[64]

Marshall suggested at Harvard that the new program not be unilateral, and he invited the European nations to draw up a list of their needs. A call went out from the British and French foreign ministers for a meeting of the states of Europe in Paris at the end of June. The European leaders convened in secret with Molotov representing Soviet Russia. Poland, Hungary, and Czechoslovakia were also present. If there were still some equivocation in Stalin's mind about the motivations underlying Western policy after the March 1947 Moscow Foreign Ministers' meeting, it may well have been resolved by the proposed European Recovery Program.[65] The full implications of this program became clear to the Russians when the foreign ministers of the Big Three met to decide how best to respond to the American initiative.

Marshall made it clear that European recovery should be based not on a country-by-country basis, but rather on an all-European plan. The French and British indicated a desire to set up a multinational committee which would examine the aid requests of all European states and then coordinate them, so as to make the most efficient use of the aid. The Russians, on the other hand, simply wanted to aggregate all the individual requests and forward them to Washington. They did not want to create any multinational institutions, which they arged would infringe upon the "sovereignty" of individual states. In addition, the issue of Germany again proved devisive. Molotov wanted assurances that any German participation in the aid program would not jeopardize possible reparations payments or lead to an increase in German industrial capacity.

Although the use of America's economic strength was probably not unexpected in Moscow, it appears that the Russians believed at first that Marshall's offer was one designed essentially to locate and guarantee markets for American products. The Russians ultimately concluded, however, that something else was involved, namely, an ambitious strategy designed to bring as many states as possible into a binding relationship with Washington, and to lure these countries away from the Russian orbit.[66]

When the Russian response was rebuffed, it would appear that Stalin decided that the best way to cut his losses was to refuse to participate in the plan at all (and to prevent the countries of Eastern Europe from doing so as well). On June 29, Molotov broke the secrecy of the conference and issued a public denunciation of its work, attacking the proposed program as an attempt to violate Russia's industrial plans for itself and its allies in Eastern Europe. He rejected the plan on the dual ground that it infringed the national sovereignty of European states and that it ignored the issue of German reparations. He also suggested that the real purpose of the aid was to increase America's role in Europe, leaving the impression that the Politburo of the CPSU had now come to the view that the plan was an indication of America's "intention to restore the economy of Germany and Japan on the old basis [pre-1941] provided it is subordinated to the interests of American capital."[67] On July 2, 1947, Soviet Russia and its Eastern European co-participants withdrew from the conference, branding it a "capitalist plot." [68]

From this point on, each side became increasingly the prisoner of its own propaganda and of the domestic climate of opinion that it created. Russia's leaders had only to review the events of the previous spring in Western Europe—events that must have seemed to them to convey the full meaning of Rostow's use of the adjective "offensive" in connection with the Marshall Plan. In particular, it must have appeared clear to the Russians, against the background of Europe's economic crisis, that America's failure to channel its economic assistance through established international organizations carried ominous implications. In July, a series of bilateral trade agreements were hastily carried forward by Moscow, serving to link Soviet Russia with its erstwhile new allies in Eastern Europe. Four days after his return from Paris, Molotov announced the establishment of the Cominform. In late August new, get-tough actions in Hungary were initiated, culminating in the silencing of all anti-communist opposition in that country.[69]

Solidifying the Break. Meanwhile, back in Washington, it was decided that additional dialogue between the White House and the American people was called for. In July, having been called back to Washington by Secretary Marshall to head the newly-created Policy Planning Staff, Kennan, speaking in the role of a chief policy maker, wrote an article for the journal Foreign Affairs entitled "The Sources of Soviet Conduct." Published anonymously, the article sketched out what soon became known as the policy of containment.

The containment concept, as Kennan viewed it, was based on several assumptions: first, there was an innate antagonism between capitalism and communism; second, because Marxist-Leninist ideology, the most militant existing expression of the communist credo, was an inherently messianic and expansionistic one, and because Soviet Russia was the leading communist-party state, America therefore must seek to throw up a barrier to Russia's expansionist policies; and, third, that in so doing, the aim must be to mellow Moscow's power, not to overthrow it.

His idea that America must change Russian behavior, not defeat it, caught on immediately. This was to consist of a two-stage policy: initially, containment or the application of counterforce to meet Russian aggressive actions in a timely manner in the appropriate places and, second, a positive approach involving an American initiative to pose solutions to the outstanding problems between them, after Soviet Russia had hopefully been changed from a revisionist to a status quo state—that is to say, converted to a position where it would be willing to negotiate meaningfully its differences with the liberal, democratic Western world.

The theory of containment, then, as translated into operational policy, was based first of all on the assumption that a substantial effort to rebuild Western strength had to precede any further serious negotiation with the Russians; negotiations of any kind would be futile until that time. Secretary of State Acheson would later put it succinctly:

> What we must do is to create situations of strength; we must build strength; and if we create that strength then I think the whole situation in the world begins to change. . . . With that change there comes a difference in the negotiating position of the various parties and out of that I should hope that there would be a willingness on the part of the Kremlin to recognize the facts . . . and to begin to solve at least some of the difficulties between East and West.[70]

Given the atmosphere of disillusionment after the wartime hopes of a reconciled humanity, this view of the nature of future relations, one supposes, was understandable when it was eventually worked out in Washington—this despite the fact that it was America itself that had made a major contribution to the impasse.

The Russian Reaction

The Truman Doctrine and the Marshall Plan precipitated a major shift in Russia's outlook. There now can be little doubt that in the Kremlin Truman's speech quickly came to be regarded as a significant "turning point in American foreign policy, a clear departure from Roosevelt's policies." [71] Just as there had been different schools of thought in the West about how best to approach the Russians, so, too, there were different orientations in Moscow concerning how best to understand American policy. The stonewalling on reparations in the Council of Foreign Ministers, and the eviction of the Communist Party members of the French and Italian coalition governments, hard on the heels of the Truman Doctrine, appear to have finally convinced Stalin that the West had indeed taken the offensive against Soviet Russia.[72] The hard line pessimists therefore moved into favor in Moscow, exemplified by the inauguration of the repressive and reactionary Zhdanovshchina later that year.

Almost on cue, Kennan's article appeared in the July issue of *Foreign Affairs*—an initiative perceived by Moscow as one essentially designed to spell out America's true intentions to its attentive public.[73] The article mentioned the Kremlin's weaknesses, suggesting that Russia's Marxist-Leninist system already possessed the seeds of its own destruction, and concluded by talking of the need to confront Soviet Russia 's aggressive policies with "unalterable counter-force." It also averred that American policy was "by no means limited to holding the line" and that American action could "influence . . . internal developments within Russia" and "increase enormously the strains under which Soviet policy must operate." For the Russians, this fit in nicely with the pattern of American behavior over the previous eighteen months, and was in concert with the attitude of the Western democracies in the interwar period.

In September 1947 a conference involving all of the communist parties of Eastern Europe was convened in Belgrade, Yugoslavia, the purpose of which was to seek a common response to the events of the previous spring and summer. One result was the establishment of the Cominform. This organization would be aimed at the coordination of policies among the Communist parties of the world in order to challenge the West on a global scale. Its "two camps" vision of a world divided between "progressive" and "imperialist" forces mirrored the growing bipolar view and use of the Nazi analogy in the West. As Georgi Malenkov put it, the "Hitlerite West . . . has taken the path of outright expansion . . . [in] Europe and the colonial and dependent countries."[74] Unlike the Third Communist International (1919–1943), however, the Cominform was limited in geographic scope to Europe, and its organization was a response to the perceived threat of the Marshall Plan, rather than an expression of a new period of revolutionary drive.

Andrei Zhadanov, a rising star in the CPSU, who presided over the conference, called the Truman Doctrine and Marshall Plan "the embodiment of the American design to enslave Europe." What action would Soviet Russia take? His answer was that Moscow would "lend every effort in order that [the Marshall Plan] be doomed to failure. The communist parties of France, Italy, Great Britain and other countries . . . must take up the standard in defense of the national independence and sovereignty of their countries."[75] It is in this sense that Zhadanov's speech reflected a mirror image of America's two-world attitude.

In retrospect, the winter of 1947–1948 appears to have been a pivotal moment for the Russians. By the early months of 1948, Moscow came to believe that the long-term implications of the Marshall Plan were even more ominous, namely, that its real character was a military one designed to provide America's Western European allies with the wherewithal to roll back Russian influence.[76] Russia might then be faced with a most unfortunate Hobbesian choice—either acquiesce in the pushing back of Russian influence to its Western borders, or of intervening and risking an American nuclear attack. Viewing the rapidly hardening American attitude since the war as a vindication of what it had suspected all along—a real, dangerous, and unrelenting hostility in the West toward legitimate Russian security interests—it was not long in addressing itself to the task of buttressing its newly-won territories in Eastern and Central Europe against the onslaught it felt was sure to come. The issue seemed clear enough to Moscow: Confronted by a revitalized West Berlin deep inside the Russian zone in Germany, and by the prospect of losing control in Eastern Europe, a real crisis was at hand. How to deal with it?

If Soviet Russia's actions in Hungary in the late summer and fall of 1947 represented the harbinger of change, Czechoslovakia turned out to be the decisive turning point. Russia had signed a treaty in late 1943 with the Czech leaders that obligated that country to cooperate with Russia. In an election in 1946, the Czech Communist Party received only 38 percent of the vote. By late 1947, the lure of Western aid and internal political changes began to pull the Czech government away from Russia. The Czechs, virtually alone among the East European states, had indicated a real desire to participate in the Marshall Plan, only to be pressured by Moscow to pull back from their initial acceptance. At this point, Stalin decided to put the 1943 treaty into effect. This was accomplished by the coup in February 1948 that eliminated the last non-communist elements in the government.[77] It was not long before bloody purges proceeded all over Eastern Europe—a house-cleaning that would drag on for the rest of the decade. From Moscow's perspective, its actions in Czechoslovakia were entirely "defensive"[78] and therefore appropriate. Soviet Russia wanted to be able to count on the relatively advanced, undamaged Czech industrial infrastructure and, above all, be able to utilize its uranium reserves and the military lines of communication that a secure hold on that country would entail.

Thus, the basis for the "vicious circle" of the Cold War was precipitated—mutual hostility and suspicion, reinforced by the actions taken by first one side and then the other. And it was not as if American intelligence officials were not aware that Washington's initiatives might well magnify tensions and, by placing Soviet Russia on the defensive, make the prospect of war more likely. In July 1947 intelligence analysts in the War Department pointed out that the Truman Doctrine and the Marshall Plan had provoked a more aggressive Russian attitude toward America. And they were also well aware that the Russians would react very negatively to plans for currency reform in Germany and to any unilateral attempt to create a West German state.

In March 1948 an agreement of principle on Germany had been reached in London by the Conference of Six Powers (America, Britain, France, and the Benelux countries). Reconvening in April, the participants on June 7 issued a statement, based on the preliminary agreement reached two months earlier, authorizing the Ministers-President of the German *Länder* to convene a constituent assembly by September 1, 1948, for the purpose of drawing up a constitution for a federal form of government, to be submitted to the German people in a referendum. The Ruhr was to remain a part of Germany, but a six-power International authority was to allocate the products of its coal and steel industries between German domestic consumption and export.[79]   The three western occupying powers agreed not to withdraw their forces from Germany until the peace of Europe was secured or without prior consultation. On June 17 the French National Assembly, by a narrow majority, gave the government the support it needed for what amounted to a reversal of French policy toward Germany over the previous three years. On the following day a currency reform in the three western zones of Germany was announced.

Moscow's response to this sequence of events was a predictable one. A Russian note on March 6 asserted that the London Conference had violated the Potsdam Agreement and, therefore, its recommendations were invalid. From the end of March the first Russian measures to cut off the western sectors of Berlin began, culminating in the suspension on the night of June 23–24 of all rail traffic between Berlin and the West. Russian particpation in the Allied Commandant in the city ceased on July 1. By August the blockade of the Western sectors of Berlin was complete. Within days the West responded. "The whole Berlin crisis," army planners informed General Eisenhower in June 1948, "has arisen as a result of . . . actions on the part of the Western Powers."[80]

THE EVOLVING AMERICAN WORLD VIEW AND
THE QUESTION OF RUSSIAN INTENTIONS

"The greatest danger to the security of the United States," the CIA reported in mid-1947, "is the possibility of economic collapse in Western Europe and the consequent accession to power of Communist elements."[81] During 1946–1947, as officials in the Truman Administration looked on, there seemed to be taking place an inexorable unraveling of the geopolitical foundations and socioeconomic structure of the international system, as evidenced by a number of disturbing developments, all viewed as destabilizing in nature: The sudden collapse of Britain's traditional role in the eastern Mediterranean, India's disruptive independence movement, the worsening civil war situation in China, nationalist insurgencies in Indo-China and the Dutch East Indies (the one in the former place apparently controlled by communists), an intensifying struggle among Arabs and Jews in Palestine, German and Japanese economic stagnation if not paralysis, and Communist electoral gains in France and Italy.

In this disturbing postwar envrionment, American assessments of long-term Russian intentions underwent a major transformation. Spurred by Kennan's long telegram, it soon became commonplace for policy makers, military officials, and intelligence analysts to state that the ultimate aim of Moscow's foreign policy was nothing less than the creation of a Marxist-Leninist world.[82] Evidence cited for this included Moscow's moves toward establishing a sphere of influence in Eastern Europe; stonewalling of the agreement to withdraw its troops from Iran; the turning over of captured Japanese weapons to the Chinese communists; a brutal approach to the extraction of reparations from their occupation zone in

Germany; diplomatic overtures for bases in the Black and Mediterranean Seas; persistent demands for a role in the occupation of Japan; and an apparent renewed verbal emphasis on Marxist-Leninist doctrine, with its accompanying verbiage trumpeting the vulnerability of capitalist economies, and the inevitability of future war.[83] All of this would lead to a growing belief in Washington that the American way of life could only succeed in a stable global environment receptive to American interests.

These assessments, however, did not seriously take into account a litany of existing contradictory evidence pointing up Russia's inherent weaknesses, and the evident moderation and caution exhibited by the Kremlin. Documentation existed on the withdrawal of Russian troops from northern Norway, Manchuria, and Iran, plus intelligence reports pointing to sizeable reductions of Russian troops in Eastern Europe and an extensive demobilization within Russia itself.[84] In early 1947, for example, CIA intelligence pointed to more than a half-dozen instances of Russian moderation including limiting their involvement in the Middle East, toning down the ideological rhetoric, and providing only limited support to the Chinese Communist Party (CCP) in its struggle with the Kuomintang.[85]

In point of fact, throughout the late 1940s, there was nearly universal agreement that the Russians, while desirous to expand their influence, nevertheless wanted no military confrontation with the West. In the spring of 1947, during a time of deep concern about a possible communist uprising in France, military intelligence concluded that the Kremlin would not try to stage a coup d'état, lest it lead to war.[86] In September 1947, the CIA stated that the Russians would not seek to conquer Western Europe for several reasons: recognition that it would be unlikely they could control hostile populations; fear of triggering a war with America that could not be won; and a preference for the achievement of political control by non-military means.[87]

Although Truman administration officials recognized that Soviet Russia possessed significant military capability,[88] it was understood within the administration that their strength was limited. As American intelligence reports clearly showed, they possessed no atomic bomb or the long-range strategic air force to deliver it. Their air defenses were highly suspect. Moreover, the Russian navy was known to be third rate except for its submarine forces. Indeed, throughout the years 1945–1948 American analysts and intelligence experts believed that extensive transportation bottlenecks, widespread industrial inadequacies, a pervasive technological backwardness, and enormous problems in the agricultural sector would effectively preclude military adventurism.[89]

If American officials did not really expect any Russian military initiatives, why, then, were they so afraid of losing control of the non-communist world? Melvyn Leffler, in a careful and persuasive study,[90] argues that the answer resides less in American assessments of Russian military capabilities and short-term intentions than in their view of the economic and political conditions in Europe and the rest of the world at that time. In their overall assessments of Russia's long-term intentions, Truman administration policy makers dismissed this record of weakness, moderation, and restraint. In fact, as 1946 wore on, these officials appeared to spend less time analyzing Moscow's intentions and more time preoccupied with its capabilities. They became less and less interested in exploring ways of addressing the Russian state's legitimate strategic requirements or in considering how America's own initiatives could impact Soviet Russia's conception of its interests. Information not confirming prevailing assumptions either was ignored in overall assessments of Russian intentions or was employed to make the case that Moscow was simply shifting tactics.

Kennan would later echo this viewpoint. "[T]he idea," he said, "that in doing things disagreeable to our interests the Russians might be reacting to features of our own behavior was one to which the mind of official Washington would always be strangely resistant. Our adversaries . . . had always to be demonic, monstrous, incalculable, and inscrutable. It was unthinkable that we, by admitting that they sometimes reacted to what we did, should confess to a share in the responsibility for their behavior."[91]

Thus, the combination of socioeconomic turmoil throughout the world and a perceived renewed Russian ideological drive contributed to the growth of a shortsighted view of Moscow's long-term policy objectives and to enormous apprehension lest the Russians gain control of strategically important resources. In this environment, there could be little room for equivocation or compromise. Action was mandatory—in particular, action aimed at shoring up those areas of the world not already under Moscow's sway. Thus, during late 1946 and 1947, the Truman administration took the initiative by calling for the creation of an economic zone in the western sectors of Germany, providing military and economic assistance to Greece and Turkey, and offering massive economic aid to Western Europe.

CONTAINMENT OPERATIONALIZED:
THE NORTH ATLANTIC TREATY, NSC-7, 20/4, AND 30

Once the decision to confront Soviet Russia with all the intensity at America's disposal had been made, it remained only to take the necessary steps to put teeth into it. Specifically, it remained for the Russian rejection of Marshall Plan aid in 1947, not only for themselves but for the countries under their influence, to push Washington over the edge to the adoption of the definitive apolitical course toward Soviet Russia that would lie at the core of American foreign policy thereafter. In the process, it became increasingly irrelevant to discuss the political goals for which the Cold War was ostensibly being fought. Indeed, with the final goal of containment (the mellowing of Moscow's aggressive intentions) appearing more and more remote by the day, and as the actual approach came to be applied in the Truman (and, later, the Eisenhower) administrations, what had originally been considered the condition of policy—security against aggression—seemed to become its only goal.

The Russian clamp-down on the Czechs in February-March, 1948 had a tremendous psychological impact on the President and his advisors. In the wake of the coup, Czechoslovakia assumed, like Poland a decade earlier, a symbolic importance out of all proportion to its value to America's security.[92] "We are faced with exactly the same situation with which Britain and France were faced in 1938-39 with Hitler," Truman wrote to his family.[93] The events in Czechoslovakia led the National Security Council, on its own initiative, to undertake a reexamination of the country's grand strategy. The result was NSC-7, entitled "The Position of the United States with Respect to Soviet-Directed World Communism."

This was the first administration document to employ the term "cold war." Its opening sentence set the tone for the whole: "Today Stalin has come close to achieving what Hitler attempted in vain." Eschewing a defensive strategy in the coming struggle, NSC-7 advocated a broad counter offensive against world-wide communism including the rearming of America through universal military training, the continuance of "overwhelming U.S. superiority in atomic weapons," and strengthening of American assistance efforts in Europe, including a "coordinated program to support underground resistance movements in countries behind the iron curtain." Vague as to both the creation and implementation of these programs, NSC-7 was rather a suggestion as to the form that the American reaction to the Russian threat might take.[94]

The first months of 1948 found the administration busy seeking to shore up potential weak spots in what was now clearly recognized in Washington as a requirement to establish a defensive perimeter around the Russian state. Negotiations were conducted with the British to gain access to bases in the Middle East and North Africa, and with the Turks to build a series of highways and airfields and to transfer fighter bombers to that country. In June, Washington moved quickly to resuscitate the Japanese economy, funds being requested from Congress to procure imports of raw materials for Japanese industry so that Japanese exports might be increased.[95] That same month the Selective Service Act was extended for a year.

Meanwhile, an important step in beginning to shore up Western Europe's defenses against any Russian adventurism was taken in the form of the Brussels Treaty. To this particular arrangement must go the distinction of being the first postwar European coalition of mutual defense against the perceived threat now posed by Soviet Russia. Britain took the lead in the winter of 1947–1948 in urging Washington to consider a permanent military alliance to guarantee Western Europe's security. While American policy makers were at first reluctant to support this proposal, mainly because there still existed in Washington a traditional conception of alliances as immoral, not to mention a lingering hope that the deadlock with Soviet Russia could be broken, Marshall in December 1947 encouraged Ernest Bevin, the British Foreign Minister, to go ahead with the plans to organize a collective system of defense for Western Europe.[96] This led to the signing of the Brussels Pact in March 1948 involving the Benelux states, France, and the United Kingdom.[97] Combined with the currency reform undertaken within the Western zones of Germany in order to stem inflation and clamp down on a burgeoning black market, this had the effect to begin to bring these areas within the scope of the economic and political reconstruction of Western Europe.

That same month the U.S. Senate passed the Vandenburg Resolution expressing the willingness of America to associate "by constitutional processes, with such regional and other collective arrangements as are based on continuous and effective self-help and mutual aid, and as affect its national security." This resolution paved the way for that support of the Brussels Pact that Truman had promised shortly after the signing of that instrument.[98]

One explanation for the fateful American decision in 1948 to undertake the erection of a military shield against a Russian invasion of Western Europe is to set forth the view that something drastic was deemed necessary to bolster European morale and to encourage the will to resist, regardless of any threat either in being or imminent. This explanation would be offered in later years by those who saw in NATO an important instrument of national power but who found it necessary to justify their support on other grounds.[99] This, however, would not be the standard American explanation. The official line quickly became and remained that Soviet Russia was planning a military conquest of Western Europe in 1949 and that only the creation of NATO forced the Kremlin to abandon the project.[100]

In point of fact, at the outset there was genuine confusion within the administration as to what NATO's role should be. Would it require more American troops in Europe? No, said the administration. Would it involve the rearming of Germans? No, they said. Was it aimed at countering internal subversion? Absolutely not, was the reply. According to Harriman, "there would be a reorientation" in Europe climaxing in "a restrengthening of those who do not believe in appeasement and neutrality." But during the Congressional hearings on the proposed North Atlantic Treaty, a consensus seemed to develop that NATO was to create not merely a balance of power, but a preponderance of power. Senator Tom Connelly, Chairman of the Senate Foreign Relations Committee, put it this way: "The Atlantic Pact is but the logical extension of the principle of the Monroe Doctrine," he said.[101]

Initially, the North Atlantic Alliance possessed no unified strategy. It consisted of separate armies joined together in the style of a traditional alliance. It remained for congressional suspicion that American assistance might be diverted to "selfish" national purposes rather than to the common defense, as well as the outbreak of the Korean War, to provide the needed impetus for the creation of the Organization itself. Interestingly, the Alliance was at first defended on purely military grounds. In his testimony on the North Atlantic Treaty before the Senate Foreign Relations Committee, Acheson sought to distinguish between the proposed alliance and its traditional, old style counterpart. The following exchange took place between Mr. Acheson and Chairman Connally:

> Sec. Acheson: The system of military alliances to which you refer was usually embodied in treaties which provided that if one of the signatory parties—they were usually bilateral treaties—became involved in war.

> The Chairman: It was not limited to attack on them, but extended also to an enterprise to make war on somebody else, is that true?

> Sec. Acheson: I think that is true; yes sir. The idea of arrangements to prevent aggression is somewhat modern. In the old treaties it was if you became involved in war, then the other signatory party would come to your help. . . . The conception of this treaty, and the conception of the Rio Treaty, and the conception of the Brussels Treaty is a newer one, and one which grows out of principles and procedures of the UN Charter.[102]

Addressing himself to the same question at this time before the Committee, John Foster Dulles asserted:

> I do not interpret this as a military alliance. If I thought it were a military alliance, I would oppose it unqualifiedly. The distinction, it seems to me, is this, that as you say, most military alliances are made between powers as a matter of temporary expediency in pursuit of some particular ambition that one or the other of them has. This is a treaty for the common defense which grows out of a common unity.[103]

Other witnesses, too, tried to draw this distinction between the North Atlantic Treaty and traditional military alliances. The distinction was not a valid one. What Messieurs Acheson and Dulles had in mind, perhaps, was the contrast between "defensive" and "offensive" alliances. American public opinion had never been well informed regarding the nature of alliances, the popular view (and one reflected in the Congress as well) being that alliances as such are intrinsically offensive and therefore major contributing factors to war. Fear of "entangling" foreign commitments was still a widespread sentiment in the country. The Atlantic Pact, therefore, had to be sold to the American people.

The final details of the treaty were worked out after Truman's election in November, 1948. The treaty itself was signed on April 4, 1949, and in September of that same year the Congress approved the Mutual Defense Assistance Act appropriating one billion dolllars for arms and equipment for the signatories and an additional $211 million for Greece and Turkey. Thus, by the beginning of the 1950s the framework for a peacetime integrated military organization comprising the armed forces of all the member states of the alliance had been created.

All of this, not unnaturally, generated considerable concern within the administration as to how the Russians might react. The available evidence indicates that intelligence officials were greatly worried in 1948 that the passage of the Selective Service Act and/or adoption of universal military training, additional appropriations for the air force, military assistance for Western Europe, the resolution endorsing American support for the West European Union, and the movement toward creating a military shield for Western Europe, might trigger a Russian attack. America's policies in seeking to prolong her nuclear monopoly as long as possible should be seen in this light.[104]

Moscow, of course, protested vigorously. From March 10 to October 12, 1949, a stream of communications flowed from Moscow to Washington. On September 19, 1949, the Soviet *chargé d'affaires* in Washington sent a strongly worded note to Acheson, protesting the "aggressive intentions of NATO" as confirmed, for example, by allowing the Italian government to join NATO, thus violating the peace treaty.[105]

The difficulty with this spate of offensive-mindedness, however, was that it would inevitably carry with it certain implications. For one thing, it would not come cheap, for it was predictable that America's accelerating confrontation with Soviet Russia would lead to calls for increased military spending. Recognizing that Washington's ever more militant actions, aimed at insulating its international interests from communist encroachment, might be perceived as endangering vital Russian interests, it was all the more vital to be prepared for any eventuality. The Truman administration's new assertiveness, it should be emphasized, did not stem merely from Moscow's actions in Berlin during the summer of 1948, although the Russian blockade of the Western sectors of the German city certainly represented an important catalyst. The new-found aggressiveness also stemmed from apprehensions that the ongoing American initiatives themselves might provoke an aggressive response from Moscow. It was this sort of reasoning that would lead eventually to the generation of NSC 20/4.

The attempt by the Russians to prevent Western access to the city presented the administration with a series of dilemmas. How to respond? Universal military training had yet to be implemented and was unlikely, given congressional reluctance. A direct attack on Russian forces in Berlin, or even sending an armored column down the highway through the Russian zone, posed serious risks of escalation. In the end, these options were rejected as too inflammatory. What happened was that the Berlin crisis, and the undesirability of the available options open to the administration, convinced a number of leading administration officials of the need to bring our capabilities into line with America's evolving commitments by increasing the military budget. But how to justify increased military spending to a president reluctant to jeopardize his domestic programs?

Defense Secretary Forrestal, greatly alarmed about Russian actions, and under enormous pressure from his own military chiefs (especially the Air Force) for more resources, in early summer requested a special study on how to plan for American defense expenditures in view of predicted Russian initiatives. This paper, appearing in November, would be adopted as the definitive statement of American foreign policy for the next two years, proclaiming it to be American policy: "To create situations which will compel the Soviet Government to recognize the practical undesirability of acting on the basis of its present concepts and the necessity of behaving in accordance with precepts of international conduct, as set forth in the purposes and principles of the UN Charter." While reiterating the long standing estimate that Soviet Russia was not likely to resort to war to achieve its objectives, it nevertheless stated that war could erupt as a result of "Soviet miscalculation of the determination of the United States to use all the means at its command to safeguard its security, through Soviet misinterpretation of our intentions, and through U.S. miscalculation of Soviet reactions to measures which we might take."[106] It is interesting to note that the language of NSC 20/4 did not spell out clear priorities but simply projected American interests almost everywhere in the world. America had to be ready to fight a war it did not want, but which might well arise as a result of the pursuit of its own national security goals. Although 20/4 did not seek a larger military budget, it nevertheless underlined the importance of restricting Russian power and influence to the borders of the Russian heartland and of underwriting the strength of non-Russian states in the area.

Meanwhile, as Gregg Herken points out, American strategy on atomic warfare had evolved incrementally since the demise of the Baruch Plan.[107] The adoption of NSC-30 in September signaled the administration's final abandonment of international control of atomic weapons. NSC-30 reflected a determination that we would use atomic weapons in the event of war with Soviet Russia, even if we initiated the conflict. When the president ordered the dispatch of American B-29 bombers to Britain in June, at the height of the Berlin crisis, thus placing American atomic capability within range of the Russian heartland, this, de facto, established the practice of nuclear deterrence in advance of the development of later theory.[108] The year 1948 signaled the first tangible integration of the atomic bomb into America's political strategy for dealing with Russia—a marriage achieved under the pressure of perceived urgent necessity, not necessarily by rational planning.[109]

Thus, foreign policy officials in the Truman administration over the course of 1947–1948 came to the view that it was imperative to develop our military capabilities to meet a full range of contingencies that might flow from further Russian initiatives or from indigenous communist-led upheavals. Such contingencies, it was felt, might very well occur because American strategy called for the rebuilding of Western Europe (including a resuscitated Germany carved out of the West's occupation zones), and the rehabilitation of Japan, Russia's two most important traditional enemies, as well as the development of our airpower and atomic weapons, and the placement of military bases on Russia's borders.

The dynamics of the Cold War after 1946 are easier to understand when one evaluates the scope of America's conception of national security that emerged between 1945 and 1948. This conception included the creation and preservation of a strategic sphere of influence within the Western hemisphere, the elaboration of a dominant naval presence in the Atlantic and Pacific oceans, an extensive system of overseas military bases designed to flesh out the country's strategic frontiers and project American power abroad, dependable and easy access to the resources and markets of Europe and Asia (including, of course, denial of those resources to the Russians), and the maintenance of nuclear superiority. Not every one of these pieces of the stragegic pie was considered vital at the outset, but, over time, challenges to these evolving concepts of national security were certain to produce hard line reactions. This occurred initially in 1947–1948 when decisions were made in favor of the Truman Doctrine, the Marshall Plan, the Rio Pact, the Atlantic Alliance, German and Japanese rehabilitation, and, finally, increased military spending.

And, yet, before the creation of the North Atlantic Treaty, and before the "Sovietization" of Eastern Europe by Moscow had been fully consummated, an event took place which would serve to strip the veil from some of the pretenses under which the more intensified phase of the Cold War was to be waged. In June 1948 the so-called "great schism" occurred between Yugoslav leader Tito and Stalin, followed by a vast purging of Titoist "heretics" in the communist parties of Eastern Europe. This episode, and the respones it elicited from Moscow, would serve to undercut the main justification for the eventual creation of NATO and the rearming of the West Germans.

The failure of the Red Army to invade the renegade state ("I will shake my little finger—there will be no more Tito. Tito will fall," Stalin had said) contained at least two implications. For one thing, the Russians apparently were not willing to invade a country possessing well-organized, well-equipped forces and presenting a strong national front (the Finnish experience still being fresh in their minds). Even assuming the intention to invade, existing American and British military capability, located precisely where it was at that time apparently was deemed sufficient by Stalin to deter him from any armed foray in Europe, East or West. Thus, before Western rearmament, before the spiraling arms race had seized hold of both America and Soviet Russia, Moscow felt itself effectively restrained from aggressive actions by the circumstances in which it found itself in the immediate postwar era.[110]

POST-NATO DEVELOPMENTS: TOWARD NSC-68

Beginning in the spring of 1949, the overt militarization of the containment policy, following hard on the heels of the Russian gambit in Berlin, served to put the capstone, as it were, on this concept of the Cold War. The struggle for Europe now took on an added intensity. In August, elections in West Germany for a national parliament took place and, at the same time, discussions were begun on the feasibility of building a large conventional European army with

German military units included. But how to proceed? Within the Administration there was considerable controversy, the State Department and Pentagon disagreeing over whether such an action would provoke strong countermeasures from Poland and France, let alone Russia.[111]

Meanwhile, infighting among the Western allies became rife. The French came out with a plan for an iron, coal and steel community—foreign minister Maurice Schuman's plan for a "little Europe"—designed, hopefully, to keep Germany weak and integrated into Western Europe while forestalling possible American and British domination. Washington had other ideas, seeking to influence events in Germany and Western Europe through NATO. These two approaches would pose the major alternatives for European development for the next quarter-century.[112]

On September 22, 1949, the Russians exploded their first atomic bomb, prompting Truman to order on March 10, 1950 the speed-up of development of a hydrogen bomb. The six-month interval between the detection of the Russian atomic test and the president's decision to go ahead with the "super bomb" was due largely to the fact that the opinions of his advisers were divided.[113] This decision, coupled with a parallel Russian push to develop a thermonuclear weapon of its own, may be said to mark the beginning of the era of the balance of terror. It was a decision that stood on its own. Taken by Truman over three months before the beginning of the Korean War, at a time when he was still insisting on holding the defense budget to around the $13 billion mark, it did not in and of itself form part of the general Western rearmament that followed the outbreak of that war. There was, however, a bridge between the two—NSC-68.

By the winter of 1949–1950, the American mood was both surly and defensive—essentially locked in a conservative mode of reaction. Once again Truman found himself equivocating on the question of what to do about Russia. On the one hand, he was committed to his "Fair Deal" for the American people—a series of new economic and social initiatives that he had proposed after his inauguration in January. Recognizing that there wasn't enough money in the Treasury to underwrite costly new programs in both the domestic sector and in defense, Truman ordered a ceiling on military spending. On the other hand, hounded by domestic critics over the "loss" of China to the communists and plagued by an intensifying anti-communist hysteria in great measure manipulated by both well-meaning and unscrupulous politicians in both parties, he felt compelled to do something lest he be perceived as a "do-nothing" president. The result was a demand for a thorough reevaluation of America's Cold War policies.

In December 1949 Kennan was replaced as director of the Policy Planning Staff in the State Department by Paul Nitze[114]—an individual who had great reservations about the ceilings on military spending that Truman had ordered. Conversations with European leaders had convinced Nitze that they needed reassurances beyond the mere words of the North Atlantic Treaty. NSC-68 was Nitze's first assignment—a situation that gave him an opportunity to put the case for increased military spending before the President and his top advisors. In early 1950 the National Security Council began work on "68," the rationale being that a further military buildup was now necessary to fully prepare the country for any eventuality. In April a seventy-page paper was handed to the State Department. Entitled, "United States Objectives and Programs for National Security," the document was an analysis of the Cold War Russian-American relationship to date, including an examination of the courses of action open to the country. After reviewing arguments for maintaining the current course, retreating to isolation, or attacking Soviet Russia, NSC presented an argument for a fourth alternative, namely, a "Rapid Build-up of Political, Economic, and Military Strength in the Free World."

The hallmark of the document is its apocalyptic warning: "The issues that face us are momentous, involving the fulfillment or destruction not only of this Republic but of civilization itself." As Acheson was to put it later, "The purpose of NSC 68 was to so bludgeon the mass mind of 'top government' that not only could the President make a decision but that the decision could be carried out."[115] As a result of carefully cultivating leading decision makers in both the Pentagon and the civilian sector of the government, Nitze, Acheson, *et al.* were able to lay the groundwork for the eventual acceptance of the premises underlying the document: that communism represented a continuing, mortal threat to the American way of life, that the only thing Soviet Russia could be made to understand was strength and our willingness to use it, and that a massive increase in defense spending would be required to bring it off. To that end, Acheson and his allies were determined to launch a global offensive to reclaim the initiative in the Cold War and to shut up the critics at home. But justification was needed, as both the mood of the public and that of their Congress at this time was hardly conducive to underwriting the expenditures that would surely be needed for any significant military buildup. For a time NSC-68 was a policy in search of a *raison d'etre*. As Acheson would admit later, "Korea came along and saved us." [116]

THE KOREAN EPISODE

Meanwhile, events taking place in East Asia during this period were certainly of some concern to the administration. The situation, viewed from Washington, was not going well as relations with the Chinese Communist Party (CCP) leadership continued to deteriorate. During the summer of 1949, CCP leader Mao Zedong indicated a desire to have diplomatic relations with Washington. But our ambassador was not allowed to talk with the Chinese Communist Party leader. Donald Zagoria has argued that if Washington had recognized the new Chinese Communist regime in 1949, exploited Mao Zedong's long-standing suspicions of Stalin, and catered to China's national interest and expressions of desire for American support, the split between Russia and China would have occurred much earlier, the Chinese might not have intervened in the Korean War, and America might not have felt compelled to intervene later in Vietnam against what it thought to be a concerted international communist conspiracy. The available evidence now indicates that Mao desired some sort of accommodation with Washington to counter-balance his relationship with Moscow.[117] Such was not to be the case. After China "fell" to the communists in October, a policy of non-recognition was decided upon.[118] In November, Mao traveled to Moscow for what proved to be a very long negotiation session with Stalin, culminating the following February in a treaty of friendship and cooperation between the communist party-state giants.[119]

Throughout the spring and early summer of 1950, however, the strategic situation in East Asia, while volatile and full of potential danger, did not appear to observers in the West to be one of imminent danger of an outbreak of war. All of that suddenly changed on June 25 when North Korea, without warning, attacked South Korea. The consequences of this action would have enormous implications for the future course of the Russian-American Cold War conflict.

Looked at from Moscow's perspective, the Korean War can be fully under-stood only in the context of Stalin's growing frustrations in Europe, the takeover of China by its indigenous Communist Party without the support of (and control by) Moscow, the statements of General MacArthur and Secretary Acheson in early 1950 that Korea fell outside our defense perimeter,[120] and the American decision to proceed with the negotiation of a separate peace treaty with Japan—to which the Russians would not be a party—and to link such a settlement with an indefinite stationing of American armed forces in that country. We also now have considerable evidence that the North Korean strongman Kim Il-sung had some not inconsiderable success in exerting leverage over the Kremlin in pursuing his own interests. By relentlessly pushing and prodding a somewhat reluctant and cautious Stalin for many months prior to June 1950, Kim was able to eventually gain the Russian leader's assent for an attack against the south by skillfully playing on the wily Russian leader's obsessive preoccupation with China's Communist Party leader.[121]

As background for all of this, it must be remembered that a civil war had been raging ever since 1946 between the regimes of Kim in the north and Syngman Rhee in the south—a struggle that had claimed some 100,000 lives by the eve of the June 1950 attack. The struggle pitted left-wing elements (both communists and other, non-communist, radicals) against right-wing groups in the south. Moreover, the confrontation involved excessive violence by both sides, including highly authoritarian methods by Rhee to suppress his opponents. By 1948 Truman, wearying of the mess, endeavored to pull out the remaining American troops in the south and turn over the problem to the UN.[122] Stalin also withdrew his forces from the north, but left behind some advisors to train the North Korean army. By 1950 the conflict had escalated into several conventional battles, with armed forays across the 38th parallel by elements from both sides. By early 1950 the fighting had died down, but only, apparently, until Kim believed he was sufficiently strong to launch a final campaign against the south to unite the country.

It was this situation which led Kim by the summer of 1950 to believe that Rhee, under increasing attack by his domestic opponents, was most vulnerable. The South Korean strongman had lost control of his legislature in May, and it may well have been that Kim, fearful that an embattled Rhee might stage an attack against the north, launched a preemptive strike of his own. When Truman would decide in June 1950 to respond to Kim's assault upon the south, it was not therefore a question of responding to Russian initiatives, but, rather, one of involving America in an internal civil war that had been going on for some time.[123]

We do know that in early 1950 Kim traveled to Moscow to seek Stalin's blessing for an attack against the south. Stalin's response was to give Kim the green light, but to state that in any event Russian forces would not be involved. The evidence points to at least two reasons for Stalin's acquiesence in Kim's plans at that time.

First, Stalin was greatly concerned when in May Truman announced that discussions on a Japanese peace treaty would now receive top priority. Such a treaty would amount to a formal alliance between America and Japan—an arrangement that would lead to the overt independence of Japan and the presence of American military bases on its territory. And Russia would not be invited to participate in the negotiations. The Russian press fairly bristled with accusations pointing out that Truman was trying to "draw the Asiatic and Pacific countries into aggressive military blocs."[124] A quick North Korean victory, perhaps, might well serve to blunt the American effort at lining up East Asia against Moscow.

Second, the evidence also points to Stalin's fear and jealousy of Mao's position in China, especially his efforts at encouraging revolutionary upheavals in Asia. The possibility that some of these revolutions might triumph, with Chinese assistance, was something that Stalin could not countenance. While Stalin, therefore, may have been somewhat reluctant to underwrite Kim Il-sung, he nonetheless did so, ultimately, both as a function of his rivalry with Mao, and only after becoming convinced that the Americans would not intervene. Moreover, Stalin appears to have calculated that Kim's mission to unify Korea might well intensify the split between the CCP and America.[125]

Militarization of Containment

The year 1950 was crucial—a pivotal moment the substance of which was in large measure to determine the shape of history for the next two decades. The events of that year may be said to constitute together a kind of quantum leap into the last half of the twentieth century, for that year saw the beginning in ernest of the nuclear arms race that Stimson had foreseen five years earlier. It also witnessed the commencement of the West's conventional rearmament, the conclusion of the Chinese-Russian treaty of alliance, the launching of NATO in Europe, the first significant initiative in the process of Franco-German reconciliation, the outbreak of a major war in Asia; and, not least, the beginning of a sustained economic expansion without precedent in the history of the industrialized Western world.

The creation of the North Atlantic military shield and the onset of the Korean War "solved" whatever controversy continued to linger between the capabilities and intentions schools of thought concerning Soviet Russia's foreign policy. For America, the North Korean attack on South Korea represented an unacceptable affront to her moral and ideological preconceptions. In this sense the impact of the Korean events on American sensibilities cannot be overestimated. From the very outset, the administration's conviction was that the North Korean attack was the work of "centrally directed Communist Imperialism," and in his special message to Congress on July 19, Truman said that "the fateful events of the Nineteen-thirties, when aggression unopposed bred more aggression and eventually war, were fresh in our minds."[126]

Korea also greatly intensified Washington's anti-communist fears at home, serving to freeze America into a militant Cold War posture for the next twenty years. In this vein, the year 1950 also saw an accelerated intensification of the anti-communist witchhunt, centering on the person of Dean Acheson. It was in January of that year that Alger Hiss was convicted of perjury. Only hours after Hiss's conviction, Acheson announced publicly that he did not intend to turn his back on his former State Department colleague—remarks seized upon by Senator McCarthy days later in launching his anti-communist crusade against "communists in government." McCarthyism would provide the worst possible accompaniment to the dramatic sequence of events that took place during that year.

Over the short term, it resulted in a remarkable spurt of activism. The fourth meeting of the North Atlantic Council having, in May, already laid the foundation for NATO, from June-December, 1950, a number of new initiatives resulting from the shock of the Korean invasion flowed out of Washington: a revitalization of the country's alliance commitments, with an associated increase in aid to the French in Indochina and the issuing of guarantees to the Chinese Nationalists on Formosa, an attempt to transform the UN by doing an end-run around the Security Council, not to mention an invasion of North Korea with the intent to liberate it from the communists, leading to a paralysis of Chinese-American relations for many years.

Indeed, the Administration's previous ambivalence about the importance to America of the security of Korea and Formosa now having been swept away, leading both to a new relationship between Washington and Tokyo and to the conclusion of an alliance with the Chinese Nationalist authorities in Taipei, the immediate result, viewed from Peking's perspective, was, in effect, to plunge America into the middle of the Chinese civil war. As part of Truman's new guarantees to the Kuomintang, not only was the Seventh Fleet interposed between Formosa and the mainland, but the determination of Formosa's status, he said, "must await the restoration of security in the Pacific."[127]

But the most important result of the Korean episode was the operationalization of the NSC-68 blueprint. Indeed, both domestic and international forces coalesced in 1950 to make the logic of NSC-68 irresistible. On September 30, Truman ordered that NSC-68 be taken as a statement of policy to be followed over the next four or five years and that the implementing programs be put into effect as rapidly as possible.[128] In December, the president requested emergency powers to expedite war mobilization, seeking a $50 billion defense budget, including a doubling of air groups to 95, and called for the establishment of new military bases in Morocco, Libya, and Saudi Arabia. The immediate result was a tripling of defense spending. For the next four decades it would remain two to three times higher, as a percentage of GNP, than in any previous periods of peace.

In Europe the Korean aggression gave rise to fear of an all-out war that few had previously regarded as a serious possibility.[129] What was more important, key individuals in positions of leadership on both sides of the Atlantic suddenly felt after June 1950 that the West was deliberately handicapping itself in the developing struggle with Soviet Russia as long as Europe was left defenseless.[130] It was only natural, one supposes, that American and European leaders, "rushing backward into the future," would unearth the experiences of the previous world conflict, crying aloud that this time the democratic West must be prepared.

It was this situation that raised the crucial question: What was to be the function of NATO? One point of view argued that NATO troops themselves should be used to off-set the approximately twenty-five divisions that Soviet Russia had maintained in the eastern half of Germany. Even a partial counterweight, it was hoped, would bring about changes in the total picture. For one thing, it would prevent Russian military action even on the local level without prior concentration of troops transported from Russian soil itself—a move that would, apparently, quickly alert the West and thus eliminate the surprise factor essential to any operation aiming at partial conquest with a minimum risk of all-out war.

After the fall of 1949 the development of nuclear weapons by the Russians tended to render obsolete the idea of NATO as a military force serving as a primary deterrent to Russian attack. A new rationalization for the continued existence of NATO was needed and was not long in forthcoming—the so-called "trip-wire" theory. This view defended NATO not on the grounds that it substantially increased the military capability of either America or of Europe, but that it "symbolized" an American commitment to defend Europe. Thus, the trip-wire rationale constituted an admission that the impact of NATO was not as important militarily as it was symbolically.

According to this view, NATO forces would serve as a sort of fire-alarm triggering mechanism, being able to resist a Russian advance with enough strength to create the necessary *casus belli atomici*, at which point America's

Strategic Air Command would take over and presumably unleash a devastating blow upon the heartland of Soviet Russia. It would be this approach that would strike the most responsive chord among Europeans anxious to have the benefits of an American defense commitment but not at the price of prohibitive economic cost or of political subservience.

Finally, it was argued by some that NATO troops alone could and should counter any aggression on the part of Soviet Russia without recourse to nuclear arms. This desire for equilibrium at the level of conventional forces was justified in the name of "defending" Europe, rather than "liberating" it—an approach which attracted European support in NATO councils early in the institutionalization process. It was this last approach which American policy makers pushed most insistently in the early 1950s, the goal to be reached over a period of several years.[131]

And it was this strategy that led Washington to put forth specific proposals as early as September 1950 for a West German army. The American government, then and later, could see no other solution to the problem of defending Western Europe. The decision to equip the West Germans with arms contained a logic all its own when taken in the context of the whole American approach to Soviet Russia after 1945. The notion was an extremely controversial one, however. It would require many months of negotiations among the British, French, Americans and the West Germans to come to some sort of understanding. Finally, in February 1952 in Lisbon the basic ground rules for a new Western alliance were agreed to.

The vehicle for accomplishing this, as it turned out, came from the French. This was not surprising, given the fact that no European state could view with alacrity the prospect of Germans in uniform again so soon after the end of World War II. In late 1950 the French premier, René Pleven, proposed a plan that would create a highly integrated European Defense Community (EDC), linked to NATO, with West German military contingents submerged in a supranational army under joint control of the member states. Once the EDC went into force, the joint occupation would be ended, and a larger measure of sovereignty granted to the Federal Republic.

For his few remaining months in office, Secretary Acheson would be hard pressed to operationalize the agreement. The French would exact a high price for their cooperation. The bottom line was that they were not willing to be in any defense organization virtually alone with the Germans, and they did not think that an American and British presence in NATO would be sufficient to counterbalance the possibility of German domination of the new grouping.[132] Acheson would eventually get the French to go along with a proposal to have half a million German troops in twelve divisions enter the EDC, but only with the understanding that Western forces would be permitted to remain in Germany, that the Germans would never deal with the Russians unilaterally, and that the Allies continue to govern West Berlin. As an added incentive to the French, Washington agreed to provide additional military assistance to Paris to help underwrite its commitments both in Europe and Indochina.

The Russian reaction to these initiatives was one of considerable alarm. From the beginning the Russians objected strongly to the formation of NATO, favoring instead an all-European security conference to conclude a nonaggression, collective security treaty in lieu of two opposed systems of alliances. Signatories to this treaty would pledge themselves to refrain from attacking one another and renounce the threat and use of force. Hostile coalitions would be prohibited, and in the case of an armed attack on one or several of the signatories, the others would regard this as an attack on themselves and would render the necessary military aid. This system would be maintained by the setting up of political military consultative committees. The West consistently rejected this proposal, doubting Russian intentions.

Between September 1950, when America first specifically demanded West German rearmament, and May 1952, when the EDC Treaty was signed, the Russians made a number of overtures which, if explored to the fullest, might have led to an all-German settlement. These gestures indicated, at the very least, that the reunification of Germany on terms acceptable to the West might have been had at the price of the abandonment of West German rearmament and of German participation in the NATO alliance. On March 10, 1952 a remarkable new initiative suddenly emanated from Moscow when the Russians proposed to the three Western powers that discussions begin among them with the aim of reaching an agreement on a German peace treaty—an agreement that would create a united and independent Germany. To that end, the Russians said, they would not be adverse to allowing Germany to have a national army with ties to neither East nor West. In the context of all this, foreign troops would be removed, and Germany admitted to the United Nations.[133]

The Russian proposal caught the administration completely by surprise. What was its purpose—a propaganda ploy, delaying tactic, or a genuine opportunity to meet Moscow on some sort of common ground to the end of unifying and neutralizing Germany and thereby reducing East-West tensions significantly? The astonishing offer was not responded to, and the motivations behind the proposal went unaddressed.[134] A treaty creating the EDC was signed in Paris on May 27, 1952, by France, Belgium, the Netherlands, Luxembourg, Italy, and West Germany, while the French agreed to the ending of the Western occupation of Germany. It now only remained for the respective parliaments to ratify the agreement for it come into effect.

We did not see fit to let the matter rest there, however. In prosecuting our version of the Cold War, America's decision makers in 1951–1952 spawned a second category of mutual security treaty aimed at extending protection to certain "key" states by means of a Monroe Doctrine-type formula. In these treaties, a particular region was declared to be so important that any attack in this area would be regarded as a threat to the peace and security of the free world. Presumably such an attack would mean war, but the situation would turn out to be less clear than with the NATO or OAS-type guarantees. The initial application of this second approach occurred in the so-called ANZUS Treaty of September 1, 1951, involving America, Australia, and New Zealand. In it the signatories recognized that an armed attack on any one of them in the Pacific arena would imperil the security of each, declaring that they would act to meet the common danger in accordance with their constitutional processes. They also promised to develop by mutual aid their individual and collective capacity to resist armed attack.[135]

In like manner, a similar type of guarantee was extended on August 30, 1951, to cover the Philippines. As such, it remained for the Eisenhower administration to bind up the few remaining fuzzy edges of an already well-entrenched and forbidding monolithic alliance structure by seeking to press the entire noncommunist world more tightly to the American breast. This was accomplished by the signing of bilateral treaties to cover Japan, South Korea, and the Republic of China. The formula would later be applied collectively to parts of Southeast Asia by means of the Manila agreement in September, 1954.

Thus, by the end of the Truman administration, the basic guidelines and structures for America's alliance policy had been put in place—a rationale and organizational infrastructure that would later be enlarged upon but not altered significantly. In two multilateral treaties—the Rio and North Atlantic agreements—America had agreed that an attack on any state actor member would be regarded as an attack on its own territory. Although both treaties provided that aggression would produce a declaration of war only if Congress acted, it was widely understood by the allied members that this was only a formality.[136]

Where the North Atlantic Treaty differed substantially from its counterpart in the Western Hemisphere lay in the fact that after 1950, in response to the Korean crisis, an elaborate organizational intrastructure was created to give the former more substance. The political reality of the situation was that the members of NATO were more firmly bound together for mutual defense than they had been disposed to state in the explicit clauses of the treaty—a situation accomplished by the institutional and organizational development of the treaty's apparatus. Thus, while America insisted upon maintaining the fiction that it reserved the sovereign right to decide for itself whether it would take military action in defense of its Atlantic allies, it had at the same time promoted and participated in a process of organizational involvement and entanglement that amounted to a curtailment, if not forfeiture, of that right.

If NATO had remained, as at the outset, essentially a traditional guaranty pact, simply committing its members to come to one another's assistance and calling for minimal peacetime collaboration, the dual task of reconciling the requiremeents of security and cohesion that came to mark its internal operation would not have been so formidable. But during the Korean War and the establishment of a central command shortly afterward, NATO acquired the characteristics of an integrated military political organization that would later exact unprecedented peacetime contributions and commitments.

The American preference for a regional security organization consonant with its own Cold War interpretation of the UN Charter, rather than for selected and restrictive bilateral pacts resembling "old fashioned" balance of power agreements, goes a long way in accounting for the multilateral character of NATO, and for the consequent difficulties in which Washington would find itself, with both the Russians and its allies. In addition, its own peculiarly intense obsession with communism, combined with a latent distrust of old-world politics, would account for the fact that the alliance was not only a guaranty pact but also an organization for extensive military collaboration and supervision. Ultimately, one can note in retrospect that the Korean War turned the policy of first deploring and then resisting the Russians and seeking to restore a balance of power in Europe into an all-out militarized confrontation with the forces of international communism around the globe.

SUMMARY: THE AMERICAN APPROACH
IN CRITICAL PERSPECTIVE

The unfolding Cold War conflict between America and Russia beginning at the end of World War II was not a simple matter of a conspiracy disguised as a state—Soviet Russia—being confronted by a largely benign and reasonable America. While ideology played an important role in shaping Russia's perceptions of the West, the decision makers in the Kremlin were neither dedicated to nor preoccupied with promoting global revolution. Rather, they were concerned with the security of the Russian state including, above all, a continuing preservation of the power and position of the governing elite.

Twice in a quarter-century the Russians found themselves faced with a highly destructive German presence in their land, the second time losing over 20 million of their people. They quite naturally were fearful of a resurgence of German (and Japanese) power after 1945. And then there was America, largely untouched by the war and possessed of a monopoly of the atomic capability. Mainly as a result of America's own conduct, Soviet Russia emerged from that conflict unsure of our intentions but, nevertheless, hopeful that the bonds forged during the fighting with the British and Americans would prove to be durable and a basis for postwar peace and cooperation.

While it is true that their Marxist-Leninist ideology imposed itself on their thinking from time to time, especially in regard to their felt need to exploit the "natural" contradictions inherent in the capitalist camp, they nevertheless proceded essentially from a realpolitik orientation. That this was so is evident when one peruses Russia's conduct in Eastern Europe from 1944–1947. The available evidence indicates that while Moscow desired certain security guarantees and friendly neighbors in Eastern Europe, they in no sense set out to convert the region to Marxism-Leninism as a means to those ends. Consequently, there was a window of opportunity in the immediate postwar period for America and its allies to constructively influence the outcome in places like Poland, Hungary, and Czechoslovakia. Unfortunately, American words and actions themselves exacerbated Russia's deep-seated anxieties, contributing to the intensification (e.g., militarization) of their conflict beginning in 1948.

Perhaps the key mistake made by both America and Soviet Russia in those initial crucial months after the war was their failure to recognize and explicitly legitimize the essential and bona fide national interests of the other. But this matter, so stated, is not so simple. In America's case, this situation was compounded by the fact that there had never been any clear-cut, unambiguous interest articulated in the first place. It certainly would have been in our national interest to negotiate an explicit quid pro quo with the Russians—one that would have recognized Russian paramount influence in Eastern Europe, and that of America and her allies in Western Europe. But President Truman pursued the worst of all possible courses in that he permitted, de facto, Soviet Russia to exercise hegemony in Eastern Europe while simultaneously refusing to legitimize this process publicly. The result was a monumental misunderstanding with the Kremlin in that each side was perceived as being unwilling to accept the legitimate security interests of the other. Each heard the other to say "no" to their preeminent roles within their own spheres. It was in this context that the unfortunate mirror imagery that came to represent the chief characteristic of postwar Russian-American relations had its origin.[137]

In looking back at American foreign policy during these years, one must ask why was America so concerned about events in Europe? That, after all, was in contrast with earlier American foreign policy when American security was not deemed to be inextricably linked to that of Europe. The 1940s saw a greatly expanded definition of American interests, drawing on two main lines of thought. First, Hitler's victories seemed to show that Americans could not allow a potential foe to control western Europe—the leading economic center outside America. If that happened the Western hemisphere might be forced into economic isolation and their security eventually eroded by enemy control of Europe's industrial resources. The decision in July 1946 to fuse the British and American zones of occupation in Germany was made for that reason. In this, the British played an important role in urging America to become more proactive. Without economic recovery, the British feared disaster. Not only would communism increase its appeal among discontented and impoverished people, but the burden of running the zone would become unbearable for Britain's weakened economy. With British and American perceptions in line on the issue, the two governments agreed to fuse their zones.[138]

Linked to this new concern for the European balance was the conviction that air power had revolutionized security. America now needed an extended defense perimter with bases across the Atlantic in Germany and Britain. While these claims had only limited support in 1945–1946, even within the Pentagon, and they were partly advanced for bureaucratic reasons (e.g., to strengthen the case for an air force independent of the army), by 1948–1949 they had become widely accepted within the Administration.

For the Russians the crucial early issue was the settlement of Germany's reparations payments, including substantial amounts from the industrialized western zones controlled by the Allies. In reacting to the stalemate, Washington was initiallly divided in 1945–1946. The State Department's European Desk, anxious to restore French power, was sympathetic to their arguments, but the War Department and the occupation authorities under General Lucius Clay wanted to get Germany back on its feet economically and end the military regime. Clay's decision to stop reparations payments from the American zone to the Russians (May 1946) was not aimed exclusively at Soviet Russia but was also intended to force the German deadlock to a head in the Allied councils.

Given all of these events, we are now better able to understand the decisive crisis of 1947. It was a process of action and reaction in which the primary catalysts came from within Europe. Of particular importance was the abrupt British retreat amid economic crisis in February 1947. Unable to sustain the costs of its overseas commitments, the British were forced to abandon the Palestine mandate, pull out of India, and end financial aid to Greece and Turkey.

What is most puzzling about America's attitude in those initial years after World War II is why the Truman administration thought it important to try to persuade the Russians to sponsor Western-style free elections in Eastern Europe. We were certainly not unaware of the fact that the Balkan states had engaged in provocative anti-Bolshevik policies during the interwar period. It was naive to think that free elections would have resulted in governments friendly to Soviet Russia, as the record of the interwar years so clearly demonstrates. And yet we apparently expected the Kremlin to go ahead and hold such elections—impartial elections that would have in all probability eventuated in regimes likely to pursue tough, anti-Russian policies. Certainly our own record of intervening in the domestic affairs of Caribbean and Central American countries should have given us some sort of appreciation of where Moscow was coming from. Why did we assume that the Russians could be made to extend such an act of forgiveness toward their western neighbors? And did we really think that legitimate democratic systems could be established in this part of the world—a region whose history of authoritarianism was undeniable?

The Truman Doctrine Reconsidered

This writer has taken the position in these pages that the Truman Doctrine was not a constructive contribution to Russian-American relations in the immediate postwar period. Certainly one reason why the Truman Doctrine proved to be so destructive is that it represented in a very real sense the first official manifestation of the Manichean orthodoxy that was to dominate American thinking for the next four decades. This outlook defined the world in terms of a vaguely postulated Russian communist conspiratorial evil, and a vaguely conceived American anti-Communist good.[139] Kennan would later criticize:

the congenital aversion of Americans to taking specific decisions on specific problems, and by their persistent urge to seek universal formulae or doctrines in which to clothe and justify particular actions. We obviously dislike to discriminate. We like to find some general governing norm to which, in each instance, appeal can be taken, so that individual decisions may be made not on their particular merits but automatically, depending on whether the circumstances do or do not seem to fit the norm. We like, by the same token, to attribute a universal significance to decisions we have already found it necessary, for limited and parochial reasons, to take.[140]

It is certainly true that the Russians reverted at this time to the sort of inflated and moralist verbal strategy in regard to America (and its capitalist ideology) that had marked their approach at various points in time during the interwar era. Stalin's February 1946 speech was most provocative in this regard, conjuring up old images of inevitable capitalist wars and degeneration. More importantly, and unfortunately, Stalin failed to fully clarify just what specific geophysical arrangements would have been acceptable to Moscow—an initiative that might have served to assuage American concerns regarding the future of Western Europe, the Middle East, and other non-Western zones of potential conflict. Unfortunately, Stalin's expectation of Western enmity was now amply fulfilled by the opposing coalition that his own shortsighted and insensitive moves had helped to provoke. Yet, given the deteriorating political situation between Soviet Russia and America, the inflated tone of Truman's speech must have had an even more devastating impact on Russian perceptions than would have otherwise been the case.

One of the more cogent of the critiques of the Truman Doctrine is that it helped to establish a mental outlook in America in which all future crises would be viewed as inherently part and parcel of a worldwide Russian-American struggle. This can be seen over time as Truman's formulation of Russian motives became more and more simplistic and ideological. Whatever Truman's private views about spheres of influence in post-World War II Europe, official American foreign policy by the time of the enunciation of his doctrine reflected a view of the international system as one world, open to democratic values—a world in which the universal ideals of order and stability should prevail—a utopian image, indeed. It was this cognitive outlook, for example, that led American policymakers to perceive the North Korean invasion of South Korea as a Russian-sponsored operation, and, later, to America's involvement in Vietnam as necessary to counteract an "international communist conspiracy."[141]

There can be little doubt, of course, that Truman's perception of American public opinion at this time influenced the way he couched his speech before the Congress. Gaddis and others point out that the domestic political situation dictated the kind of verbal strategy that Truman and his chief lieutenants adopted at this time.[142] The Republicans were in control of the Congress, and many of them were still unreconstructed isolationists—a mood set that reflected the atttitudes of many of their constituents. Having "brought the boys home from Europe," it would certainly have been difficult to even consider a reversal of the demobilization policies of those immediate postwar months.[143] Shock therapy was required.

And so Washington found it necessary to administer "the adrenalin of great anxiety" (Acheson's phrase) into the public forum because it was feared that the American people could not be sufficiently galvanized by measured intellectual analysis to achieve the strengthening of Western power. Thus, the Doctrine was designed to "prod Congress and the American people into accepting the responsibilities of world leadership." [144] In so doing, the Doctrine, not coincidentally, turned out to be the first successful salvo in a long process of reversing the recent postwar shift of power and responsibility in foreign affairs to the Congress—a transformation that would lead to what Arthur Schlesinger would later call the "imperial presidency."[145]

The Doctrine was a milestone for several other reasons, not the least of which was that this was the first time in the postwar era that America substantively intervened in another country's civil war. As such, the Greek intervention was the prototype in a long series of such initiatives—all to be justified as part and parcel of necessarily large aid programs to prevent the collapse of "free world" economies and institutions. Yet, when all was said and done, the intervention in Greece succeeded only because Tito withdrew his aid for the communist guerrillas as a result of his expulsion from the communist party bloc in 1948. It was still a close call, putting America at the brink of military intervention.[146]

Finally, the Doctrine was based implicitly on the domino theory approach—on the assumption that Stalin, like Hitler, by way of analogy, was intent on unlimited conquest. Only raising a wall would suffice to dam the red tide. Perhaps the most lasting and deleterious consequence was that from 1947 onward any threats to the West's political-economic well-being could be easily explained as communist-inspired, not as problems that arose from difficulties inherent in the international order itself.

The Marshall Plan in Perspective

Soviet Russia's rejection of the Marshall Plan, of course, has long been regarded as a major turning point in the evolution of the Cold War. At the time, American officials viewed Moscow's response to the Plan as overt evidence of inherent Russian hostility and aggressiveness. The so-called "orthodox" or traditional scholarly view on this would reflect this perspective, namely, that Soviet Russia's action in rejecting the Plan was ideologically-driven, and was quickly fitted into their long-standing view of the inherent nature of Western aggressive intentions.[147]

But new evidence from the opened archives in Moscow suggest the need for a more nuanced interpretation—one that squares more precisely with Marshall Schulman's and William Taubaman's interpretations. Russian policy from late

1945 to early 1947 was largely defensive and reactive in character. Far from pursuing grandiose plans of expansion, Stalin and his associates regarded themselves as vulnerable, well aware that their country was much weaker in both economic and military capability than America. That is why a policy of confrontation with the West would not serve any expansionist proclivities.

Prior to the summer of 1947, the available evidence suggests that Stalin still hoped to pursue some sort of detente with the West. In particular, he may well have desired to reach a negotiated settlement on most areas of difference, especially on the future of Germany. The Marshall Plan, however, following hard on the heels of the Truman Doctrine, radically changed Stalin's calculus, and led him to shift away from this more moderate line and to adopt a strategy of confrontational unilateral action to secure Moscow's interests. And he did so primarily out of fear of his own vulnerability to American economic power.

The hard reality in all of this is that this turning point was the result of neither Russian or American "aggression." Rather, it lay in the unstable international economic and political conditions in Europe which led both sides to believe that the current status quo was unacceptable. As Scott Parrish points out, it was in this environment that the Western powers felt compelled to design the details of the Plan in such a way that it would stabilize Western Europe, but only at the cost of provoking a confrontation with Russia. And it was this same environment that compelled Stalin to respond to the plan by means of a series of tactically offensive maneuvers which fanned the flames of confrontation even higher.[148]

In retrospect, as Mikhail Narinsky points out, implementation of the Marshall Plan without Russian involvement to a certain extent suited both sides. Moscow retained and consolidated its influence in the countries of Eastern Europe, while America and its allies now had an opportunity carry out a set of measures to stabilize the soico-political situation in Western Europe and, later, to create a military-political alliance. Ironically, the notion of dividing Europe into spheres of influence, an idea which Washington had long opposed, in the end triumphed.

Containment Reassessed

The theory of containment, as enunciated and practiced by the Truman and subsequent administrations, came to be regarded as the "answer" to the threat posed by an aggressive and threatening Soviet Russia. The model invoked by America's leaders was the seizure of power by minority communist parties in Eastern Europe—a yardstick that overlooked the fact that these takeovers were made, at least in part, as a result of prior American misperception and indecision, including an unwillingness to clarify our most important national interests in the region, and that they were made ad hoc and incrementally. In the face of all this, the Truman Doctrine, Marshall Plan, and North Atlantic Treaty all seemed to be reasonable and prudent measures for preventing a similar fate in Western Europe.

Against the immediate background of communist takeovers in Eastern Europe, the myth of the conspiratorial nature of what was, in fact, a situation endemic to the ambiguities and uncertainties that almost always occur in the aftermath of a long and ruinous war, sank deep roots in the American popular consciousness, and in McCarthyist terms, the enemy became International Conspiratorial Communism. This international conspiracy was seen as nothing more than a clique of gangsters—the Kremlin gang—operating without any purpose save to perpetuate their power, without any design but to extend their domination, without any capabilities other than to engage in subversion and suppression.

As the Cold War grew in intensity and lengthened in time, the American people (and their representatives in Congress) began to be increasingly impatient and irritable with the progress of the "struggle."[149] In the course of the trying contest of attrition that was becoming more apparent by the day, it was little wonder that the cry of "there can be no substitute for victory" would begin to exert considerable pressure upon the decision-making elite. The mostly inflexible Cold War posture adopted by the Truman Administration after 1947 contributed, as nothing else could have done, to the institutionalization of the struggle. There soon developed around Kennan's first stage an elaborate intellectual rationale eventually leading America to the position that this was the only viable approach that could be taken with respect to the Russians. Since Washington knew their intentions anyway, so the reasoning went—to conquer the world, of course—it would be a waste of time to fool around with them, at least on the vital issues dividing the two countries. The most important requirement was to evaluate adequately their capabilities and to counter them with some semblance of effectiveness. Accordingly, it remained for the subsequent complete militarization of the Cold War in the early 1950s to mark the final domination of the capabilities school—a situation that would continue to pertain until the disappearance of Soviet Russia in 1991. Indeed, it can be said in retrospect that the institutionalization of the Cold War became a reality at the moment when this first tenant of containment, as a frame of reference, became the *grundnorm* of American policy toward the Russian state.

Looked at more critically, the concept of containment itself, in both its original formulation as Kennan saw it, and in later interpretations, contained a number of ambiguities and contradictions—all of which represented a kind of tension level reflective of the American tradition of foreign affairs. At one level of analysis, one may say that the concept was only a derivative of a broader point that Kennan was trying to make, namely, pointing up the instrumental nature of Russia's ideology under Stalin. There never was any Marxist timetable for world conquest, Kennan always argued, but rather a complex interplay between traditional Russian zenophobia and the revolutionary state, and the Russians' need to justify the retention of the dictatorship by stressing the

capitalist threat from abroad. At this level, most of America's opinion makers
at this time went far beyond Kennan's views, embracing the notion that the
Russians were in fact hell-bent on world domination in order to accomplish their
revolutionary *raison d'etre.*

On the other hand, in the "X" article, and in Kennan's later writings on the
subject, one can discern language that seems to indicate that he regarded at the
time the extension of Russian and/or communist influence *anywhere* as a threat
to American interests.[150] His assumption, for example, that any success of a
local communist party, or, indeed, any extension of communist influence any
place, ought to be regarded as an extension of the hegemony of Moscow, falls
into this category.[151] In other commentary, by way of contrast, he emphasized
the view that we ought to be in the business of denying only certain areas to
Russian influence. In his Memoirs, Kennan observes:

> My objection to the Truman Doctrine message revolved largely around its failure
> to draw [a distinction between various geographic areas]. Repeatedly at that time and
> in ensuing years, I expressed . . . the view that there were only five regions in the
> world—the United States, the United Kingdom, the Rhine valley with adjacent
> industrial areas, the Soviet Union, and Japan where sinews of modern strength could
> be produced in quantity; I pointed out that only one of these was under Communist
> control; and I defined the main task of containment . . . as one of seeing to it that
> none of the remaining ones fell under such control.[152]

Yet this distinction was not made clear in the "X" article. More importantly,
one may detect in the "X" article something else that bothered Kennan--
something that goes to the heart of America's historic preference for order and
the rule of law in international affairs. It is almost as if what Kennan found
most objectionable about Russian foreign policy was the Kremlin's *conduct* of
that policy—"the secretiveness, the lack of frankness, the duplicity, the wary
sucpiciousness, and the basic unfriendliness of purpose,"[153] and not so much
Soviet Russia's so-called expansionist tendencies. In this he had drunk deeply at
the well of America's historic distrust of Europe, of power politics, and its
concomitant deviousness.

Kennan's "X" article, and the thinking that grew up around it, exemplifies
what might be called the mechanistic approach to an understanding of Soviet
Russian conduct—a fundamentalist conception of the dark and impure forces
lurking in the environment to which we must give battle. He described "the
whole Soviet government machine, including the mechanism of diplomacy," as
moving "inexorably along the prescribed path . . . stopping only when it meets
with some unanswerable force." He spoke of Russian expansionism in almost
Newtonian fashion, its "political action [being] a fluid stream which moves
constantly, wherever it is permitted to move, toward a given goal." In his
approach to the role of the CPSU, Kennan, moreover, accepted Stalin's own
image of Russia—a Soviet Russia monolithic in orientation, highly cohesive
and based on the principle of infallibility.[154]

The impermeability of Soviet Russia to outside influence was an equally important aspect of Kennan's mechanistic image. So, too, one sees a strong sense that the world communist movement throughout the Truman years was little more than an instrumentality of Russian foreign policy. But this view is at variance with both the realities of the communist party-state world during the 1945–1948 period and, for that matter, Russia's own conduct. Joseph Starobin's study of the world communist movement at the end of World War II calls this view fundamentally into question. Starobin rightly points to the fact that polycentrism was, as a result of the war, an incipient reality in 1945–1946—a reality cut short with the onset of the Cold War, the establishment of the Cominform in 1947, and the consolidation of the Soviet Russian communist party-state bloc—a consolidation that would, nevertheless, take several years (1948–1953) to consummate.[155]

Containment must also be seen as central to what might be called the second great Red Scare in twentieth-century American history. In this sense, what took place in this country in 1946–1952 was a complex psychological process reflective of many deep-rooted aspects of America's tradition of foreign affairs. "Containment [was] the product not so much of what the Russians have done," says Gaddis, "or of what has happened elsewhere in the world, but of internal forces operating within the United States."[156]

Indeed, American society as a whole did not lend itself well to the new dispensation after World War II. Among the American people, traumatized by the Great Depression and two world wars, the age of innocence was fast disappearing as traditional small-town values were perceived to be under assault. Many religious groups came to view Russia's official atheism as the wellspring of a new fundamental attack on America's core traditions. It would not be long before Americans began to see communist subversion everywhere. Living in a tension-filled society, Americans found it increasingly easy to make a vague and unseen enemy the scapegoat for their sundry fears. Unfortunately, unsavory politicians, pandering to America's worst instincts, exacerbated the situation.

America's leaders, all the while, frightened and anxious about their new superpower obligations, did not have the luxury of retreating once again into an isolationist mode. President Truman and most of his advisors, untutored in Marxist-Leninist revolutionary ideology and tactics, found it relatively easy to read Marxism-Leninism as aggression and to see Stalin as another Hitler. Reasoning by analogy set in rather quickly, proving to be irresistible to both the elite and the masses alike.

Certainly, in putting together a balance sheet on the impact of containment, one can say in a positive sense that it steered all three major Axis countries (except for a quarter of Germany) toward democracy; that it helped to preserve their capitalist economies and allied them with America; and that in Korea it showed that armed force could be stopped with action limited to the original locus. It surely helped to make the world safe for American business. Moscow's backdown in the Berlin blockade episode seemingly validated the theory of containment, while Yugoslavia's successful breakaway from Moscow's orbit served to confirm the potential disintegration of the communist party-state bloc, if we only would keep applying the pressure.

On the other hand, containment left Soviet Russia dominant in its area of wartime operations, while America failed to prevent the division of the world into spheres of influence. At the same time, we had to accept the existence of repressive Moscow-sponsored regimes in a variety of places. And for a long time, Soviet Russia was quite successful in identifying itself (and its ideology) with movements for self-determination in the Third World.

Did containment keep Russia out of Western Europe? Doubtful. We know now that Soviet Russia demobilized almost as rapidly as America did, even though the Kremlin sought to hide it.[157] As we have seen, there is little evidence to buttress the view that in the absence of Western rearmament the Russians were prepared to move against Western Europe.[158] From the earliest postwar days, Stalin made no effort to challenge Anglo-American influence in Italy or American control of Japan, except to cite these situations as justification for his position in the Balkans. Russia's principal cold war effort was directed mainly at preserving its postwar gains. Certainly, in the wake of the Truman Doctrine, Marshall Plan, the response to the Berlin blockade, and the inauguration of collective defense agreements by the West, there are data to support the view that Stalin backed off at that time, in effect formulating his own version of containment to keep his newly won sphere intact, while avoiding general war. Ironically, it may well be that the Allied response to the Berlin blockade, and Tito's defiance forced Stalin to question his previous posture of confrontation.[159] If that is true, NSC-68 failed to recognize that Stalin was retreating to his own containment strategy. Bohlen, Acheson, and Kennan knew better, as Acheson admitted in his memoirs, but felt they had to "bludgeon" the administration and the Congress with the "pervasive impact" of the world domination theory.

In regard to economic relations, America's approach to the Russians from the very beginning consisted of a bewildering array of ignorant, naive and unrealistic atitudes and policies. Containment, with its downgrading of trade with Russia (and its communist party-state allies), reinforced the already evident propensity for Moscow to go it alone, for economic autarky, and for the siege mentality that would characterize Soviet Russia during Stalin's last years. At the outset, Washington chose to withhold the one instrument that might have influenced Russian behavior—a postwar reconstruction loan—in the hope of extracting political concessions. Moscow responded by taking what it needed from its German occupation zone.

Moreover, our early belief that Russia could be persuaded to integrate its economy with those of the capitalist world betrayed a basic lack of sophistication. Moscow's refusal to participate in the Bretton Woods system, of course, was an effect of the Cold War—not a cause. Ultimately, the West's effort to employ economic power for political purposes rested on two shaky assumptions: that other countries needed reconstruction aid so badly that they would accept whatever political conditions Washington imposed and that Congress (and the American taxpayer) would foot the bill.

The Incremental Nature of the Response

The conspiracy principle represented a perception of the nature of a growing global threat by a society and government that were quite unprepared to accept the global responsibilities thrust upon them in the wake of World War II. Governmental decision makers during the Truman administration began the postwar period with no clear policy consensus for dealing with Soviet Russia. The years 1946–1950 were a period of initial policy confusion that gradually became clarified by the adoption of a hard-line global containment policy, of which the conspiracy principle was an integral part. Though the adoption of the hard-line consensus brought greater clarity of purpose to containment, it did not immediately end dissension within the government over the allocation of resources and which areas of the world were most important to the containment effort.

From 1946 to 1950 decision makers were severely constrained in the adoption of a broader containment policy by the availability of relatively few of the resources felt to be required to carry out a more ambitious policy. The Truman administration was fiscally conservative and under consistent congressional pressure for more austerity still. Perceptions of an increased threat to America gradually led to attempts to gain more resources for containment. Truman felt keenly the fiscal constraints that would inevitably be involved if the country mounted a major military rearmament program. His commitment to the legacy of Roosevelt's New Deal programs precluded for a long time the funding of any all-out confrontation with Moscow. Throughout his first term, he sought to hold the line against any major increase in defense spending. But Truman felt he was boxed in, vulnerable to criticism from the right and in his own party. All he could do was try to hold down the increase in military spending so that there was something left for the Fair Deal.

Yet, in the end, he himself became totally convinced of the necessity for massive spending in order to sustain a global containment policy. In this sense, the Truman Doctrine (1947), the Czech coup and Berlin blockade (1948), the "fall" of China (1949), Russia's nuclear detonation (1949), and the outbreak of the Korean War (1950) represented watershed events in the evolution of a greater willingness by America to allocate more resources to containment as that policy came to be applied on a global scale.

America's Russia Policy as Reflection of Her World View

World War II and the years immediately thereafter constituted a seminal period in American history, reflecting at one and the same time the full contradictory complex of America's traditions of foreign affairs. In retrospect, it appears that American assessments of Russia's actions were less a consequence of Moscow's exasperating and strident diplomatic demands than a result of increasing anxiety about the perceived precariousness of American strategic and economic interests in an unpredictable, disorderly, and dangerous world. Greatly concerned about the prospects for the outbreak of famine, disease, anarchy, and revolution, a growing number of officials in the Truman administration after 1945 believed that indigenous Communist parties might well successfully exploit these problems and that the Russians could thereby take advantage of the situation. Moreover, with a fuller range of declassified American documents from this period now available, a greater case than heretofore thought possible can now be made that economic considerations at this time led a growing number of high level officials in the Truman Administration to begin to dwell on the need to preserve American access to world markets and, to that end, to forestall undue Russian influence in these areas.[160]

For America, the facts of the split with Soviet Russia were quite plain. For us, the moral breach came over Poland, while the Greek-Turkish crisis was the trigger for our psychological mobilization, leading to the universalization of the conflict. The events in Greece and Turkey signaled a tightening of ranks in the West, and was certainly a factor in forcing the communist parties in France and Italy into opposition in the spring of 1947. The final break occurred over Germany. Soon, the "loss" of China, Russia's detonation of an atomic bomb, and the North Korean attack on South Korea intensified the perception of threat underlying these evolving concepts of national security. The Truman administration responded with military assistance to Southeast Asia, a decision to build the hydrogen bomb, direct military intervention in Korea, a commitment to station troops permanently in Europe, expansion of the American alliance system, and a massive rearmament program at home.

Unfortunately, America's decision makers did not believe in the type of logic associated with the concept of counterbalancing national interests so central to an effective balance of power. We had not lost faith that conflicts of interests among nations would yield to good intentions and good will. Instead, the notion of world responsibility, and its necessary concomitant sense of mission, became the hallmarks of an activist, interventionist foreign policy. Justification for this centered on the notion that while other countries have interests, America has responsibilities. And what better way to rationalize her responsibilities then to perpetuate the self-image of America's existential uniqueness as the guarantor of freedom and human dignity upon the world's stage. Indeed, the future of the planet would reside in America's ability to act on behalf of mankind. In the process, she would go abroad in search of monsters to destroy.

Regarding the nature of Soviet Russia's conduct, we did not grasp the fact that the essence of America's Cold War problem was not Marxism-Leninism but Russian power, which might well find itself opposed by foreign communists as well. According to Djilas, "Stalin felt instinctively that the creation of revolutionary centers outside Moscow could endanger its supremacy in world communism. . . . He was always ready to leave them in the lurch whenever they slipped out of his grasp."[161] Our giving up on Chiang in 1948 acknowledged that in the absence of an effective if not popular government in an area threatened by communist insurgencies, containment would not work, certainly not without direct American military intervention. Had there existed in Washington an operative image of Russian behavior that assumed the existence of divergent opinions among the Communist Party elite in Moscow, and that further recognized that external behavior affected internal politics within Soviet Russia, it would have enabled America's decision makers to be better prepared to respond to changes in Russian conduct after Stalin's death. A less mechanistic image might therefore have prepared America to respond to new initiatives that came from the Kremlin during the the Eisenhower era.

To say all this is not to suggest that Russian foreign policy during and after World War II was either enlightened or benign. Ideology certainly influenced Russia's behavior. In general, they believed that economic and class interests determined the policies of capitalist systems, and they assumed that these countries were dedicated to the destruction of socialism. They also believed that rivalries would inevitably come to mark the relationships among the capitalists themselves—situations that would sooner or later result in bloody wars. The trick was to stay out of their wars, all the while exploiting their hatreds until the inevitable day when communism would come to prevail throughout the world.

These beliefs certainly colored Russia's leaders' view of their contemporaries and served to intensify their sense of threat. But these beliefs were always subject to manipulation by the Kremlin—by a leadership commitment to realpolitik as the most appropriate method of insuring their own survival. Ideology, rather, usually played the role of legitimizing or sanctifying policy, not determining it. Moscow's approach to other communist movements outside Russia itself perhaps best illustrated the essential secondary role of ideology in their mindset. In general, the rule prevailed that if the Russians could not control such movements, they usually found excuses to oppose them or, at best, to reluctantly give some support.

Certainly, Russian behavior in Eastern Europe was frequently shortsighted, insensitive, and obtuse. Moscow did seek to exploit strategic opportunities wherever possible (for example, in northern Iran), and the Kremlin did from time to time employ local, indigenous communist parties to expand Russian influence in areas beyond the periphery of the Russian land mass (e.g., Rumania and Bulgaria). On the other hand, Stalin's main problem with Yugoslavia's Tito was his reluctance to underwrite the militant partisan's ideas for revolution from below at the end of the war. Stalin refused to bail out the Greek left, was a constant thorn in Mao Zedong's side, and made it clear that he expected the French and Italian communists to play ball with their bourgeois breathren after the war. In the end, of course, Stalin failed to keep Germany neutral, failed to prevent the merging of the Western zones, failed to take over West Berlin, and failed to prevent West German rearmament.

It is now more apparent that the decision makers in the Kremlin for some time after the end of World War II really were not sure what they wanted to do and how to behave. In late 1949, for example, there occurred a Politburo debate over Stalin's policies, specifically whether possession of the atomic bomb and the CCP victory had so weakened capitalist circles that internal controls could be eased and consumer production increased. In a speech given on November 6, Malenkov remarked that the West was collapsing of its own contradictions, and that Soviet Russia could now follow the path of peaceful competition. Suslov countered by arguing that the West could very well attack in Eastern Europe, China, and North Korea precisely because of these reverses. Stalin, after some equivocation, came down on the side of continued control.[162] This was certainly not a recipe for messianic behavior. Thus, if the Kremlin's policies tended to be inherently nationalistic, reactive, opportunist, and even contradictory, as the record seems to indicate, then it is not inappropriate to ask whether America's own conception of national security tended, albeit unintentionally, to engender anxieties and to provoke countermeasures from a proud, suspicious, insecure, and inhumane government that was at the same time legitimately apprehensive about the long-term implications arising from the rehabilitation of traditional enemies and the development of foreign bases on its borders.

And the Truman administration's handling of public opinion only exacerbated the situation. By portraying the Russian-American conflict as a clash between two mutually irreconcilable ideologies,[163] Truman and his advisors managed to shock the public into providing support necessary to implement a tough policy, but in the process trapped themselves in a new cycle of rhetoric and response that in subsequent years would restrict America's flexibility in dealing with Moscow.

Each of the protagonists viewed the other as untrustworthy aggressors and, each, consequently, misperceived defensive or reactive measures for aggressive ones. This syndrome is especially evident in the Russian reaction to the Marshall Plan. After some initial interest, Molotov and Stalin quickly concluded that Washington had embarked on a sinister crusade designed to seduce Russia's East European colleagues and to rearm Germany. So, too, the West's move to create the Federal Republic of Germany and NATO. It was this view of America's initiatives that led Moscow to create the Cominform, extinguish opposition in Hungary, Poland, and Czechoslovakia, and to blockade Berlin. These actions in turn served to confirm for America its essential image of a dangerous and calculating Soviet Union.

If America had acted to reinforce the most favorable of the Russian images of our foreign policy, events might have taken a different tack. At the very least such a strategy might have resulted in a more limited adversarial relationship of the sort that is generally reflective of great power interaction in periods of conflict, rather than the total monolithic confrontation that in fact resulted. At best, it would have headed off the Cold War before it started.

RUSSIA'S POLICY RECONSIDERED

Fifty years later it is much easier to see where Russia was coming from and, from its perspective, what had gone wrong after the war. There were certainly certain grundnorms that underlay Russia's approach to the West at the end of and immediately after the war, the first being the primacy of Russian security interests as they were believed to relate to that country's strategic position. Understandable for any country under these circumstances, this concern was especially pronounced in the Russian case as that country's traditional insecurities were magnified by the terrible trauma of the war. Yet, it is crucial to note that security was seen not in absolutist terms of some sort of global hegemony or promotion of world revolution, but one rather limited and realistic in a true Realpolitik sense—reestablishment of the country's 1941 borders, an emasculated Germany and Japan, and friendly regimes along the Russian periphery, especially in the West.

What is impressive about this list is its traditionalism dating back to Tsarist diplomacy. And it was a strategic outlook that was clearly understood at the time by experienced Russian observers in the West. Kennan, for one, in September, 1944 defined the Kremlin's basic goal after the war as one designed "to prevent the formation in Central and Eastern Europe of any power or coalition of powers capable of challenging Russian security."[164]

A second grundnorm was Moscow's acceptance of Big Three cooperation as a prerequisite for a stable postwar peace. Only such an arrangement, it was felt, would suffice in support of Russia's national interests. Implicit in this view was a substantive revision of the traditional Bolshevik notion of the Western threat to the point where it was now felt to be manageable if not passé.

NOTES

1. Memorandum by Raymond E. Murphy on "Possible Resurrection of Communist International, Resumption of Extreme Leftist Activities, Possible Effect on U.S.," June 2, 1945, *FRUS, 1945, Potsdam*, I, pp. 267–280.

2. Kennan to Byrnes, July 15, 1945, *FRUS, 1945*, V, pp. 866–867. Assuming the No. 2 position in the embassy, he had just then returned to Moscow after a hiatus of several years and was shocked to find that little had changed for the better, especially the propensity of the regime to employ terror and lies against the population.

3. Memo by E.F. Willett on "Dialectical Materialism and Russian Objectives," January 14, 1946, Forrestall Papers, Box 17, "Russia study" folder.

4. See James Reston, *New York Times*, September 30 and October 14, 1945.

5. Beginning with an exchange of messages between Truman and Stalin in late April 1945, until their last "wartime" communication on December 19, the interaction on Eastern Europe between the new American president and the wily Russian leader reads increasingly like a dialogue of the deaf.

In his April 23 message, Truman asked Stalin to accept the Yugoslav precedent as a model for Poland. Stalin's reply, one that seems in retrospect to be especially heartfelt and emotional, appears to have reflected the dictator's true feelings: "You are asking too much," he said. "You want me to renounce the interests of the security of the Soviet Union; but I cannot provide against the interests of my own country." Correspondence between the Chairman of the Council of Ministers of the USSR and the Presidents of the USA and the Prime Ministers of Great Britain During the Great Patriotic War of 1941–1945, Vol 2. Correspondence with Franklin D. Roosevelt and Harry S Truman, August 1941–December 1945 (Moscow: Progress Publishers, 1957), No. 298, hereafter cited as *Correspondence*.

6. Minutes of the meeting of the Secretaries of State, War, and Navy, October 10, 1945, *FRUS, 1945*, II, pp. 55-56.

7. Cited in Robin Edmonds, *Setting the Mould: The U.S. and Britain, 1945–1950* (New York: W. W. Norton, 1986), p. 72.

8. *FRUS, 1945*, II, pp. 55–57.

9. "Summary Report on Soviet Policy in Rumania and Bulgaria," December 7, 1945, *FRUS*, V, pp. 633–637. See also Mark Etheridge and C .E. Black, "Negotiating on the Balkans, 1945–1947," in Raymond Dennett and Joseph E. Johnston, eds., *Negotiating with the Russians* (Boston: Houghton Mifflin, 1951), pp. 200-202.

10. "Intelligence Estimate of the World as of December, 1945," National Archives, Decimal Files, Record Group 59, *Marshall Mission Records, 1944–1948*: Box 2.

11. Truman memorandum of conversation with Byrnes, January 5, 1946, Harry S Truman, *Memoirs*, Vol. 1, Year of Decisions (Garden City, N.Y.: Doubleday, 1955), pp. 551–552.

12. Charles de Gaulle, reflecting French fears of a resurgent Germany, very strongly disliked the Yalta agreement's emphasis on economic unity and called for the detachment of the Rhineland and the Ruhr. See in this regard John Gimbel, *The American Occupation of Germany: Politics and the Military, 1945-1949* (Stanford, Calif.: Stanford University Press, 1968), in which Chapters 1–4 underline the importance of the French attitude. See also Lucius D. Clay, *Decision in Germany* (Garden City, N.Y.: Doubleday, 1950), and Robert Murphy, *Diplomat among Warriors* (Garden City, N. Y.: Doubleday, 1964).

13. Norman Naimark, *The Russians in Germany: A History of the Soviet Zone of Occupation, 1945–1949* (Cambridge, Mass.: Harvard University Press, 1995).

14. American Institute of Public Opinion polls of August 8, October 17, 1945 and February 27, 1946, cited in Hadley Cantril and Mildred Strunk, eds., *Public Opinion, 1935-1946* (Princeton, N.J.: Princeton University Press, 1951).

15. Although not everyone saw it that way. Joseph Davies pointed out that "Russia in self-defense has every moral right to seek atomic bomb secrets through military espionage if excluded from such information by her former fighting allies." *New York Times*, February 19, 1946.

16. *Speeches by J. V. Stalin and V. M. Molotov Delivered at Election Meetings in Moscow in February, 1946* (London: Soviet News, 1946), pp. 6–7.

17. Given on February 9, he suggested that the unevenness of development among capitalist countries could lead to violent upheavals and even war among them. War was therefore inevitable as long as capitalism existed. In this sense, the speech

reflected the orthodox Marxist view that these capitalist states are bound to quarrel among themselves, particularly over control of dwindling raw materials and over colonial territories still existing in the world. Soviet Russia would not be normally part and parcel of such quarrels within a decaying imperialist system save for the fact that even Russia is a member of the international system and may be affected by such death struggles within the capitalist world. Above all, there is the danger that some leaders of the capitalist world might seek to unite their countries for an attack on the Russian state, if only to distract attention from their own internal problems.

The speech contributed greatly to the evolving American perception of the Russian state as a messianic threat. That Stalin's remarks may well have been intended primarily for domestic consumption as part of a new effort both to mobilize Russian society and to re-introduce controls as a prerequisite to rebuilding the country was not seriously considered. The American reaction to the speech displayed an embarrassingly unsubtle lack of understanding of the nonoperational functions of ideological verbalizing by Russia's policy makers. We could not understand the concept of "manipulative threatmanship" routinely employed by the Kremlin in its dealings with the outside world.

18. "Mr. Truman's Balloon," *Time Magazine*, March 18, 1946, pp. 17–19.

19. As Frank Roberts, British *charge d'affaires* in Moscow, pointed out in a "long telegram" to Whitehall in early 1946 that Stalin and his associates did not object to the ideas in the speech, but felt that it was unnecessary and undesirable to state these obvious facts in public in a way that appeared to many Russians as needlessly provocative. See his comments in his March 18, Section 3 cable, cited in Kenneth M. Jensen, ed., *Origins of the Cold War: The Novikov, Kennan and Roberts 'Long Telegrams' of 1946* (Washington, D.C.: United States Institute of Peace, 1991), p. 66.

20. Margaret Truman, *Harry S Truman* (New York: William Morrow, 1973), p. 312.

21. George Kennan to Byrnes, February 22, 1946, *FRUS, 1946*, VI, pp. 705–706.

22. Kennan to Byrnes, March 20, 1946, *FRUS*, 1946, VI, p. 723. Roberts was at this time similarly advising his government on the Russian mind set. Our "very forbearance and cooperative spirit have been misinterpreted as weakness," he said, concluding that the Russian push "is partly an attempt to profit from the present fluid state of postwar Europe," and also an attempt to seize opportunities to dig in "before the inevitable reaction against high-handed Soviet actions sets in."

In regard to Moscow's approach to the nonsocialist world, Roberts observed that "[T]he small group ruling Russia believe that the end justifies the means, and that they are at the head of a chosen people, with a chosen system destined to spread throughout the world. In their view relations with the outside world and even alliances are short-term arrangements for definite objectives, and can be modified or rejected as soon as they no longer suit the purpose of the Soviet Union."

As to negotiations, "She approaches a partner, whom she regards as potentially hostile, endeavors to exact the maximum advantage for the Soviet Union, if possible without any return, and, having obtained what she wants, reopens the issue or raises another at the earliest possible moment in order to achieve the next item on her programme. There is, therefore, no degree of finality about any agreement reached with the Soviet Union." *FRUS*, 1946, VI, March 14, 1946, Section 1, p. 38.

23.   Stalin's speech certainly convinced a number of the skeptics.   Navy Secretary James Forrestal had already concluded that it would be impossible for democracy and communism to coexist, believing, according to Michael Sherry, *Preparing for the Next War: American Plans for Postwar Defense, 1941–1945* (New Haven, Conn.: Yale University Press, 1977), p. 35, that the aggressive nature of Russia's inten-tions had become so evident that he professed amazement when others had difficulty "preparing for the war just over the horizon." The exact point in time at which Forrestal became a Russophobe is unclear, but Stalin's behavior at Yalta seems to have been one factor. In early 1945 he was apparently influenced by Harriman's cables, as indicated by the following underlined citation in his *Diaries*: "[W]e now have ample proof that the Soviet government views all matters from the standpoint of their own selfish interest. . . . [W]e must clearly realize that the Soviet Union's program is the establishment of totalitarianism, ending personal liberty and democracy as we know and respect it." "Russia" File, *Forrestal Papers*.   See Walter Millis, ed., *The Forrestal Diaries* (New York: Knopf, 1951), pp. 134–135.

24.   For an overview of the American actions during the crisis, including correspondence between Byrnes and Molotov, see *FRUS*, 1945, VIII, pp. 388–522; *FRUS*, 1946, VII, pp. 289–304; FRUS, 1946, VII, p. 317, 340–342, 346–348, 356–415.   An excellent analysis of the crisis is Mark Lytle, "American-Iranian Relations 1941–1947 and the Redefinition of National Security," unpublished Ph.D dissertation, Yale University, 1973.

25.   American Institute for Public Opinion poll, March 26, 1946, cited in Cantril and Strunk, *Public Opinion, 1935–1946.*

26. Joint Intelligence Staff, hereafter cited as JIS, "Areas Vital to the Soviet War Effort," February 12, 1946, Record Group 218, National Archives, Washington, ser. CCS 092 (3-27-45), JIS 226/2.

27. The American perception of the Turkish crisis may be seen in *FRUS*, 1946, VII, pp. 837-50.   For background on the evolving American concern about Russian actions in the region, see the memorandum of Loy W. Henderson, head of the Office of Near Eastern Affairs, Department of State, December 28, 1945, pp. 1-6.

28.   Andrei Zhadanov hoped to use it as a base for expanding Russian influence, while the more pragmatic Georgi Malenkov preferred to keep it as a Russian outpost while exploiting it economically.   Malenkov prevailed. See Werner Hahn, *Postwar Soviet Politics: The Fall of Zhadanov and the Defeat of Moderation, 1946–1953* (Ithaca, N.Y.: Cornell University Press, 1982).

29.   Acheson to Byrnes, May 9, 1946, *FRUS, 1946*, V, p. 549.

30. *Department of State Bulletin*, No. 376 (September 15, 1946), pp. 496–501.

31. "American Relations with the Soviet Union," a report prepared by Clark M. Clifford and submitted to Truman on September 24, 1946, printed in Arthur Krock, *Memoirs: Sixty Years on the Firing Line* (New York: Macmillan, 1968), Appendix A, pp. 431–448.

32. Vladislav Zubok and Constantine Pleshakov, in an important recent book, *Inside the Kremlin's Cold War: From Stalin to Khrushchev* (Cambridge, Mass.: Harvard University Press, 1996), pp. 74, 125, and 276–277, argue that at the end of the war there was no great motivation in the Kremlin for a massive ideological confrontation with the West. They make the case that Soviet Russia's foreign policy orientation at that time was still based on the realpolitik assumption of seeking to balance British and American power and, if possible, to take advantage of their

anticipated rivalries in a renewed and fluid balance of power situation.

Vladimir Pechatnov, a former Soviet diplomat, has recently revealed that top Russian Foreign Ministry officials at the end of the war believed that a continuation of the wartime alliance among the so-called Big Three was an absolute prerequisite for the protection of Moscow's interests in the postwar era. Based on his uncovering of three heretofore secret memoranda written by top officials Ivan Maisky, Maxim Litvinov, and Andrei Gromyko during the latter days of the war, it is apparent that the foreign policy making elite were thinking in terms of spheres of interest and not Sovietization—something they knew would be unpalatable to the West. See his "The Big Three after World War II," *Cold War International History Project Working Paper No. 13*, Woodrow Wilson International Center (Princeton, N.J.: Princeton University Press, 1995).

33. Stalin, in particular, was apparently having some difficulty deciding whether he wanted a unified Germany overseen by the German communists, a demilitarized, neutral Germany along the lines of the Weimar Republic, or a Sovietized eastern zone subject to the complete domination of Moscow. According to Naimark, *The Russians in Germany*, p. 467, this ambivalence was manifested in the contradictory actions taken in their zone by their military people, the secret police, officials of the Foreign Ministry, and reparations teams.

Among the more recent works in the West that have extensively reviewed Soviet Russia's threat perception at the end of the war and its conduct in Eastern Europe during the 1945–1948 period and that, with varying degrees of characterization and emphasis, point out that the Kremlin's attitude was one of uncertainty, equivocation, and conservatism regarding the future of this region, see Michael McGwire, "National Security and Soviet Foreign Policy," in Melvyn P. Leffler and David S. Painter, eds., *Origins of the Cold War: An International History* (London and New York: Routledge, 1994), pp. 54–76, William C. Wohlforth, *The Elusive Balance: Power and Perceptions during the Cold War* (Ithaca: Cornell University Press, 1993) ,and Amos Perlmutter, *FDR and Stalin: A Not So Grand Alliance, 1943–1945* (Columbia and London: University of Missouri Press, 1993). More dated but still valuable treatments include Fernando Claudin, *The Communist Movement: From Comintern to Cominform* (New York: Monthly Review Press, 1975), Adam Ulam, *Expansion and Coexistence: Soviet Foreign Policy, 1917–1973,* 2nd ed. (New York: Praeger, 1974), Franz Borkenau, *European Communism* (New York: Harper and Brothers, 1953), and Zbigniew Brzezinski, *The Soviet Bloc: Unity and Conflict*, rev. ed. (Cambridge, Mass: Harvard University Press, 1960). See, also, Charles Gati, "The Democratic Interlude in Postwar Hungary: Eastern Europe before Cominform," *Survey* (Summer, 1984): 99–134.

34. A good case can be made that from 1945 through early 1947, polycentrism characterized Russia's relations with the other communist parties of Eastern Europe. Brzezinski, *The Soviet Bloc*, p. 186, quotes Joseph Revai's comments in 1949 about Hungary's political evolution in which Revai observed that the party did not possess ". . . a united, clarified, elaborated attitude in respect to the character of the People's Democracy and its future development" and suggests that Stalin ". . . was not very helpful before the autumn of 1947" in establishing the nature of the Hungarian People's Democracy.

In Poland, Communist Party documents from late 1944 and early 1945 reflect an intense ongoing debate over the most appropriate approach to take for mobilizing support from the population. Stalin's relationship with Mikolajczyk reflects this uncertainty. As late as early 1946, Stalin may have perceived Mikolajczyk as an acceptable alternative to the rather bumbling, fumbling communists. Wladyslaw Gomulka was talking in 1945–1946 about a necessarily lengthy struggle before the establishment of socialism. On May 15, 1945, Gomulka sent a message to Stalin, reviewing the political situation in Poland at that time and pointing out that it would be necessary to create a broad national front to free Poland, with a unified working class to lead it, adding that the Polish Workers Party did not necessarily need a monopoly of power. A cover letter by Georgi Dimitrov, the de facto head of the Communist International [officially disbanded in 1943], notes that there was serious sectarianism in the party over sovietization of Poland, and over the nature and pace of agricultural collectivization. On this matter, see the Central Party Archive of the Institute of Marxism-Leninism, Central Committee of the Communist Party of the Soviet Union, Special Collection, File 17, Opus 128, Unit 1206—*Polish Party Situation*, November 16, 1941 to May 15, 1945.

Paul Zinner, *Communist Strategy and Tactics in Czechoslovakia, 1918–1948* (New York: Praeger, 1963), p. 186, observes that during this same period "the revolution . . . had definitely come to a stop." It was for that reason that the CCP was "subjected to severe criticism from Yugoslav Marshal Tito" who pressed the Czech communists to get on with building socialism.

35. See his "Choices in the Postwar World: Containment and the Soviet Union," in Charles Gati, ed., *Caging the Bear: Containment and the Cold War* (New York: Bobbs-Merrill, 1974): 85–108.

36. *Ibid.*, pp. 102–103.

37. *Ibid.*, Eugene Varga, *Izmeneniya v ekonomike kapitalizma v itage mirovoi voiny (Changes in the Economy of Capitalism as a Result of the Second World War)* (Moscow: Gospolitizdat, 1946. For an English summary, see Leo Gruilow, trans. *Soviet Views on the Post-War Economy* (Washington: Public Affairs Press, 1948). For a discussion of the debate on economics in Soviet Russia in 1945–1948, see Werner Hahn, *Postwar Soviet Politics: The Fall of Zhadanov*, pp. 84–94.

38. Roberts cable of March 14, 1946, Section 1, in Jensen, *Origins of the Cold War*, p. 34.

39. *Ibid.*

40. On this point, see Eduard Mark, "Charles E. Bohlen and the Acceptable Limits of Soviet Hegemony in Eastern Europe," *Diplomatic History* (Spring, 1979), pp. 201–213, and his "American Policy toward Eastern Europe and the Origins of the Cold War, 1941–1946: An Alternative Interpretation," *Journal of American History* (September, 1981), pp. 313–336.

41. Brynes speech of October 31, 1945, *Department of State Bulletin*, XIII (November 4, 1945), pp. 709–711.

42. The statements by Acheson and Dulles are cited in Charles W. Kegley, Jr. and Eugene Witthopf, *American Foreign Policy: Pattern and Process* (New York: St. Martin's Press, 1987), pp. 50–51.

43. Roosevelt-Churchill agreement of September 19, 1944, cited in Margaret Gowing, *Britain and Atomic Energy, 1939–1945* (New York: Oxford University Press, 1964).

44. Brynes, quoted in Truman, *Year of Decisions*, p. 87.

45. Henry L. Stimson, *Diary*, June 6, 1945.

46. David E. Lilienthal, *The Journals of David E. Lilienthal* (New York: Harper & Row, 1964), Vol. II , January 24, 1946, p. 14. See, also, Richard G. Hewlett and Oscar E. Anderson, Jr., *A History of the United States Atomic Energy Commission: The New World, 1939–1946* (University Park, PA.: Pennsylvania State University Press, 1962).

47. Baruch was appointed by Truman, in part to defuse growing congressional criticism of any plan that would abandon America's monopoly of atomic weapons.

48. In June 1946, The Joint Chiefs of Staff, Untitled Document, JCS to Baruch, June 5, 1946, "Atomic" Series", (8–15–45), Sec. 3, US JCS Records, wrote Baruch that the bomb was "the one military weapon which may for the period until Russia obtains it exert a deterrent effect upon her will to expand."

For a detailed and comprehensive analysis of the approach taken by the Roosevelt and Truman administrations toward the political use of atomic weapons, see Greg Herken, *The Winning Weapon: The Atomic Bomb and the Cold War, 1945–1950* (New York: William Morrow, 1980). A provocative analysis of the thinking of President Truman, his Secretary of War, Henry Stimson, Dean Acheson and others may be found in Walter LaFeber, *America, Russia and the Cold War, 1945–1984*, 7th ed. (New York: Knopf, 1993), Chapter 2. Margaret Gowing, *Science and Politics* (London: Birkbeck College, 1977), p. 11, puts it this way: "If Russia had been formally consulted about the bomb during the war . . . it might have made no difference. The fact that she was not, guaranteed that the attempts made just after the war to establish international control, which might have failed anyway, were doomed."

49. Senate Committee on Foreign Relations, Legislative Origins of the Truman Doctrine, p. 95, quoted in Robert Donovan, *Conflict and Crisis* (New York: W. W. Norton, 1977), p. 286. On the gestation and unfolding of the American involvement in the Greek situation, see Lawrence S. Wittner, *American Intervention in Greece, 1943–1949* (New York: St. Martin's Press, 1982).

50. See, in this regard, George F. Kennan, *Memoirs, 1925–1950* (Boston: Little, Brown, 1957), pp. 311–324, and Walter LaFeber, "American Policy-Makers, Public Opinion, and the Outbreak of the Cold War, 1945–1950," in The *Origins of the Cold War in Asia*, ed. Yonosuke Nagai and Akira Iriye (New York: Columbia University Press, 1977), pp. 53–54.

51. Cited in D.F. Flemming, *The Cold War and Its Origins, 1917–1960* (Garden City, N. Y.: Doubleday, 1961), Vol. I, pp. 448–455.

52. *New York Times*, March 28, 1947, p. 7.

53. Joseph M. Jones, *The Fifteen Weeks* (New York: Viking, 1955), p. 155. For splits between the soft-line and hard-line approaches in the early postwar days, see Larsen, *Origins of Containment*, pp. 66–125.

54. *The Cold War: A Study in United States Foreign Policy* (New York: Macmillan, 1947), pp. 14–16.

55. Although Scott Parrish argues that the promulgation of the Truman Doctrine did not have an appreciable impact on Russian thinking at the time. As far as Stalin was concerned, he says, Truman's declaration did not alter substantially the underlying dynamic of Russian-American relations. For his view of the summary impact on Russian thinking of both the Truman Doctrine and the Marshall Plan—and the relationship between the two, see "New Evidence on the Soviet Rejection of the Marshall Plan, 1947," *Cold War International History Project Working Paper No. 9,*

Woodrow Wilson International Center for Scholars (Princeton, N.J.: Princeton University Press, 1994).

56. *The United States in the World Arena* (New York: Harper, 1960), p. 208.

57. *War or Peace* (New York: Macmillan, 1950), p. 105.

58. *Ibid.*, pp. 208–209. Rostow goes on to say, pp. 209–210, that "On April 29, the day after his report to the nation on the failure of the Moscow Conference, Secretary Marshall instructed the Policy Planning Staff to prepare a general plan for American aid in the reconstruction of *Western* [author's emphasis] Europe."

59. *Ibid.*, p. 208.

60. *The State of Europe* (New York: Alfred Knopf, 1949), pp. 118–123.

61. *FRUS, 1947*, III, pp. 225–229. See also U.S. House of Representatives, Foreign Affairs Committee, 80th Congress, 1st and 2nd sessions, *U.S. Foreign Policy for a Post-War Recovery Program* (Washington, D.C.: Government Printing Office, 1948), I: pp. 354–359. On the British attitude and role, see Michael Hogan, *The Marshall Plan: America, Britain and the Reconstruction of Western Europe, 1947–1952* (New York: Cambridge University Press, 1987). More generally, Terry H. Anderson's *The United States, Great Britain, and the Cold War, 1944–1947* (Boston: Houghton Mifflin, 1981) is instructive.

62. In a speech given wide circulation in the press, Acheson made clear the philosophy behind the proposal and its consistency with subsequent American policy. "These measures of relief and reconstruction have been only in part suggested by humanitarianism. Your Congress has authorized and your Government is carrying out a policy of relief and reconstruction today chiefly as a matter of national self-interest. . . . Free peoples who are seeking to preserve their independence and democratic institutions and human freedoms against totalitarian pressures, either internal or external, will receive top priority for American aid." Cited in Kenneth Ingram, *History of the Cold War* (London: Darwen Finlayson, 1955), pp. 58–59.

63. See Jones, *The Fifteen Weeks*, pp. 145–167. Actually, the Marshall Plan was a product of two internal State Department memoranda—those of William Clayton and George Kennan. Clayton's assessment was predicated on the notion that "there will be revolution" in Europe if something was not done. It would therefore be necessary for the administration to make a "strong spiritual appeal to the American people . . . in order to save Europe from starvation and chaos." His memorandum ended with the words "we must avoid getting into another UNRRA. The United States must run this show." It is well to note that he specifically did not mention the Russians. For his views, see *FRUS, 1947*, III, p. 233.

Kennan's paper (the first issued by the newly created Policy Planning Staff) shared Clayton's premise that "the root of the difficulties of western Europe" was not "communist activities." He went on to say that "what the press has unfortunately come to identify as the 'Truman Doctrine' should be clarified"; in particular, the "effort to restore sound economic conditions in others countries" was not to be regarded as "only a by-product of a defensive reaction to communist pressure; nor was the Truman Doctrine a blank check to give economic and military aid to any area in the world where the communists show signs of being successful."

The paper went on to point out that "it may be necessary for the key countries of western Europe to find means of conferring together without the presence of the Russians and Russian satellites." *FRUS, 1947*, III, pp. 223–230.

64. *Department of State Bulletin*, No. 415 (June 15, 1947), p. 1160.

65. For the author's observations in the following three paragraphs, he is indebted to the comments of Michael MccGwire, "The Genesis of Soviet Threat Perceptions," in Melvyn P. Leffler and David S. Painter, eds., *Origins of the Cold War: An International History* (New York: Routledge, 1994), pp. 73–75.

66. See, in this vein, Scott D. Parrish, "The Turn toward Confrontation: The Soviet Reaction to the Marshall Plan, 1948," *Cold War International History Project Working Paper No. 9*, Woodrow Wilson International Center, (Princeton, N.J.: Princeton University Press, 1994), and Mikhail M. Narinsky, "The Soviet Response: The Turn to Confrontation," *Cold War International History Project Working Paper No. 11*, Woodrow Wilson International Center, (Princeton, N. J.: Princeton University Press, 1994).

67. Quoted in telegram from Molotov to Secretary of State Marshall, May 26, 1947, *Papers of Joseph Jones*, President's Secretary File, Harry S.Truman Library.

68. There is some evidence to indicate that there was division in the Kremlin as to how to respond, and that it may have been Stalin's personal decision, overruling Molotov, that decreed the breakdown of the meeting. See *FRUS, 1947*, III, pp. 319–320, in which is printed the text of a telegram by Czech Communist Party leader Klement Gottwald to that effect. See also Ulam, *Expansion and Coexistence*, p. 434.

69. That the Russians in the spring of 1947 had not yet decided what to do is now quite apparent. It must be remembered that Eastern Europe at this point had by no means reached full satellite status. A democratic government of sorts existed in Prague; in Warsaw all manner of Polish nationalists, inside and outside the Communist Party, had not yet been brought to heel; and in Yugoslavia, Tito, who had indicated designs on Albania, had already begun to stir the Bulgarian and Hungarian communists with ideas about a Balkan alliance, quasi-independent of Moscow.

The ambiguity of this situation is ably summarized by Charles Gati when he points out the willingness of the Hungarian communists to cooperate with non-communist elements in the country during this time. Right up to the September 1947 convening of the Cominform gathering, they were unsure of Moscow's intentions. See his conclusions based on a number of more recently available Hungarian sources in "The Democratic Interlude in Postwar Hungary: Eastern Europe before Cominform."

70. Hearings before the Committee on Armed Services and Committee on Foreign Relations, U.S. Senate, 82nd Congress (Washington, D.C.: Government Printing Office, 1950), "Military Situation in the Far East," p. 2083.

71. Evgenni Varga's phrase, cited in his article in *Foreign Affairs*, "Anglo-American Rivalry and Partnership: A Marxist View," (July 1947), p. 583, four months after the president's message. Parrish takes a different view, pointing out that a number of documents recently gleaned from Russian archival sources point up the fact that Moscow regarded continued cooperation with the West a distinct possibility in late spring, 1947, despite the troublesome shift in American policies suggested by the Doctrine. See his *New Evidence on the Soviet Rejection of the Marshall Plan, 1947*, Cold War International History Project Working Paper No. 9, Woodrow Wilson International Center for Scholars (Princeton, N. J.: Princeton University Press, 1994, especially pp. 7–12.

72. On this point, see Joseph Starobin, "Origins of the Cold War," *Foreign Affairs* (July, 1960), pp. 228–254.

73. *Ibid.*
74. Quoted in Louis Halle, *The Cold War as History* (New York: Macmillan, 1967), pp. 150–151. On the application of the Nazi analogy to the Russians in Eastern Europe, see Ernest May, *"Lessons" of the Past: The Use and Misuse of History in American Foreign Policy* (New York: Oxford University Press, 1973), p. 50. For a discussion of the essentially non-ideological character of the Cominform, see Natalya Yegorova, "From the Comintern to the Cominform: Ideological Dimensions of the Origins of the Cold War," paper presented at the *Conference on New Evidence on Cold War History,* Moscow, January, 1993.
75. Andrei Zhadanov, "The International Situation," reprinted in *The Strategy and Tactics of World Communism*, Supplement I (Washington: Government Printing Office, 1948), pp. 212–230.
76. On this point, see William Taubman, *Stalin's American Policy: From Entente to Detente to Cold War* (New York: Norton, 1982), pp. 172–173.
77. For the Czech-Russian background see Vojtech Mastny, *Russia's Road to the Cold War: Diplomacy, War, and the Politics of Communism, 1941–1945* (New York: Columbia University Press, 1979), pp. 133–142, 281–282.
78. This was the word that would be used by Kennan later to describe both the Prague takeover and the Berlin blockade. See his "The United States and the Soviet Union, 1917-1976," *Foreign Affairs* (July, 1976): 683–684.
79. The Ruhr Authority never actually functioned, being replaced in 1950 by the Coal and Steel Authority set up under the Schuman Plan.
80. "National Military Establishment Views on Germany," June 30, 1948, RG 319, P&O, 092 (top secret). See also Hillenkoetter, Memoranda for the President, March 16, 1948, and June 9, 1948, HTL, HSTP, PSF, box 249.
81. For assessments by the Central Intelligence Agency during this period, including those prepared for meetings of the National Security Council (NSC), see *Harry S Truman Papers*, President's Secretary's File, Harry S Truman Presidential Library, Independence, Mo., hereafter cited as HTL, HSTP, PSF, boxes 249–260, and 203–207, in this instance, CIA, "Review of the World Situation as It Relates to the Security of the United States," September 26, 1947, box 203.
82. It must be remembered that traditional, mainstream thinking about the Russians had two distinct sources. On the one hand, there was the older isolationist and anti-European tradition of "Middle America." Then there was the legacy of the first Red Scare which perpetrated the view that Marism-Leninism was a virulent ideological poison threatening the entire world with its rotten contagion. The second interpretation appeared validated by Russia's actions after 1945.
83. Joint Chiefs of Staff (JCS), "Presidential Request for Certain Facts and Information Regarding the Soviet Union," July 25, 1946, Record Group (RG) 218, National Archives, Washington, D.C. ser. Combined Chiefs of Staff (CCS) 092 USSR, JCS 1696.
84. For the withdrawal of Russian troops, see, for example, Military Intelligence Division (MID), Joint Logistic Plans Committee (JLPC), "Soviet Intentions and Capabilities in Scandinavia as of 1 July, 1946," April 25, 1946, RG 319, P7O, 350.05 (top secret). For reports on reductions of Russian troops in Eastern Europe and demobilization within Soviet Russia, see MID, "Review of Europe, Russia, and the Middle East," December 26, 1945, RG 165, OPD, 350.05 (top secret). How many Russian divisions were then capable of offensive operations in

Europe is still a matter of debate—perhaps thirty but nowhere near the 175 with which the Russian armed forces were credited by some Western observers at the time. For two views of the figures, see Samuel F. Wells, Jr. "Sounding the Tocsin: NSC 68 and the Soviet Threat," in *International Security* (Fall, 1979): 152–153, and Hannes Adomeit, *Soviet Risk-Taking and Crisis Behaviour* (London: Allen & Unwin, 1982), pp. 138–141.

85. For an overall intelligence summary of these events, see Central Intelligence Group (hereafter CIG), "Revised Soviet Tactics in International Affairs," January 6, 1947, HTL, HSTP, PSF, box 254. See, also, MID, "World Political Developments Affecting the Security of the United States during the Next Ten Years," April 14, 1947.

86. Georgi Kornienko, first vice foreign minister of Soviet Russia in the late 1970s and early 1980s, commented at a 1994 symposium in Norway that "All of our leaders whom I knew from the late 1940s and early '50s—all of them feared war and were willing to go to great lengths for peace." See his comments in Odd Arne Wested, ed., "U.S.-Soviet Relations and Soviet Foreign Policy Toward the Middle East and Africa in the 1970s: Transcript from a Workshop at Lysebu," October 1–3, 1994, Norwegian Nobel Institute, 1995, pp. 79–81.

Former Russian Premier and CPSU First Secretary Nikita Khrushchev, in remembrances published during the glosnost years, wrote that Stalin "was afraid of war. . . . Stalin never did anything that might provoke a war with the United States. He knew his weakness." Cited in Jerold Schecter and Vyacheslav Luchkov, trans. and ed., *Khrushchev Remembers: The Glasnost Tapes* (Boston: Little, Brown, 1990), pp. 100–101.

87. CIA, "Review of the World Situation," *Ibid.* David Holloway, in *Stalin and the Bomb* (New Haven, Conn: Yale University Press, 1994), p. 271, argues that "there is no evidence that Stalin intended to invade Western Europe, except in the event of a major war." British Foreign Secretary Bevin as late as December 1947 could still observe in private that he "doubted whether Russia was as great a danger as a resurgent Germany might become." Cited in Alan Bullock, *Ernest Bevin: Foreign Secretary, 1945–1951* (London: Routledge, 1983), p. 269.

88. JIS, "Russian Military Capabilities," October 25, 1945, RG 218, ser. CCS 092 USSR (3-27-45).

89. As early as November, 1945, American intelligence analyses of Soviet Russia's military problems began to arrive on the policy makers' desks. See, for example, JIS, "Estimate of Soviet Postwar Military Capabilities and Intentions," November 8, 1945, RG 218, ser. CCS 092 USSR (3-27-45), JIS 80/14; JLPS, "Russian Capabilities," November 15, 1945; and MID, "Intelligence Estimate of the World Situation for the Next Five Years," August 21, 1946, RG 319, P&O, 350.05 (top secret). A superb analysis of Moscow's problems in this regard may be seen in Mathew A. Evangelista, "Stalin's Postwar Army Reappraised, *International Security*, VII (Winter, 1982–1983), especially pp.121–122.

90. Melvyn P. Leffler's "The American Conception of National Security and the Beginnings of the Cold War, 1945–1948," *The American Historical Review*, 89 (April, 1984): 346–381, is a path-breaking study of postwar American policy, drawn from a wealth of declassified documents from the armed services and intelligence agencies. Leffler makes an excellent case for the view that, after the denials and confusions of the World War II period, America developed very rapidly a rather clear

conception of its national security—a conception based on a fear of international systemic instability and strife. It was this concern, he argues, and the fact that Soviet Russia might be able to exploit it for its own purposes, that led the Truman administration to undertake the fateful steps during these years that brought America into a massive confrontation with the Russian state. See also Lloyd Gardner, *Architects of Illusion: Men and Ideas in American Foreign Policy, 1941–1949* (Chicago: University of Chicago Press, 1970).

91. *Memoirs*, p. 498.

92. In November 1947 Kennan, in a State Department Policy Planning Staff assessment, predicted that Russia might soon have "to clamp down completely on Czechoslovakia" because the danger to that country "could too easily become a means of entry of really democratic forces into Eastern Europe in general." But he thought that "all in all" the Cold War was going well for America and viewed Czechoslovakia as no direct threat to American interests. Cited in Herkin, *The Winning Weapon*, p. 245.

93. *Memoirs*: Vol. II, *Years of Trial and Hope*, p. 350.

94. NSC 7 may be found in *FRUS, 1948*, I, 2, pp. 546–550, and also in Thomas H. Etzold and John Lewis Gaddis, eds., *Containment: Documents on American Policy and Security, 1945–1950* (New York: Norton, 1978), pp. 164–169.

95. *FRUS, 1948* (Washington, D.C., 1974), 6: pp. 654–566, 694–695, 712–717, 733–734, 750–751, 964–965. See also, "Strategic Importance of Japan," May 24, 1948, HTL, HSTP, PSF, box 255.

96. In one form or another, the idea of a Western Europe security bloc had been promoted by the British ever since 1944, Washington at that time taking the position that until the Russian postwar attitude was clear, America would not commit itself one way or another. By the end of 1947, however, with the Yalta-Potsdam mechanism for dealing with the German problem grinding to a halt, the perceived Russian military threat had now come to outweigh the fear of a German resurgence almost everywhere in the West. See, in this regard, Robert M. Hathaway, *Ambiguous Partnership: Britain and America, 1944–1947* (Boston: Little, Brown, 1981).

97. In this defense arrangement each signatory promised to aid one another with all the military and other aid "in their power" in the event of an attack.

98. U.S. Congress, Senate Resolution 239, 80th Congress, 2nd Session, (Washington, D.C: Government Printing Office, June 11, 1948). See also Harry Truman, *Memoirs*, Vol. II, p. 244.

99. See John Lewis Gaddis, *Strategies of Containment* (New York: Oxford University Press, 1982), Chapter 3, especially pp. 71–83.

100. U.S. Department of State, *NATO: 1949–1959: The First Ten Years* (Washington, D.C.: Government Printing Office, 1960).

101. U.S. Congress, 81st Congress, 1st Session, Senate Committee on Foreign Relations, *Hearings on NATO*, Part II (Washington, D.C.: Government Printing Office, 1949), p. 231.

102. *Ibid.*, Part I, pp. 14–15.

103. *Ibid.*, Part II, p. 350.

104. In March, General S.J. Chamberlin, director of army intelligence, warned the Chief of Staff that American actions might provoke a Russian reaction. See his Memorandum to the Chief of Staff, March, 14, 1948, and Chamberlin, Memorandum

for Wedemeyer, April 14, 1948, RG 319, P&O, 092 (top secret).

105. See Fund, *U.S., 1949*, Opus 33, File 218, Subfile 20, p. 29.

106. NSC 20/4 may be found in Etzold and Gaddis, *Containment*, pp. 173–211.

107. See Herkin, *The Winning Weapon*, especially Chapter 11. In June 1946 the Joint Chiefs of Staff had written Baruch that the bomb was "the one military weapon which may for the period until Russia obtains it exert a deterrent effect upon her will to expand." (untitled document, JCS to Baruch, June 5, 1946, "Atomic" Series, (8-15-45), Sec. 3, USJCS Records).

108. This despite the fact that there were no bombs on those initial planes sent to Europe. Indeed, the country at that time had precious few bombs to ship anywhere, nor were the Air Force's bombers modified to carry what atomic bombs we had. And it would not be until July 1950 that Truman permitted even the non-nuclear components of atomic bombs to be sent overseas. On this point, see Richard G. Hewlett and Francis Duncan, *Atomic Shield: A History of the U.S. Atomic Energy Agency, II, 1947–1952* (University Park, Pa.: Pennsylvania State University Press, 1969), pp. 521-23. See also "U.S. Air Power Flowing Back to Europe," *Aviation Week*, August 2, 1948.

109. In early 1948, for example, Kennan recommended that the Baruch Plan be replaced by direct and secret negotiations with Russia. See Hewlett and Duncan, *Atomic Shield*, pp. 266–270.

110. Stalin's mood during this period would later be documented for us. Six days after the Czech coup, Milovan Djilas was in the Kremlin as a witness to the following conversation: "Stalin then turned to the uprising in Greece: 'The uprising in Greece will have to fold up. . . . Do you believe,' he turned to Kardelj [Vice-Premier of Yugoslavia], 'in the success of the uprising in Greece?'

Kardelj replied, 'If foreign intervention does not grow, and if serious political and military errors are not made.'

Stalin went on, without paying attention to Kardelj's opinion: 'If, if! No, they have no prospect at all. What do you think that Great Britain and the United States—the United States, the most powerful state in the world—will permit you to break their line of communication in the Mediterranean? Nonsense. And we have no navy. The uprising in Greece must be stopped, and as quickly as possible.' " *Conversations with Stalin* (London: Hart-Davis,1962), pp. 164.

111. Laurence W. Martin, "The American Decision to Rearm Germany," in Harold Stein, ed., *American Civil-Military Relations: A Book of Case Studies* (Birmingham: University of Alabama Press, 1963), pp. 646–651.

112. In 1949–1950 Kennan offered a third alternative, calling for an approach designed to contain Russia, but at the same time ease the Cold War, by neutralizing Central Europe. Kennan from this time forth would regard NATO as an obstacle to a settlement in Europe by its insistence on dividing and rearming Germany. See his *Memoirs*, pp. 446–449.

113. In October 1949 six members of the U.S. Atomic Energy Commission's general advisory committee, including James Conant and Robert Oppenheimer, signed a statement pointing out that such a bomb might become a "weapon of genocide." Their views were eventually endorsed by the commission. Their recommendation, however, would soon be overtaken by events.

114. But not without making a case for the international control of atomic energy in a memorandum to the Secretary of State. Entitled "International Control of

Atomic Energy," it was submitted by Kennan as a personal paper because Nitze was "not entirely in agreement with the substance." See *FRUS, 1950*, III, pp. 22-40.

115. Dean Acheson, *Present at the Creation: My Years at the State Department* (New York: Norton, 1969), p. 375. Kennan opposed the proposed military buildup, arguing that Stalin had no grand design for world conquest, that his attention was now almost wholly focused within the Russian bloc, and that as a reactionary thinker he really feared overextending Moscow's reach. See George Kennan to Dean Acheson, February 17, 1950, *FRUS, 1950*, I: pp. 1160, 1163–1164. See also in this vein, Paul Y. Hammond, "NSC-68: Pro-logue to Rearmament," in Warner P. Schilling et al., *Strategy, Politics and Defense Budgets* (New York: Macmillan, 1962), pp. 308–311.

As for Kennan's views of Nitze: "He had no feeling for the intangibles—values, intentions. When there was talk of intentions, as opposed to capabilities, he would say, 'How can you measure intentions? We can't be bothered to get into psychology, we have to face the Russians as competitors, militarily.' " Cited in Strobe Talbott, *The Master of the Game: Paul Nitze and the Nuclear Peace* (New York: Alfred A. Knopf, 1988), p. 23.

116. Princeton Seminar, July 8–9, 1953, *Acheson Papers*, Truman Library. Nitze's role is ably reviewed and analyzed in Ernest R. May, *American Cold War Strategy: Interpreting NSC 68* (Boston: St. Martin's Press, 1993). See especially his Introduction, pp. 1–19.

117. See Donald Zagoria, "Choices in the Postwar World: Containment and China," in *Caging the Bear: Containment and the Cold War*, ed. Charles Gati (New York: Bobbs-Merrill Co., 1974), pp. 109–127. The record reveals that from 1945 right up to the middle of 1949, a number of Chinese bids for American recognition and support were made and rejected. For a review of the 1945–1946 overtures, see Barbara Tuchman, "If Mao Had Come to Washington: An Essay in Alternatives," *Foreign Affairs* (October, 1972): 44–64. A report released by the Senate Committee on Foreign Relations in 1973 revealed that Mao sought recognition as late as the summer of 1949, after America had disengaged from the civil war in China, only to be rejected by Truman himself under political pressure at home. See Committee on Foreign Relations Report U.S. Senate, *The United States and Communist China in 1949 and 1950: The Question of Rapprochement and Recognition* (Washington, D.C.: U.S. Government Printing Office, 1973). See also William W. Stueck, Jr., *The Road to Confrontation: American Policy Toward China and Korea* (Chapel Hill: University of North Carolina Press, 1991), and Dorothy Borg and Waldo Heinrichs, eds., *Uncertain Years: Chinese-American Relations, 1947–1950* (New York: Basic Books, 1980).

118. Certainly a major factor influencing Truman's decision to stonewall the CCP was the domestic political situation, most especially the existence of a vociferous and influential "China lobby" in America. Composed of a wide range of conservative Republicans and Democrats, Truman could ill afford to completely ignore their strong efforts to ensure a hardline approach to the Chinese communists. For an interesting review of the Sino-American interaction during this period in the context of domestic American politics, see H. B. Westerfield, *Foreign Policy and Party Politics: Pearl Harbor to Korea* (New Havan, Conn: Yale University Press, 1955), p. 356–361.

119. The agreement called for, among other things, military assistance to one

another in case of armed attack by another country, singling out Japan in particular as a potential threat to Asian communism.

120. In March 1949 as reported in the *New York Times* on March 2, p. 2, General MacArthur had defined America's essential security zone in Asia to include Japan, the Ryukyu Islands, and the Philippines. On January 12, 1950, Acheson, in a speech before the Overseas Press Club in Washington, D.C., stated the administration view that Soviet Russia did not now pose a specific threat to spread communism in Asia by force of arms as much as by subversion, echoing MacArthur's view that Japan was of paramount importance economically to America. Reprinted as "Crisis in Asia," *Department of State Bulletin*, XXII (January 23, 1950: 111–117.

121. The relationship between the two men was a difficult one from the outset, beginning in the 1920s when Stalin sought to have the CCP subordinate itself to the Kuomintang. An excellent review of the long-standing suspicion and rivalry between Stalin and Mao is Zagoria's, "Choices in the Postwar World: Containment and China." According to Sergei Goncharov, John W. Lewis and Xue Litai, *Uncertain Partners: Stalin, Mao and the Korean War* (Stanford, Calif.: Stanford University Press, 1993), realpolitik was the ground on which their relationship foundered.

122. Kennan was also concerned at this time about Korea's unsettled internal politics, recommending that Washington consider an evacuation of that country. *FRUS, 1948*, 1, 2, pp. 523–526.

123. An insightful review of these events may be found in Masao Okonogi, "The Domestic Roots of the Korean War," in Nagai and Iriye, *The Origins of the Cold War in Asia*, pp. 299–320.

124. See on this matter Walter LaFeber, *America, Russia and the Cold War*, pp. 102–103. LaFeber's three reasons for the Korean attack: North Korea's belief that Rhee was vulnerable in the south; Kim's belief that he could break free of Chinese influence; and Stalin's concern that Japan was now proving to be a threat to Russian hegemony in the region, while at the same time serving as a brake on Chinese ambitions to lead the non-Western world revolutionary movement.

125. See in this regard Kathryn Weathersby, "Korea, 1945-1950: To Attack or Not to Attack? Stalin, Kim Il Sung, and the Prelude to War," *Cold War International History Project Bulletin*, 5 (Spring, 1995): 1–9. See, in addition, her "The Soviet Role in the Early Phase of the Korean War: New Documentary Evidence," *Journal of American-East Asian Relations*, (Winter, 1993): 425–458. The close relationship between the North Korean regime and the CCP is also an important theme of Bruce Cummings, *The Origins of the Korean War: The Roaring of the Cataract, 1947–1950* (Princeton, N. J.: Princeton University Press, 1990), pp. 528–562.

The actual circumstances of the June 25 invasion are still not fully clear. Cummings suggests, for example, that the timing of North Korea's attack was fortuitous in that the actual assault might well have grown out of a series of local incidents. On this point, see his *The Roaring of the Cataract*.

An excellent treatment of the well-springs of the Korean War may also be found in Robert R. Simmons, *The Strained Alliance: Peking, P'yongyang, Moscow and the Politics of the Korean War* (New York: Knopf, 1975). A useful earlier survey of what was known about the conflict in the 1980s may be found in Burton I. Kaufman, *The Korean War: Challenges in Crisis, Credibility, and Command* (New York: Macmillan, 1986), especially pp. 31–33.

Research in Chinese documents has borne some interesting fruit recently. For the Chinese perspective, see Jian Chen, *China's Road to the Korean War: The Making of the Sino-American Confrontation* (New York: Columbia University Press, 1994), and Shu Guang Zhang, *Deterrence and Strategic Culture: Chinese-American Confrontations, 1949–1958* (Ithaca, N.Y.: Cornell University Press, 1992).

As Chen points out, the CCP ultimately decided to send in its troops in order to prevent the complete destruction of North Korea's military forces, thereby creating a most unfavorable strategic situation in the East—one entailing an ascendent American influence at the expense of Chinese interests. What was not known in the West at this time is that Stalin reneged on his promise to provide air cover for the intervening Chinese forces—a "betrayal" that would be an important factor in the future Sino-Soviet split. On this last point, see Chen, "The Sino-Soviet Alliance and China's Entry into the Korean War," *Cold War International History Project Working Paper No. 1*, Woodrow Wilson International Center for Scholars (Princeton, N.J.: Princeton University Press, 1992).

126. Presidential Papers of Harry S. Truman, 1950, pp. 527. Acheson reiterated the view that the invasion "was ordered by the Kremlin and is being actively directed by key Soviet personnel in Korea." See his *Present at the Creation*, p. 418.

127. Presidential Papers of Harry S. Truman, 1950, p. 492.

128. *FRUS, 1950*, I, p. 400.

129. For a review of European reactions, see Charles Maier, "Alliance and Autonomy: European Identity and U.S. Foreign Policy Objectives in the Truman Years," in Michael Lacey, ed., *The Truman Presidency* (New York: Woodrow Wilson International Center and Cambridge University Press, 1989), pp. 273–298, and Geir Lundestad, "Empire by Invitation?: The United States and Western Europe, 1945–1952, *Journal of Peace Research* (September, 1986): 263–277. See also Charles O. Lerche, Jr., *Last Chance in Europe* (Chicago: Quadrangle Books, 1967).

130. The views of Paul Nitze and Dean Acheson, for example, are well-documented in this regard. See John Lewis Gaddis, *Strategies of Containment.* esp. his Chapter 4, "NSC-68 and the Korean War."

131. A total of ninety divisions was agreed upon at Lisbon in February 1952, but subsequently was reduced to thirty—a figure that would never be met subsequently, due to Western European reluctance to undertake the necessary costs (e.g., tax increases) to sutain those numbers.

132. For an accounting of these debates, including the European concerns, see Richard J. Barnet, *Roots of War* (Baltimore: Penguin Books, 1972), esp. pp. 125–137 and 243–251. French president Vincent Auriol told Acheson several months after the Lisbon conference that "our policy toward Germany was a great mistake. . . . We were wrong in thinking that the greater danger came from Russia. It came from Germany." Cited in Dean Acheson, *Sketches from Life of Men I Have Known* (New York: Knopf, 1961), p. 53.

133. In particular, the draft treaties on Germany promulgated by the Russians on May 24, 1952 (just before the signing of the EDC), and on August 23 of the same year, indicated, on the surface at least, a desire by the Kremlin to arrive at a mutually satisfactory solution. On the Russian reaction to Western rearmament in the early 1950s, see Philip Noel-Baker, *The Arms Race* (London: Atlantic, 1958). This is a classic early work in the field of arms control, and one that goes to the heart of the issues.

134. Acheson would later refer to the Russian initiative as the "golden apple"

tactic—one designed to disorient the Allies and prevent them from reaching their intended goals. See his "Progress Toward International Peace and Unity," *Department of State Bulletin* (April 28, 1952), p. 648.

135. Britain, conspicuous by its non-involvement, was not even asked to participate.

136. This formula was first used in the 1947 Rio de Janeiro Treaty of Reciprocal Assistance which provided that an "armed attack by any state against an American state shall be considered as an attack against all the American states" (Article 4). Each state was required to assist in meeting the attack in exercise of its inherent right of self-defense. The same type of commitment was included in the 1949 North Atlantic Treaty. That treaty declared that an attack on the territory of any European or North American member would be considered an attack on all, and each was to take such action as it deemed necessary, including the use of armed force (Articles 5 and 3).

137. Robert Jervis would later provide a theoretical framework of analysis for an understanding of such dynamics. "When the state believes that the other knows that it is not threatening the other's interests, disputes are likely to produce antagonism out of all proportion to the intrinsic importance of the issue at stake. Because the state does not think there is any obvious reason why the other should oppose it, it will draw inferences of unprovoked hostility from even minor conflicts." in *Perception and Misperception in International Politics* (Princeton, N. J.: Princeton University Press), p. 72.

138. For the case that Britain forced the pace over Germany, see Anne Deighton, "The 'Frozen Front': The Labour Government, the Division of Germany and the Origins of the Cold War, 1945–1947," *International Affairs*, 15 (Summer 1987): 449–465.

139. In his own defense of the Truman Doctrine, to cite one instance among many, Truman clearly revealed the Manichean orientation: "The world reaction to it proved that this approach had been the right one. All over the world, voices of approval made themselves heard, while Communists . . . struck out at me savagely." *Memoirs*, Vol. II, *Years of Trial and Hope*, p. 106. Truman, Acheson, et al., of course, assumed that Soviet Russia was primarily responsible for the revolutionary uprising in Greece. See also in this context Edward Weisband and Kent Trachte, "The Truman Doctrine: A Neo-Revisionist Critique", Paper delivered at the Annual Meeting of the International Studies Association, St. Louis, Mo., March 18, 1977.

140. *Memoirs*, p. 322.

141. Thomas Schelling, in addressing America's intervention in Korea, has argued that "saving face" and creating expectations for future behavior was also an important motivation. Schelling believed that the American role in the Korean conflict was not simply designed to prevent a communist takeover, but was also aimed at preserving American credibility as a system maintainer. See his *Arms and Influence* (New Haven, Conn: Yale University Press, 1966), p. 124.

142. John Lewis Gaddis, *The United States and the Origins of the Cold War*, p. 351. See in this regard Thomas G. Paterson, "Presidential Foreign Policy, Public Opinion, and Congress: The Truman Years," *Diplomatic History* (Winter, 1979): 31–49.

143. The fact that we had demobilized our armed forces significantly after the war now had begun to worry a number of people in the administration. In June 1945, the numbers totaled 12 million. One year later they stood at 3 million, and by June 1947

at 1.5 million. But our later fears were exaggerated on this score. Russia, as we now know, also demobilized rapidly after World War II.

144. Gaddis, *The United States and the Origins of the Cold War*, pp. 357–358.

145. Dean Acheson certainly epitomized the elitist view of politics that came to dominate the foreign policy-making establishment in the postwar era. The basic role of Congress, he once observed, "is the function of people who don't know and don't care and are obstructive, and they are just generally raising hell around." Princeton Seminar, October 10–11, July 22–23, 1954, *Acheson Papers*, Truman Library.

146. On the strategic situation facing America at this time, and the country's capacity to act, see Robert A. Garson, "American Foreign Policy and the Limits of Power: Eastern Europe, 1946–1950," *Journal of Contemporary History* (July, 1986: 73–91.

147. See, for example, Ulam, *Expansion and Co-existence*.

148. On this point, see Narinsky, "The Soviet Union and the Marshall Plan," p. 41, in which a telegram is quoted from Nikolai Novikov to Molotov on June 24, 1945 stating that "...the main goals of U.S. foreign policy, the essence of the 'Truman Doctrine,'—to check the process of democratization in European countries, to stimulate forces hostile to the Soviet Union and to create conditions for the buttressing of the positions of American capital in Europe and Asia—remains without any substantial changes. A thorough analysis of the 'Marshall Plan' shows that...it is directed toward the establishment of a West European bloc as an instrument of American policy."

149. See, in this vein, M. Brewster Smith, "The Personal Setting of Public Opinion: A Study of Attitudes Toward Russia," Public Opinion Quarterly (Winter 1947–1948): 507–523. For a broader commentary, see Gabriel A. Almond, *The American People and Foreign Policy* (New York: Harcourt, Brace, and World, 1950).

150. *Memoirs*, pp. 272–282.

151. *Ibid.*, p. 385.

152. *Ibid.*, p. 378.

153. Cited in Harold K. Jacobson, *America's Foreign Policy* (New York: Random House, 1965), p. 260.

154. *Ibid.*, p. 261–262. This perception, of course, misunderstood the Marxist gospel on the question of world revolution, insofar as the Marxist theory of world revolution was from the beginning a socioeconomic prediction, not a military prescription. Furthermore, the devotees of this view failed to grasp the important changes in the relationship between revolutionary theory and state practice that had taken place under Stalin. On these matters, see Helmut Gruber, *Soviet Russia Masters the Comintern: International Communism in the Era of Stalin's Ascendency* (Garden City, N.Y.: Doubleday, 1974); and William G. Rosenberg and Marilyn B. Young, *Transforming Russia and China: Revolutionary Struggle in the Twentieth Century* (New York: Oxford University Press, 1982).

155. Joseph Starobin, "Origins of the Cold War," pp. 275–288.

156. *Strategies of Containment*, p. 23.

157. See Nikita Khrushchev's comments in *Pravda*, January 15, 1960. His numbers for the demobilization and remobilization of Soviet Russia's armed forces were: May, 1945, 365,000; 1948, 2,874,000; and 1955, 5,763,000. See also Ulam, *Expansion and Co-existence*, p. 414.

158. Even the disturbing developments of the first half of 1948 did not change

these assessments.   The CIA concluded that the communist takeover in Czechoslovakia would not increase Russian capabilities appreciably and would lead to no alteration in the Kremlin's tactics.   In December of that year, Acting Secretary of State Robert Lovett, summed up this American perspective when he said that he saw "no evidence that Soviet intentions run toward launching a sudden military attack on the western nations at this time.   It would not be in character with the tradition or mentality of the Soviet leaders to resort to such a measure unless they felt themselves either politically extremely weak, or militarily extremely strong." Cited in John Prados, *The Soviet Estimate: U.S. Intelligence Analysis and Russian Military Strength* (New York: Dial, 1982), p. 82.

159.   This shift may be seen to have coincided with the death of Zhadanov in August, 1948, and of the purge of Zhadanov's entourage following his death—events which, in combination with the demotion of Molotov in the spring of 1949, redounded to the benefit of the Malenkov faction and the policy of retrenchment. Later in the year, Malenkov delivered a speech in which he argued that "capitalist encirclement" was crumbling, and that Stalin no longer had to apply pressure as before. On this point, see Marshall D. Shulman, *Stalin's Foreign Policy Reapparised* (Cambridge, Mass.:   Harvard University Press, 1963).

160. James Forrestal, Henry Stimson, John McCloy, and others, for example, argued at this time that long-term American prosperity required open markets, unhindered access to raw materials, and the rehabilitation of much, if not all, of Eurasia along liberal capitalist lines.

161. Djilas, *Conversations with Stalin*, p. 48.

162. On this debate, refer to the Russian Centre for Keeping and Studying Documents of Modern History (former Third Communist International Archive), Central Committee of the Communist Party of the Soviet Union, General Department. Fund N17. Inventory No. 128. File 749.   Report N 40, pp. 133–135.

163. Certainly, the growing tendency to view Moscow's actions as motivated chiefly by ideology had an enormous impact on the general public. Wartime opinion polls revealed that most Americans regarded security from attack as the main motivation of Russian foreign policy. By July 1946 more than half now believed the Kremlin wanted to dominate the world. It would decline further from there.

164. "Russia—Seven Years Later," in his Memoirs, p. 520.

3

The Eisenhower Years: Nothing Fundamental Has Changed

An absolute principle is as absurd as absolute power.
—Lord Acton

THE VIEW FROM WASHINGTON

The decade of the 1950s ushered in a new era of possibilities for addressing the manifold problems associated with the Russian-American Cold War relationship. Within two months of Dwight Eisenhower's inauguration Joseph Stalin was dead, and with him, ultimately, the system that bore his indelible imprimatur. As a result, opportunities would present themselves for meaningful conflict resolution—occasions in response to which the assumptions and attitude of the new administration would go a long way toward determining whether the world would continue to be plagued by endemic conflict and crisis or somehow find a way to live in relative peace and security.

The Odd Couple

Whether intended or not, the new administration's world view reflected from the very beginning a divergent, if not contradictory, orientation toward the Cold War—a divergency centering on the backgrounds and personalities of the two men who would dominate the country's foreign policy for the next six years—Dwight D. Eisenhower and John Foster Dulles. Eisenhower manifested at one and the same time in his own personality and style the moralist and

pragmatic strains of the country's foreign affairs tradition. Deeply committed to
the efficacy of middle America's traditional values of democracy and the rule of
law, Eisenhower was also prone to seek the middle ground and to look for
compromise in his dealings with others. Above all, he believed in the potential
benefits to be had from "sitting down and reasoning together." His wartime
experiences of dealing with contentious Allies had demonstrated the value to be
derived from face-to-face discussion.[1]

Dulles, on the other hand, was a true believer—a fundamentalist whose
basic approach to world affairs was to reduce its complexities to a handful of
black-and-white simplicities. Dulles's policy would be based on a bipolar view
of the world—a world divided between good and evil, free versus slave—above
all, a world dominated by Washington and Moscow. In such a world, there
would be inevitable conflict and confrontation between America and Soviet
Russia. His perception of the Russian state was a simple, straightforward one:
In Ole Holsti's words, it "was built on the trinity of atheism, totalitarianism,
and communism, capped by a deep belief that no enduring social order could be
erected on such foundations."[2] That Soviet Russia's leadership was "bad" (insincere, immoral and brutal) and their creed was "Godless," is why he believed
that the Cold War was basically a moral, rather than a political, conflict. There
could be no compromise with such people.[3]

In the election campaign of 1952, Dulles had promised that a new
Republican administration would seek to reshape American foreign policy. In
the foreign affairs plank of the Republican platform which he largely drafted,
Dulles condemned Yalta by promising to repudiate all "secret understandings,"
indicted the Roosevelt and Truman administrations for "neglect of the Far East,"
and promised that Republicans would find a "dynamic" substitute for the
"negative, futile and immoral" policy of containment.[4] In the ensuing months
he spoke confidently, if somewhat vaguely, of a "rollback" of Russian power in
Eastern Europe and "liberation" of countries under the Kremlin's domination.
He also helped to popularize the notion that Chiang Kai-shek and his
Nationalists on Taiwan would be "unleashed" to attack the Chinese mainland.

It is therefore one of the ironies of this period that while Eisenhower's
nomination was a victory for the so-called moderate wing of the Republican
Party, his election to the presidency served to confirm in power its right-wing
viewpoint on foreign affairs The Manichean assumptions on which the global
war against communism was firmly based in the American mind virtually
assured the ascendence of the right. Confronting an "absolute" and "uncom-
promising" evil, it was only natural to assume that a tough, fearless, absolute
counter-position would eventually carry decisive weight. It was the moderate
Eisenhower whose first inaugural address set a precedent by beginning with a
prayer and then went on to state America's vision of the Cold War in classic
terms: "Here then is joined no argument between slightly differing philosophies.
This conflict strikes directly at the faith of our fathers and the lives of our sons.
No principle or treasure that we hold, from the spiritual knowledge of our free

schools and churches to the creative magic of free labor and capital, nothing lies safely beyond the reach of this struggle. Freedom is pitted against slavery; lightness against the dark."[5]

Thus, while Eisenhower came into the White House holding fast to the view that the Cold War was the result of Moscow's essential hostility and perfidiousness, years of dealing with the Russians at the military level had nevertheless left him with the impression that they could perhaps be reasoned with. His secretary of state, on the other hand, believed such efforts would be pointless, so long as "Godless Communism" held sway in Moscow. The result, during their time together in Washington, was to impart to American foreign policy a quasi-schizophrenic character, exhibiting a pattern of ambivalence toward Soviet Russia and the Cold War—one that combined a certain flexibility of outlook and willingness to talk associated with the new president, counterbalanced by the more confrontationist, suspicious attitude and aggressive actions of his Secretary of State.[6]

The foreign policies adopted by the new administration during its initial months in office reflected this dualism. They also mirrored the internal ideological dynanmics of the Republican Party at that time—a set of viewpoints that were not at all consistent.[7] Moreover, the climate of public opinion of the country as a whole was a particularly volatile one, expressive of many of the conflicting traditions of foreign affairs under which the nation had labored for so long.[8] Consequently, the image and message of the country projected abroad in its foreign relations was an ambiguous one—a situation that only served to confuse and irritate America's allies and to exacerbate and intensify the hostile relationship with Soviet Russia.

The New Look

Eisenhower and Dulles came into office determined to take a fresh, new approach toward waging the Cold War with the Russians—an orientation that was de facto a function of these factors. At the domestic level, a fundamental aim of the new president was to cut governmental expenditures. This meant, of course, a rejection of deficit spending—an indication of mainstream Republicanism's fiscal conservatism, and of its longtime aversion to New Deal-Fair Deal economics. In terms of foreign policy, this orientation in its broadest sense appeared to conflict with Truman's commitment to global containment, which in fact could be maintained only by a hefty armament budget. In microcosm, it dovetailed nicely with the expressed desire by the American people at the time to "bring the boys home" from Korea.[9] The solution to this problem worked out by the foreign policy experts was a new strategy which its principal author, Secretary Dulles, dubbed the "New Look"—an approach that would rely essentially on military sufficiency or parity, not across-the-board superiority vis-à-vis the Russians.

The New Look shaped the administration's foreign policy. For starters, it repudiated the Truman administration's reliance on NSC-68's premise that America could successfully spend up to 20 percent of its GNP on arms.[10] At the same time, the basic military premise of the New Look was recogition of America's substantial lead in nuclear weapons and the means of delivering them. Since nuclear arms appeared to represent the country's only effective weapons in any future military conflict with Soviet Russia, and with the NATO forces then in place being too small to effectively restrain a Russian attack in Europe, it came to be assumed that Washington would have to rely on such weapons in order to deter aggression.[11] To counter Moscow's plans, the New Look policy emphasized both the role of strategic airpower and the importance of tactical nuclear weapons as deterrents to aggression. "Massive retaliation" became the framework for response, with the methodology for employing it taking on the connotation of "brinkmanship."[12]

Actually, the "new look" for the most part consisted of old policies obscured by new language. In retrospect it is difficult to avoid the judgment that the promises of change were given mainly to assuage public dissatisfaction and frustration with previous policy, and to give vent to the conservative Republican credo that "there can be no substitute for victory."[13] The truth of the matter is that the Eisenhower Administration did not have a workable alternative to containment. In fact, the fundamental principles of the Truman-Acheson diplomacy—substantial military rearmament, an emphasis on regional alliances, and permissive enforcement through the United Nations, predicated upon an all-out ideological Cold War with Soviet Russia and its Marxist-Leninist allies—were not only maintained but extended during the Eisenhower era. Continuity, rather than change, marked the transition from Democrat to Republican rule. Thus, containment was not only not rejected, but brinkmanship should be seen as a tactic designed to support containment at an acceptable cost, given the domestic climate of opinion that conditioned the administration's approach to foreign affairs.

From the beginning, many in the military opposed the New Look, criticizing its undue reliance on the concept of massive retaliation as its most obvious limitation. Who would do the fighting, they asked? Moreover, they said, it was not a suitable strategy for protracted conflict.[14] In this, they echoed Walter Lippmann, who had foreseen as early as 1946 that the military requirements of containment would put inordinate strains on American capabilities:

American military power is distinguished by its mobility, its speed, its range and its offensive striking force. It can only be the instrument of a policy which has as its objectives a decision and a settlement . . . it is not designed for, or adapted to, a strategy of containing, waiting, countering, blocking, with no more specific objective than the eventual "frustration" of the opponent.

The Americans would themselves probably be frustrated by Mr. X's policy long before the Russians were.[15]

Recognizing these pitfalls, Eisenhower and Dulles realized that they had to compensate. Husbanding the country's resources, and pandering to public opinion, the new administration sought ideological refuge in the semantics of "liberation politics" while seeking to sign up as many allies as possible to do the fighting. Since there was no point in seeking an accommodation with the Russians—how can one negotiate with evil, Dulles argued—the country's capabilities needed to be continually stressed.

It was this dual emphasis on the efficacy of power, and a distrust of traditional diplomacy, with its historic emphasis on compromise, that would lead the Secretary of State to avoid, block, disrupt, and negate efforts to stabilize and pacify the international situation in the years when he was at the foreign policy helm.[16] Such policies, and the attitudes which supported them, led Kennan to declare in the spring of 1954 that Americans had become "wholly absorbed with power values to the point where they are impatient of any discussion of international affairs that tries to take account of anything else."[17]

The Death of Stalin: Whither Goeth Moscow?

Joseph Stalin died suddenly in early March 1953, and with his passing an opportunity for a new beginning appeared to present itself—one that appealed to the new president's basic instincts. Within days of the Russian dictator's demise, the new leader of Soviet Russia, Georgi Malenkov, suggested in a series of public statements that the Russians might be receptive to tension-reduction measures from Washington.[18] Eisenhower reacted with evident interest. "Look," he said, "I am tired . . . of just plain indictments of the Soviet regime. . . . The past speaks for itself. I am interested in the future. . . . The slate is clean. Now let us begin talking to each other."[19] This attitude was reflected later in the spring in a new peace initiative launched from the White House.

Eisenhower's initial public response to Malenkov's comments took the form of a major presentation on April 16, 1953, before the American Society of Newspaper Editors. In an eloquent speech—one that conjured up visions of a world "under the cloud of threatening war," and of "humanity hanging from a cross of iron,"—Eisenhower asserted that this was no way for mankind to live. He then called upon the Russians to take a few "clear and specific steps" to demonstrate the sincerity of their professed new commitment to peace, suggesting that the signing of an Austrian peace treaty, concluding an armistice in Korea, and the reunification of Germany based on the principle of democratic elections would be excellent examples.[20] The climax of the speech was a call for nuclear disarmament, but one predicated upon proposals, including comprehensive and verifiable on-site inspection measures, that Moscow had long rejected.[21]

Churchill responded to the speech in early May by calling for a summit with the Russians as soon as possible. In contrast to the American president, however, Churchill specifically repudiated the notion that the Russians had to undertake specific deeds as an indication of their good faith. "It would be a mistake," he said, "to assume that nothing could be settled with Soviet Russia unless or until everything is settled."[22] Eisenhower's immediate reaction to the holding of a summit was a negative one: "This idea of the President of the United States going personally abroad to negotiate—it's just damn stupid. Every time a President has gone abroad to get into the details of these things, he's lost his shirt."[23]

But the Russians appeared to be serious in trying to reach out to the West. Over the next several months, the Russians moved in a number of areas to lessen tensions and to create opportunities for dialogue: Soviet Russian citizens married to foreigners were now allowed to leave the country; diplomatic relations were reestablished with Greece and Israel; claims to Turkish territory were renounced; political controls in East Germany were relaxed and, most importantly, promotion of revolution by the international proletariat was downgraded.[24]

Dulles reacted suspiciously to the seeming new line coming out of Moscow, warning the president that the Russians were playing for time in order to hide internal problems. The Russians were nothing but a bunch of tricksters, he said, their overtures merely designed to minimize the chance of war while Soviet Russia rebuilt its strength, and to lull the West into relaxing its own strength and unity. The Secretary of State urged caution, and recommended a policy of increased toughness, arguing that what Moscow really wanted was to torpedo the proposed European Defense Community as a vehicle for the rearming of West Germany. Ultimately, he was able to convince Eisenhower to meet with the British and French first, with the possibility of a future summit with the Russians to be discussed at that time.[25] And, thus, an opportunity was lost very early in the Eisenhower administration to test Russian intentions in the wake of Stalin's death.[26]

Meanwhile, an opportunity presented itself very early in Eisenhower's first term to employ the nuclear card in the guise of brinkmanship. During the 1952 election campaign, Eisenhower issued a dramatic announcement that he would go to Korea to try to end the impasse. Wanting to extricate the country from a protracted conventional war on that peninsula, and anxious to cut the defense budget so as to eliminate the federal government's deficit spending habits, he announced that in order to extricate itself from Korea, Washington might raise the ante significantly. This led to a series of negotiations in the spring. By May, however, the administration, frustrated by the slow progress of the talks, hinted it might use nuclear weapons if a peace were not forthcoming. The Chinese responded, the talks continued, leading to a final armistice in July.[27] While the policy of brinkmanship appeared to have been validated, it may well have been that in the wake of Stalin's death, the Korean "settlement" was brought about by Moscow's desire to facilitate an easing of tensions.[28]

In early summer 1953 riots broke out in East Germany. The outbreak of violence was brought about by Moscow's loosening of political controls, but at the price of demands for increased production at the same wages for workers. The workers rebelled, necessitating a military crackdown by the Russians. In the face of these events, Eisenhower and Dulles took no action other than to rachet up propaganda activities in support of the rebellion. But with the failure of the administration to do more than offer verbal support for the workers' uprising, the essential limits on what America could actually do became apparent. Thus, in Germany, the professed policy of liberation and rollback came to be seen for what it really was—empty rhetoric. Liberation politics had failed its first significant test.[29]

Pressure for a meeting with the Russians slowly grew in the ensuing months. In November 1953 French Premier Pierre Mendes-France, in a speech before the United Nations, called for a summit—a move rejected by Eisenhower who insisted upon "adequate" preparations by the foreign ministers before he would even consider such a meeting. A more important reason for Eisenhower's reluctance was the fact that there was at that very moment an ongoing series of delicate discussions taking place between Washington and its major European allies regarding the most appropriate security measures to take in regard to the Russians. Russian behavior at this time can only be understood in this context. Unfortunately, what was not well comprehended in Washington at that moment was that Malenkov's interest in exploring with the West areas of possible convergence flowed from Moscow's overwhelming concern about German rearmament.[30] To grasp where the Russians were coming from at this time, it is necessary to put into perspective the new administration's European policy—a policy that served to set the tone for the whole.

The Approach to Europe and the Question of Germany

From the very beginning, Secretary Dulles insisted on pursuing the twin goals of arming the Federal Republic of Germany (FRG), closely tied to NATO, while seeking to unify the two halves of the country through the principle of free elections. This was essentially the policy that President Truman and Secretary of State Acheson had followed since the beginning of the decade. In the process, they bequeathed to their successors a rationale that was at the very least one unlikely to promote a rapprochement with Moscow, for the progressive achievement of the former inevitably made the latter more difficult to bring off.

The vehicle for linking the FRG to NATO was the European Defense Community (EDC). From the beginning the EDC was in major trouble in the French parliament. After the French agreed to the approach in May 1952, three separate governments in Paris refused to bring the agreements to a vote, in part due to British reluctance to commit its troops to a permanent garrison role on the continent as a counterweight to German rearmament. As the delay in ratification stretched out, the French public's hostility grew. Dulles tried to force their hand in December 1953 by publicly warning Paris that failure to ratify would lead to an "agonizing reappraisal" by Washington of America's commitments to Europe. Throughout the following year, as the French dithered and Dulles applied pressure, the situation simmered. Finally, on August 30, 1954, after more than two years of debates and delays, the French National Assembly rejected the treaty.[31]

While Dulles stewed, the British came forward almost immediately with an alternative which soon won acceptance from all quarters. The British proposal was hammered into final form in London in September 1954, signed in Paris in October, ratified by the states concerned during the next few months, and put into force in May 1955. The Paris agreement ended the joint Western occupation of Germany, restored full sovereignty to the West German government, and admitted the Federal Republic of Germany to NATO. It also provided for the contribution of a maximum of twelve West German divisions to NATO forces and expanded NATO's authority over the armed forces of all member states. The most innovative features of the Paris agreement were a substantive commitment by Great Britain—far more binding than its earlier pledges to the EDC—to maintain substantial armed forces on the continent while, at the same time, the major European states were prepared to accept some limitations and controls upon the size and disposition of their armed forces.[32]

The proposed creation of the EDC did have one immediate result—one that had been envisoned by Mr. X from the beginning: It created a bargaining counter with respect to the Russians. The main thrust of Russian policy in Europe during this time was to obtain a settlement that, in effect, would have resulted in some degree of German neutrality, albeit at the price of unification. To that end, the Russian government waged an intensive campaign throughout the 1953–1955 period to keep a reunified western Germany from joining any anti-Russian military alliance. A number of approaches and tactics were tried—all either rejected out of hand or responded to half-heartedly by an administration determined to throw up a ring of steel around the Russian state. On several occasions during this period, the Russians offered German reunification on the basis of free elections as long as the reunited state held aloof from military alliances.[33] Such a settlement, along the lines of the Locarno Treaty, was proposed by Churchill in his call for a summit in May 1953. But Secretary Dulles, echoing the strategy of the Truman administration in refusing to negotiate a German settlement until we could do so from a "position of strength,"[34] sought to avoid any serious negotiations with Soviet Russia until the West could confront Moscow with German rearmament within an organized European security framework as a *fait accompli*.

On February 4, 1954, Molotov repeated the offer of German unification at the Big Four Foreign Ministers Conference—one responded to by Secretary Dulles by insisting that a reunified Germany be permitted to join the EDC. Not surprisingly, the American initiative was rejected by the Russians out of hand.[35]

In June 1954 Russian Premier Nikolai Bulganin proposed a progressive reduction of troops on German soil, leading to their total withdrawal. It would be repeated in a Russian government statement of January 23, 1955. Eisenhower and Dulles remained firm, agreeing on unification only with the price tag of its involvement in Western security arrangements attached. There was little the Russians could do but try to make the best of it.

In early December 1954 Moscow announced the Russians would form a counterpart to NATO if the Paris Agreements were ratified. When it became apparent that the reality of full West German independence was imminent, on May 5, 1955, they invited West German Chancellor Konrad Adenauer to Moscow, out of which came the establishment of diplomatic relations with the Bonn government. This was followed by a strengthening of the East German army, the announcement of plans to seek a rappprochement with Yugoslavia, and the move toward the establishment of a counterpart security organization in Eastern Europe—the Warsaw Pact. Most importantly, Khrushchev broke a ten-year logjam by agreeing to withdraw Russian troops from Austria as part of a deal to unify and neutralize that country—an arrangement concluded and signed on May 15.

It was Moscow's willingness to acquiesce in Austrian unification that led Eisenhower to agree to a summit—a concession now shared by the new British Prime Minister, Anthony Eden, who had succeeded an ailing Churchill in May. But it was a very reluctant American administration indeed, Dulles insisting on an approach that the Russians would be sure to reject: unification of Germany "under conditions which will neither 'neutralize' nor 'demilitarize' united Germany, nor subtract it from NATO."[36] A tripartitite note was issued to the Russians on May 10, 1955, inviting them to a conference. The note suggested that the purpose of the meeting should be to have an exchange of views, and "not [to] undertake to agree upon substantive answers to the major difficulties facing the world."[37] After further exchanges of notes, and several meetings at both the ambassadorial and foreign minister levels, an agenda was agreed to—one that reflected to a considerable degree Moscow's concerns: reunification of Germany, European security, disarmament, and East-West contacts.

At the conference (July 18–23, 1955) Eisenhower sought to explain the American position on the German question:

> Ten years have passed since the German armistice, and Germany is still divided. That division does a grievous wrong to a people . . . it creates a basic source of instability in Europe. Our talk of peace has little meaning if at the same time we perpetuate conditions endangering the peace. . . . In the interest of enduring peace, our solution should take account of the legitimate security interests of all concerned. That is why we insist a united Germany is entitled at its choice, to exercise its inherent right of collective self-defense.[38]

In other words, a "just" solution to the problem of Germany meant leaving a united Germany free to join the West's principal military alliance in Europe. But such a solution would have meant complete Russian capitulation on the German question and would have required no negotiation at all, since the Russians could achieve Eisenhower's "settlement" simply by withdrawing their forces.

The contradiction inherent in this approach was recognized by Kennan in 1957:

> The Western governments have insisted that such an all-German government must be entirely free to continue to adhere to the NATO Pact. . . . The Soviet Union is, of course, not a member of NATO; and while British, French, and American forces would presumably remain in Germany under the framework of the NATO system, one must assume that those of the Soviet Union would be expected to depart. If this is so, then Moscow is really being asked to abandon—as part of an agreement on German unification—the military and political bastion in Central Europe which it won by its military effort from 1941 to 1945, and to do this without any compensatory withdrawal of American armed power from the heart of the continent.[39]

The summit itself produced nothing in the way of substantive agreements.[40] The final communique took the form of a directive to the foreign ministers to pursue negotiations on three issues: European security and Germany, disarmament, and development of contacts between East and West.[41] The ministers in fact met in Geneva from October 27 through November 16, but achieved little, if anything. With the Western allies maintaining their approach, the Russians rejected all of the West's initiatives on German reunification and European security. Eisenhower concluded that "The clear breach of [the] Summit directive creates a condition where no confidence can be placed on agreements with [the] Soviet government and . . . we shall have to conduct our relations accordingly." [42]

Arms Control Treadmills

Thus, by the fall of 1955, after some promising breakthroughs, the Cold War relationship remained frozen in place. Despite the fact that the Russians had acquiesced in an Austrian settlement and, after Stalin's death, helped to facilitate an honorable exit by America from Korea, it appeared in Washington that nothing fundamental had changed. This mood colored and set limits on America's halfhearted, sporadic, and uncoordinated efforts to arrive at some sort of detente with Soviet Russia in the arms race. Moscow's disarmament proposals were habitually greeted with much the same suspicion and hostility in Washington with which Moscow itself tended to view all proposals emanating from the West. No major Russian proposal could be accepted at face value without searching scrutiny of the alleged ulterior motives concealed behind it; disarmament projects were commonly viewed as traps for the unwary, designed to strengthen Moscow's relative power position. More particularly, it was contended that, even granted effective Russian compliance with a disarmament agreement, the "natural" arsenal of weapons available to Soviet Russia and its

Marxist-Leninist allies—sabotage, intrigue, promotion of revolution, and guerrilla warfare—would, ironically, be enhanced by any meaningful disarmament.[43]

Eisenhower's first major attempt in this area was the so-called "atoms for peace" plan. In a major address before the UN General Assembly on December 8, 1953, the president proposed establishing an international agency for the control of atomic energy which, among other things, would be the recipient of periodic contributions of fissionable material for peaceful purposes. The proposal was certainly motivated in part by the fact that the Russians had exploded their first thermonuclear device in August, thereby jeopardizing the American monopoly. While the Russians dragged their feet for a while, in 1957 such an agency was in fact created—the International Atomic Energy Agency—an organ that would ultimately be responsible for spreading nuclear technology around the world, contributing in the process to the proliferation of nuclear weapons.[44] Just what actually motivated Eisenhower's initiative is open to debate. Eisenhower himself would later admit that he received advice that Russian participation in the program would be more detrimental for them "since the United States could afford to reduce its atomic stockpile by two or three times the amount the Russians might contribute, and still improve our relative position."[45]

By the fall of 1954 it was apparent that the Russians were approaching parity with America in nuclear technology, if not in the actual number of warheads in hand, and that Churchill's characterization of the peace of the world resting on a "balance of terror" was beginning to come true. The Russians now had begun to operationalize a long-range bomber capacity, and had moved rapidly ahead in thermonuclear capability. But throughout this period, as was the case with the German issue, the Eisenhower Administration accorded negotiations on arms control a lower priority than such other aspects of its strategy as maintenance of a credible nuclear deterrent, the preservation of harmony among its allies, and the determination to score "debating points" wherever possible at Moscow's expense.

It was this attitude that was prevailing within the Eisenhower administration when, in 1955–1957, America was presented with not one, but three Russian plans for general, internationally controlled and inspected disarmament. Each plan was based on an originally developed Western plan, each made substantial efforts to meet the West on a common ground of agreement, each was unconditionally rebuffed. On May 10, 1955, after nine years of resistance to all Western plans, Soviet Russia reversed itself and accepted the Western plan for manpower ceilings, reduction in conventional armaments, the Western timetable, the Western arrangement for the abolition of nuclear stocks and other weapons of mass-destruction, and the Western demand that government appropriations for armed forces and conventional armaments be reduced correspondingly.[46]

While there were problems in the Russian proposal, most notably restricting inspection posts to large infrastructure sites, the fact that they seemed prepared to address Western notions of international control and supervision was encouraging. The timing of the unprecedented disarmament proposal was no coincidence, for an awareness of the sequence of initiatives undetaken by both sides during the month of May is crucial for a proper understanding of what would ultimately transpire. Much as in the spring of 1947 involving the Truman Doctrine and the Marshall Plan, these actions did not have lives of their own but should be seen for what they really were—a series of reactive measures in context. On May 9, 1955, West Germany became a formal member of NATO, followed the next day by Moscow's dramatic arms control initiative. On May 14 Soviet Russia and the Eastern European states signed the Warsaw Pact. The next day, the Austrian State Treaty was signed. On May 26 Khrushchev and Bulganin flew to Belgrade to seek an understanding with the Yugoslavs.

When faced, however, in essence with its own proposals for complete and general disarmament, Washington responded by declaring its opposition to any plan for general disarmament, despite the fact that it had previously committed itself to this goal in a mutually agreed upon statement of principles with the other negotiating states.[47] The Russian proposals of 1955 were made, moreover, against a background of the specific "deeds" which had been demanded by Eisenhower at the outset of his administration as a test of Russian intentions with respect to peace. Even after the Russians signed the Austrian State Treaty, Washington would not even consider serious negotiations on disarmament, nor on Moscow's proposals, urged from 1952 to 1955, for an evacuation of troops from Germany on terms similar to that of the Austrian treaty.[48]

As for the controls proposed by the Russians:

[I]f they meant anything at all, they would have made an immense breach in the Iron Curtain—hundreds, if not thousands, of UN inspectors, chosen by the UN, "on an international basis," permanently in residence in Russia, with wide powers of access to military and other installations, and with the right to full information about all aspects of Russian military finance—in itself a powerful instrument of control. But for full measure the Russians also put forward their plan for the establishment of ground "Control Posts" at large ports, at railway junctions, on main motor highways and in aerodromes. This was to guard against the danger of surprise attack by modern weapons; it was to start before any measures of armament reduction began; it was a spontaneous Russian suggestion, which made a further great breach in the Iron Curtain.[49]

Eisenhower, recognizing that the American side had to make some sort of response to the dramatic Russian initiative, and that a summit conference was now the place to do it, instead of seeking to explore Moscow's offer, went to Geneva with his so-called "Open Skies" proposal. This inspection scheme called for unimpeded overflights of one another's territory for the purpose of verifying nuclear weapons development and troop deployments. The Russians did not bite. Given the open nature of American society, Eisenhower's proposal could hardly be said to be an even-handed approach to the issue. Since the Russians already knew the location of most American military bases, Eisenhower said, "mutual agreements for such overflights would undoubtedly benefit us more than the Russians, because we know very little about their installations."[50] Thus, the Geneva Conference failed to achieve much in the way of detente in the field of arms control as well. Perhaps the only real significance of the conference on this issue was the development of the beginning of a genuine mutual understanding of the dangers of nuclear war.

On May 14, 1956, new deeds were forthcoming from the Russians. Premier Bulganin announced that Soviet Russia was reducing its armed forces by another 1.2 million men, in addition to the 640,000 mustered out of the service in 1955. He also announced the withdrawal of 30,000 troops from East Germany, the placing of 375 warships in reserve, and the closing of several military schools.[51] Asked at a press conference what his reaction was to these statements, Dulles replied: "Well, it's a fair conclusion that I would rather have these men standing around doing guard duty than making atom bombs."[52] Other American officials echoed this view, pointing out that Russian military strength would not be significantly reduced, since so much depended on H-bombs and missiles. Few in official circles in Washington could find cause for optimism in these Russian initiatives.

In 1957, the Russians did accept the principle of aerial surveillance over portions of Russian territory and Eastern Europe (in return for similar rights over Western Europe and the Eastern part of America), only to have Washington recall its chief negotiator at these talks, Harold Stassen, for exceedling his authority in discussing counter-proposals with the Russians at the table. Arms control discussions having achieved precious little, the discussion shifted in 1957 to the possibility of limiting nuclear testing. When the Russians suddenly proposed a two-to-three-year moratorium on testing under some form of international inspection, Stassen was authorized to pursue negotiations on a separate test ban with the Russians at the UN.

But when his scientists informed him that they were on the verge of a major breakthrough on producing a "clean" thermonuclear weapon within a very few years, Eisenhower backed off his earlier support for a separate test ban agreement, reaffirming the traditional American position that a test ban would have to be part of a comprehensive treaty that included the cutting off of all nuclear weapons production. In the summer of 1957 Dulles presented an American proposal for a two-year suspension linked to a Russian agreement to cease weapons production—a proposal rejected by the Russians. Over the next year and a half, both sides jockeyed for position, each scoring occasional propaganda points at the other's expense. In the end, all that came out of these interactions was an unenforceable parallel moratorium on nuclear testing—one that was capable of being terminated at any time.[53]

To Engage or Disengage?

In a series of lectures delivered at Harvard University in the spring of 1957, the British Labour Party leader Hugh Gaitskell was among the first important figures in the West to recommend disengagement. The best hope for world peace, he said, lay in the evacuation of the danger area in Central Europe and the creation, by stages, of a disengaged zone until it covered the whole of Germany, Poland, Czechoslovakia, and Hungary. Within this zone armed forces would be subject to inspection and control. Finally, together with a permanent control on arms in these territories, there should be a multilateral European security plan, in which the various states in the neutral zone would have their territories guaranteed by the great states as well as by each other.

The three conditions necessary for the success of such a withdrawal, said Gaitskell, were, first, that Germany must accept her existing frontiers; second, that NATO must remain in being and American forces remain in Europe; and, third, that any such plan be put forward only after full agreement on it had been reached by all the members of the Atlantic Community.[54]

Kennan also addressed this issue in his Reith Lectures in London in November and December of the same year, arguing that the only realistic hope for a rollback of the Iron Curtain was disengagement. If Soviet Russia and America could somehow be persuaded to pull back from Germany, he said, a general withdrawal from Europe might follow. In the process, NATO and the Warsaw Pact could be dismantled, and an integration of the whole European economy along Common Market lines could be instituted. Ultimately, he declared himself prepared to see all American military forces withdrawn from the continent and eventually from Britain, so long as America's NATO obligations still remained. The "atomic deterrent," he maintained, would become operable at once if there were any attempt by the Russians to re-invade Europe.[55]

The views expressed by Gaitskell and Kennan touched off a heated debate on both sides of the Atlantic. Not surprisingly, the orthodox cold warriors were not amused. Acheson, articulating the view of the Cold War establishment, led the attack. "Mr. Kennan has never, in my judgment, grasped the realities of power relationships. . . . To Mr. Kennan there is no Soviet military threat in Europe."[56] More importantly, however, the comments by Gaitskell and Kennan apparently resonated in the Kremlin. In February, 1957, Khrushchev took up the question in an interview that he gave to columnist Joseph Alsop and Chester Bowles in Moscow. Both Russian and American troops should be withdrawn from Central Europe, he suggested, and the countries of Western Europe should withdraw their forces from each other's soil. Peace could then be assured by agreements between the Warsaw Pact and the NATO states. Fearful that West Germany would obtain nuclear weapons, the Polish foreign minister Adam Rapacki, with the evident blessing of Moscow, responded to the disengagement argument by calling for the creation of a nuclear-free zone in Central Europe. The so-called Rapacki Plan never had a chance.[57]

On October 4, 1957, Soviet Russia launched the world's first man-made satellite in space—a scant two months after they had fired the world's first intercontinental ballistic missile. These two events precipitated a virtual panic in the West. Suddenly "gaps" between American and Russian capabilities were found virtually everywhere. That same fall, the findings and recommendations of a committee headed by Ford Foundation member Rowan Gaither, Jr., were leaked to the newspapers. The Gaither Report painted a bleak picture of the future of American security, pointing out that Soviet Russia was developing weapons systems at a much faster pace than America, and that she might be in a position to launch a successful nuclear attack by the end of the decade.

Much like NSC-68 earlier, the Gaither Report called for a dramatically enhanced defense capability for America, advocating a major increase in offensive nuclear warmaking capacity, more conventional armed forces, improved civilian defenses, and a reorganization of the Defense Department. For starters, it advocated an increase in defense spending to $48 billion.[58] To his credit, Eisenhower rejected most of the report's recommendations, refusing to turn the country "into a garrison state." It would later become evident that he had another reason for going slow with Gaither's recommended buildup. Beginning in 1956, the CIA had initiated a series of high-altitude reconnaisance flights over Soviet Russia—overflights which proved conclusively that notions of missile and bomber gaps were greatly exaggerated. America, it seems, still retained a signi-ficant lead in stragegic weapons.[59]

On December 10, 1957, Premier Bulganin wrote a long letter to Eisenhower, reviewing the events of the previous several months, and making a number of suggestions for an improvement in relations. Reacting to the American administration's relentless buildup of nuclear weapons, and the announced intent to station tactical nuclear weapons in Europe, including West Germany, the note pointed to these military preparations as part of a war scare based on the alleged aggressive actions of Soviet Russia. Pointing out that the possession of these weapons might result in an arms race among the Europeans, with consequences that might not be expected or controllable, the note reminded Eisenhower that major wars have sometimes resulted from such situations.

Arguing that the so-called position-of-strength policy had not had positive results for either side, and that something dramatic was needed to break the vise of the Cold War, Bulganin went on to propose that there be an agreement by both sides not to station nuclear weapons on German soil, that both Germanys commit not to produce such weapons, that Czechoslovakia and Hungary also agree not to station such weapons on their territories, that NATO and the Warsaw Pact conclude a non-aggression treaty among themselves, that both sides stop propaganda in the mass media, and that, ultimately, the goal should be to withdraw all military forces from NATO and Warsaw Pact countries, and employ collective security as an alternative.[60]

Nothing substantive resulted from this proposal. Throughout 1958 both sides continued to develop their respective nuclear arsenals, engaging from time to time in propaganda exchanges of nuclear missile bluff. One particular aspect of these developments would prove to be particularly controversial—the stationing of nuclear missiles in West Germany. As a result of its reluctance to put together the conventional forces required of it under its NATO obligations, Bonn, beginning early in 1957, demanded nuclear-armed missiles, artillery capable of firing nuclear shells, and fighter bombers able to carry nuclear bombs. This in turn precipitated a flurry of concern among European leaders, worried about the danger of a full-fledged arms race in Central Europe. Proposals were soon forthcoming from the capitals of Western Europe calling for the reunification and neutralization of Germany.

Meanwhile, in June 1958 Charles de Gaulle returned to power in France. Harboring deep reservations about British and American pre-eminence within the Western alliance, and still embittered over Eisenhower's conduct in the Suez crisis of 1956, de Gaulle made it perfectly clear that what he would be about was the reestablishment of French *grandeur*. From Washington's perspective, what that might mean in practice was the advancement of "neutralist" policies within the NATO alliance—something that would in fact come to pass. NATO was beginning to lose its monolithic (that is to say American-dominated) character. The widening split within NATO became even more apparent in late 1958 when France, West Germany, Italy, and the Benelux countries prepared for the formal commencement of the European Economic Community (EEC) to officially commence January 1,1959.

Signed in early 1957, the EEC agreement called for the establishment of an economic customs union within fifteen years. The immediate impact of the plan was as much political as economic, for the EEC, by creating a middle bloc of states between Moscow and Washington—one in which West Germany would now be more firmly tied to Western Europe—represented a kind of clarion call for independence from American domination of Europe.[61] The Russians viewed these developments with considerable anxiety. The future potential of the EEC, combined with the now distinct possibility of West German hands on nuclear weapons, raised for Moscow once again the specter of a militarized and economically aggressive Germany. In the fall of 1958 the Russians decided to act and, in so doing, focused on the fulcrum that could well affect the balance of power in Europe—Berlin.

Crisis in Berlin

On November 10, 1958, Khrushchev reignited the long-simmering Berlin problem by announcing Moscow's intentions of signing a separate treaty with East Germany. The move caught the West by surprise—one which, if carried out, might well put into jeopardy the occupation rights of the Western allies in that city. On November 27, a note was sent to the Western occupying powers specifying that if a negotiated solution to the Berlin problem could not be brought off, such a treaty would be signed within six months. Why did

Khrushchev issue the ultimatum at that moment? In all probability it came about for several reasons.[62]

Certainly, the Russians had long harbored a deep-seated fear of a rearmed Germany. After 1949 Moscow's German policy had always been two-pronged: propping up the East German regime and containing the Federal Republic. When it became apparent that there was little that the Russians could do to forestall a West German integration into NATO, Moscow at first sought to normalize its relationship with the Bonn government, with an emphasis on undermining Chancellor Konrad Adenauer's staunchly pro-Western line. This is what prompted a meeting, at the Russian's suggestion, between Khrushchev and Adenauer in Moscow in September, 1955.

However, by the spring of 1957 the Russians had begun to move in a different direction, spurred by comments by Adenauer and his state-secretary fof foreign affairs, Heinrich von Brentano, that the FRG was on the verge of adopting a program of nuclear armament.[63]   The Russians were particularly irritated by Adenauer's new assertiveness in demanding the return of old German lands annexed after the war by Soviet Russia, Poland and Czechoslovakia. This so-called "revanchism" in the FRG, in combination with the burgeoning "economic miracle" of West German economic recovery, could not be ignored by the Russias, who viewed all of this as a growing threat to geopolitical stability in central and eastern Europe.[64]

Second, the menacing rise of West Germany coincided with an aggravation of the economic situation in the GDR. The disparity in living standards between the two German states produced an ever growing flight of skilled workers and professionals from the GDR through the open border in Berlin.   Ever since 1949, some three million East Germans had fled for the West in what amounted to a veritable brain drain of its best educated and most productive people. It now came to be suspected that the FRG had more economic leverage over the GDR than was generally recognized. There was, in other words, a danger of "conquest without war" by means of economic strangulation.   The communist party regime in the East had been imploring Moscow for some time to do something about it.[65]

Third, there was the internal political situation in Soviet Russia itself. In June, 1957, hardliners in the CPSU, proceeding from the view that Khrushchev was weak and had endeavored to make too many compromises with the West, sought to remove him from power. Although the coup leaders, led by former foreign minister Molotov, failed, the abortive coup may well have strongly affected Khrushchev's subsequent foreign policy. As America had not responded to his initiatives and continued to support the FRG's rearmament, all of this may very well have been on Khrushchev's mind as the Berlin showdown was unfolding.[66]

Finally, and perhaps most importantly, the strategic situation now seemed to require some sort of decisive action. At one level, it appeared to favor Moscow. The Russian success with Sputnik, hard on the heels of their successful testing of a prototype ICBM, may well have convinced the Russian Politburo that a major shift in the military balance of power had taken place, and that it was a good time to try to take maximum advantage of a situation in which Moscow had some strategic trump cards to play. While the events of 1955–1956 in Europe were a cause for concern, they also represented an opportunity to play on the growing splits within the Western bloc to the end of obtaining advantages for Soviet Russia. But on another level worrisome developments had taken place within the socialist camp itself. With the apparent shift in the balance of power in favor of the Russians, Moscow now was under increasing pressure from China to play hard ball with the West.[67]

Ever since coming to power, Khrushchev had regarded Sino-Russian relations to be one of the cornerstones of his foreign policy. Preserving and strengthening Soviet Russia's alliance with Peking was a long-standing priroity. Beginning in the fall of 1957, however, the PRC leadership had begun to challenge Khrushchev's authority in the international arena. Arguing that Russia's superior strength cast her in a unique position to challenge Western hegemony throughout the world, the Chinese urged a tougher line on the Russians. Any temporizing with the Americans was simply unnecessay and uncalled for.

In August, 1958, immediately after Khrushchev's visit to Peking, and without his knowledge, the PRC began preparations for retaking several off-short islands occupied by the Kuomintang government. The resulting crisis involving the United States, was a shock for the Russians who now faced the possibility of a major war between its main ally and the U.S. Only after some not inconsiderable diplomatic exersion were the Russians able to disuade the Chinese to refrain from attacking these islands. But as compensation, Khrushchev now had to demonstrate he was decisive in confronting the West and the FRG in their campaign against the GDR.[68]

By forcing the issue of Berlin, Khrushchev may have been gambling that by getting the West to agree to a permanently-divided Germany, he would remove for all time the specter of a united Germany aligned with the West and armed with nuclear weapons aimed at Soviet Russia. That this ultimatum came at this time is not coincidental, as Washington had only just recently begun stationing in Western Europe artillery and aircraft capable of employing nuclear warheads.[69]

There was considerable division among the Western allies as to how best to respond to the Russian demand. The British, fearing for their safety in the face of Soviet Russia's new-found capability to devastate their island nation, expressed a willingness to explore the idea of making Berlin a free city.[70] The French, with Charles de Gaulle now back in power, exhibited little enthusiasm for a unified Germany but agreed that confronting the Russians over Berlin was necessary. After some difficult discussions, the Allies agreed to reject the six-months ultimatum, reaffirming their occupation rights in Berlin on the basis of the agreements reached at the end of World War II. They did, however, indicate a willingness to bargain on the subject, but only as part of a broader settlement the full range of issues concerning Germany.

There the matter rested until the following March when the British passed along the word that the Russians would agree to call off the May 27 deadline if the West committed to a new summit conference. Eisenhower stonewalled, recalling the results of the 1955 meeting, but ultimately agreed to a foreign ministers conference with the Russians. While nothing substantive came of those meetings, an invitation was issued to Khrushchev to visit America in 1959. As a result of that visit, tensions over Berlin eased, and Khrushchev was prevailed upon to remove the time limit on those discussions. At the same time, Eisenhower acquiesced to a summit conference, scheduled for May 1960.

The May 1960 summit conference was a disaster. The ill-fated CIA reconnaisance flight of Francis Gary Powers on May 1, 1960, doomed the conference before it began.[71] Two issues headed the agenda: Berlin and a comprehensive test-ban treaty. Neither issue was addressed at the conference, as Khrushchev used his opening remarks to denounce Eisenhower's authorization of overflights in Russian airspace and his refusal to apologize for them, and then walked out of the talks. In the ensuing months, Khrushchev ruled out any further negotiations on Berlin, while the test-ban talks at Geneva dragged on to an inconclusive end in August. For the remaining months of his presidency, Eisenhower concluded, there was "nothing left for him to do."[72]

The 1960 summit conference debacle clearly demonstrated how deeply entrenched Cold War interests could block any meaningful resolution of the longstanding impasse. The Russians could have waited until the results of the conference before interdicting one of the CIA overflights. The Americans could have suspended the flights in the period preceeding the meeting. Or Moscow could have kept quiet in the meantime, hoping that the CIA had learned its lesson and would stop the flights.

In any event, it may well be that Khrushchev decided in the final days before the conference that there was more to be gained at that time from embarrassing and humiliating the American president publicly. Several weeks before the summit, the Chinese published a militant manifesto that represented a barely disguised attack on what they called Russian "revisionism"—a euphemism for a catalogue of sins that were charged to Moscow. The whole international Communist Party movement now appeared headed for a major upheaval, as various parties had already begun to choose up sides. Khrushchev may have calculated that, in order to forestall a major split and to line up support for his own policies, a get-tough policy toward America was in order.[73] Then, too, an equally influential factor in Khrushchev's conduct may have stemmed from pressure by domestic Communist Party (CPSU) hard liners, in alliance with the Russian military, who viewed any accommodation with the West as under-mining Soviet Russia's security. Taking a tough stand would therefore serve to shore up his political base of support at home.[74]

Thus, although there is no conclusive evidence that either Eisenhower or Khrushchev deliberately provoked the incident, both sides conducted themselves in a manner which seemed designed to antagonize the other. Prior positions assumed on other issues, plus the unfolding dynamics of the rhetoric of response, may well have preordained the outcome of the meeting, once the plane was shot down.[75]

Covert Action—The New Cold War Weapon

For America, the fundamental challenge of the Bolshevik revolution had never been Russian military power but rather the threat it posed to Western political and economic institutions that had developed and ripened over many decades. Militarily, the West was never on the defensive in the Cold War; philosophically it was a different matter as the Western democracies had not shown up well in confronting fascism before World War II. Moreover, the "left" had never really disappeared during the war, leading the struggle against German occupation and the collaborationist regimes in many of the countries occupied by the Germans. Now, in the first postwar decade, came the added challenge of decolonization and the great upheaval in China.

Success could not be assured without first grasping the essential point that this was a global ideological crisis. For some, the contrast between a divided West, still suffering from past mistakes and facing the challenge of decolonization, and the seemingly single-minded purposes of Russian communism was frightening, to say the least. And because, it was felt, the Kremlin recognized no moral standard except "that which serves the revolution," it was therefore mandatory to counter this unbridled evil by intervening wherever necessary to thwart it. What that came to mean in practice by the time of Secretary Dulles was a kind of charter for American subversion of communist regimes, eventually to be defined only by reference to the Russian "design." During the Eisenhower administration distinctions between direct actions against Soviet Russia and frustrating the "design" became functionally irrelevant.

Flowing from this mindset, it should not be surprising that the Eisenhower administration would perfect another method of achieving its foreign policy objectives—covert action. The attraction of covert action in support of anti-communist elements in the Third World held a particular attraction for Eisenhower and Dulles, because the application of a little manipulation rapidly came to be viewed as one tactic that could have dramatic results for relatively little expenditure of the country's resources. Thus it came to pass that the Central Intelligence Agency, created by President Truman in 1947, would play a significant role under President Eisenhower in the country's overriding interest in containing communism.

The 1950s were the golden age of the CIA. Few questions were asked and even fewer answers given. The budget for its activities was well hidden, and congressional oversight committees preferred not to be told about its activities. Ultimately, the CIA operated on the basis of an understanding by all concerned that, because the other side engaged routinely in "dirty tricks," covert action on our part was certainly called for. It did not take long in this regard for the Eisenhower administration to get the ball rolling.

The CIA's initial efforts were deemed successes. The first one took place in Iran. In 1951, a nationalist regime led by Mohammed Mossadegh had come to power in that country and forced the Western-backed Shah Mohammed Pahlavi into exile, while nationalizing that country's oil field, and appeared in early 1953 to be moving closer to that country's indigenous Communist Party—all to the chagrin of the British who had heretofore controlled Iranian oil production. CIA agents were sent into the country and anti-Mossadegh riots were instigated, leading to his downfall. With the Shah restored to his throne and oil supplies to the West secured, the "communist tide" had been stopped in Iran.[76]

In Guatemala, as well, the CIA was authorized by the President to intervene in a domestic situation that appeared to bode ill for American interests. In 1951, Jacob Arbenz Guzman had become president of the country. An anti-American leftist, Arbenz worked closely with that country's Communist Party in carrying out an agrarian reform program. Thousands of acres of the United Fruit Company's holdings were expropriated. In response to American pressure to back down, Arbenz announced that he would purchase weapons from Czechoslovakia in self-defense. Concerns about the security of the Panama Canal were soon forthcoming. Eisenhower then authorized a covert operation designed to remove Arbenz from office. Training and military support were provided to a designated opponent who, in due course, succeeded in overthrowing Arbenz.[77]

These early successes came to be emblamatic of the administration's approach to dealing with non-Western reform movements—reflective, as they were, of an orientation toward the Third World that would prove over time to be extremely destructive for America's national interests.

THE THIRD WORLD: WAR BY PROXY

Because Dulles believed that the two superpowers should make the decisions for their respective camps, he refused to accept, perhaps even to recognize, the world's diversity. For Dulles, what was happening elsewhere in the world, outside the immediate sphere of Russian-American conflict, was essentially unimportant and peripheral to the morality play taking place on center stage. Everything else should only be seen through the prism of the Cold War struggle.[78] What this meant in practice was the triumph of a view that saw these other actors as pawns to be manipulated by the two giants. A number of implications flowed from this perspective, not the least of which was that the revolution of rising expectations then under way in the non-Western world was at the very least downplayed, if not having escaped the notice of the Eisenhower administration altogether.

America had provided verbal support for the anti-colonial revolutions that had gripped Africa and Asia in the immediate post-1945 period, but we found it much more difficult to adjust to the burgeoning social and economic revolutions that followed. These transformations were necessary in order to get out from under their dependence on the West that still controlled their principal sources of income by means of extractive industries. To do that required monetary capital which could be obtained in only one of two ways—massive loans from the outside, something America was not willing to undertake, or nationalization of their major foreign holdings. This transformation also would necessitate more centralized state control and planning in order to utilize most effectively what resources they had.

This hard reality posed a series of dilemmas for America. As nationalizations began to occur more frequently, and American business corporations lost money when their plants, mines and plantations (and those of their allies) were expropriated, demands for action resonated on Wall Street and Capitol Hill. And as most of these emerging polities did not pay for what they seized, either because they did not have the money to do so, or because as a result of their long experience with Western exploitation they felt they deserved whatever they took, the pressure for getting tough with these people became enormous. This, combined with America's pervasive anti-communist orientation, would lead to a fundamental misperception by the president and his advisors of the basic positions and policies of not a few of these newly-emergent non-Western countries.

What this meant in practice was that throughout Eisenhower's two terms in office America sought to follow a policy designed in general to discourage radical change and to aid any government in power, including its incorporation into the country's anti-communist alliance network, regardless of its ideological nature, provided it was avowedly anti-communist.[79] This orientation flowed from certain assumptions that both Eisenhower and Dulles held concerning the nature of social change in the world—views expressive of America's conception of stability and order. Under Dulles, America developed the habit of defining social change as communist aggression and/or subversion. As Richard Barnet and others have ably pointed out, there were a number of reasons for that, the two principal ones being the need of American business to maintain an extractive economy in the Third World, and the administration's desire to construct bases around Russia and China.[80] Unfortunately, American decision-makers more often than not defined the issues in such a way that for most revolutionary social movements then in progress elsewhere in the worl, to pursue what they desired both nationally and internationally was, in effect, to oppose America.

Most of the anti-communist governments during this period were those that feared fundamental change at home and that were more than willing to join America's military arrangements in order to receive the necessary support that would bolster them against the constructive forces making for constitutional internal change.[81] On the other hand, because many of the new states proved to be very weak politically, as well as underdeveloped economically, their leaders could well remember their periods of colonial subjugation. Fearful that their new independence would be compromised, they sought rather to insulate their new sovereignties from the major quarrels that they refused to recognize as their own. Thus, most of the national leaders of the newly-emergent Third World states had a genuine interest in attempting to shift the burden of defense against Russian "aggression" to others.[82]

But the administration was adamant. It was absolutely mandatory that all work together to build bulwarks against the aggressive "world communist bloc," and any state that had the temerity to profess neutrality in the struggle quickly earned the wrath of the American State Department. In addition, since even many Western states opposed the American policies that produced these results, the process served to weaken Washington's ability to counter Russian probes in the so-called Third World. As a result, coalition problems tended to be exacerbated, and the more enligthened elements in the non-Western world disaffected. Nowhere was this attitude in dealing with the emerging countries of the Third World more destructively exemplified than in the Eisenhower administration's ongoing attempts to forge alliance blocs in these regions.

Dulles and the Collector's Approach to Alliances

During the eight years of the Eisenhower presidency, a firmly-rooted approach to alliances came to be institutionalized into an intricate web of concrete policies. In the aftermath of the Korean War, and with new crises seemingly occurring everywhere at once, the traditional view of alliances as "mere" pacts of mutual military cooperation for limited purposes lost its attraction. Under Dulles's whiplash leadership, America sought to transform its alliances into citidels of capability directed against specific enemies rather than against aggression in general. And in the face of a perceived intensifying Russian and Chinese threat to America's well-being, its alliance policy, while still couched ostensibly in defensive terminology, was to be directed toward the overt development of an extensive system of offensive alignments in which military pacts would form the iron core.[83] Thus, under Dulles's guidance, American alliance policy during the Eisenhower era became more affixed than ever before to the idea that communism in the world was the great menace which required the mustering of all the forces available to the "free world" to counter. It did not take long for the new administration to indicate where its initial priorities lay.

The Latin American Prototype. At the Tenth Inter-American Conference of Hemispheric States, held in Caracas, Venezuela, in the spring of 1954, the American delegation introduced a resolution designed to prevent the spread of communist imperialism in the Western Hemisphere. Known as the Declaration of Caracas, the resolution was officially labeled a "Declaration of Solidarity for the Preservation of the Political Integrity of the American States Against

International Communist Intervention."[84] The American mood at the conference was a decidedly somber one. In the course of the debate over the proposal, the foreign minister of Guatemala asked Secretary Dulles what was meant by "international communism." Dulles replied: "International communism is that farflung clandestine political organization which is operated by the leaders of the Communist Party of the Soviet Union. Since 1939 it has brought fifteen once independent nations into a state of abject servitude. . . . The total constitutes not a theory, not a doctrine, but an aggressive, tough, political force, backed by great resources, and serving the most ruthless empire of modern times."[85]

Dulles addressed the conference several times and was successful in the end in having his resolution passed, but only in the face of considerable uneasiness and some opposition. A number of delegates felt that "the condemnation of a particular type of political arrangement in the Americas—even one abetted or inspired from outside the hemisphere—was difficult to reconcile with the principle of non-intervention in internal affairs."[86] Still others felt that the primary problems of Latin America were social and economic rather than political: "Our peoples expect something more than a new way of fighting Communism . . . something appropriate to improve their welfare and progress. In the absence of constructive economic and social measures, more opposition to Communism might even give it prestige and . . . spread it."[87]

Those comments would prove to be prophetic. Throughout his tenure in office, Eisenhower's neglect of Latin America, except as a function of preventing communist infiltration of the region, would prove to a growing source of embarrassment and frustration for his administration. To the degree that America ignored the growing demands for political, economic, and social justice in Latin America, their very lack of realization erupted into increasing anti-American hostility. The bird would come home to roost in Cuba. As events unfolded in that country beginning in 1953 with little known Fidel Castro's abortive assault on a government army barracks in Santiago, Cuba would come to epitomize Eisenhower's limited world view. That upheaval would also demonstrate the constraints within which every American president thereafter would have to operate in dealing with Third World revolution.

Castro's revolution was the culmination of a long winter of discontent among Cuban liberals and nationalists who had had their fill of indigenous dictators trampling over their people, and who inevitably did Washington's bidding. Throughout most of the first half century of Cuban independence, American economic interests controlled the island's suguar, rum, mining, and utility industries. Fulgencio Batista had come to power by democratic means in 1940, serviing one term before stepping aside. But as army chief of staff, he nullified the 1952 election, placing himself in office by *golpe de estado*, and choosing to rule as a dictator thereafter. His primary support was the army, trained and equipped by Washington, and his policies became more repressive. The 1952 *golpe* proved to a major turning point in Cuban history, for Batista's actions represented a clear violation of the great 1940 Cuban constitution—one of the most democratic documents of its kind in Latin America—and one which had taken many years of struggle to consummate.

Castro emerged in the mid-1950s at the head of a coalition of anti-Batista opponents, determined to reinvigorate the guarantees of the 1940 document. The dictator was driven from power by January 1959. At first, Castro was welcomed by the American public as a democratic reformer, his American supporters banking on him to restore civil liberties, continue to look to Washington for guidance, and even to introduce gradual and adequately compensated land reform, but not at the expense of tampering with America's monopoly of Cuba's plantation economy. But from the beginning, the Eisenhower administration had doubts about Castro's credentials. Warned by the CIA that "communists" might well be involved in the new Cuban government, Eisenhower and Dulles began to look for a third alternative—neither a Batista nor a Castro. In this mindset, the whole American approach to the non-Western world would be encapsulated: locate a liberal who would not upset the prevailing economic order but who would govern in a reasonably democratic manner. It was not to be. In Cuba, as in many other similar places, there could be no point in having a genuine social revolution if the basic underlying economic infrastructure was left untouched.

In the spring of 1959, Castro sought an audience with Eisenhower to sort things out. The president refused, instead sending his vice-president, Richard Nixon, to New York City to meet with the Cuban leader. It would prove to be a dialogue of the deaf. Washington rejected Castro's request for a loan, and relations steadily deteriorated thereafter. In the ensuing months, American-owned property in Cuba began to be expropriated without adequate compensation, although some payments were offered by the Cuban government. Incrementally, Havana's policies became more blatantly anti-American in character, leading in the summer of 1960 to a wholesale nationalization of foreign economic interests. In June, Washington cut off the annual sugar quota subsidy and, finally, severed diplomatic relations in January 1961.

Beginning in early 1960, the Russian government saw an opportunity to become involved in Cuba as a substitute for traditional American domination. Welcoming Castro as a new force to be reckoned with in Latin America, Khrushchev pronounced the Monroe Doctrine dead, and in February signed a trade agreement to exchange Cuban sugar for Russian oil and machinery. Over the next two years, as American involvement and influence in Cuba waned, that of Soviet Russia grew, culminating in 1961 with Castro's public statement that he was now a Marxist-Leninist, and that Cuba's relationship with Moscow would be the centerpiece of its foreign policy. Thus, America's approach to Cuba would come to represent the quintessence of the self-fulfilling prophecy.[88]

On Dealing with the Middle East.   Whatever else may be said about President Truman's decision to sponsor the creation of Israel in 1948, by making it, he thereby involved American Middle East policy in a serious inner contradiction. The Truman administration apparently was not fully cognizant that American support of Israel's creation would represent a basic conflict with the policy of containment of Soviet Russia, at that very moment being worked out in Washington. Like a number of foreign policy decisions since that time, the decision to recognize Israel was made impulsively and not as the result of a deliberate intention to subordinate one set of interests to another.[89] Having thrown in their lot with Zionism in aiding the creation of Israel, American decision makers, in the waning months of the Truman administration, proceeded at the same time to seek ways and means to arm the Arabs as allies against Russia, not realizing that arms in Arab hands were more likely to be used against Israel than in defense against communist subversion. The consequent dilemma in American Middle East policy did not, however, become readily apparent until the succeeding administration seriously undertook in the mid-1950s to build a Middle East alliance against Moscow.

When Dwight Eisenhower took office in January 1953 his initial moves only complicated these problems. Far more preoccupied than his predecessor with security pacts, Secretary Dulles proceeded to act in the Middle East as if Israel did not exist. The rapidly proliferating investment of American oil companies in this part of the world doubtless was partly responsible for the new emphasis. In even larger measure, however, the growing pro-Arab orientation of American foreign policy in the 1950s was born of a new American preoccupation with completing, through a Middle Eastern military alliance, the band of physical encirclement of the Russo-Sino periphery. Yet, perhaps in no other area of the world was America's commitment to the containment of communism more inimical to the best interests of the American people.

An early example of this approach occurred in Egypt in 1954–1955. In 1952 the Egyptian monarchy was overthrown in a military coup led by an obscure young army officer, Gamal Abdel Nasser. Heretofore pro-British, Egypt began to assert itself as a non-aligned country. More disturbingly, from Washington's perspective, Nasser, in a desire to modernize his military in the context of the Arab world's hostility toward Israel, opened negotiations with both the West and the Russian bloc for weapons. This would eventually lead in September 1955 to an arms deal with Czechoslovakia.

Partly to counter this potentially destabalizing development, Eisenhower and Dulles expressed an interest in helping Egypt finance a proposed massive hydroelectric project on the lower Nile River designed to modernize the Egyptian economy. Negotiations among the British, Americans and Egyptians culminated in February, 1956 in a $1.3 billion loan. Unfortunately, Dulles had miscalculated, running into a firestorm of domestic opposition from special interest groups and members of Congress.[90] Under pressure to provide arms to Israel as compensation for possible Russian-bloc military assistance to Egypt and Syria, Dulles refused. The deal languished for five months, while Dulles tried to explain his policy to a growing array of critics. Dulles finally began to back off when in April 1956 Nasser forged a military pact with Saudi Arabia, Syria, and Yemen, while refusing to repudiate the Czech arms deal. When

Nasser the following month extended diplomatic recognition to the Peking regime as the *de jure* government of China, that was the last straw.

Assuming that Soviet Russia could not and would not step into the breach and bail out the Egyptian leader, Dulles announced on July 19, 1956, that the dam project offer was now withdrawn. One week later Nasser seized the Suez Canal, nationalizing the British-controlled holding company that had run the canal since its opening in 1867, and in a single stroke gaining access to the $25 million annual operating revenue from the canal. Nasser's action provoked a strong negative reaction from the British and French, dependent on the canal for the movement of oil from the Persian Gulf to Europe. Demanding restoration of control over the canal, London and Paris received scant support from Washington. Difficult and protracted negotiations ensued. Warned by the British in late summer that they might take military action if the matter was not resolved quickly, Dulles failed to apply pressure on Egypt, refusing to take the British comments seriously.[91]

In October 1956 the Israelis, British and French launched a sudden surprise attack on Egypt, Israeli armor quickly overrunning the Sinai peninsula, while British and French paratroopers landed in the canal zone to neutralize Egyptian forces. Not having been consulted about the operation, Eisenhower reacted furiously, ultimately working in concert with Soviet Russia at the UN to compel the invaders to withdraw. The upshot of all of this was that Nasser emerged from these events a hero in the Arab world, and Soviet Russia entered the scene as a major player for the foreseeable future.[92] The administration's policies on this issue turned out to be a disaster, as Washington misjudged the importance of the dam project to Nasser, misunderstood his attitude toward the Russians, and, above all, confused Egyptian nationalism and nonalignment with a pro-communist orientation. Most importantly, we alienated our most important allies, Great Britain and France, who would thereafter never again deal with America in quite the same way.[93]

Perhaps the most injurious example of this Pyrrhic policy was Dulles's attempt to construct a military alliance in the area that would link NATO in the West with SEATO in the East. What Dulles did in fact accomplish with this design was to sponsor the one idea predictably certain to make Egypt hostile to the West: the arming of Iraq, Egypt's chief rival for Arab leadership at the time, and to link it with Britain, Turkey, Iran, and Pakistan in the so-called "Northern Tier" Alliance. The product of this inept piece of Cold War strategy, the Baghdad Pact, was incipient weakness rather than manifest strength.

The pact split the Arab world without erecting even the shadow of a military barrier to Moscow's policies. Moreover, it was the arming of Iraq that caused Egypt to seek and obtain arms from Moscow and its allies, thus opening the door to Russian political penetration of the entire Middle East area.[94] Russia's arming of Egypt, in turn, upset the Arab-Israeli balance of military power, which helped pave the way for war in the fall of 1956. The Baghdad fiasco illustrates clearly how self-defeating it is to arm states against a danger the existence of which they do not recognize, or at least subordinate to other policies, especially when such states have unresolved disputes with their neighbors.

In like manner, Pakistan, in opting in 1954 for membership in the Southeast Treaty Organization, had not been particularly interested in obtaining American military assistance because it was afraid of a Russian or Chinese invasion but because she wanted to strengthen her position with respect to India. The point is that rearming Pakistan added little strength to the anti-Russian *cordon sanitaire*; what it did accomplish was to exacerbate the precarious balance between India and Pakistan, contributing to a major skirmish in 1965 between those two states over Kashmir. In the Pakistani instance, the arrangements with that country so alarmed neighboring India that America was soon forced to declare that none of the military equipment given Pakistan could be used against India in case of war between the two sub-Asian countries. That this ban would prove to be difficult to enforce became rather apparent when one reviews the Kashmir fighting in the fall of 1965, and the major military conflict between the two countries in 1971 over Bengladesh.[95]

After Eisenhower's reelection in the fall of 1956, he felt that it was time to shore up American interests in the Middle East. The Suez debacle had seriously weakened the Baghdad Pact, and in its wake Nasser had begun pushing for a political unification of the Arab peoples—an approch that would bear some fruit two years later in the union of Egypt, Syria, and Yemen in the guise of the so-called United Arab Republic (UAR). In early January 1957, the president asked Congress for authorization to extend economic and military aid and, if necessary, to employ American military forces in the region if any country there asked for help against "communist-instigated armed aggression." The resulting resolution, to be known as the "Eisenhower Doctrine," was agreed to in March, but only after some difficulties in the Senate.[96]

Within a month of its passage, King Hussein of Jordan came under assault from pro-Nasser elements inside his country who he labeled communists. Eisenhower, invoking his doctrine, dispatched $10 million in assistance and ordered the Sixth Fleet to steam close to Jordan. The official State Department justification for the action was that America was acting to safeguard the "independence and integrity of the nations of the Middle East."[97] America's strident anti-communism had now become sanctified into a policy dogma, legitimized by the Congress, wherein America itself would determine where, when, and under what conditions it would intervene to save others from the scourge of communist subversion.

It would not end there. Throughout the first half of 1959, Dulles frequently expressed concern that the growing influence of the UAR might endanger friendly Iraq, Jordan and Lebanon. On July 14, a military coup overthrew the pro-Western Iraqi monarchy and established a regime friendly to the UAR. Now the Baghdad Pact suddenly had a large fissure in it. Repercussions were immediately felt in Lebanon, where pro-Nasser factions had been fighting the

Christian-dominated government. After receiving an urgent telephone call that same morning from the Lebanese president, and after hurried consultations with congressional leaders, Eisenhower authorized the landing of some 14,000 American troops in Lebanon to quell the threat of civil war. Nasser journeyed to Moscow seeking Russian assistance, but Khrushchev refused. As Dulles would later explain to the cabinet, America had once again frustrated Stalin's and Lenin's prophecies that communism would triumph by getting at the capitalist West through the non-Western world.[98]

The decision to intervene in Lebanon displayed America's historic unilateralism to the full—an action that risked general war on behalf of a less-than-democratic government that was not truly representative of the Islamic elements in the country. While Eisenhower said he had no desire to take the place of the UN as the primary peacekeeping body in the world, America had acted alone because it was felt that only swift action would suffice. The Lebanon action also displayed reasoning by analogy to the fullest. In justifying the intervention in Lebanon in 1958, Eisenhower, invoking the precedent of Greece and the Truman Doctrine, called attention to the "Communist takeover of Czechoslovakia, the Communist conquest of the China mainland in 1949 and their attempts to take over Korea and Indochina."[99]

In the Middle East, as in Asia, the natural role for America would have been to act as a constructive force for moderation between the reactionary tendencies of the colonial states and the haste with which their colonies sought to attain national independence, all the while seeking to facilitate the politics of compromise. The Eisenhower Administration failed to play this role chiefly because of its single-minded concern with the building of a military retaining wall against Russian-inspired aggression and subversion, often in almost total disregard of local sentiments, social conditions, and the attendant political implications.[100]

Seeking to Align Southeast Asia. For much the same reasons, America's involvement in Southeast Asia was problematical. The obstacles to alliance-building in 1954 were substantial. Yet Secretary Dulles insisted upon a treaty, the effects of which would prove to be at best superfluous and at worst, contributory to the subsequent American tragedy in Vietnam.

The American desire to forge an anti-communist pact with the countries of Southeast Asia was born of the French military involvement in Indochina, and of the undesirable conclusion, in our view, to that struggle at the conference table in July of that year. President Eisenhower had warned that a communist victory in Indochina might topple other free governments in Asia like "a row of dominoes,"[101] but the growing supremacy of the Vietminh in most of Vietnam and the French government's determination to come to terms after Dienbienphu in May, precluded any chance of continuing the struggle.[102]

The armistice, signed in July 1954, duly recognized Vietminh military successes in Indochina. Vietnam was divided at the seventeenth parallel, with the Vietminh in control of the northern "regroupment zone" and the Western-

backed regime of Emperor Bao Dai installed in the South, while all the
Indochinese states became fully independent. The armistice called for internationally supervised elections by 1956 to determine the reunification of
Vietnam. As for Laos and Cambodia, while they lost no territory and retained
non-communist governments, they were in effect neutralized by agreeing not to
join regional alliances or to allow foreign bases and troops on their soil.

But Washington had other ideas. The Eisenhower administration refused to
sign the Geneva agreements. Dulles acquiesced in them because he had no
choice, but avoided actually endorsing the final product, announcing instead that
America would resist future communist attempts to overrun any part of
Southeast Asia.[103] When the time came, Washington supported Bao Dai and his
successor, Ngo Dinh Diem, in their refusal to join in the electoral procedure. In
September 1954 Dulles announced that henceforth American aid would go
directly to the government in the southern regroupment zone. The next month
American military advisers began training a South Vietnamese army. In July
1955 the French pulled out of Vietnam altogether and, with American support,
Diem announced that elections would not be held in the South. Recognizing
that Ho Chi-minh would most likely win any free election rather easily,
Eisenhower and Dulles rationalized the cancellation of the election by stating
that the people of South Vietnam were in no position to make a real choice
since they did not understand the alternative to Ho, or even that he was a
communist agent of the Russians and Chinese.[104] Thus Vietnam, like Germany
and Korea before it, remained divided between communist and pro-Western
regimes, with little prospect of peaceful reunification as long as America insisted
on pursuing its monolithic anti-communist foreign policy.

Anxious, therefore, to forestall this possibility, Dulles strove to erect a
regional defense system for the area patterned loosely on the NATO model. The
result of his efforts was the Southeast Asia Collective Defense Treaty, signed at
Manila on September 8, 1954, by eight states. Transformed into the Southeast
Asia Treaty Organization a few weeks later, the Manila Pact included Great
Britain, France, Australia, New Zealand, the Philippines, Thailand, and Pakistan
as signatories. Each member agreed that its own safety would be endangered by
an armed attack on any other member within the carefully defined treaty area, or
on any additional state or territory in that area which the members, *acting
unanimously*, might later designate. The signatories promised to consult in the
event of threatened subversion, and to act together against the common danger in
accordance with their respective constitutional processes. The pact also called for
economic cooperation among the members and for the strengthening of free
institutions and military defenses of each member. Finally, a declaration endorsing equal rights and self-determination, designed to remove any colonialist taint,
was signed in conjunction with the treaty.

Dulles hailed the SEATO agreement as the capstone of a rapidly developing
Pacific regional defense network. The alliance, however, was far from being a
replica of NATO; its weaknesses were numerous from the outset, thereafter

serving to nullify whatever value it may have ever possessed. In the first place, an effective system of regulating security in Asia would have had to include a far larger area than it was possible to bring within the scope of the treaty. Such a bloc would have logically had to involve more than Southeast Asia—Japan, Korea, and Formosa, for example.

The problem was that Japan and Korea at that time were extremely hostile toward one another; that it would have been difficult to include Formosa since it was then the subject of considerable differences of opinion between America and Great Britain; that some of the nonaligned states of southern Asia, notably India, Ceylon, Burma, and Indonesia, refused to join any arrangement that would appear to ally them with one side or the other in the Cold War; and that the noncommunist states of Indochina, at any rate, must be precluded from membership because of their status under the Geneva Agreements.

Moreover, the continental Asian parties to the treaty, as well as the Philippines, were not particularly strong militarily. Their capacity for continuous self-help and mutual aid—an important element in the North Atlantic Treaty—was at the very least questionable, and would remain so for some time. Finally, there were certain persistent political problems that stood in the way of such a strong and comprehensive treaty, including a general Asian fear of Western imperialism with which France and Britain were long associated; a British reluctance to undertake any obligations that might alienate the Commonwealth; and a French unwillingness to take action that might provoke communist violations of the Geneva Agreements.

The treaty was signed, nevertheless, although on a substantially reduced scale of membership, and an additional wall of confrontation was erected—unfortunately, at the expense of many of the important interests of the non-Western world. The paradox of this creation of Secretary Dulles's fertile mind was that it was, in effect, stillborn. The ostensible aim of SEATO was to protect neutral Laos and Cambodia—who refused to join it—while truncated Vietnam later became devastated by SEATO's chief protector, America. Just as an early French compromise with Ho Chi-minh in 1945–1946 might have produced a "Titoist" Vietnam with which the West could have lived in peace, so after 1954, a more far-sighted American policy toward the Vietminh would have, in all probability, proved to be the least risky option for the future. That future, instead, witnessed a vast and destructive involvement in an Asian country, the consequences of which eventually spelled humiliating defeat for America.

America and the Third World in Perspective

In looking back at the Eisenhower administration's approach to the non-Western world, the question of the pre-eminence of Marxist-Leninist ideology in Russian foreign policy having become the basic assumption of the American public and its decision makers, this led to a definition of any anti-American attitude as "communistic," and to the failure to understand communism as nationalism in countries like Vietnam and Cuba. In the final analysis, this was historically wrong and diplomatically counterproductive. In its efforts, therefore, to align as much of the Third World as possible, one has to admit that the American approach was by and large a self-defeating policy. Where conservative regimes desired American aid to support internal policies, the arrangements made with them tended to identify America, sometimes to its lasting sorrow, with the policies of these regimes.[105] Where nationalist regimes existed, the attempt to induce them into alliances against their better judgment often appeared as a threat to the realization of their national goals.[106]

The reasoning behind these alliance-building attempts was mostly unsound anyway. Such states had little to add in a military sense, although some of them were able to provide bases that were of some temporary importance; and the military aid involved frequently served to unbalance the economies of these countries. What is more, the real and undervalued mediatory role that some of these states could play when uncommitted was largely neglected. Whereas they might prove to be bulwarks, as uncommitted states, in upholding desirable principles of international relations, within the Western anti-communist bloc they proved to be weak, vulnerable and even unreliable.

Thus, the Eisenhower administration bequeathed to the succeeding administration of John Fitzgerald Kennedy an array of alliances encircling the globe with a membership of some forty-four states—all dedicated to the prevention of a communist takeover of that area of the earth designated as the "free world." Among the problematical offspring of the "collector's approach" were SEATO and CENTO. And NATO, despite any short-term advantages for its European members, would possess at least two major disadvantages: It tended to obfuscate, rather than clarify, security problems in Europe, and it would hang around the neck of Russian-American relations like an albatross.

While certain "problems" of a tactical nature had indeed arisen within the sundry alliances, America's foreign policy decision makers in the 1950s did not particularly concern themselves with the serious dilemmas already quite apparent within them. This attitude was far from healthy. For one thing, the ever-present element of the unintended is greatest when policy facilitates a transformation in the process of preventing another. Such was the case with respect to the buildup of French power as a result of Washington's unilteral policies. Morever, by the day of Kennedy's inauguration in January 1961, Cuba had already been "excluded" from the inter-American system, becoming a highly troublesome irritant within the body politic of the Organization of American States for many years thereafter.

AMERICA AND RUSSIA: THE ROAD NOT TAKEN

In attempting to take any dispassionate overview of the Eisenhower administration's approach to Soviet Russia, one needs to take into account, first of all, that America possessed in these years a vast preponderance of capability vis-à-vis the Russians.   A realization of that fact confronts students of post-World War II American foreign policy with a rather clear framework within which to make sense out of the foreign policies of this period.   Second, there was little or no meaningful effort expended to look at Moscow's conduct in a rational and disapassionate manner, seeking to take into account the changes that took place in Soviet Russia's orientation and policies.

Russia after Stalin: The New Course

In looking back at Russia's foreign policy in the Eisenhower era, it is apparent that a number of important factors interacted to provide both the context and substance of that policy. The circumstances within the country itself in the wake of Stalin's passing provided the crucial framework for policy for the next five years. The struggle for power among the collective leadership that succeeded him, and an ongoing debate among his colleagues as to how best to run the country, conditioned and colored the initial policies adopted and pursued. It should not be surprising, given the dynamics associated with these events, that the country's approach to the rest of the world would have reflected in rather unique ways the individual views of the personnel involved during this period.

In a series of notes to the West representing his last major foreign policy initiative before his death in March 1953, Stalin proposed a German settlement in which Germany would be reunited and permitted to possess its own army, on the condition that it remain permanently neutral. Was this, as Western leaders believed at the time, a move designed to undermine Western defense plans by exploiting divisions among the major players on the proposed rearmament of West Germany? Or was it a genuine attempt to resolve the German problem by means of concessions on both sides—in the case of Russia, a willingness to sacrifice a communist East Germany for the larger goal of preventing Germany's rearmament within a Western alliance? While no definitive answer to these questions is yet possible, it was probably not coincidental that in the last year of Stalin's life the growing prominence given to "peaceful coexistence" in Russian foreign policy coincided with the emergence of Georgi Malenkov as a driving force within the CPSU leadership. After Stalin's death, Malenkov would emerge as the chief spokesman for the policy of peaceful coexistence. That policy imperative flowed, above all, from a desire on the part of Russia's new leadership to have a period of respite vis-à-vis the outside world so that they could begin to sort things out.[107]

Indeed, the major factor that would incline the country toward a policy of peaceful coexistence appears in retrospect to be the felt need to reform the Stalinist system both at home and abroad. A good case can be made that a compelling reason why the Russians in the those initial post-Stalin months relaxed Moscow's heavy hand in Eastern Europe was the view that Marxist-Leninist ideology needed substantial reinvigoration. Between 1947, when the

Cominform was established, and 1953, Eastern Europe, with the exception of Yugoslovaia, had undergone a thorough period of Stalinization. In the process, a heavy-handed collectivization of agriculture, and the imposition of iron-fisted political controls, all accompanied by party purges, created a pall over these countries, serving to alienate many of the younger Marxist-Leninists who had rallied to Soviet Russia's bannner after the war in the belief that the discredited political systems of the previous era needed replacing.[108]

Stalin's death placed the matter of his management of Soviet Russia's external and internal relations into question. Thus, almost immediately, moves were forthcoming from Moscow to liberalize and humanize the Stalinist infrastructure, both at home and in Eastern Europe under Moscow's domination. The word went out that party functionaries in these countries should seek active "contact" with the masses, so as not to "ossify." The initiative was predicated on the belief that Marxism-Leninism, when stripped of its worst excesses, possessed enough historical truth and attraction to warrant support in and of itself.[109] That reality would have as its core imperative the revitalization of the CPSU and, concomitantly, the downgrading of the pervasive role of the security forces in the life of the country.

Cracks within the Stalinist edifice were apparent almost from the moment the new leadership took over. They emerged in the jockeying for position within the new leadership, a process which over a period of two years eventually found Nikita Khrushchev emerging as the dominant figure. Even so, it was not until 1957 with his defeat of the "anti-Party" group that his domestic position was relatively secure. Casualties along the way included Lavrenti Beria, head of the Interior Ministry. His purge and execution in the summer of 1953 signalled a turning away from Stalinist repression, provoking a flood of demands for the rehabilitation of prisoners and victims of Stalin's terror campaigns.

The sidelining of Malenkov was a more complex affair. Malenkov, who as Chairman of the Council of Ministers initially appeared to be Stalin's chief successor, was the leading advocate of the so-called "new course" of economic reform which proposed a shift of emphasis away from heavy industry toward production of consumer goods. Khrushchev's problem was not the policy itself but Malenkov's stewardship of it. Khrushchev's strategy was to oppose the new course, use his leverage over the party to restore its power, prestige, and sense of élan, engineer the removal of Malenkov, and then adopt many of his policies.

By the early months of 1955 the outlines of Khrushchev's version of the new course were becoming plain. His policies involved controlled political and economic liberalization, coupled with the extension of these benefits to the People's Democracies of Eastern Europe. A pattern emerged by 1956 regarding Moscow's relationship to these countries: a nominal institution of the separation of government power from Party power (the chief plank of which was a call for collective leadership and the ending of the cult of personality), an economic shift from heavy industry to consumer goods, and the rehabilitation of former opponents of Stalinism. In the process, Moscow's economic controls were also to be eased.[110]

An early impact of all this was seen in East Germany in the summer of 1953 when the workers rioted against the repressive Ulbricht regime—a revolt that was crushed by Russian armor, but with the proviso that Ulbricht follow the new course and admit his past mistakes. In the case of Yugoslavia, however, there existed a fiercely nationalistic regime whose allegiance could only be won by efforts at conciliation. This Khruschev did in the spring of 1955 by visiting Belgrade in a bit of personal diplomacy.

Yugoslavia, however, proved a difficult challenge for the Russians, for Tito wanted something Khrushchev could not give. Soviet Russia, with one eye on the People's Republic of China (PRC), was more concerned about the need to maintain the leading role of the CPSU, stressing the basic indivisibility of the communist ideological bloc, albeit with the understanding that rigid Stalinism was no longer a viable option. For his part, Tito insisted that he could not subscribe to the Russian concept of a monolithic communist bloc. Behind this view, as Richard Lowenthal noted, lay a dispute between Belgrade and Moscow on the meaning of "co-existence." For Russia, co-existence meant a truce between the two great hostile blocs; for Yugoslavia, it meant active cooperation of all countries regardless of differences in their internal systems.[111]

Khrushchev's speech before the Twentieth Party Congress in February 1956 was a culmination of the new course. By launching a frontal attack on Stalin and his system (although carefully worded so as not to point to Khrushchev's own role in Stalin's crimes), he sent a shock wave through the Communist Party world, especially Eastern Europe. Its immediate impact was to foster diversity within the bloc, or "polycentrism" as it came to called, without defining clearly where its limits might be. Although Khrushchev's speech was mainly designed to consolidate his own reformist position within the party leadership by discrediting those remaining Stalinist elements in a position to oppose him, the speech would very quickly have enormous international implications. Khrushchev was walking a thin line. Going too far, too fast risked destablizing East Europe's regimes, including even the possibility of their turning away from Moscow. Not to follow through on the course already set in Moscow risked inviting outbursts of frustration which might well have the same destablizing effect.

The repercussions of the secret speech were felt especially keenly in Poland and Hungary. The constellation of competing forces in both countries were similar, though the outcomes were very different. Three elements were in contention: the Stalinist leaderships, liberal communist opposition leaders who had been rehabilitated since Khrushchev's February speech, and nonpartisan workers and students movements supported by prominent intellectuals. In each case, the inital pattern of events showed significant parallels: public demonstrations, put down with brutal force by government troops, followed by pressure on the old Stalinist leaderships to step aside.[112]

In the Polish case, however, the new "liberal" leader, Wladislaw Gomulka, was able to maintain control of the popular movement, orchestrate events to the liking of Moscow, and avert the massive repression that would befall Hungary. In Budapest a similar scenario unfolded with the "liberal" Imre Nagy becoming leader of the country. The difference was that Nagy was installed in power at a time when the momentum of the uprising was reaching its peak and when the Communist Party itself was the chief target of the rebellion. Within days of his appointment, he bowed to the revolutionary momentum, announcing the establishment of a multiparty system, withdrawal from the Warsaw Pact, and virtually complete Hungarian independence and neutrality. Russian repression followed—an intervention supported by China and Yugoslavia, both of which, while championing polycentrism, were not prepared to acquiesce in any fundamental revision of the Marxist-Leninist system, including the establish- ment of a Western parliamentary-style neutral Hungary.[113] Ironically, Soviet Russia's subsequent heavy-handed treatment of Nagy (involving his forcible removal from Yugoslav asylum and later execution) led to a worsening of relations between Belgrade and Moscow.[114]

The fruits of these events in Poland and Hungary were somewhat paradoxical. Having established the outer limits of polycentrism for these two countries, and by implication for others inclined to enter on the same course, Poland and Hungary were permitted, indeed encouraged, to develop the most liberal economic and political systems of all those in Eastern Europe. The most oppressive Eastern European regimes remained those, such as Albania, Romania, Bulgaria, and Czechoslovakia, which were in least need of Russian oversight.[115]

Schism with Peking. The dispute with China was another matter. It was inevitable, one supposes, that as soon as Marxism-Leninism would triumph in more than one country, Moscow's relationship with that state would become problematical. This was especially true in regard to China, possessed of the longest continuous state civilization in human history, and deeply proud of its cultural accomplishments. China had suffered egregiously in the nineteenth and twentieth centuries at the hands of Western imperialism, of which Russia was an integral part. The Chinese communist revolution should be seen as the culmination of a century long effort at emancipation from that domination, and of a desire to forge for itself a new identity in the twentieth century—an amalgam of modernity and traditional Chinese values.

In this, China had to contend with a Soviet Russia which after 1921 chose for its own reasons to support the Kuomintang, the CCP's mortal enemy, as the future wave of the country. What this meant in practice was the virtual elimi- nation of the CCP as an independent force in the country, its ultimate salvation and reorganization via the Long March ordeal of the 1930s, and its re-emergence on the eve of World War II as a viable, independent force to be reckoned with.[116] It would not be until late 1948 that Stalin would see fit to withdraw recognition from the Kuomintang, preferring to hedge his bets almost to the very end.[117] When, finally, Mao journeyed to Moscow in the winter of 1949–1950 to try to reach an accommodation with the Russians, the catalogue of grievances was a lengthy one, the negotiations protracted and difficult, and the results uncertain.[118]

Relations between Moscow and Peking during the Korean War were fraught with rivalry and suspicion, as Stalin sought to play the Chinese and North Koreans off against one another.[119] During that conflict it was already becoming quite apparent that China would be an independent factor in world affairs and one not easily managead from afar. In the wake of the Korean armistice, the CCP now had the opportunity to address the many domestic challenges postponed by the war: a weeding out of counter-revolutionaries, indoctrination of the population with the political mass line, implementation of its first five year plan, and the social remaking of the country.[120] The successes on all these fronts over the ensuing five years were spectacular, inculcating in this first generation of post-revolution leadership a renewed sense of *élan* and purpose. The so-called "Great Leap Forward" campaign can best be understood in this light—reflecting a self-image that China could now set about doing what even Soviet Russia had not yet been able to accomplish—the actual achievement of full communism, and without the necessary interim stage of state socialism.[121]

There were, of course, foreign policy implications in all of this, not the least of which was Peking's view that its own accomplishments, conditioned by both its historic role in Asia and its status as a developing country, ought to serve as a role model for aspiring revolutionaries in the Third World. This led Mao Zedong in 1957 to urge strong support for "wars of liberation" in the newly emerging nations, wars that could be safely fanned because America's strategic power had been neutralized by Soviet Russia. Khrushchev refused to cooperate because he knew that his ICBM program was well behind that of America at this juncture. His refusal signified to Mao that the Russians had joined the establishment powers against the underdeveloped countries.

Meanwhile, the post-Stalin reforms in Soviet Russia themselves became a bone of contention between the two communist party-state giants. Khrushchev's denunciation of Stalinism at the Twentieth Party Congress, with the Chinese sitting in the room, certainly had implications for Mao's conduct in his own country. Thereafter, China would increasingly characterize those reforms as unwarranted "revisionism"—that is to say, a needless tampering with Marxist-Leninist-Stalinist dogma. The Russians responded by riddiculing Mao's Great Leap Forward with its emphasis on forced collectivization. This issue certainly epitomized the internal differences between the two states, as Soviet Russia had traditionally emphasized industrialization, only secondarily infusing the masses with revolutionary ideology. For Mao, just the opposite was the case.

Their dispute intensified as the PRC consolidated its revolution and aspired to its own role within world communism. From China's perspective, it had ample reason to be angry with Moscow's leadership. In the wake of Moscow's spectacular achievements in weapons technology, Mao assumed that Russian successes had created a "qualitative change in the distribution of world power [which] had . . . torn apart the paper tiger of American imperialism and shattered the tale of the 'position of strength.' "[122] In 1957 he began to argue that "the international situation has now reached a new turning point. There are two winds in the world today; the East wind and the West wind . . . I think the characteristic of the situation today is the East wind prevailing over the West wind."[123]

For these reasons, Mao came to regard Khrushchev's notions of peaceful coexistence with its associated bouts of summitry with America as an unwarranted appeasement of imperialism.[124] Khrushchev's trip to America in 1959, his willingness to go to Geneva again, and Moscow's failure to keep the heat on Berlin all were barometers, from China's perspective, that Khrushchev was selling out communism and the Third World. It certainly did not help matters when Khrushchev, in the midst of all these difficulties, reneged on Moscow's pledge to help the Chinese develop nuclear weapons.[125] Nor was Moscow's refusal to come to China's aid in the 1958 Taiwan Straits crisis, or its backing of India in that country's dispute with China over disputed territory along their northeast frontier very conducive to friendly relations.[126]

From the late 1950s onward the Sino-Russian schism bore the marks of a theological dispute, each side regarding the other's version of Marxism-Leninism as heretical. By the the time Eisenhower left office, both sides had come to impasse, openly acknowledging the split, and scrambling diligently to line up support for their respective points of view.[127] Alas, if the implications of this split were essentially unappreciated in Washington, it was because of the tenacity of the Eisenhower administration's conviction that if you have seen one communist, you've seen them all—a view that led Washington to misconstrue what the Vietminh's revolution in Indochina was all about.

Treading Water in Washington

In the context of these developments throughout the 1953–1958 period, the Russians at one point or another sought accommodations with the West on a number of issues. Eisenhower and Dulles did not seem to grasp the magnitude of these changes taking place. It is one of the many ironies in the story of Russian-American relations during this period that the liberalization of the communist party-state world should have occurred at the very moment when the new leadership in America was embarking on a more aggressive Cold War approach. The disarmament issue is a case in point.

The Disarmament Issue. From the demise of the Baruch Plan in 1946 until the mid-1950s, America made no really serious effort to negotiate nuclear weapons control. This was due in part to the fact that America was reluctant to give up its perceived nuclear advantage without conventional disarmament first. It also had a palpable fear of being tricked. Meanwhile, Moscow's new approach to the West was a reflection of a desire for relaxation of tensions in the context of its domestic reorientation, but also one of uncertainty as to just what course to take. What this would mean in practice, on the one hand, was that Moscow, possessed of a continuing fear of bargaining from a position of weakness, would continue to strive to catch up, while maintaining much of its provocative and irritating drumbeat of Marxist-Leninist propaganda aimed at the West. Yet, in the post-Stalin era, Moscow very quickly sought to explore possible areas of convergence and agreement with the West.

Malenkov's call in the spring of 1953 for a broad East-West effort to negotiate differences should be seen in this light—an intiative (which Churchill welcomed) that was met with intransigence from Washington. Eisenhower and Dulles simply went ahead with plans to implement a grand design for containment by increasing troop commitments for NATO, bargaining for Spanish bases, preparing for German rearmament, and working on the paper chain of anti-Russian treaties. Thus, the institutionalization process, begun so hopefully with NATO in 1950, provoked a massive escalation in the competition for armaments, contributed in the succeeding decade to an immense stockpile of obliteration weapons, while bringing little in the way of meaningful security to anyone. And underpinning this massive superstructure of threat and counterthreat came to exist a whole complex of vested interests that were built into America's defense policies after 1947.[128]

In the 1954–1958 period a potential breakthrough occurred and foundered on the inspection issue and the West's reluctance to accept limitations on nuclear weapons, even though the Russians offered to make cutbacks in their conventional forces. The Rapacki Plan and the Berlin Crisis of 1958–1961 both resulted from this situation—initiatives flowing from Moscow's desire to prevent the Federal Republic of Germany from getting a finger on the nuclear trigger. The West's response in late 1957 was to step up deployment of tactical nuclear weapons in Europe and to accept intermediate range ballistic missiles under collective NATO command.

Khrushchev went a long way in 1956–1959 in extending the olive branch of arms limitations to the West. He offerred concessions in the very areas in which Stalin had been most rigid—inspection and conventional force reductions. During these years, Soviet Russia took unprecedented initiatives in both foreign and domestic security affairs, in distinct contrast to the past, including unilateral troop reductions, a unilateral nuclear test moratorium in 1958, and Khrushchev's proposal for "universal and complete disarmament" in 1959—actions that were not fully and conscientiously explored by the West.

Washington did not grasp the significance of the Russian moves, ignoring what the Cold War conflict was originally about. To point out one example, while the reduction of manpower in the armed forces of Soviet Russia in 1955 was not all that major in its impact on that country's overall military capability, in terms of the critical problem of a divided Europe, the reduction was a significant step. For the reduction in manpower was really a test of whether the Russian buildup had in the first place been a move preparatory to overrunning Western Europe, or whether it was only a deterrent posture. If the posture was essentially a deterrent one, as the withdrawal from Austria would seem to have indicated, then the Russians were in a position to consider the *mutual* withdrawal of armies and reduction of forces which would end the division and occupation of Europe. If Moscow had been approached with some preliminary proposals for new negotiations, and an atmosphere of detente had been initiated, might not the tragedy in Budapest, in the fall of the year, have been avoided?[129]

The Broader Picture: A Strategic Overview

It must be remembered that throughout the 1950s and 1960s the Russians were considerably behind America in technology—a situation that, in the absence of any substantive agreements, inevitably precipitated a relentless effort to catch up. There was little else they could do. It was this situation, and as a function of its growing rivalry with the PRC, that led Russia from the mid-1950s to initiate a new approach by wooing neutral governments and movements in Third World countries. What this meant in practice was that containment might have to be applied not only to protect other countries, but to deny them a choice of a pro-Russian foreign policy. This is what prompted the CIA to engage in covert operations in some of these regions—starting in Iran in August 1953, continuing in Guatemala in 1954, and in Southeast Asia later. Massive American assistance to various European colonial states, especially the French in Indochina and the Portuguese in Africa, as well as aid to incumbent authoritarians in Latin America and the Middle East, was soon forthcoming—all designed to maintain the status quo by force, if necessary. One unintended consequence was that this led to the identification of America with imperialism and neocolonialism by younger Third World nationalists who then turned to Soviet Russia as a friend and protector.

The initiatives of Malenkov and Khrushchev, including Russia's recognition of the Federal Republic of Germany in January 1955 when their call for reunification was rebuffed, evoked only a gradual and grudging response from Washington. Surprised by Russian concessions when we least expected them, we dismissed these conciliatory gestures as tricks and deceptions. Ironically, a case can be made that containment, as practiced up to that time, may well have caused the Russians to mellow, as Kennan foresaw,[130] yet the Eisenhower administration was so wedded to its hard line it could not moderate its suspicions of Moscow. Would Khrushchev have agreed to allow verifiable inspection if he had been offered guarantees on Germany? While a conclusive answer to that question is not yet possible, American policy was so wedded to a defense strategy anchored in Germany that the possibility was never seriously confronted.

Moreover, rancor over what had happened in China blinded Eisenhower and his associates to the indications of trouble between Russia and China—trouble that made detente with America desirable for Russia. The specifics of our actions in the context of Moscow's new approach—for example, bringing the Federal

Republic into NATO in late 1954, and becoming a patron of South Vietnam in violation of the Geneva Accords after the summer of that year—were surely not ones that were well received either in Moscow or Peking. Ironically, America, by making its military pre-eminence and the security of its own political sphere its paramount goals, mirrored that of Stalinist Russia.

By not capitalizing on Russia's attempts at reaching out, America enabled the hardliners in the CPSU and military to view them as failures of monumental proportions. By increasing Khrushchev's vulnerability to the neo-Stalinist opposition in the party, as well as leaving him wide open to Chinese attacks, the West's rebuff weakened him politically and may have contributed to his 1960 switch to a hard line in order to save face. American policy made the change inevitable. Beginning in the spring of 1960, Khrushchev's inauguration of a new virulent anti-American propaganda campaign, breaking up of the 1960 summit, cancellation of planned military cuts, jostling for influence in the Congo, working out of a deal with Castro, ending their unilateral moratorium on nuclear testing and increasing pressure on Berlin—all while stepping up the Russian dispute with the Chinese—can only be understood in the context of the failures of the previous five or six years.

The years of Eisenhower's second term were marked by the height of bipolarity—a situation in which America possessed unprecedented ability to influence people and control events. Yet, unless it tries all the alternatives that offer reasonable chances of success, a state with the relative supremacy enjoyed by America in the 1950s cannot, with any real warrant or meaning, claim that it was "forced" to follow a certain approach or policy. On the contrary, America voluntarily utilized its preponderance of power during these years to insist upon resolution of the major strategic issues strictly on its own terms, and to refrain from negotiating anything with the Russians unless it could "negotiate from strength." But negotiation from strength meant in practice that there would and could be no meaningful negotiations. The very concept defined negotiation as the acceptance of America's proposals, and America's decision makers acted upon that definition. Moreover, by defining American interests in terms of an undifferentiated and worldwide Russian threat, it became difficult if not impossible to distinguish between America's vital and secondary interests.

If America could have at least made an honest attempt to meet Moscow on terms to include much of what they proclaimed to be their own criteria, and they then rejected it—the onus would then have been on the Russians, and we would have been no worse off militarily and much better off politically. Such was not the case. And it was not that there was no one who saw the handwriting on the wall. Periodically during these years the negative approach of American foreign policy was questioned by men of political prominence in America. Thus, in 1958, Senator J. William Fulbright could say:

> Our foreign policy is inadequate, outmoded, and misdirected. It is based in part on a false conception of our real, long-term interests and in part on an erroneous

appraisal of the state of the world in which we live. . . . If there is a single factor
which more than any other explains the predicament in which we now find ourselves,
it is our readiness to use the specter of Soviet communism as a cloak for the failure of
our own leadership.[131]

Certainly, the McCarthyist hysteria of Eisenhower's first term made it more
difficult for the administration to respond rationally, if not understand any
Russian initiative designed to ease tensions at this time. This mindset led to an
interpretation of containment that called for an equal and opposite reaction,
usually military, to any perceived communist threat anywhere in the world.
Dulles's "supercontainment" system, consisting of NATO-style alliances all
around Russia, was its major policy consequence. With the partial exception of
NATO, none proved to be of much significance except as evidence of an
inflexible posturing in Washington in disregard of the major changes taking
place inside Russia itself.[132]

But the mindset of America's decision-making establishment remained
frozen; logic yielded to emotional anxiety, self-assurance to fear. The mood was
such that Denis Brogan could observe that while, in the past,

America developed a self-confidence that the outside world marvelled at more
than it admired, there is now an alarming . . . combination of irritation and
resentment that reflects a growing discomfort in the face of some painful aspects of
the modern world. . . . This is an awful situation and it produces dangerous reactions.
. . . If America is in danger, it can only be through treason or incompetence verging
on treason. If 'commies' and 'reds' could be rooted out, there would be a speedy return
to the good old days when America's defeat was as inconceivable as the earth going
around the sun the wrong way.[133]

It would require another thirty years before the end of this conflict would
come to pass—a denouement that would be marked by a continuation of the
essential foreign affairs mindset that America had brought to bear in its external
relations from the beginning. Its policies would continue to reflect the strengths
and weaknesses which we have endeavored to fairly characterize in these pages.
In the final analysis, Soviet Russia would pass from the world scene, and with
its passing, the long cold war that had dominated the last half of the twentieth
century—all this in spite of America's foreign policies!

NOTES

1. For the experiences that shaped Eisenhower's approach to the presidency,
one would do well to consult Stephan E. Ambrose, *The Supreme Commander: The War
Years of General Dwight D. Eisenhower* (Garden City, N.Y.:, Doubleday, 1970);
Robert J. Donovan, *Eisenhower: The Inside Story* (New York: Macmillan, 1956);
Emmet John Hughes, *The Ordeal of Power: A Political Memoir of the Eisenhower*

Years (New York: Knopf, 1963); Herbert S. Parmet, *Eisenhower and the American Crusades* (New York: Macmillan, 1972); and Robert A. Divine, *Eisenhower and the Cold War* (New York: Oxford Univeristy Press, 1981).

2. "Cognitive Dynamics and Images of the Enemy," pp. 227-242, in Samuel A. Kirkpartrick and Laurence K. Pettit (eds.), *The Social Psychology of Political Life* (Belmont, Calif.: Duxbury Press, 1972).

3. Dulles's analysis of how communism influenced Russian foreign policy developed early. See his "Thoughts on Soviet Foreign Policy and What to Do About It," *Life Magazine* (June 3 and 10, 1946), pp. 113–126, 118–130.

Ole Holsti cites Sidney Verba to the effect that "the more ambiguous the cognitive and evaluative aspects of a decisionmaking situation, and the less a group context is used in decision making, the more likely are personality variables to assert themselves. Both the ambiguity of information concerning Soviet intentions and Dulles's *modus operandi* appear to have increased the importance of his image of the Soviet Union." p. 76.

On Dulles's thinking about foreign affairs right before becoming Secretary of State, see his "A Policy of Boldness," Life (May 14, 1952): 13–32.

On the religious influence in Dulles's thinking, see Mark G. Toulouse, *The Transformation of John Foster Dulles* (New York: Basic Books, 1985).

4. K. H. Porter, and D. B. Johnson, *National Party Platforms, 1840–1956* (Urbana: University of Illinois Press, 1961), p. 498.

5. *Department of State Bulletin*, Vol. XXVIII, No. 710 (February 2, 1953): 168.

6. See, in this regard, Richard H. Immerman, "Eisenhower and Dulles: Who Made the Decisions?" *Political Psychology* (Autumn, 1979): 3–20. See also Townsend Hoopes, *The Devil and John Foster Dulles* (Boston: Little, Brown, 1973).

7. Epitomized by the views of Thomas E. Dewey, Robert A. Taft, Harold Stassen, Douglas MacArthur, and Joseph McCarthy. The Republican Party, out of power in Washington except for a brief two year period immmediately after World War II, was a seething cauldron of frustrated and angry ideologues and opportunists, reeking with vengence and looking to concoct a recipe for victory at the polls. Thus, unlike 1948, foreign policy played a major role in the 1952 presidential campaign. The Republican victory, both for the White House and in the Congress, provided an opportunity at long last for the Republican Party to give vent to these viewpoints from a position of power. On this point, see Ronald J. Caridi, *The Korean War and American Politics: The Republican Party as a Case Study* (Philadelphia: Lippincott, 1968).

8. On the nature of public opinion at the outset of the new administration, see Angus Campbell, Gerald Gurin, and Warren E. Miller, *The Voter Decides* (Urbana: University of Illinois Press, 1954), especially pp. 46, 67, and 119.

9. See Robert A. Divine, *Foreign Policy and U.S. Presidential Elections, 1952–1960* (New York: Norton, 1974).

10. At the outset of Eisenhower's presidency, he ordered a review of Cold War options. Called the "Solarium Exercise," alternatives to the Truman policy were discussed, including negotiation and rollback. The conclusion was NSC-162/2, adopted in the fall of 1953. In the process, some of the ongoing and projected programs of NSC-68 were either rejected or modified. See *FRUS, 1952–1954*, II, pp. 577–597. See also William B. Pickett, "The Eisenhower Solarium Notes," *Society for Historians of American Foreign Relations Newsletter* (June, 1985): 1–8.

11. In a speech in January 1954 Dulles quoted Lenin and Stalin to show that the Russians planned to overextend the free world and then destroy it with one blow. It would now be necessary, he said, for the country hereafter to rely upon nuclear weapons instead of ground forces in responding to any and all "communist" aggressions. Cited in New York Times, January 17, 1954, p. 1. A more in-depth explanation is his "Policy for Security and Peace," Foreign Affairs (April, 1954): 349–361, esp. pp. 357–358.

12. A policy Dulles later candidly explained to the American people, New York Times, December 30, 1956, Section IV, p. 3. On the formulation of the policy of massive retaliation, see Robert E. Osgood, Limited War, The Challenge to American Strategy (Chicago: University of Chicago Press, 1961), pp. 189–214.

13. A clarion call first given wide public articulation by Douglas MacArthur in a speech before a joint session of Congress in the spring of 1951. On the hard line sentiments widespread in the Republican Party at this time, see Richard Rovere, Senator Joe McCarthy (Cleveland, Ohio: Athenium, 1959), and Daniel Bell, The End of Ideology: On the Exhaustion of Political Ideas in the Fifties (Glencoe, Ill.: The Free Press, 1960).

14. During Eisenhower's presidency, three Army Chiefs of Staff resigned in protest over this issue, for the Army suffered most from his refusal to increase the Defense Department budget. The Army wanted enough flexibility to be able to meet the communist threat at any level. The trouble with the New Look, they said, was that it locked America into an all-or-nothing approach. Wherever and whenever conflict broke out, the chiefs wanted to to be able to counter it. To do so, they needed a large standing army with specialized divisions, a wide variety of weapons, and an extensive transportation capacity.

A definitive study of this issue, including a review and analysis of the various viewpoints, may be found in Samuel P. Huntington, The Common Defense: Strategic Programs in National Politics (New York: Columbia University Press, 1961). One of the most important critiques of the New Look was that of Maxwell D. Taylor, The Uncertain Trumpet (New York: Harper & Row, 1959).

15. The Cold War, pp. 13-14.

16. An interesting commentary on this point is that of Chalmers Roberts, "The Pious Truculence of John Foster Dulles," The Reporter (January 23, 1958): 220–223.

17. New York Times, March 24, 1954, p. 8. Robert R. Bowie, Director of the State Department's Policy Planning Staff from 1953 to 1957, argues that the New Look, as a necessarily more patient and moderate strategy than that of the previous administration, would eventually "win" the Cold War. See his comments in Ernest R. May, ed., American Cold War Strategy: Interpreting NSC 68 (Boston: St. Martin's Press, 1993), pp. 110–116.

18. See Current Soviet Policies: The Documentary Record of the Nineteenth Communist Party Congress and the Reorganization after Stalin's Death (New York: Basic Books, 1953), especially pp. 249-260. See also Donovan, Eisenhower: The Inside Story, p. 41.

19. Cited in Hughes, The Ordeal of Power, pp. 103–104.

20. Such steps, Eisenhower said, cited in The White House Years: Mandate for Change, 1953–1956 (Garden City, N.Y.: Doubleday, 1963), p. 36 "would be impressive signs of sincere intent. They would carry a power of persuasion not to be matched by any amount of oratory."

21. In large measure because of a fear of penetration and destabilization of the Stalinist system by outside states.

22. House of Commons, Parliamentary Debates, Fifth Series, Vol. 515, Cols. 883–898, as cited in Keith Eubank, *The Summit Conferences, 1919–1960* (Norman: University of Oklahoma Press, 1966), pp. 136–137.

23. Hughes, *The Ordeal of Power*, p. 151.

24. *Current Digest of the Soviet Press*, V (September 5, 1953), pp. 3–12, 26.

25. The meeting of the "Big Three" took place on the island of Bermuda in December, where Churchill unsuccessfully urged that a summit with the Russians be arranged.

26. Charles Bohlen, the American ambasador to Soviet Russia at the time, later regretted the fact that Eisenhower did not respond positively to Malenkov's overtures and to Churchill's call for a summit conference. See his *Witness to History, 1929–1969* (New York: Norton, 1973), p. 371.

27. On the progress and significance of the armistice talks, see David Rees, *Korea, The Limited War* (New York: St. Martin's Press, 1964).

28. Upon his return from Stalin's funeral in Moscow, Chou En-lai, the Chinese prime minister, announced his willingness to break the deadlock in the Korean settlement talks and to discuss one of the major issues of contention—the return of POWs. See statement by Chou En-lai in *Pravda*, March 31, 1953, quoted in *Current Digest of the Soviet Press*, Vol. V, no. 30, pp. 3–12 and p. 26.

29. On the bankruptcy of Dulles's "liberation" strategy, see Bennett Kovrig, *Myth of Liberation* (New York: Basic Books, 1973).

30. The Russians viewed the May 26, 1952, EDC treaty as an "open military union pursuing aggressive policies." According to a Russian foreign office official, "West Germany constitutes a real threat, especially because the ruling circles of the USA consider the future of a West German revanchist army as the basic aggressive core of the North Atlantic bloc." Cited in Archives of the Foreign Ministry of the Russian Federation, *Foreign Policy of USSR Related to the U.S.*, Opus 39, No. 53, File 292, "On the State of Relations between USSR and US, 1950–1954," Reg. No. 37, pp. 29-30.

31. There is some evidence to indicate that the Russian and French governments may have negotiated some sort of informal quid pro quo involving the proposed EDC treaty and an honorable French exit from Indochina. The Russians believed that by moderating Vietminh demands at the Geneva peace conference taking place at that very moment, she might be able to induce the French to stay out of the EDC. Thus Soviet Russia brought pressure to bear on the Vietminh to adjust their negotiating demands sufficiently to make them minimally acceptable to France. In that way, the Mendes-France government might well survive, and the chances of rejection of the EDC in the parliament made more likely.

On this linkage, see Donald Lancaster, *The Emancipation of French Indo-China* (London: Oxford University University Press, 1961), pp. 336–337; Daniel Lerner and Raymond Aron, eds., *France Defeats the EDC* (New York: Praeger, 1957), pp. 16–17; Donald S. Zagoria, *Vietnam Triangle: Moscow, Peking, Hanoi* (New York: Pegasus, 1967), pp. 28 and 40. See also the report by New York Times correspondent Tillman Durdin, *New York Times*, July 25, 1954.

32. The Paris agreement embodied these unprecedented features in a complex series of arrangements. First, it enlarged and revised the Brussels Pact of 1948, under

which France, Britain, and the Benelux countries had formed the Western European Union (WEU). Italy and Germany now became members of the WEU, which in turn became a subdivision of NATO, as the actual military direction of WEU forces was vested entirely in the NATO high command. The Brussels Pact was amended by deleting reference to German aggression, and its purpose was redefined as that of promoting unity and encouraging the "progressive integration" of Europe.

The old Consultative Council of the WEU was reconstituted and empowered to fix the maximum size of the armed forces which each member country could contribute to NATO. These limitations could be increased only by unanimous consent, and compliance with them would be verified by a newly created Agency for the Control of Armaments. In addition to this general limitation, the German Federal Republic specifically agreed not to manufacture atomic, biological, or chemical weapons, and to refrain from producing certain other types of weapons save upon request of NATO with the approval of the WEU.

Finally, the German Federal Republic was admitted to NATO once the powers concerned had ratified these changes in the Brussels Pact, plus the arrangements to end the joint occupation and restore full sovereignty to the FRG.

33. This was the policy originally set forth by Moscow in its March 1952 draft for a peace treaty.

34. Churchill evidently had come to the view that while continued Anglo-American cooperation was essential, a certain distancing from the new administration's policies was in Britain's best interests, especially in regard to the problems of colonialism in the Third World. A good accounting of the British-American dialogue at this time is M. Steven Fish, "After Stalin's Death: The Anglo-American Debate Over a New Cold War," *Diplomatic History* (Fall, 1986): 343–353.

35. For a discussion of this exchange, see Walter LaFeber, *The American Age* (New York: W. W. Norton, 1989), Chapter 16, especially pp. 513–517.

36. "Estimate of Prospect of Soviet Union Achieving Its Goals," July 1, 1955, Conference Dossiers, *Dulles Papers*, Princeton University, pp. 1–27.

37. *U.S. Department of State Bulletin*, Vol. 32, No. 830 (May 23,1955): 832–833.

38. Eisenhower, *Mandate for Change*, pp. 124–125.

39. *Russia, the Atom and the West* (London: Oxford University Press, 1958), pp. 38–40.

40. Bohlen saw the conference as an opportunity to gain valuable insights into Russia's thinking. On June 12 he sent a lengthy dispatch emphasizing Russian preoccupation with two main objectives: retention of control over their East European satellites and avoidance of war with the West. He pointed out a change in Moscow's attitude toward a relaxation of tensions, noting that the arms race was straining their economy, that they would not allow atomic inspections on their territory, and that they would seek to get rid of NATO. See his *Witness to History*, p. 381.

41. *U.S. Department of State Bulletin*, Vol. 33, No. 840 (August 1, 1955): 176–177.

42. Eisenhower, *Mandate for Change*, p. 529.

43. Dulles was especially prone to this sort of attitude. See in this regard Douglas Stuart and Harvey Starr, "The 'Inherent Bad Faith Model' Reconsidered: Dulles, Kennedy and Kissinger," *Political Psychology* (Fall/Winter, 1981–1982): 1–33.

44. On the ultimate impact of this proposal for nuclear proliferation, see Ralph Lapp, *The Weapons Culture* (Baltimore: The Johns Hopkins University Press, 1969).

45. Quoted in Peter Lyon, *Eisenhower: Portrait of the Hero* (Boston: Houghton Mifflin, 1974), p. 584. See also in this regard Thomas F. Soapes, "A Cold Warrior Seeks Peace: Eisenhower's Strategy for Nuclear Disarmament," *Diplomatic History* (Winter, 1980): 51–64, here, p. 62. Robert Divine, *Eisenhower and the Cold War*, p. 114, argues that this motivation nevertheless misses the ultimate significance of the initiative—to get the deadlocked talks off dead center by developing areas of mutual trust.

46. The Russian initiatives are carefully catalogued and analyzed by Philip Noel-Baker, *The Arms Race* (London: Atlantic, 1958). This is a classic early work in the field of disarmament studies, and one thast goes to the heart of the issues in the mid-1950s.

47. The so-called Six Principles—proposed by the American delegate on April 24, 1952, and accepted by the Russians on May 10, 1955. On this point, see Noel-Baker, *The Arms Race*, pp. 12–20.

48. An excellent accounting of this situation may be found in Sebastian Haffner, "Germany, Russia and the West," *Encounter* (October, 1961): 14–21.

49. Noel-Baker, *The Arms Race*, pp. 20–21.

50. In 1965, Eisenhower told an interviewer that "We knew the Soviets wouldn't accept it. We were sure of that." Quoted in Parmet, *Eisenhower and the American Crusades*, 406. Divine, *Eisenhower and the Cold War*, p. 122, calls the proposal a "flawed but sincere attempt . . . to reduce international tension."

Khrushchev, according to Ambassador Bohlen, *Witness to History*, p. 384, took Eisenhower aside at the conference and said who was the American president "trying to fool?" He went on to state that as "this [was] a very transparent espionage device. . . . You could hardly expect us to take this seriously."

51. *Current Digest of the Soviet Press*, III, (May 15, 1956), pp. 2–13. See also Fred J. Cook, "Juggernaut—the Warfare State," *The Nation* (October 28, 1961), p. 313.

52. Quoted in D.F. Fleming, *The Cold War and Its Origins, 1917–1960* (Garden City, N.Y.: Doubleday, 1961), p. 789.

53. Indeed, it would last for some three years until 1961 when the Russians resumed testing. For a succinct overview of the nuclear weapons inspection negotiations, see Charles C. Alexander, *Holding the Line: The Eisenhower Era, 1952–1961* (Bloomington: University of Indiana Press, 1975), pp. 94–98, 201–210. For the nuclear testing debate, see Robert A. Divine, *Blowing on the Wind: The Nuclear Test Ban Debate, 1954–1960* (New York: Norton, 1978). On the broader issue of the continuing failure of high-level meetings to resolve much of substance between the two sides, see Patricia Dawson Ward, *The Threat of Peace* (New York: Oxford University Press, 1979).

54. His comments were subsequently published under the title, *The Challenge of Co-Existence* (Cambridge, Mass.: Harvard University Press, 1957).

55. Kennan's proposals would later be published as *Russia, the Atom and the West*.

56. Quoted in *U.S. News and World Report*, January 17, 1958, p. 63.

57. For a summation/analysis of the various proposals, see James W. Robinson, "Disengagement in Europe: An Evaluation of U.S. Policy," *Columbia Essays in*

International Affairs, ed. Andrew W. Cordier (New York: Columbia University Press, 1966), pp. 31–58.

58. The text of the report is entitled, "Deterrence and Survival in the Nuclear Age" (Washington, D.C.: Government Printing Office, 1976). Paul Nitze, the primary author of NSC-68, was also a major contributor to the Gaither study.

59. Eisenhower had the report shelved and it did not become public information until 1973.

60. Cited in Archive of the Foreign Ministry of the Russian Federation, Op. 43, File 82, Subfile 21, "On Political Interrelations" (1957), pp. 15–25.

61. The implication of this reality would become evident during 1960 when the states of Western Europe, for reasons of economic gain, would ship some $1 billion worth of strategic goods to Soviet Russia, much to the dismay of Washington.

62. Western scholarship on this question has tended to center upon several factors: One school of thought argues that the Russian leadership was essentially concerned with blocking the nuclearization of West Germany. See, in this regard, Ulam, *Expansion and Coexistence*, Jack M. Schick, *The Berlin Crisis, 1958–1962* (Philadelphia: Lippincott, 1971), Jean Edward Smith, *The Defense of Berlin* (Baltimore: Johns Hopkins University Press, 1963), and Marc Trachtenberg, "The Berlin Crisis," in *History and Strategy* (Princeton, N.J.: Princeton University Press, 1991): 169–234. Another perspective avers that Khrushchev provoked the crisis in order to restore his authority at home—an authority in question because of setbacks in Russian agricultural policies and in its missile build-up. This view is echoed by Robert Slusser, *The Berlin Crisis of 1961: Soviet-American Relations and the Struggle for Power in the Kremlin* (Baltimore: Johns Hopkins University Press, 1973), and Carl Linden, *Khrushchev and the Soviet Leadership* (Baltimore: Johns Hopkins University Press, 1966). A third orientation, primarily coming out of Western Europe, is that Khrushchev unleashed the crisis in response to pressures from the "hawks" in the Kremlin and, above all, from GDR leader Walter Ulbricht. This view is reflected by Michael Tatu, *Power in the Kremlin: From Khrushchev to Kosygin* (New York: Viking Press, 1971), and Norman Gelb, *The Berlin Wall* (London: Michael Joseph, 1986).

Recent studies have emphasized a more multi-faceted orientation, contending that the Kremlin's actions were shaped by a combination of perceived threats, including Western German nuclearization and the possible collapse of the East German regime, and a number of more offensive-minded temptations, mostly linked to a perceived shift of the "correlation of forces" in favor of Soviet Russia. See, in this vein, Michael Beschloss, *The Crisis Years, Kennedy and Khrushchev, 1960–1963* (New York: HarperCollins, 1989), Hannes Adomeit, *Soviet Risk-Taking and Crisis Behavior. A Theoretical and Empirical Analysis* (Boston: George Allen and Unwin, 1982), and McGeorge Bundy, *Danger and Survival: Choices About the Bomb in the First Fifty Years* (New York: Random House, 1988), esp. pp. 359–364.

Older studies pointing up Moscow's growing rivalry with Peking for leadership of the international communist movement as the decisive factor in the Berlin intiative include William E. Griffith, *The Sino-Soviet Rift* (Cambridge, Mass.: Harvard University Press, 1964), pp. 445–447, and Adam Ulam, *Expansion and Coexistence*, pp. 629–644.

63. Evidence for this comes from a paper delivered by Zoya Vodopyanova and Vladislav Zubok, "The Berlin Crisis, 1958–1962: New Evidence from Soviet

Archives," presented at the Conference on New Evidence on Cold War History, Moscow, January 12–15, 1993, sponsored by the Cold War International History Project.

64. See a memo by Valentin Falin to the Soviet Presidium (Politburo) in November, 1956 in which he stated that "In case of a settlement of disputed issues between the FRG and Poland, the Polish government would no longer be interested in hosting Soviet troops on Polish territory," and the GDR would find itself isolated and vulnerable "to subversive activities and sabotage from within." Archive of the Ministry of Foreign Affairs, fond 595, Opus 6, Box 789, Vol. 78, 1. 437.

65. See, in this regard, A.G. Mileykovsky, ed., *International Affairs after the Second World War*, I (Moscow: Progress Publishers, 1962), especially pp. 291, 534.

66. Based, among other factors, on interviews by Zubok with Oleg Troyanovsky, who became a Khrushchev confident in 1958.

67. On this point, see Hope Harrison, "Ulbricht and the Concrete 'Rose': New Archival Evidence on the Dynamics of Soviet-East German Relations and the Berlin Crisis, 1958–1961," *Cold War International History Project Working Paper No. 5*, Woodrow Wilson International Center for Scholars (Princeton, N.J.: Princeton University Press, 1993).

68. For recent documentation on Russian policy toward the offshore islands crisis, see Konstantin Pleshakov, "Khrushchev as Counter-Revolutionary: The Taiwan Straits Crisis of 1958 and the Sino-Soviet Schism," and I.N. Shevchuk and M. Yu. Prozmenshchikov, "Soviet-Chinese Relations, 1953–1959, two papers presented at the Conference on New Evidence on Cold War History, January 12–15, 1993.

69. In response to the urging of the Gaither Report, the president had agreed in early 1958 to deploy Intermediate-Range Ballistic Missiles to Western Europe. See Eisenhower, *The White House Years: Waging Peace*, pp. 221–223.

70. On this point, see Smith, *The Defense of Berlin*, p. 178.

71. As to the impact of the U-2 overflights on Russian-American relations at the end of Eisenhower's presidency, see David Wise and Thomas B. Ross, *The U-2 Affair* (New York: Columbia University Press, 1962).

72. Cited in an interview with George B. Kistiakowsky, *A Scientist at the White House* (Cambridge, Mass.: Harvard University Press, 1976), p. 282.

73. Edward Crankshaw, *Khrushchev* (London: Collins, 1966), pp. 272–273, argues that from 1960 until the end of Khrushchev's career his foreign policy was dominated by the quarrel with China.

74. This is the point made by Michael Beschloss in *Mayday: Eisenhower, Kennedy and the U-2 Affair* (New York: Harper and Row, 1986), pp. 376–377 and 381.

In his comprehensive analysis of the U-2 affair, Beschloss avers that both sides were culpable for the failure of the conference and, with it, the failure of detente. In Eisenhower's case, he could not bring himself to accept Khrushchev's offer of a way out, namely acknowledging that the U-2 was a spy plane but that he had not authorized the flight, since that would appear to the world that he was not in control of American foreign policy. Moreover, he saw no reason to suspend the flights in the weeks before the conference, based on the assumption that the Russians did not possess the capability to do anything about them in any event. *Mayday*, pp. 371–372, and 376–377.

75. Certainly foreign policy making is rarely the end product of a logical chain of reasoning. Many studies of the bureaucratic context of decision making have pointed out that such factors as endemic parochialism; a tendency to define objectives in light of their own needs, values, and traditions; decisions made on the basis of ritual and precedent; avoiding risk and honoring the status quo; decision making by mechanical procedure rather than by reflection; and preoccupation with doing what was assigned initially regardless of its present usefulness, are examples of some of the "pathologies" inherent in the process. Among the many works that emphasize the bureaucratic model as an explanation of foreign policy behavior, see I. M. Destler, Leslie H. Gelb, and Anthony Lake, *Our Own Worst Enemy: The Unmasking of American Foreign Policy* (New York: Simon and Schuster, 1984); Charles F. Hermann, "Bureaucratic Constraints on Innovation in American Foreign Policy," in Charles W. Kegley, Jr., and Eugene R. Wittkopf, eds., *Perspectives on American Foreign Policy* (New York: St. Martin's Press, 1983); Dan Caldwell, "Bureaucratic Foreign Policy Making," *American Behavioral Scientist* (September-October, 1977): 87–110; John Oneal, *Foreign Policy Making in Times of Crisis* (Columbus: Ohio State University Press, 1982); Irving L. Janis, *Groupthink: Psychological Studies of Policy Decisions and Fiascoes* (Boston: Houghton Mifflin, 1983); and Paul A. Anderson, "What Do Decision Makers Do When They Make a Foreign Policy Decision?" in Charles F. Hermann, Charles W. Kegley, Jr., and James N. Rosenau, eds., *New Directions in the Study of Foreign Policy* (London: Allen and Unwin, 1986).

76. On the American involvement, see Mark H. Lytle, *The Origins of the American Alliance, 1941–1953* (New York: Holt, Rinehart and Winston, 1987), and Kermit Roosevelt, *Countercoup: The Struggle for the Control of Iran* (New York: Praeger, 1979). See, also, Robert Engler, *The Politics of Oil: A Study of Private Power and Democratic Institutions* (New York: Macmillan, 1961), and Leonard Mosely, *Power Play: Oil in the Middle East* (New York: Atheneum, 1973).

77. Two excellent books that delve into the Guatemalan intervention are Richard Immerman, *The CIA in Guatemala: The Foreign Policy of Intervention* (Austin: University of Texas Press, 1982), and Stephen Schlesinger and Steven Kinzer, *Bitter Fruit: The Untold Story of the American Coup in Guatemala* (New York: Anchor Books, 1981). On the president's personal involvement in covert actions, see Blanche Wiessen Cook, *The Declassified Eisenhower* (New York: Atheneum, 1981).

78. His negative expression of this belief was his denunciation of neutrality, or nonalignment, which he characterized as immoral.

79. "American policy was designed to create maximum change behind the Iron Curtain and to prevent it elsewhere," said Norman Graebner, cited in Stephan Ambrose, *Rise to Globalism: American Foreign Policy Since 1938*, 6th ed. (New York: Penguin Books, 1992), p. 204.

80. Richard J. Barnet and Ronald E. Muller, *Global Reach: The Power of the Multinational Corporations* (New York: Simon and Schuster, 1974). See also Richard Barnet, *Roots of War: The Men and Institutions Behind U.S. Foreign Policy* (Baltimore: Penguin Books, 1972).

81. The roster of misfits, incompetents, and unsavory characters supported by Washington in the name of anti-communism during the 1950s reads like a "Who's Who" from a Damon Runyon short story: Trujillo in the Dominican Republic, Batista in Cuba, Somoza in Nicaragua, Jimenez in Venezuela, Odria in Peru, Pinella in

Colombia, Stroessner in Paraguay, Magloire in Haiti, Franco in Spain, Salazar in Portugal, Diem in South Vietnam, Rhee in South Korea, Chiang in Taiwan, Aya Khan in Pakistan, and Menderes in Turkey, for example.

82. This was the primary motivation underlying Indian foreign policy under Jawarhalal Nehru, and that of Indonesia under Ahmed Sukarno in the 1950s.

83. An orientation that prompted a scathing critique from Hans Morgenthau, "Alliances in Theory and Practice," in *Alliance Policy in the Cold War*, ed. Arnold Wolfers (Baltimore: Johns Hopkins University Press, 1959), p. 210. "Our alliance policy," he said, "partakes of the doctrinaire, legalistic, and mechanical character of much of American foreign policy. . . . Instead of recognizing that there are useful, harmful, and superfluous alliances according to circumstances and discriminating among them in view of the interests to be served and policies to be pursued, we have followed the collector's approach to alliances: the more, the better."

84. "The Declaration of Caracas," *Department of State Bulletin*, Vol. 30, No. 769 (March 22, 1954): 420.

85. *Ibid.*, 419.

86. Cited in Richard P. Stebbins, *The United States in World Affairs* (New York: Harper, 1961), p. 376.

87. A quote from a Bolivian delegate, cited in Stebbins, *The United States in World Affairs*, p. 373.

88. On Eisenhower's understanding of and approach to the events in Cuba, see Robert F. Smith, *What Happened in Cuba? A Documentary History* (New York: Praeger, 1963), and Richard E. Welch, Jr., *Response to Revolution: The United States and the Cuban Revolution, 1959–1961* (Chapel Hill: University of North Carolina Press, 1985).

89. Truman's recogition of Israel was tendered over the opposition of his Secretaries of State and Defense, who were afraid that recognition might turn Arab oil producers against America. As Soviet Russia was also then urging recogition of a separate Jewish state, Marshall and Forrestal also believed that close Russian-Israeli ties might turn the new state into a pro-communist outpost in the Middle East. For that reason, Marshall advocated a UN-sponsored trusteeship over Palestine that would mandate Arabs and Jews living together in one country. Truman, however, opted for a separate Jewish state, in part with the hope of offsetting potential Russian influence. Meanwhile, inspite of this, the State Department and America's oil corporations hustled to improve their relations with the Arab oil producers. On Truman's approach to this issue, see Forrest C. Pogue, *George C. Marshall: Organizer of Victory* (New York: Holt, Rinehart and Winston, 1973). For more critical appraisals, consult Cheryl A. Rubenberg, *Israel and the American National Interest* (Boston: St. Martin's Press, 1986), and Edward Tivnan, *The Lobby: Jewish Political Power and American Foreign Policy* (New York: The Free Press, 1987).

90. See U.S. Senate Committee on Foreign Relations, 84th Congress, 2d Session, "Hearings on the Situation in the Middle East," February 24, 1956 (Washington, D.C.: Government Printing Office, 1956), pp. 43–68.

91. On his reaction to the British concern, see Interview with Robert Murphy, Dulles Oral History Project, *Dulles Papers*, Princeton University.

92. Negotiations would take place shortly thereafter leading to the establishment of a Russian naval base in Egypt.

93. For the various positions and roles in all of this, including implications for

subsequent American foreign policy, see Herman Finer, *Dulles over Suez* (New York: The Free Press, 1964), and Robert W. Stookey, *America and the Arab States: An Uneasy Encounter* (New York: Holt, Rinehart and Winston, 1975).

94. This development possesses even more importance when one remembers that before 1955 Soviet Russia had opted, in the words of Walter Z. Laqueur to "keep aloof from Middle Eastern affairs and to maintain an attitude of studious unconcern in relation to that quarter." Cited in his "Soviet Policy in the Middle East," *The World Today*, II, No. 12, p. 37. In any event, Iraq withdrew from the Baghdad Pact in March 1959 and the alliance was transformed five months later into the Central Treaty Organization, or CENTO, with headquarters in Ankara, Turkey.

95. For a discussion of American policy toward this region at this time, and its implications for the countries involved, see John C. Campbell, *Defense of the Middle East: Problems of American Foreign Policy*, rev. ed. (New York: Macmillan, 1970). On the issue of American arms sales being employed by recipients in ways that have served to be destablizing in their regions, see Philip J. Farley, Stephen S. Kaplan, and William H. Lewis, *Arms Across the Sea* (Washington, D.C.: Brookings Institution, 1978), and Michael T. Klare, *American Arms Supermarket* (Austin: University of Texas Press, 1984).

96. U.S. Senate, Committee on Foreign Relations, 85th Congress, 1st Session, *Hearings . . .* to Authorize the President to Undertake Economic and Military Cooperation with Nations in the General Area of the Middle East, Parts 1 and 2 (Washington, D.C.: Government Printing Office, 1957), especially pp. 4–41.

97. Department of State, *American Foreign Policy: Current Documents, 1957* (Washington, D.C.: Government Printing Office, 1961), p. 1024.

98. Sherman Adams, *Firsthand Report* (New York: Knopf, 1961), p. 293.

99. Quoted in Stanley Hoffmann, *Gulliver's Troubles: Or the Setting of American Foreign Policy* (New York: McGraw-Hill, 1968), p. 137, n. 52.

100. See in this regard Richard J. Barnet, *Intervention and Revolution: America's Confrontation with Insurgent Movements Around the World* (Cleveland: Mentor Books, 1968).

101. Public Papers of the Presidents of the United States, *Dwight D. Eisenhower, 1954* (Washington, D.C.: U.S. Government Printing Office, 1960), p. 383.

102. On May 7, 1954, the French garrison at the remote northwest town of Dienbienphu surrendered to the besieging Vietminh forces, thus breaking the back of an eight-year struggle by the French to hold on to their colony. During the course of the seven-week siege, the French requested American military assistance to bail them out—a request that triggered a tumultuous debate in America and among its Western Allies. At various points during the review of what options to pursue, recommendations for air strikes, including the use of tactical nuclear weapons, were forthcoming from a number of the president's advisors. As a result of the refusal of the British to go along, combined with congressional opposition and internal dissent from within the administration, Eisenhower ultimately opted not to intervene.

On the American debate to intervene in the spring of 1954, see Chalmers Roberts, "The Day We Didn't Go To War," *The Reporter* (September 14, 1954): 31–35, and Matthew B. Ridgway, *Soldier: Memoirs of Matthew B. Ridgway* (New York: Harper and Bros., 1956), p. 278. For a full account of the French position, see Jean Lacouture and Philippe Devillers, *La Fin d'une Guerre, Indochine 1954* (Paris:

Editions du Seuil, 1960), Chapters 5–7.   On the genesis of the American involvement, see Andrew J. Rotter, *The Path to Vietnam: Origins of the American Commitment to Southeast Asia* (Boulder, Colo.: Sage Publications, 1987).

103. For a critical analysis of the Eisenhower administration's approach to Vietnam, see George McTurnan Kahin and John W. Lewis, *The United States in Vietnam* (New York: Delta Books, 1967), especially Chapters 1–5. See, also, Melvin Gurtov, *The First Vietnam Crisis: Chinese Communist Strategy and United States Involvement, 1953–1954* (New York: The Free Press, 1967).

104. *U.S. Declaration on Indochina*, Department of State Press Release 394 (July 21, 1954). See also Dulles News Conference of July 13, 1954, Department of State Press Release 400.

105. American decision makers were not able to perceive the ambiguities inherent in these agreements. Thus, for example, Spain, in 1953, agreed to permit the construction of American bases within its territory in return for economic and military assistance grants that amounted to over one billion dollars in the 1953-1960 period. The bases constructed there remained under "Spanish flag and command," and there was no published legal guarantee by the Franco government that would automatically permit their use in time of war. On more than one occasion in future years, America would find itself hard-pressed to obtain Spain's acquiescence for permission to utilize its territory (including its air space) in support of military operations deemed necessary by Washington.

106. This would be particularly the case in the years after World War II with countries such as India, Indonesia, Argentina, Burma, and Libya.

107. *Current Soviet Policies: The Documentary Record*, pp. 24–28. See also Ulam's commentary on this matter in his *Expansion and Coexistence*, pp. 546–547.

108. See, in this vein, Karl Reyman and Herman Singer, "The Origins and Significance of East European Revisionism," in *Revisionism: Essays on the History of Marxist Ideas*, ed. Leopold Labedz (New York: Praeger, 1962), pp. 215–222, and Edmund Stillman, ed., *Bitter Harvest: The Intellectual Revolt Behind the Iron Curtain* (New York: Praeger, 1959).

109. Russian policy toward Tito during the post-1952 period, for example, freely envisaged the abandonment of a certain amount of control in the expectation of considerable ideological gains.

110. Zbigniew Brzezinski's treatment of this period, *The Soviet Bloc: Unity and Conflict* is informative.

111. See his *World Communism: The Disintegration of a Secular Faith* (New York: Oxford University Press, 1964), p.15.

112. On the situation in Eastern Europe after the speech, especially the patterns that were replicated in various places, see Brzezinski, *The Soviet Bloc*.

113. For a general review and analysis of polycentrism and its significance at the time, see Walter Z. Laqueur and Leopold Labedz, eds., *Polycentrism* (New York: Praeger, 1962). That Tito was first and foremost a polycentrist and not a revisionist, see Ernst Halperin, *The Triumphant Heretic* (London: Heinemann, 1958), and George W. Hoffman and Fred W. Neal, *Yugoslavia and the New Communism* (New York: Praeger, 1962). The classic critique of Tito's policies in this regard remains Milovan Djilas, *The New Class* (New York: Praeger, 1957).

114. See Roy Medvedev, *Khrushchev, A Biography* (Oxford: Blackwell, 1982), p. 109.

115. See Stephen Kertesz, *East Central Europe and the World: Development in the Post-Stalin Era* (East Bend, Ind.: University of Notre Dame Press, 1962).

116. On Soviet Russia's policies toward China between the world wars, see Richard C. Thornton, *The Comintern and the Chinese Communists, 1928–1931* (Seattle: University of Washington Press, 1969), and Xenia J. Eudin and Robert C. North, *Soviet Russia and the East, 1920–1927* (Stanford, Calif.: Stanford University Press, 1957), the latter as part of a broader treatment of the Russian approach to the Far East. See, also, Charles B. McLane, *Soviet Policy and the Chinese Communists, 1931–1946* (New York: Columbia University Press, 1958), and Conrad Brandt, *Stalin's Failure in China* (Cambridge, Mass.: Harvard University Press, 1964).

117. On this point consult Max Beloff, *Soviet Policy in the Far East, 1944–1951* (New York: Oxford University Press, 1953), and Griffith, *The Sino-Soviet Rift* (Cambridge, Mass.: MIT Press, 1964).

118. An excellent analysis of those difficult negotiations may be found in David Floyd, *Mao against Khrushchev* (New York: Praeger, 1963).

119. See my discussion in Chapter 2.

120. On China's internal policies at this time, see Franklin W. Houn, *To Change A Nation: Propaganda and Indoctrination in Communist China* (Glencoe, Ill.: Free Press, 1961); A. Doak Barnett, *Communist China: The Early Years* (New York: Praeger, 1964), and Stuart Schram, *The Political Thought of Mao Tse-tung* (New York: Praeger, 1969).

121. See, on this point, A. Doak Barnett, *Chinese Economic Strategy: The Rise of Mainland China* (Washington, D.C.: National Planning Association, 1959), and Arthur G. Ashbrook, Jr., "Main Lines of Chinese Communist Economic Policy," in *Profile of Mainland China*, Studies Prepared for the Joint Economic Committee, U.S. Congress, 1967 (Washington, D.C.: Government Printing Office, 1968), I, pp. 17–27.

122. Cited in Donald Zagoria, *The Sino-Soviet Conflict, 1956–1961* (Princeton, N.J.: Princeton University Press, 1962), pp. 160–162.

123. Quoted in William Zimmerman, "Russia and the International Order," *Survey* (January, 1966): 209–213.

124. Zagoria, *The Sino-Soviet Conflict*, pp. 21–22, argues that at the root of the split with Moscow was Mao's fear of a Russian-American accommodation at China's expense.

125. On this issue, see Raymond L. Garthoff, "Sino-Soviet Military Relations," *Annals of American Academy of Political and Social Science* (September, 1963): 76–93.

126. The Russian-Chinese-Indian triangular relationship at this time is covered well by George W. Patterson, *Peking Versus Delhi* (New York: Praeger, 1964).

127. For a while both protagonists avoided attacking each other directly, preferring to criticize important allies as surrogates. In Soviet Russia's case that meant castigating Albania; for China, the designated victim was Yugoslavia. See William E. Griffith, *Albania and the Sino-Soviet Rift* (Cambridge, Mass.: The MIT Press, 1963).

128. A situation which Eisenhower was sensitive to at one level or another throughout his presidency. He once said that the country was fortunate to have someone in the White House who could say no to the military—something that he did with regularity during his two terms. Of course, his farewell address to the American

people in January 1961 constituted a solemn warning about the "coincidence of interest" tying together important elements of the American business community with government and military leaders.

129. Imre Nagy's proposals to the Russian Presidium that Hungary become nonaligned would perhaps have been better received in Moscow if there had been indications that Washington was interested in a neutral belt involving some of its own allies in the Central European area.

130. This is the point made by Georgi M. Kornienko in May, *American Cold War Strategy*, pp. 125–128.

131. *Progressive* (September, 1958), p. 21.

132. The triumph of the capabilities school of thought during the Eisenhower era became a *fait accompli*. The effect of military thinking upon American foreign policy after 1945, in this regard, became increasingly pervasive and problematic. For one thing, it was due largely to military influence that the idea that every "loss" for America was automatically a "gain" for the enemy became ingrained into the American mind. Another contribution of the military mentality was a preoccupation among American decision makers in seeking to shift "fixed" amounts of security in their day to day policy making. It was also the American military that argued that it is good to have Soviet Russia in a more insecure position than America. The difficulty with this sort of reasoning, of course, was its logical outcome: If America were to live in absolute security, Soviet Russia would have to live in total insecurity. It is also apparent that Moscow might well go to war before letting such a situation come to pass.

133. "A Historian Questions Our Mood," *New York Times Magazine* (December 3, 1961), p. 26.

4

Babylon Revisited

On December 7, 1941, America was dragged onto the center stage of world history. The era of "effortless security," as Walter Lippmann put it, was over. That most destructive and dehumanizing of twentieth-century conflicts demonstrated that the American people were no longer guaranteed easy security or prosperity by their favored geographical setting. Thus the war and its immediate aftermath was a seminal period in America's history. As the tangled events that took place during and immediately after that conflict required a central American involvement, how the country would respond to the manifold challenges confronting it would go far in determining the kind of world that would emerge thereafter. It was in the midst of this strategic sea change that Russian-American relations would come to play a central role in the history of the next two decades. The world quickly discovered that its problems were much more foreign to the American tradition than to that of the Russian.

As we have seen, America's conduct during that struggle, reflected most especially in its approach to dealing with Soviet Russia, contributed significantly to the problems that would follow. Its own long tradition of foreign relations did not serve it well, as Franklin Roosevelt and his chief foreign policy advisors labored under the twin handicaps of lack of experience with and understanding of the proven requirements of *realpolitik*. This reality was especially manifest in the moralist policies pursued toward friend and foe alike after 1939. America's moralism led to the assumption of injurious ad hoc postures like unconditional surrender, total victory, no appeasement, and the Atlantic Charter—postures encouraged by a long record of self-indulgence made flesh by America's geographical distance from danger, and its enormous technological accomplishments during the war.

More importantly, America emerged from the conflict without a very clear, well worked out conception of the role it would play in the postwar world. In the process of dealing with a series of "crises" that arose as a result of Soviet Russia's actions in 1945–1946, America's policy makers slowly elaborated a series of "worst case" predictions about Russian intentions. By 1947–1948, these predictions reflected what had by then become a fairly widespread set of assumptions about Russian behavior.

The core assumption was that Soviet Russia was a dangerous country—one motivated essentially by the requisites of its official Marixst-Leninist political ideology. Marxism-Leninism itself, as a structured, doctrinaire belief system, was by definition felt to be diametrically opposed to our way of life. That this was so was because it was historically totalitarian, anti-democratic and anti-capitalist and, therefore, a real threat to the freedom, liberty and economic well-being of people throughout the world. Moreover, as it was a cohesive, monolithic force to which all adherents were bound in united solidarity, much like Islam after the seventh century, Marxism-Leninism was therefore inherently an expansionist, crusading ideology intent on converting the entire world to its beliefs.

As the fountainhead and leader of this international movement dedicated to the conversion of the non-communist world, Soviet Russia was felt to be inevitably in control of a great many subservient communist parties and insurgencies on a worldwide scale. A second assumption, consequently, was that any country vulnerable to subversion and contiguous to the Russian sphere of influence, was *ipso facto* assumed to be a target for communist penetration. This perception, it was argued, was fostered by Soviet Russia's own behavior and that of its so-called fifth columns, first in the Middle East, especially in Greece and Iran, then in Eastern Europe, especially in Czechoslovakia, and in Western Europe, especially in France and Italy, and ultimately in Asia, particularly in China and Southeast Asia. This was the essence of the so-called conspiracy theory which was explicitly verbalized by President Eisenhower early in his administration, but which had already become a *grundnorm* of American policy early in the Truman administration.

The country, however, did not arrive at this view all at once. While Moscow's behavior during the war confused and exasperated American policy makers, preoccupation with waging the war, along with a particular concern about avoiding the mistakes of the past, led the president and his top advisors to believe that something could be worked out with the Russians. As that conflict dragged on, Roosevelt came to realize that Russian power flowing into the vacuum left by the defeat of Germany would have to be accepted as a *fait accompli.*[1] As Kennan would later write, no one could have denied Stalin "a wide military and political glacis on his Western frontier . . . except at the cost of another war, which was unthinkable." Since the West could not defeat Hitler without Stalin's aid, which "placed him automatically in command of half of Europe, Roosevelt endorsed the new dimensions of Soviet power, in the hope that it would encourage future friendship with the West."[2]

One problem, however, was the universalist ideologies publicly espoused by both America and Russia during the war. Whereas in private both countries may well have been prepared to consider if not adopt a sphere of influence policy, which on Eastern and Western Europe (if not on Germany) involved some acknowledgement of the other's interests and sensitivities, that is not what they said in public. Privately Roosevelt by 1945 spoke the language of spheres of influence, but official American foreign policy was couched in terms of one world, open only to democratic values. Roosevelt and Truman believed the American people would not tolerate conducting the nation's business in the language of Europe's traditional diplomacy, but by encouraging misleading, even utopian, expecta-tions they paved the way for growing public disenchantement with what the Russians were doing and, in the process, unwittingly played to Moscow's suspicions. FDR's death cleared the way for a revision of strategy he himself would probably have executed in time, but perhaps not in as abrupt and confused a manner as was actually done. Ironically, Truman, at first, embraced a *quid pro quo* approach in the belief he was implementing FDR's policy, but in so doing he convinced the Russians that he had changed it.

As the Cold War developed steadily, the available evidence indicates that policy makers on both sides had not been following confrontational blueprints from an early stage; rather, they gradually lost faith in the strategy of collaboration without having anything clear-cut to put in its place. Over time the basic assumptions each side had developed about the other were allowed to dictate policy. In the case of America, the basic assumption was that Russia's intentions were revolutionary. As for Russia, it assumed fundamental capitalist antipathy. As a result, each side's attitude and approach toward the other underwent significant if not inexorable changes from the summer of 1945 through the winter of 1947–1948, leading the two countries down the path to the all-out confrontation that would follow. In this, President Truman and his advisors pointed to the realities of history, seeking to employ its lessons to prevent another tragedy from happening. There can be little doubt that their readings of recent history played a crucial role in the subsequent transformation.

AMERICA'S APPROACH TO HISTORY: REASONING BY ANALOGY

Inadequately armed with any deep historical sense of cause and effect in world affairs, America plunged into a vigorous leadership role possessed of the solid conviction that it had now come to understand the object lessons of history. Two events during the post-World War I period made lasting impres-sions on America's World Wa II-era leadership and led to widely and strongly held assumptions about what our policy should be after that conflict: the failure of the League of Nations to oppose Japan's aggression in Manchuria in 1931, and the Munich Agreement of 1938. Secretary of the Navy Forrestal, for example, in September 1945 dismissed the idea "that we should endeavor to buy their [Russian] understanding and sympathy. We tried that once with Hitler. There are no returns on appeasement."[3]   Moreover, Russian actions were fitted into America's dominant image of totalitarian regimes. If you've seen one totalitarian regime, it was said, you've seen them all. Repression at home implied aggression abroad. As Truman observed in May 1947: "There isn't any difference in totalitarian states . . . Nazi, Communist or Fascist, or Franco, or anything else—they are all alike."[4]   Given these views of appeasement and totalitarianism, there was a tendency for America's decision makers to focus on those aspects of Soviet Russia's conduct in 1945–1946 that fitted the paradigm—Poland, Rumania, Bulgaria, for instance, but not Finland, Iran, Czechoslovakia, or Greece.

When faced with Russian pressures in Iran, Turkey, and Greece in 1946–1947 that eventually led America to intervene with economic and military assistance, the Truman administration took the position that these events were analogous to developments in the interwar years (especially the Manchurian, Italo-Ethiopian, and Czechoslovakian crises). Inferences were made from those analogies as guides for policy. A further analogy was made between North Korea's attack on South Korea and the Japanese, Italian, and German aggressions prior to World War II serving as a basis for the American decision to confront the North Korean assault. And in the case of the Vietnam conflict, a loosely-knit mass of inferred historical parallels underlay the escalating American intervention—the "loss" of China, the earlier French defeat at Dienbienphu, and communist behavior in the Quemoy-Matsu, Berlin, and Cuban crises.

While the real importance of the Munich episode stemmed from Czechoslovakia's strategic location, it came to be identified in America with the abstract proposition that *any* aggression anywhere could/would have disastrous results. This simplification would lead America to a whole strategic rationale on how to handle Soviet Russia's actions, fairly indiscriminately applied. America saw object lessons in how not to do things and then more or less literally began to apply these new prescriptions under circumstances that, from a shallow perspective, they seemed to fit.

One of the problems of such an approach is that it encourages applying the principle out of context. Another complication is that the assumed remedy is utilized whenever the principle seems to apply. A third difficulty is a state's previous unfortunate experience with a particular type of danger can sensitize it to other examples of that danger. While this sensitivity may lead the state to avoid the mistake it committed in the past, it may also lead it inadvertently to believe the present situation is like the past one.

It is as though America believed that what it did or did not do would be decisive in world affairs without any real corresponding feeling for how these problems were handled in an earlier age, or who handled them then. Thus the Chinese-Russian conflict of the late 1950s which, after all, had a considerable history going back into the nineteenth century, was thought unlikely until its existence could finally not be denied. Many Americans tended to look on these events as though they were brand new, had no roots, and only came to exist when we were there to perceive them and formulate some policy toward them.

Then, too, because what was done from 1919 to 1939 was considered essentially wrong, it was assumed that doing the reverse after 1945 would be essentially right. If before 1939 we refrained from membership in the League of Nations, from making alliances, from sending troops outside our own hemisphere, from offering substantial and continuing aid to other countries far from our own shores, after 1945 we did all of those things, and with a vengeance. Moreover, convinced that America had erred in the interwar period by "sitting it out," we moved after 1945 quite close to taking a stand on any and every international dispute, and we did it with astonishing rapidity.[5]

IMAGES, PERCEPTIONS AND REALITY

In policy making, perceptions often dictate behavior and realities sometimes count less than beliefs, myths, and obsessions. American-Russian relations certainly reflected this fact. The Cold War developed not so much from the actions of the protagonists as from the way their actions were interpreted or misinterpreted. More often than not, however, the images held by one side about the other did not correspond to reality.[6]

In regard to Soviet Russia's conduct during and immediately after the war, her foreign policies can only be understood in light of the experiences of her people over many years. While doctrinal demands and neurotic personal ambition certainly influenced Stalin's policies during these years, the overriding requirement underlying Soviet Russia's foreign policy was her need for security and economic reconstruction.[7] Indeed, the behavior of Soviet Russia after 1917 was not markedly different from that of Czarist Russia before that time—the same centralization and authoritarianism, the same conspiratorial approach to international relations, the same profound mistrust of the outside world, the same obsession with secrecy and espionage, the same cautiousness, the same capacity for retreat, the same attempt at trying to push back the menacing presence of foreigners across the Russian border, and the same effort to achieve security by expanding Russian space.[8]

If Russia's communists were more successful than its tsars, the difference is more readily accounted for by their material power and by weakness and vulnerability in the world around them than by some new compelling sense of mission. They focused their efforts, afterall, on the same areas of proximate geographical interest as their predecessors—Eastern Europe, the Middle East and the Far East—with markedly greater success only in the first of these. They would ultimately engage in some far flung adventures in places like Cuba and Africa, yet, allowing for a half-century of communication and transportation systems transformation, it cannot be said that they did anything incompatible with tsarist aims and practices.

The Bolshevik Revolution, of course, appeared to friend and foe alike at the time to have changed everything in Russia's external relations—proclaiming, as it did, an international crusade against capitalism, imperialism, and war. It launched an international movement of revolutionary parties that, in form at least, acknowledged this mission. And it is true that it succeeded in digging a political chasm between communist and anti-communist that significantly colored the nature of an enormous array of internal changes in countries all over the world. But America's view that Soviet Russia's behavior after World War II was essentially an ongoing attempt to apply Marxist-Leninist revolutionary ideology was a mistake. Rather, the character of Russian foreign policy after the revolution was a dictatorial amalgam of revolutionary rhetoric, internal conservative policies, and traditional Russian behavioral orientations. By the eve of World War II, Russia was in no sense any longer a revolutionary society.

Indeed, it may be said in retrospect that over a period of two decades after 1917 Bolshevik foreign foreign policy underwent a basic reorientation. Beginning with Lenin and accelerating under Stalin from the mid-1920s forward, there evolved in the Soviet Russian state a species of postrevolutionary leadership presiding over a relatively deradicalized socialist movement—one that went quite a distance toward accommodating itself to the world that it remained ideologically committed to transform. The deradicalization of Bolshevik communism contained important foreign policy implications, the major one being that Soviet Russia ceased being a revolutionary power since at least the waning of Trotsky's influence on the decision making process in the mid-1920s. During Stalin's hegemony the commitment to world revolution became weak as a political motivation and ceased to be a mainspring of Soviet Russia's initiative in world affairs. What was vital to Stalin was the maintenance of his own personal power and to rebuild Russia to the point where it would be strong enough to withstand capitalist penetration. While its leadership would remain ideologically committed to the goal of a world-wide transformation along Marxist-Leninist lines, the pattern of Russian conduct in world affairs would become that of a traditional great power, infused with considerations of both national interest, ideology, and internal politics.

The list of faulty images held by one side about the other was extensive. In America's case, during the war we mistook Stalin's determination to ensure Russian security through spheres of influence as an unfortunate renewed emphasis on power politics—something that the nation's foreign affairs tradition had historically rejected, Latin America notwithstanding. After the war, Moscow's policies in this regard came to be viewed as a renewed effort to spread communism outside the borders of Soviet Russia.

In 1945–1946, Russia's intransigence and uncooperative behavior manifested in its German occupation policies confused and angered Americans. So, too, did her hard line policies on the Eastern European peace treaties—this despite the fact that our own conduct in both the Italian and Japanese cases served to set precedents for Soviet Russia's own actions. And when we came to the view that Germany required economic reconstruction—a view largely dictated by the severe economic drain that the occupation had begun to engender for both the American and British economies—we could not fully grasp how our efforts to rehabilitate Germany, made necessary in our view by Soviet Russia's intransigence, fed Moscow's anxieties.

Stalin's two-camps speech in early 1946, the Russians' infuriating conduct at the various Council of Foreign Ministers meetings during the 1945–1948 period, Russia's refusal to cooperate with the Marshall Plan in the summer of 1947, the coup in Czechoslovakia in early 1948, followed by the Berlin blockade in 1948–1949, the explosion of a nuclear device in late 1949, and the North Korean attack on South Korea in June 1950, all served to confirm in the American mind an image of Soviet Russia as nothing more than a conspiracy disguised as a state, possessed of a single-minded determination to take over the world. But it is crucial to remember that America came to this worst-case scenario piecemeal, and only in the fullness of time to wholly believe it.

All of this precipitated, in our view, an entirely rational and necessary response by the West, led by Washington. The Truman Doctrine in the early spring of 1947, the Marshall Plan the following June, the formation of the Western European Union in the summer of 1948, the formation of NATO and the merging of the Western zones of Germany in 1949, the response in Korea, the massive arms buildup of 1949–1953, the creation of the EDC in 1954 and, with its failure, the inclusion of West Germany in NATO in 1955, were all viewed as appropriate reactions to this long series of Russian provocations and aggressive actions.

Nor were we able to comprehend that the Russian communists did not always, everywhere, control events or dictate policies within their own area of hegemony. Thus, for example, Tito's demands for Trieste, his funneling of support to the Greek communists and his shooting down of two U. S. transport planes in August 1946 were among the actions that the Western powers readily but erroneously assumed were orchestrated by Stalin. So, too, Soviet Russia's culpability for and involvement in the North Korean attack in June 1950 was misunderstood by an America already in the process of looking for an excuse to operationalize NSC-68. Moscow's role in Indochina and, later, with Castro's revolution in Cuba were likewise misinterpreted. In each instance, Russia's involvement came *after* that of America and occurred essentially as a function of Moscow's growing rivalry with the People's Republic of China for influence in the Third World, for leadership of the revolutionary forces in that world, and as a function of its worldwide competition with America which by the 1950s had taken on a dynanmic all its own.

As for Russia, their leadership during World War II seems to have misread the relationship between Britain and America. Russia, guided by its Leninist proclivities, was too ready to assume inevitable Anglo-American discord and to look constantly for ways to exploit it. Washington's exasperating propensity to postpone decisions on a postwar territorial accommodation, its delay in opening up a second front in Western Europe, and its failure to share the atomic bomb secret with Moscow undoubtedly fueled Russian apprehension and doubt concerning Western motivations.

Then, too, Anglo-American conduct in the Italian armistice matter did not help matters. By refusing to involve the Russians from an early stage in these negotiations, we created a framework of precedent for her later actions in Rumania, Bulgaria, and Hungary. French intransigence on the Allied Control Council for Germany—actions that went unrenounced by her Western partners—went not unnoticed by Moscow, serving to encourage her own hard line conduct in that country.

The Truman Doctrine, with its unfortunate amalgam of ideological rhetoric and tough proposals, was read in Moscow as a call to arms. The subsequent Marshall Plan thus came to be viewed in Moscow as an economic declaration of war and as an attempt to subvert Soviet Russia's legitimate role in Eastern Europe. Washington's approach to the atomic bomb issue was perceived in Moscow as nothing more than a thinly disguised attempt to maintain and perpetuate a nuclear monopoly on behalf of an aggressive West, with the ultimate intent of employing it to destabilize Soviet Russia itself.

This is not to say, however, that Soviet Russia's own conduct did not contribute significantly to the growing impasse. The renewed Marxist-Leninist rhetoric emanating out of the Kremlin in early 1946 certainly had a perverse effect in America. Whether or not those exhortations were sincerely entertained by Stalin and his colleagues or merely tactics employed as part of their domestic politics, as now appears to be the case, they had a deeply unsettling effect on the outside world. Throughout the 1945–1961 period, Moscow's persistent tendency to cloak and rationalize its policies by reference to the canons of Marx and Lenin only served to confuse Washington's elite, thereby confirming among them the idea of conspiracy. It is well to remember, however, that Britain and France would come to this conclusion later than America, and only to varying degrees and with divergent perceptions along the way.

A number of Western scholars doubt whether there was ever much we could have done to prevent the Cold War. The Russians, according to Adam Ulam, were not easily dissauded from "their suspicions about the intentions of the Western Powers. Not the most intensive credits, not even the turning over to the Russians of sample atomic bombs, could have appeased them or basically affected their policies. Suspicion was built into the Soviet system."[9] Perhaps, but in the absence of a genuine, sustained effort to that end, Moscow's bottom lines were never seriously tested. It would therefore follow that what America did after World War II made a difference and that the image of Soviet Russia advanced by Kennan in the long telegram to explain the sources of Russian conduct was itself in part reflective of growing Cold War thinking in Washington, and, ironically, contributed to the Russian image of an intensifying hostility from the West.

THE APPEAL OF DICHOTOMOUS REASONING

The transformation of policy during the Truman years was nothing short of remarkable. Starting out in the spring of 1945 full of doubt and uncertainty as to what to do and how to proceed, and under the leadership of a president embarrassingly inexperienced in the field of foreign policy, the administration was transformed within the short space of five years into a gaggle of implacable zealots possessed of a singleminded collective determination to fight Soviet Russia on all fronts. It was a transformation deeply and pervasively informed by some of the more retrograde aspects of the country's tradition of foreign affairs. As such, the metamorphosis was in the grand tradition of pendulum swings in American history—about-faces that long mirrored the range of contradictory values deeply embedded in America's collective cultural psyche.

The whole of American history may be seen in this sense as a series of juxtapositions of value/mood swings, each a reaction to the one that preceded it—transformations that have been inevitably reflected in policy orientations. In some periods certain values have tended to be predominant, in other periods the opposite values have prevailed. The list of these warring opposites is a lengthy one: moralism and pragmatism, optimism and pessimism, change and stability, isolationism and interventionism, war and peace.[10] The war-peace dichotomy is particularly instructive regarding the mood of the country at the end of World War II, as the nation would undergo yet another such about face.[11]

The country's attitude toward conflict has been especially reflective of this tendency. Here, the world for America has always tended to be black or white: either there is peace or there is war. Intermediate shades of gray, involving conflict at one or another level, and peace and cooperation at other levels, have always been difficult to comprehend. For Americans peace is regarded as the normal human condition, war an aberration. But when wars must be fought, once committed, all-out struggle is mandatory. The enemy having been vanguished, however, the "normal" state of affairs is reinstated. What was so difficult to take for many Americans so soon after the end of World War II was the idea that it was time to gear up again for another such confrontation. Is it any wonder that the challenges facing the country after 1945 would call forth the interventionist impulse with impunity—a response this time, however, that must be different. Now, it was argued, American foreign policy should be colored by a good dose of healthy realism.

AMERICA'S NEW REALISM: GLOBALISM IN MORALIST CLOTHES

As the conflict with Soviet Russia intensified and lengthened in time, many of those who were "present at the creation" of the country's confrontationist policy toward the Russians argued that it was time to jettison the naive, utopian, and idealistic policies of the interwar period. A new realism was now called for. The "realist" message proclaimed that the impotent and impatient moralism characteristic of America throughout much of its history was obsolete. Force and policy now had to be integrated, in contrast to what had happened from 1941 to 1945. One could no longer count on the ability of force to put an end to the history of force and to bring forth an age of harmony. And one could no longer vacillate from isolationism to world utopianism. One therefore had to say goodbye to Kellogg-Briand pacts that excommunicated war, to policies of nonrecognition without sanctions, and to the rule of law among states through the ministry of a genuine collective security.

But what should the new perspective be? The 1945–1948 years brought forth two rather disparate responses, sequential in nature, the second flowing out of the first. In the process, the first response in opposition to the old European politics was finally rejected. Initially, those entrusted with the responsibility for the country's foreign policies began to speak of ending the balance of power and doing away with the very rivalries and power politics that had played such an important role in buttressing America's own security early in her history. But, In order to "sell" the new realism, one had to present it in moral terms. This was felt to be the necessary condition for obtaining the support of the people. It was therefore required that the Cold War be transformed into a crusade. It was doubly moral because it would save the world from the inevitable castastrophe that would occur if the communists faced only procrastinators and weaklings, and because it would gradually provoke the transformation, if not the conversion, of the enemy. While the dream of final harmony was postponed, it was not put aside.

It was in this context that the elements of a new world order were presented for the first time as contributions to the moral success of the new realism. Aid to underdeveloped nations, support for the UN, and European integration were stations on the way to a world that would be more and more like that of America. Moreover, the methods that were made to serve the new realism were appreciably characteristic of America's exceptionalism: its instinct for violence in the face of conflicts of ends expressed in terms of the build-up of nuclear forces far beyond the requirements of adequate deterrence, and resort to covert operations designed to "destabilize" and "deactivate" potential enemies.

The evolving Cold War, interpreted as a mortal contest of values in a moral context, seemed to offer endless struggle. The power that this vision came to hold over America's imagination was that it promised an endless peace as the reward for that struggle. When unfreedom was finally defeated, the world would come to enjoy that new condition which was the ultimate end of America's foreign policies in the first place—a just ordering of society, a world of legality, prosperity, consensus, and harmony. Interpreting the Cold War as a competition among values thus gratified the old belief of an America above the corruption and compromise of other nations.

The new globalism forced Americans to realize that they could no longer escape involvement in an imperfect world. But because the Cold War, like World War II, was conceived as a moral crusade, it inflated an involvement that should have been essentially limited and pragmatic into a moral mission. Since we were accustomed to victory in battle and were stronger than any nation had ever been before in history, we believed that the world's problems could be resolved if only we willed hard enough and applied enough power. Thus, American military power, consecrated by the victory of World War II and re-confirmed by the development of the atomic bomb, joined forces with the power of American idealism to inaugurate a policy of global interventionism.

The new credo was rationalized and sanctified by means of the notion of global responsibility. Imbued with a strident missionary zeal, the idea of responsibility came to be an accepted assumption of American foreign policy that few effectively challenged. The political rhetoric at the time characterized the American mission in the world as one inspired by philanthropic motives. "Other nations have interests," Dean Rusk would later pronounce, "the United States has responsibilities."

Pursuant to this new operational notion of global responsibility, America became active in virtually every sphere of international relations. It was the primary sponsor and supporter of the United Nations. It pushed hard for the expansion of foreign trade and the development of new markets for American business abroad. It engineered the creation of a vast complex of alliances and regional institutions, while simultaneously solidifying American hegemony in areas regarded as its traditional spheres of influence. In all of these activities, three common denominators came to be emphasized: America has global duties and responsibilities; America stands as the doorkeeper of freedom and morality on the world stage; and the future viability and peace of the world is dependent upon America's willingness and readiness to act abroad for the good of mankind.

The ideological rhetoric of the Truman Doctrine, though exaggerated for political reasons, provided a new justification for the evolving policy which then helped shape the American outlook. Containment was the first major policy manifestation of the new approach. But as the strategy of containment gradually evolved, the impact of the old Puritan evangelism or world mission intruded. This was reflected in the rhetoric of the Marshall Plan, which Joseph M. Jones described as "infinitely more than a policy of containment of Soviet-Communist expansion," but also "a constructive policy of building throughout the free world the conditions not only of peace but of a good life."[12]

But as the struggle lengthened in time, many of America's easy-going beliefs, its innate optimism, and, above all, its image of the inevitability of victory came to be sorely tested. The perceived nature of an apparent expanding series of Russian orchestrated challenges along a constantly shifting line of containment led to a perception of a worldwide threat against which Kennan's original notion of the application of selected counterforce was deemed to be increasingly inadequate. The sudden shift in the Truman administration's understanding of the amount of resources required for containment in the fall of

1949 culminated in the planning goals of NSC-68. It remained for the North Korean attack on South Korea in mid-1950 to push America over the edge to the adoption of the definitive integrated response to the threat. Once the image of the wholly international scope of the Russian-inspired and orchestrated communist onslaught became fully internalized in the American psyche, the conspiracy theory became writ large. America's commitments now became interdependent. If successfully challenged in one area, so the reasoning went, they would inevitably be challenged in others.

Combating this threatening, adversarial ideology became almost an obsession. The varied reasons for American fear and hatred of communism rested on a set of corollary assumptions about "the nature of the beast." The policy rhetoric—like that employed to rationalize religious wars and persecutions in the past—advocated "sleepless hostility to Communism—even preventive war."[13] In short, the world came to be viewed in zero-sum terms: what one side won, the other side necessarily lost. Such an outlook almost guaranteed permanent conflict by recognizing no virtue in conciliation or cooperation with an ideological foe. Thus, wars of righteousness in which compromise and limited objectives are looked upon as treason came to the fore in the world of the 1940s and 1950s—modern counterparts to earlier historical wars of religion. By the time Dulles took over, distinctions between direct actions against Soviet Russia and frustrating the "design" had become blurred beyond recognition.

Conspiracy, having been linked intimately with containment as a strategic concept, came to serve several important functions for America's decision-makers. First, it allowed decision-makers in both the Truman and Eisenhower administrations to see patterns in communist behavior through the prism of reasoning by analogy. The Korean episode, along with increased communist insurgency elsewhere in Asia, served to illuminate the handwriting on the wall, and the earlier experiences with the Russians in Europe and the Middle East came to be viewed within the context of a global pattern of aggression, only this time through the use of internal subversion.

Second, the notion of conspiracy provided a crude but serviceable strategic framework for decision makers to employ in situations characterized by a high degree of ambiguity. It was very difficult, of course, to determine ahead of time the strategic value, or the relative vulnerability to communist subversion, of individual countries. The conspiracy theory resolved that psychological and political problem by making all regions and, by extension, each state within a region, strategically important.[14] The country's evolving alliance policy, for example, reflected this orientation.

Third, the notion of conspiracy provided decision makers with the necessary arguments for cultivating domestic support for the resource allocation necessary for the operationalization of a global containment policy. Because it was difficult to explain, let alone justify, the need for the ever-growing resources to expend in areas that seemingly had little or no direct connection to the country's security, the notion of conspiracy provided a vehicle for making those connections and thus preventing the public, and Congress, from ignoring potential trouble spots that might lead later to dangerous security challenges.[15]

Ultimately, the notion of conspiracy reflected only too well the country's dominant Puritan ethic, pandering, on the one hand, to the public's fundamentalist tendencies, while, on the other, serving as a means to socialize those members of the attentive public (and their representatives in the Congress) who remained skeptical. By Eisenhower's first term, it had gained an incredible momentum of its own because it had by then provided a strategic calculus for America's decision makers as a means of winning the necessary support for the application of containment worldwide. It came to epitomize in the popular consciousness the basis for national consensus in waging the Cold War. A virtually complete consensus on this point, the boundaries of which were sharpened by the hysteria of the McCarthy period, held for at least a decade, and weakened only slowly thereafter. Unfortunately, it trapped the country into a containment strategy with very little flexibility.

NSC-68 was at the center of this development, epitomizing much of what was injurious and destructive in America's foreign affairs traditions. The goal of NSC-68 was to "light the path to peace and order." Americans must "bear witness" to their values. The moralist appeal to righteousness, the self-image of uniqueness, and the fundamentalist conception of a central evil with which we must necessarily do battle, were all reflected in that document.[16] Nitze argued in NSC-68 that America must take the lead in trying to "bring about order and justice by means consistent with the principles of freedom and democracy." One also sees in NSC-68 a strident statement of militant nationalism. The concept of the evil "other" so assiduously cultivated in that document is centrally germane in America's tradition of foreign affairs—a symbolism one first detects in the Truman Doctrine. NSC-68's power derived not from any original formulations but from its clever reworking of the powerful tradition of American nationalism.

What made NSC-68 significant was its timing. Its military estimates are certainly open to question. Even at the time, the assumption about the "fundamental design of the Kremlin" was not shared by everyone in Washington, including Charles Bohlen, who questioned whether Moscow really did plan to dominate the world, pointing out that, if this was indeed the basic Russian design, this "leads inevitably to the conclusion that war is inevitable."[17]

Certainly the British had a different view of the Russian "threat" at the time. What was particularly unsettling for London was the document's notion that communism was monolithic, especially in regard to China. In a speech before the House of Commons in December 1950, Foreign Secretary Bevin reaffirmed that it was British policy "not to become obsessed with the Communist conception of China but rather to bear in mind that the mass of Chinese scarcely understood what Communism means, and try if we could to bring them along and keep them in association with the other nations of the world."[18] But with the China Lobby in full swing, McCarthy already lusting for blood, and

Secretary of State Acheson well on the way to becoming a palpable domestic liability for the Democratic Party, this doctrine was perhaps understandable in the climate of Washington in 1950.

The fundamentalist urge to reduce complex reality to black and white simplicities became a dominant feature of the Cold War under Truman and Eisenhower. Over time one sees the idea of a "Kremlin design" more frequently employed by America's leaders. For Forrestal, Acheson, Nitze, and Dulles, for example, debate over Russia's intentions was not necessary. And because human beings tend to attribute greater logic and coherence to others' behavior than actually exists, it was not difficult to move to the next step and conclude that Moscow had a clear strategy to take over the world, and was now beginning to develop the capacity to bring it off. It was only required, therefore, to move to counteract what they might be capable of doing. And a single-minded, persistent emphasis on such an approach would surely bring forth dividends.

Beginning in 1947, the Rio de Janeiro Pact, Truman Doctrine, North Atlantic Treaty, Southeast Asia Collective Defense Treaty, Caracas Declaration, Taiwan Resolution, Baghdad Pact, and Eisenhower Doctrine all marked distinct but related steps in a policy that appeared unable to articulate any purpose other than preventing a military expansion of the Russian sphere of influence—all at the expense of ignoring numerous, palpable opportunities to successfully manage the conflict at lower levels of intensity, if not settle it altogether. One can only conclude that the rhetoric of response—that is to say the quantification of means over ends—was allowed in the end to dictate the policy followed by America toward Soviet Russia.

QUESTIONS OF POWER POLITICS, SPHERES OF INFLUENCE, AND COLLECTIVE SECURITY

America's understanding of the requisites for successfully stage-managing the vagaries and vicissitudes of power was never a consistent and logical one. In this, the country's foreign affairs tradition hindered the adoption of reasonable policies. In miscrocosm, this confusion may be seen in the country's approach to Soviet Russia. In a larger sense, this fact was amply demonstrated in the contradictory approach taken toward the questions of spheres of influence and collective security.

What neither Truman nor Eisenhower was able to grasp is that the problems between Soviet Russia and America were not ones that could be resolved by means of the general goals of opposing aggression and upholding some version of collective security. They were concrete political and military problems that required the coherent management of national power according to an overall strategic plan for achieving specific security objectives. The handling of the spheres-of-influence question illustrates this point well. It is truly ironic that America had difficulty with spheres of influence during World War II in regard to

Soviet Russia's role in Eastern Europe—all in the context of a history of our own Monroe Doctrine becoming transformed over time into an ideological justification for an American sphere of influence in the Caribbean and Central America.[19]

After the war, as relations with Soviet Russia floundered, Washington acquiesced *de facto* in a sphere of influence, balance of power approach, but America's grudging tolerance for spheres was compromised by its universalist ideology and by its rapidly expanding definition of security to include the stability of the whole of Eurasia. Moreover, the Korean and Vietnam wars, and the German problem with its chronic friction over Berlin, whatever else they were, reflected the inability of both Washington and Moscow (and their major allies) to draw acceptable lines between their respective spheres of influence in the power vacuums created by World War II.

More generally, a country long suspicious of the unbridled use of power for state ends, once ensconced as the world's leading "great power," had considerable difficulty in handling it with realism. In particular, the notions of self-restraint and limitations in the exercise of that power were difficult to swallow. The idea that there are limits to what we can and should do runs counter to the American national character, especially as we view the outside world. Our tendency has been to have everything or nothing to do with the world—and to be anxious about anything in between. The League of Nations was supported as an American political invention and rejected as a grave threat to the country's national sovereignty. Americans fought one war to make the world safe for democracy and another for unconditional surrender, but dismantled a mighty army after World War II with alacrity. And respected military and political leaders responsible for America's strategy during that war chose not to conduct its last stages in such a way so as to secure territorial boundaries that might have assured the creation of an effective balance of power in Europe.

Nor did the concepts of limits to power generally commend themselves to the wider public. They have about them an air of compromise and weakness; they require the use of language—detente, neutralization, tacit agreements, privileged sanctuaries, and equilibrium—which has a more European flavor than an American one. And the concept of limited warfare conducted for limited objectives and ending with the achievement of those objectives by compromise with the enemy of the moment was not only foreign but deeply repugnant to the American mind.

Then, too, America's view of the international system betrayed an ignorance and misunderstanding of the requirements for the maintenance of an effective international order. Because of our own relatively short historical experience as a nation-state and our even shorter active participation in world affairs, we did not have the perspective to assess the very unusual features of the post-1945 world. Lacking that perspective, we were encouraged to overstress its bipolarity. What was not appreciated was the degree to which bipolarity itself was the temporary reflection of a postwar aberration, that it deviated from the norm of international relations experience, and that it could not and would not last.

The country's worldview that emerged was Wilsonian, ideological, and impressed with military power. It was also heavily ethnocentric and it misperceived much of the nature and the framework of conflict among states. Its central weakness was its assumption that conflict is somehow unnatural, that violent changes in government anywhere are unnecessary and therefore unacceptable, and that to reconcile clashes of interest by the diplomatic method is less honorable than to discover the alleged "causes" of conflict and attack them root and branch either by military means or by direct appeals to peoples over the heads of their governments.

America's neo-Wilsonian view was a natural one to have in 1945 because Hitler had just provided the world with its most vivid example of the evil genius as statesman. The more active American foreign policy that commenced in 1947 and the extensive reorganization in Washington that accompanied it were deeply influenced by this newer perception of international relations. The emerging "born again" military-ideological theorists won most of the battles in the bureaucratic fights of 1945–1947. They would be Washington's main organizational planners thereafter for the duration of the Cold War.

America's concept of collective security also foundered on these attitudes. The original UN system never worked because it rested on the assumption of a five power concert in charge of the undertaking. When the original concept became hostage to the Russian-American conflict, a substitute system was quickly established, employing the General Assembly more significantly. Improvisation of UN emergency forces would serve to play a soothing role that supported American interests, either by moderating clashes that involved America's allies and friends (e.g., over decolonization) or by preventing direct Russian interventions. In this way, the "long peace" could be sustained—an international community in which we stressed reasonableness, the need to cooperate as equals and to subordinate selfish national interests to the higher common good. Yet at the same time, we came to the view that our very disinterestedness and international responsibilities thrust upon us the role of interpreter and trustee of the common good. We were the only country that could view the whole picture, while at the same time demanding nothing for ourselves. It was others who posssessed parochial and self-serving viewpoints.

AMERICA, THE THIRD WORLD, AND REVOLUTION

America during the Truman and Eisenhower years consistently displayed an unwillingness/inability to understand the burgeoning revolutionary experience then underway in the non-Western world. That incomprehension consisted of at least two misconceptions. Initially, we insisted upon interpreting these upheavals as if they were simply pale reflections of our own. They were not. They were, at bottom, intensely nationalist, anti-Western and even anti-rational movements. Tocqueville was one of the first to perceive the underlying reason for our negative responses to revolution: Americans, he noted, "feel no natural inclination for revolutions, but are afraid of them." Indeed, they "fear a revolution as the greatest of evils."[20] This attitude may be seen early in the century in the approach taken toward the Russian Revolution. "The inability of the Allied statesmen to picture to themselves the passions of the Russian civil war," said Kennan "was caused by the fact that we represent . . . a society in which the manifestations of evil have been carefully buried and sublimated in the social behavior of people. . . . For this reason . . . despite our widely traveled and outwardly cosmopolitan lives, the mainsprings of political behavior in such a country as Russia tend to remain concealed from our vision." [21]

In the early days of the country's involvement in Indochina, Louis Hartz would write that "it is the absence of the experience of social revolution which is at the heart of the whole American dilemma. . . . In a whole series of specific ways it enters into our difficulty of communication with the rest of the world. We find it difficult to understand Europe's 'social question'. . . . We are not familiar with the deeper social struggles of Asia and hence tend to interpret even reactionary regimes as 'democratic.' " [22] Vietnam represented the quintessence of our cultural inability to see some conflicts as revolutionary wars, and our un-willingness to honor our historical commitment to the right of self-determin-ation and equality in freedom.

From the beginning of our history, we supposed that the revolutionary impact of the American experience was our democracy, but in reality it was our abundance. The so-called "revolution of rising expectations" that came to mark the post-1945 era was an American-inspired phenomenon.[23] In response to this situation, the most effective means by which we could have promoted humanitarian and democratic principles abroad was not by merely applauding revolutions conducted in the name of such principles but by imparting to other parts of the world the means that we have developed for raising the standard of living. But we threw away this opportunity by failing to hold out the processes which others might emulate and by showing, instead, the end product—our standard of living—which they could only envy. Then we deepened the alienation by blaming other peoples for failing to embrace the political ideals which our standard of living supports.

But our misapprehension of revolution goes deeper than that. In the most ironic of senses, it may be fairly said that the only revolutions with which the American people have felt completely satisfied are the ones that did not succeed. After every revolution that failed, we indulged ourselves in assuming that its success would have fulfilled our ideals and were thus free to extend our hospitality to the revolutionists who were no longer welcome at home.[24]

The country's instinctive reaction in the face of movements for basic social transformation would betray an endemic incapacity for understanding and sympathy, since such experiences are alien to the American society's own traditions and needs. As such, America exhibited over time an unwillingness (some would say incapacity) to make a clear distinction between the commitment of Third World societies to revolutionary change and the occasional efforts by Moscow to expand its influence. America's foreign policy makers tended to see a communist involvement in every attack on the capitalist status quo anywhere. Moreover, Washington tended to misjudge the nature of the changes likely to occur in these situations, deceiving itself in the view that a majority of Third World countries could in fact achieve modernization by copying America's own approach of gradual and "peaceful" reform based on programs formulated, of course, in cooperation with America itself. The fact that this did not always happen and, further, that the forces of modernization were sometimes violent and therefore at odds with America's interests, was particularly difficult for Americans to comprehend.

Thus, uncomfortable with radical revolutionary programs of one sort or another, we set about implementing a policy designed to frustrate their consummations. The early experiences in Indochina and Guatemala would later be replicated in Cuba, the Dominican Republic, and Grenada. What resulted from the Korean War and the adoption of NSC-68 was an open-ended charter for intervention and covert activities worldwide, often in opposition to those who professed nonalignment in the developing struggle. An interesting paradox in this regard is that America, with its Puritan Ethic's moralist condemnation of war, would become an unrelenting critic of latter-day neutralists and non aligners, castigating them as immoral.

America's evolving foreign aid program mirrored these emphases. National pride and cultural arrogance, mixed with a dose of liberal humanitarianism, faith in progress, and above all, fear of communism, produced the nation's multibillion-dollar aid program.[25] This confusion of motive hampered the effort from the beginning. When a program is sold on conflicting ideological, military, and humanitarian grounds, it becomes hard to conceive let alone administer on national interest grounds. Confusion became institutionalized.[26] The net effect of all this aid tended to stimulate instability and dictatorship.

As aid, primarily in the form of military assistance, came to the fore during the Eisenhower era, some of the strongest partisans for such aid were "technology's own Maoists"—academics and politicians who gave new life to the missionary impulse. These ideologues argued that American military might, technological supremacy, and benevolent intentions gave our nation the opportunity and obligation to ease the nations of the earth toward modernization and stability: toward a full-fledged Pax Americana Technocratica. This doctrine appealed to the traditional prejudices of the American people. It contained and catered to an enormous self-satisfaction about the achievements of American society and the presumed uniqueness of our mission in the world. Unfortunately, these patriotic sentiments did not help us to understand the complex and varied problems of economic growth and social change in other lands. They partook of what Walter Lippmann called a fatal "universalism" in American thought, fueled by ignorance and a long experience of world isolation.

FOREIGN POLICY ELITES AND PUBLIC
OPINION: DANGEROUS LIAISONS

As the country became obsessed with extending the range of its ideology and protecting the American way of life, domestic American politics contributed heavily to the virulence and depth of the Cold War antagonism. There can be little question that Truman and the Republicans both sought to exploit the other's alleged "softness" on communism. Truman's early haste to brand opposition to his policies as "communist-inspired" contributed significantly to the politicization of the conflict, and was a major factor in the inauguration of a witchhunt in the country that was to culminate in the McCarthy era hysteria—a monster chase that had an enormously destructive impact on the country's foreign affairs structures.

Whatever else it was, the McCarthy phenomenon demonstrated that neither by history nor tradition was America prepared to play a world power role, and that the frustrations caused by this novel experience could be blamed on the very people who represented us overseas. This view, of course, was a direct challenge to the professional diplomat who by training is bound to see things differently. It is the tendency of the diplomatic profession to regard one's own country as simply one nation among many, not as a unique and exemplary "way of life" that exists to transcend vicious and/or irrelevant foreign traditions. In this sense, McCarthy was correct in calling the country's diplomats "un-American," for their experience tends to lead them to question the traditional self-image of American politics—the notion that ours is a unique society that the rest of the world should regard as the model for its own aspiring development. Instead, the insights of diplomacy suggest that other countries also have a sense of self-esteem and even mission, that the self-evident truths of the American experience are not always so evident to others, and that diversity rather than uniformity may be the best of all possible worlds. Moreover, those diplomatic services with the longest experience in handling international affairs are most prone to consider that problems left alone will go away—and sometimes they do. It is this sense of reality that the diplomat brings to the domestic, internal scene—one which is often viewed as threatening by the true believer.

As public opinion experts have long known, the most influential propaganda is that which reinforces pre-existing belief inclinations and persuades people to accept ideas (perhaps tentatively held) toward which they are already favorably predisposed. This was certainly the approach taken by the militants in the Truman and Eisenhower administrations. There is no question that the apparent sinister intentions of Soviet Russia played into the hands of the diehard anti-Bolsheviks in the country. "The threatening behavior of hawkish groups in rival countries becomes a most potent bargaining counter in domestic politics. It provides a most telling justification for large defense budgets and relaxation of controls over how military appropriations are spent. There is something for everybody and corresponding status benefits for those high in the political,

industrial, military and labor hierarchies."[27] Strong words and/or action is often
felt to be necessary to overcome domestic roadblocks. The result is that, in
Joseph Nye's words, "in order to shorten the lags in formulating consensus in
our democracy, the political leadership must exaggerate the degree of external
threat."[28]

The dynamics of the unfolding public consensus on the nature of
communism and Soviet Russia's role had another deleterious impact on the
country's ability to conduct rational foreign policy—the phenomenon of
bipartisanship. Few orientations in the post-World War II era would play so
destructive a role as the idea that when it came to issues of foreign policy, the
proper role of the "loyal opposition" was to avoid undue criticism of prevailing
policy. Because opposition in the Congress (and in the country as a whole)
might very well play into the hands of the enemy, it came to be viewed as un-
American for the opposition political party (not in possession of the White
House) to rock the boat. This pernicious viewpoint would prove to be
especially seductive in the wake of the Korean War, and would be contributory to
the ability of succeeding administrations to obtain enormous sums of money to
fund the country's Cold War controntationist policies. It would only be in the
midst of the Vietnam conflict in the 1960s that bipartisanship would finally
come under concerted attack—two decades after the Cold War had begun.

AMERICA'S TRADITION OF FOREIGN AFFAIRS AND THE ECONOMIC INTEREST

One question that continues to fascinate observers is the degree to which
America's decision to wage cold war with Soviet Russia was motivated by
economic considerations. As is usual in such matters, the record is a mixed bag.
Certainly at one level, the preponderant body of evidence points to the view that
the American foreign affairs tradition was a far more powerful influence on
foreign policy behavior than economic interes—a conclusion that came to be
shared by most members of America's intellectual elite themselves.[29]

Looking at this issue more broadly, a case can certainly be made that
America's aggressive policies were derived from the imperatives of its capitalist
free-enterprise system. There can be no doubt that America's economic needs
contribued to producing an activist, globalist, interventionist foreign policy.
This fact may be best understood in a reactive sense regarding Soviet Russia's
conduct. Russia's fundamental challenge had never been felt to be simply its
military power, but the threat it posed to the political and economic institutions
that had flourished during the Pax Britannica and were now the legacy of
America. And this reality is even more compelling when one examines the
country's approach to the question of revolution in less developed countries. But
the arguments of America's early Cold War revisionists that either a desire for
foreign markets for America's goods or capital, or a need for heavy military

spending to maintain aggregate domestic demand, fueled American foreign policy in the Cold War, have not stood well the test of time.

While there is some evidence for the view that competing institutional interest groups (for example, the Air Force in the late 1940s) impacted the elaboration of the country's Cold War policies, the notion that in America ideology was (and is) merely a superstructure erected (consciously or otherwise) to promote economic interests of the capitalist class needs to be rejected.[30] The growing disjunction of ends and means, locked in place in a mammoth civil-military bureaucratic machine, is a much more plausible explanation of our troubles than economic greed or imperialism. The bottom line remains that a small elite, with a long record of holding power and a monopoly of communication, would dominate American public life for much of the Cold War era. The social backgrounds of the authors of America's Cold War policies were nourished by a cultural ambience that stressed moderation, order, stabilitry, the rule of law—the progeny of a reformed protestantism that pervaded the institutions where Acheson, Nitze, Dulles, and many of their colleagues were educated.

MORALITY AND POLICY

The crucial issue of the interrelationship between morality and political action has been a fundamental dilemma of American foreign policy throughout most of the country's history.[31] Morality is not an abstract concept divorced from political reality, but flows from within that reality. It is concrete and immanent, and it is expressed in the decision maker's sense of responsibility for his actions. This viewpoint frees the decision maker from the beckoning will-of-the-wisp of moral crusades against evil that eventuate so often in strident calls for confrontation and war. Bismarck, on the eve of the Austro-Prussian War of 1866, warned those who would punish Austria for its wickedness: "Austria was no more wrong in opposing our claims than we were in making them."[32] Should not this approach have been a relevant morality for America in the Cold War?

The nation's inability to make this sort of distinction may be seen at several levels. On the one hand, for much of the twentieth century, American foreign policy was preoccupied with demons. There is a curious American belief and long-standing tendency of viewing our adversaries as implacable foes which, driven by dogmas or demons that are of their own motivation, are never open to influence by what we do. [33] Unfortunately, with regard to Soviet Russia, this led the nation into the disastrous realm of self-fulfilling prophecies. To treat Marxism-Leninism as the only serious alternative to our own form of government and society enhanced its importance far beyond any serious historical assessment. Moreover, the effect was to press toward the Leninist credo all those who, for whatever reason, tended to react against the West in general or

America in particular, or who feared our influence, rebelling against the status quo—which by and large was a status quo congenial to us.

America's conception of crisis should also be seen in this light, in particular the country's habitual tendency during these years to regard almost every Russian threat as equal and to view "today's" crisis as its primary manifestation. Due at least in some measure to this propensity on the part of American decision makers, there were far too few serious negotiations with the Russians on the major security questions during this period, and the sincerity of Moscow's positions were often left untested because of the unreadiness of Washington to get down to serious business on the terms that the Russians laid down from time to time.

Then there was the question of technology, most especially its military dimension. The stalemate in Korea led to a new emphasis on the necessity and promise of military technology—particularly the use of sophisticated electronic gear and weaponry, air power, and counterinsurgency—as the salvation of those resisting aggression.[34] Consequently, there occurred a "militarization of the thinking of the American political leadership as a result of the shibboleths of the Cold War and the new-found eminence of America as the leader of the free world."[35] Thus, one can say in this sense that over time our European policy became essentially a NATO operation, revolution viewed as a threat to be opposed with military force, that insurgency was at bottom a technical military problem, and crisis something one dealt with through the political-military machinery invented for the world of 1947.

The blind impetus that military power seems to follow once such power is acquired is almost irresistible—the need to improve it, to replace it, even exercise it like a horse. All of this contributed to the impasse. Like expanding industrial and commercial conglomerates, military establishments, given sufficient means, can become protean and insatiable, requiring vast amounts of funding just to stay in place.[36] Then, again, one of the elements in standard military thinking that is most destructive when imported into political decision making is its tendency to make "worst-case" analysis. One reason why the two sides failed in their interminable efforts to achieve meaningful disarmament was that America in particular placed too much emphasis on the purely technological aspects of arms control. While these technical issues were not inconsiderable by any means, the preponderant obstacles to disarmament were not technical or economic, but rather political and strategic—rooted in the nature of the power process and in the juxtaposition of values among the two states. Thus, in the end, while idealism continued to define the nation's purposes, the means used became increasingly expedient.

And, yet, militarization of the Cold War could not prevent expansion of Russian influence in the Middle East in the mid-1950s nor, later, in Cuba. Nor did it make the Russians behave in a way acceptable to Washington in Berlin in 1953, 1958, and 1961, or in Hungary in 1956. Nor did our many interventions abroad generate the sort of positive outcomes that one would have hoped.

Rather, all too often they contributed to an international precedent of expedient action, endorsement of ideological conflict, active sponsorship of civil violence, and conspiratorial politics. This is not to say that intervention is never legitimate, so long as we abandon the concept of a special role. But when one plays power politics and plays up the special role at the same time, trying to have the best of both worlds, then the difficulties are compounded.

AFTER THE FALL

The specter of Soviet Russia after 1945 may well have been the most stressful intrusion upon America's political consciousness since the Civil War. One has to go back to the British impact of the last century to detect a reaction to a single country that figured so deeply in America's formulation and understanding of its own being and destiny. Anticommunism and containment, and their concomitant necessity for interventionism, together constituted the heart of America's post-World War II universe, as she went out into the world at the head of those favoring preservation of the status quo. As such, we came to view international affairs framed as a contest between the pursuit of equality in freedom and totalitarianism—an approach that was, alas, outmoded almost from the beginning.

In the wake of Soviet Russia's collapse, numerous American political leaders spoke confidently of the "next American century" in which the "rule of law" will prevail as part of a "new world order." Like Henry Luce fifty years earlier, George Bush led the way in the early 1990s by predicting that America's pre-eminent world role would continue. Only the United States of America, he said, has the "moral leadership" to preside over the world's affairs.

Bush's views were echoed by a steady stream of free-flowing rhetoric, all reflecting the ageless moralist component of the American tradition of foreign policy, reiterating the notion that America continues to have a special duty to create a new world order. Shortly after Iraq's invasion of Kuwait, former Assistant Secretary of Defense Richard L. Armitage boasted that "those who so recently predicted America's imminent decline must now acknowledge that the United States alone possesses sufficient moral, economic, political, and military horsepower to jump-start and drive international efforts to curb international lawlessness."[37] This was, once again, America's "unipolar moment," with little likelihood in the foreseeable future of any other country being able to rival us.[38]

E. H. Carr once said that "the belief that whatever succeeds is right, and has only to be understood to be approved, must, if consistently held, empty thought of purpose, and thereby sterilize and ultimately destroy it."[39] He went on to point out that "any sound political thought must be based on elements of both utopia and reality. Where utopianism has become a hollow and intolerable sham, which serves merely as a disguise for the interests of the privileged, the realist performs an indispensable service in unmasking it. But pure realism can offer nothing but a naked struggle for power that makes any kind of international society impossible. The human will shall continue to seek an escape from the logical consequences of realism in the vision of an international order that, as soon as it crystallizes itself into concrete political form, becomes tainted with self-interest and hypocrisy, and must once more be attacked with the instruments of realism." [40]

For much of the twentieth century, America has struggled to locate the happy mean between these two lodestars—a search that has been greatly complicated by its tradition of foreign affairs. That she has yet to resolve the great dilemmas deeply embedded in her world view remains most unsettling indeed. The courage to change, however, is something that is learned from experience. In foreign policy, as in life, there is a "time and a season." Such courage frees a nation from the chimera of a foolish and crippling consistency. It shatters the illusion that every problem is the same as every other problem and puts a premium on political imagination. This was something that was not ever really learned or understood in the Truman and Eisenhower administrations. It is a problem that continues to plague America as the twentieth century comes to an end.

NOTES

1. He told U.S. Senators in January 1945, for instance, "that the Russians had the power in eastern Europe, that it was obviously impossible to have a break with them and that, therefore, the only practicable course was to use what influence we had to ameliorate the situation." Robert Dallek, *Franklin D. Roosevelt and American Foreign Policy*, 1932–1945 (New York: Oxford University Press, 1979), pp. 507–508.

2. "World War II: Thirty Years After," *Survey* (Winter-Spring, 1975): 35–36.

3. Cited in Ernest R. May, *"Lessons" of the Past: The Use and Misuse of History in American Foreign Policy* (London: Oxford University Press, 1993), p. 33.

4. Quoted in John Lewis Gaddis, *The Long Peace: Inquiries into the History of the Cold War* (New York: Oxford University Press, 1987), p. 36.

5. For many years after 1945, it became the practice of the State Department to react to notes from the Russians virtually as soon as they were received. Very little analysis was made of the impact of these quick responses on American foreign policy. Indeed, the fact that America possessed a more extensive and elaborate network of communications than almost any other country continued to tempt the government to react too quickly on the basis of incomplete information throughout the Cold War era. See, on this matter, John Franklin Campbell, *The Foreign Affairs Fudge Factory*, p. 73.

6. The action-reaction, perception-misperception syndrome that underlay the origins of the Cold War is ably explored by David Reynolds, "The 'Big Three' and the Division of Europe, 1945-48: An Overview," *Diplomacy and Statecraft* (London: Frank Cass & Co. Ltd., 1990): 117–136. For a presentation of a comprehensive psycho-social framework for comprehending the Russian-American confrontation, see Deborah Welch Larsen, *Origins of Containment: A Psychological Explanation*

(Princton, N. J.: Princeton University Press, 1985).

7. Russia lost one quarter of her capital equipment, 1700 towns, 70,000 villages, nearly 100,000 collective farms and more than twenty million dead during World War II. In 1945 Russia's steel production had sunk to only one-eighth that of America.

8. Louis Halle, *The Cold War as History* (New York: Macmillan, 1967), p. 11, makes this point.

9. *Expansion and Coexistence*, p. 399. On the Cold War viewed as a series of misperceptions and refractory images, see Ralph K. White, *Nobody Wanted War* (Garden City, N.Y.: Doubleday, 1970).

10. Just as the interventionism of Theodore Roosevelt and Woodrow Wilson stimulated the congressional isolationism of the 1920s and 1930s, later the memory of the deplorable congressional performance in foreign affairs during those years gave Americans in the post-1945 years an exalted conception of presidential power and pre-eminence.

11. For an interesting commentary on swings of the pendulum in American historical attitudes toward the outside world, see Knud Krakau, "American Foreign Relations: A National Style?" *Diplomatic History* (Summer, 1984): 253–272. See, also Geir Lundestad, "Commentary," in Ernest R. May's *American Cold War Strategy: Interpreting NSC–68* (Boston: St. Martin's Press, 1993), pp. 184–189.

12. *The Fifteen Weeks* (New York: Viking, 1955), p. 240.

13. On the policy semantics of the Truman era, see May, *"Lessons" of the Past*, pp. 19–86.

14. By way of contrast, if a particular state would be evaluated discreetly, it might appear unimportant to America's security. See Robert H. Johnson, "Exaggerating America's Stakes in Third World Conflicts," *International Security* (Winter, 1985-86): 32–68.

15. This approach was one pushed persistently by Dean Acheson during his years in Washington. Acheson placed his confidence in power manipulated by an elite. As a good elitist, the multitude bothered him, with the Congress and the UN not far behind in his mind's eye.

16. Notions, informed by Winthrop's original conception, that have also been reflected in many of America's greatest pronouncements—for example, Lincoln's second inaugural address, Wilson's declaration of war against Germany, Kennan's "X" article, Kennedy's inaugural address, and Bush's justification for war against Iraq.

17. *FRUS, 1950*, I, pp. 221–225.

18. See House of Commons Parliamentary Debates, Fifth Series, Col. 1456, December 14, 1950, p. 482.

19. If a sphere of influence can be defined as a determinate region within which a single power exerts a predominant influence which limits the independence or freedom of action of other political entities within it, then surely what America came to represent in the Caribbean and Central America qualifies. See, in this regard, John P. Vloyantes, *Spheres of Influence: A Framework of Analysis* (Tuscon: University of Arizona Press, 1970). For the Russian-American understanding in this regard, see Paul Keal, *Unspoken Rules and Superpower Dominance* (New York: Atherton Press, 1983).

20. Alexis de Tocqueville, *Democracy in America,* ed. Phillips Bradley (New York: Basic Books, 1958), p. 636 and pp. 638–639.

21. Kennan, *Russia and the West under Lenin and Stalin* (Baltimore, Md.: Penguin Books, 1958), pp. 142–143. See also Bernard S. Morris, *International Communism and American Foreign Policy* (New York: Atherton Press, 1966).

22. Louis Hartz, *The Liberal Tradition in America*, p. 306.

23. According to Andre Siegfried, cited in Isafel Cary Lundberg, "World Revolution, American Plan," *Harper's Magazine* (December 1948), p. 24, "The one really new gospel we introduced is the revelation after centuries of passively endured privations that a man may at last free himself of poverty, and most fantastic innovation of all, that he may actually enjoy his existence . . . and so, without our wishing it, or even knowing it, we appear as the terrible instigators of social change and revolution."

24. One wonders what sort of reception Castro would have received in America if he had failed.

25. During the long course of the Russian-American confrontation, over a thousand billion dollars of the public's tax revenues were spent on the military containment of Soviet Russia. On this point, see Ruth Leger Sivard, *World Military and Social Expenditures* (Leesburg, Va.: World Priorities, 1993).

26. One reason why our primary foreign aid dispensing agency was reorganized and/or renamed seven times after its initial conception.

27. Murray Edelman, *Politics as Symbolic Action* (Chicago: Markham, 1971), p. 73.

28. *The Making of America's Soviet Policy* (New Haven, Conn.: Yale University Press, 1984). pp. 6–7. See, also, D.W. Smythe and H.K. Wilson, "Cold War Mindedness and the Mass Media," in Neil D. Houghton, ed. *Struggle Against History: U.S. Foreign Policy in an Age of Revolution* (New York: Washington Square Press, 1968), pp. 59–78.

29. See Charles Kadushin, *The American Intellectual Elite* (Boston: Little, Brown, 1974). See also Allen Barton, "Consensus and Conflict Among American Leaders," *Public Opinion Quarterly* (Winter, 1974–1975): 23–37, in which he argues that the Cold War was maintained not by a military-industrial complex but a "political government group [consisting] of politicans and officials with a thirty-year investment in anti-communism as a political issue and a government policy."

30. See Michael H. Hunt, *Ideology and U.S. Foreign Policy* (Boston: Little, Brown, 1987), as well as Bruce Russett and Elizabeth Hanson, *Interest and Ideology, The Foreign Policy Beliefs of American Businessmen.* (San Francisco: W. H. Freeman, 1975).

31. For a provocative discussion of the relationship of morality and the nation's politics, see Henry Steele Commager, "A Historian Looks at Our Political Morality," *Saturday Review* (July 10, 1965): 15–18.

32. Quoted in A. J. P. Taylor, *Bismarck, The Man and the Statesman* (New York; Knopf, 1955), p. 115.

33. Kenneth W. Thompson, *Interpreters and Critics of the Cold War* (Washington, D.C.: University Press of America, 1978), p. 4.

34. In a study by the Brookings Institution, Barry M. Blechman and Steven S. Kaplan, *The Use of the Armed Forces as a Political Instrument* (Washington, D.C.: University Press of America, 1976), found that the U.S. deployed its military forces at least 215 times from 1945 to 1975, and Soviet Russia 115 times.

35. Bernard Brodie, book review in *Survival* (January, 1973), p. 33.

36. On this point, see Herbert York, *Race to Oblivion* (New York: Simon and Schuster, 1970).

37. Cited in Michael T. Klare, "The New World Order," *Progressive* (November, 1990), p. 16.

38. See Charles Krauthamer, "The Unipolar Moment," *Foreign Affairs* (November-December, 1991): 23–24.

39. *The Limitations of Realism, The Twenty Years' Crisis, 1919–1939* (London: Macmillan, 1962), p. 100.

40. *Ibid.*, p. 101.

Selected Bibliography

ARCHIVES AND MANUSCRIPT COLLECTIONS

Acheson, Dean. *Papers*. Harry S. Truman Library.

Archives of the Foreign Ministry of the Russian Federation (AVPRF), *Foreign Policy of the U.S.S.R. Related to the U.S*. Opus 39, No. 53, File 292, Reg. No. 37.

_____. *U. S. Embassy Notes and Letters to the Foreign Ministry*. U. S. Division Fund, Op. 128, File 154, Subfile 2.

_____. Opus 43, File 82, Subfile 21, "On Political Interrelations," (1957).

Central Party Archive of the Institute of Marxism-Leninism, Central Committee of the Communist Party of the Soviet Union, *Special Collection*, Opus 28, File 17,Unit 1206.

_____. *The United States, 1949*. Opus 133, File 218, Subfile 20.

Clifford, Clark M. *Papers*. Harry S. Truman Library.

Connally, Tom. *Papers*. Library of Congress.

Dulles, John Foster. *Papers*. Seeley Mudd Library, Princeton University.

Eisenhower, Dwight D. White House Office Files: *Office of the Special Assistant for National Security Affairs*. Dwight D. Eisenhower Library.

Forrestal, James. *Papers*. Seeley Mudd Library, Princeton University.

Hopkins, Harry L. *Papers*. Franklin D. Roosevelt Library.

Hull, Cordell. *Papers*. Library of Congress.

Jones, Joseph. *President's Secretary's File*. Harry S. Truman Library.

Kennan, George F. *Papers*. Seeley Mudd Library, Princeton University.

Roosevelt, Franklin D. *President's Secretary's File*. Franklin D. Roosevelt Library.

Russian Centre for Keeping and Studying Documents of Modern History, Central Committee of the Communist Party of the Soviet Union, *General Department*. Fund N17. Inventory No. 128, File 749. Report N 40.

Truman, Harry S. *President's Secretary's File*. Harry S. Truman Library.

U. S. Department of Defense. *Army Staff Records*. Record Group 319. Modern

Military Records Branch, National Archives.

_____. *Joint Chiefs of Staff Records.* Record Group 218. Modern Military Records Branch, National Archives.

_____. *Joint Intelligence Staff.* Record Group 218. Modern Military Records Branch, National Archives.

U. S. Department of State Archives, *1943–1945.* Record Group 59. National Archives.

_____. *Office of Intelligence Research Files.* Record Group 59. Diplomatic Branch, National Archives.

PUBLISHED DOCUMENTS

Anglo-Russian Political Conversations at Moscow, October 9-October 17, 1944, Public Record Office, London.

Baker, Ray Stannard, and William E. Dodd, eds. *Presidential Messages, Addresses and Public Papers (1917–1924)* by Woodrow Wilson, New York: Wiley, 1971.

Correspondence Between the Chairman of the Council of Ministers of the U.S.S.R and the Presidents of the U. S. A. and the Prime Ministers of Great Britain During the Great Patriotic War of 1941–1945. 2 vols. Moscow: Progress Publishers, 1957.

Current Digest of the Soviet Press.

Current Soviet Polices. Documentary Record of the Nineteenth Communist Party Congress and the Reorganization after Stalin's Death. Moscow.

Degras, Jane, ed. *Soviet Documents on Foreign Policy, 1917–1941.* London: 1951–1953.

Departments of War and Army. Record Group 165, *Records of the Operations Division, and Records of American-British Conversations.*

_____. Record Group 319, *Records of the Plans and Operations Division.*

_____. Record Group 107, Records of the Office of the Secretary of War, *Robert P. Patterson Papers*, safe file and general decimal file.

_____. Records of the Office of the Assistant Secretary of War, *Howard C. Peterson Papers*, classified decimal file.

_____. Record Group 335, Records of the Under-Secretary of the Army. *Draper/Voorhees files*, 1947–1950.

Documents on American Foreign Relations, Vols. I-IX (1939–1947). Boston and Princeton, 1940–1949.

Etzold, Thomas H., and John Lewis Gaddis, eds. *Containment: Documents on American Policy and Strategy, 1945–1950.* New York: Norton, 1978.

Ferrell, Robert H., ed. The Eisenhower Diaries. New York: Macmillan, 1981.

_____. *Off the Record: The Private Papers of Harry S. Truman.* New York: Macmillan, 1980.

Gaither Report. "Deterrence and Survival in the Nuclear Age." Washington, D. C.: Government Printing Office, 1976.

Galambos, Louis, ed. *The Papers of Dwight David Eisenhower*, 9 vols. Baltimore: Johns Hopkins University Press, 1970–1978.

Goldberg, Harold J. ed. *Documents on Soviet-American Relations*, Vol. I, "Intervention, Famine Relief, International Affairs, 1917–1933." Gulf Breeze:

Academic International Press, 1993.

House of Commons, *Parliamentary Debates*, Fifth Series, Vol. 374, Coll. 68–69.

Joint Chiefs of Staff. Record Group 218, National Archives. Washington, D.C.: Government Printing Office, 1971.

Joint Logistic Plans Committee, Military Intelligence Division.

Karalekas, Anne. "History of the Central Intelligence Agency," in U.S. Congress, Senate, Select Committee to Study Government Operations with Respect to Intelligence Activities, *Final Report: Supplementary Detailed Staff Reports on Foreign and Military Intelligence: Book IV*. Washington, D. C.: Government Printing Office, 1976.

Lilienthal, David E. *The Journals of David E. Lilienthal*. 2 vols. New York: Harper & Row, 1964.

Millis, Walter, ed. *The Forrestal Diaries*. New York: Knopf, 1951.

National Security Council. *Record Group 273*, Judicial, Fiscal, and Social Branch, National Archives. Washington, D.C.

Office of the Secretary of Defense. *Record Group 330*, National Archives, Washington, D.C.: Government Printing Office, 1977.

Rosenman, Samuel I., ed. *The Public Papers and Addresses of Franklin D. Roosevelt*. New York: Macmillan, 1941-1950.

Rush, Myron ed.. *The International Situation and Soviet Foreign Policy: Key Reports by Soviet Leaders from the Revolution to the Present*. Columbus: Ohio State University Press, 1970.

Pravda.

Proceedings, Inter-Allied Meeting Held in London at St. James Palace. London: H. M. Stationery Office, 1941.

Public Papers of the Presidents: Dwight D. Eisenhower, 1953-1961. Washington, D.C.: Government Printing Office, 1960–1961.

_____. *Harry S. Truman, 1945–1953*. Washington, D.C.: Government Printing Office, 1961–1966.

Sovetsko-amerikanskie otnosheniia. Moscow: Narkomindel, 1934.

Stimson, Henry L. *Diary*. Henry L. Stimson Papers. Yale University Library.

The United States and Russia: The Beginning of Relations, 1765–1815. Joint U.S.-Soviet Documentary Publishing Project. Washington, D.C.: Government Printing Office, 1980.

U.S. Arms Control and Disarmament Agency. *Arms Control and Disarmament Agreements*. Washington, D. C.: Government Printing Office, 1982.

U.S. Congress. Joint Economic Committee. *Profile of Mainland China*. Studies Prepared for the Committee. Washington, D.C.: Government Printing Office, 1968.

_____. House of Representatives. Committee on Armed Services. [Hearings] *Unification and Strategy*. Washington, D.C.: Government Printing Office, 1949.

_____. Committee on Foreign Affairs. [Hearings] *Assistance to Greece and Turkey*. Washington, D.C.: Government Printing Office, 1947.

_____. [Hearings] *U. S. Foreign Policy for a Post-War Recovery Program*. Washington, D.C.: Government Printing Office, 1948.

_____. Senate. Committee on Foreign Relations. [Hearings] *Assistance to Greece and Turkey*. Washington, D.C.: Government Printing Office,1947.

_____. [Hearings] *European Recovery Program*. Washington, D. C.: Government Printing Office, 1948.

_____. Historical Series: *Military Assistance Program, 1949*. Washington, D. C.: Government Printing Office, 1974.

_____. Historical Series: *Reviews of the World Situation, 1949–1950*. Washington, D.C.: Government Printing Office, 1974.

_____. [Hearings] *Legislative Origins of the Truman Doctrine*. Washington, D.C.: Government Printing Office, 1973.

_____. [Hearings] *Military Situation in the Far East*. Washington, D.C.: Government Printing Office, 1950.

_____. [Hearings] *NATO, Parts I* and *II*. Washington, D.C.: Government Printing Office, 1949.

_____. [Hearings] *Situation in the Middle East*. Washington, D.C.: Government Printing Office, 1956.

_____. [Hearings] *To Authorize the President to Undertake Economic and Military Cooperation with Nations in the General Area of the Middle East*. Parts 1 and 2. Washington, D.C.: Government Printing Office, 1957.

_____. *The United States and Communist China in 1949 and 1950: The Question of Rapproachement and Recognition*. Washington, D.C.: Government Printing Office, 1973.

_____. [Hearings] *The Vandenberg Resolution and N.A.T.O*. Washington, D.C.: Government Printing Office, 1973.

_____. *Senate Resolution 239*, 80th Congress, 2nd Session. Washington, D.C.: Government Printing Office, June 11, 1948.

U.S. Department of State. *American Foreign Policy, 1950–1955: Basic Documents*. Washington, D.C.: Government Printing Office, 1957.

_____. *American Foreign Policy: Current Documents, 1957*. Washington, D.C.: Government Printing Office, 1961.

_____. *Bulletin.*, November 4, 1945; September 15, 1946; June 15, 1947; January 23, 1950; April 28, 1952; February 2, 1953; March 22, 1954; May 23, 1955; August 1, 1955.

_____. *Memorandum on Certain Aspects of the Bolshevik Movement in Russia*. Washington, D.C.: Government Printing Office, 1919: 367–393.

_____. *NATO, 1949–1959: The First Ten Years*. Washington, D.C.: Government Printing Office, 1960.

_____. *Postwar Foreign Policy Preparation, 1939-1945*. Washington, D.C.: Government Printing Office, 1950.

_____. *United States Relations with China, with Special Reference to the Period 1944–1949*. [China White Paper]. Washington, D.C.: Government Printing Office, 1949.

_____. *Foreign Relations of the United States, 1942–1960*. Washington, D.C.: Government Printing Office, 1961-1985.

_____. *The Conference of Berlin (The Potsdam Conference)*, 2 volumes. 1945. Washington, D.C.: Government Printing Office, 1960.

_____. *The Conferences at Cairo and Tehran, 1943*. Washington, D.C.: Government Printing Office, 1961.

_____. *The Conferences at Malta and Yalta, 1945*. Washington, D. C.: Government Printing Office, 1955.

_____. *The Conferences at Washington and Quebec, 1943*. Washington, D.C.: Government Printing Office, 1970.

NEWSPAPERS AND MAGAZINES

Atlantic Monthly, February, 1942
Encounter, October, 1961
Fortune, March, 1944; September, 1945.
Life, June 3, 1946; June 10, 1946; May 14, 1952
New Republic, March 22, 1919
New York Times, September 30, 1945; October 14, 1945; February 19, 1946; March 28, 1947; March 2, 1949; July 25, 1954.
New York Times Magazine, December 3, 1961
Progressive, September, 1958; November, 1990.
Saturday Review, July 10, 1965
Survival, January, 1973
Time, March 18, 1946.
The Nation, October 28, 1961
The Reporter, January 23, 1958; September 14, 1954
U.S. News and World Report, January 17, 1958

UNPUBLISHED MATERIAL

Dulles, John Foster. *Oral History Collection*, Princeton University Library.
Hawkes, James R. "Stalin's Diplomatic Offensive: The Politics of the Second Front, 1941–1943," *Ph.D. dissertation*, University of Illinois, 1966.
Lytle, Mark. "American-Iranian Relations, 1941–1947 and the Redefinition of National Security," *Ph.D. dissertation*, Yale University, 1973.
Weisband, Edward, and Kent Trachte. "The Truman Doctrine: A Neo-Revisionist Critique," *Paper delivered at the Annual Meeting of the International Studies Association*, St. Louis, MO, March 18, 1977.
Wested, Odd Arne. "U.S.-Soviet Relations and Soviet Foreign Policy Toward the Middle East and Africa in the 1970s: Transcript from a Workshop at Lysebu," October 1-3, 1994, Norwegian Nobel Institute, 1995.

BOOKS AND ARTICLES

Acheson, Dean. *Present at the Creation: My Years at the State Department*. New York: Norton, 1969.
_____. "Progress Toward International Peace and Unity," *U. S. Department of State Bulletin*, April 28, 1952: 646–649.
_____. *Sketches from Life of Men I Have Known*. New York: Knopf, 1961.
Adams, Sherman. *Firsthand Report*. New York: Knopf, 1961.
Adromeit, Hannes. *Soviet Risk-Taking and Crisis Behaviour. A Theoretical and Empirical Analysis*. London: Allen & Unwin, 1982.
Alexander, Charles C. *Holding the Line: The Eisenhower Era, 1952–1961*. Bloomington: University of Indiana Press, 1975.
Allison, Graham. *Essence of Decision: Explaining the Cuban Missile Crisis*. Boston: Little, Brown & Co., 1976.
Almond, Gabriel. *The American People and Foreign Policy*. New York: Harcourt, Brace & World, 1950.

Alperovitz, Gar. *Atomic Diplomacy: Hiroshima and Potsdam*. New York: Simon and Schuster, 1965.

_____. *Cold War Essays*. Garden City, New York: Doubleday, 1970.

_____. *The Decision to Use the Atomic Bomb*. New York: Vintage Books, 1995.

Ambrose, Stephan E. *Rise to Globalism: American Foreign Policy Since 1938*, 6th ed. New York: Penguin Books, 1992.

_____. *The Supreme Commander: The War Years of General Dwight D. Eisenhower*. Garden City, N.Y.: Doubleday, 1970.

Anderson, Paul A. "What Do Decision Makers Do When They Make a Foreign Policy Decision?" in Charles F. Hermann, Charles W. Kegley, Jr., and James N. Rosenau, eds. *New Directions in the Study of Foreign Policy*. London: Allen and Unwin, 1986.

Anderson, Terry H. *The United States, Great Britain, and the Cold War, 1944–1947*. Boston: Houghton Mifflin, 1981.

Backer, John H. *The Decision to Divide Germany*. Durham, N. C.: Duke University Press, 1978.

Bailey, Thomas A. *America Faces Russia: Russian-American Relations from Early Times to Our Day*. Ithaca, N.Y.: Cornell University Press, 1950.

Baily, Samuel L. *The United States and the Development of Latin America, 1945–1975*. Boston: Little, Brown, 1976.

Balkhovitnikov, Nikolai N. *The Beginnings of Russian-American Relations, 1775–1815*. Cambridge, Mass.: Harvard University Press, 1976.

Barnet, Richard J. *Intervention and Revolution: America's Confrontation with Insurgent Movements Around the World*. Cleveland: Mentor Books, 1968.

_____. *Roots of War: The Men and Institutions Behind U.S. Foreign Policy*. Baltimore: Penguin Books, 1972.

_____,and Ronald E. Muller. *Global Reach: The Power of the Multinational Corpora-tions*. New York: Simon and Schuster, 1974.

Barnett, A. Doak. *Chinese Economic Strategy: The Rise of Mainland China*. Washington, D.C.: National Planning Association, 1959.

_____. *Communist China: The Early Years*. New York: Praeger, 1964.

Barton, Allen. "Consensus and Conflict Among American Leaders," *Public Opinion Quarterly*, Winter, 1974–1975: 23-37.

Bashkira, Nina N. ed. *The U.S. and Russia: The Beginning of Relations, 1765–1815*. Washington, D.C.: Government Printing Office, 1980.

Bell, Daniel. *The End of Ideology: On the Exhaustion of Political Ideas in the Fifties*. Glencoe, Ill.: The Free Press, 1960.

Beloff, Max. *Soviet Policy in the Far East, 1944–1951*. New York: Oxford University Press, 1953.

Berdyaev, Nicolas. *The Origin of Russian Communism*. London: Geoffrey Bles, 1948.

Berezhkov, Valentin. *At Stalin's Side: An Interpreter's Memoirs from the October Revolution to the Fall of the Dictator's Empire*. Birch Lane Press, 1994.

Beschloss, Michael. *Mayday: Eisenhower, Kennedy and the U-2 Affair*. New York: Harper and Row, 1986.

_____.*The Crisis Years, Kennedy and Khrushchev, 1960–1963*. New York: Harper-Collins, 1991.

Blechman, Barry M., and Steven S. Kaplan. *The Use of the Armed Forces as a Politi-*

cal Instrument. Washington, D.C.: University Press of America, 1976.

Bloomfield, Lincoln. *International Military Forces, Peacekeeping in an Armed and Disarming World.* Boston: Little, Brown, 1964.

Blum, Robert M. *Drawing the Line: The Origin of the American Containment Policy in East Asia.* New York: Norton, 1982.

Bohlen, Charles. *Witness to History, 1929–1969.* New York: Norton, 1973.

Borg, Dorothy, and Waldo Heinrichs, eds. *Uncertain Years: Chinese-American Relations, 1947–1950.* New York: Basic Books, 1980.

Borkenau, Franz. *European Communism.* New York: Harper and Bros., 1953.

Borowski, Harry R. *A Hollow Threat: Strategic Air Power and Containment before Korea.* Westport, Conn.: Greenwood Press, 1982.

Bowett, D. "The Use of Force in Self-Defence in International Law," *British Yearbook of International Law* 37, 1991: 166–183.

Boyle, Peter G. *American-Soviet Relations: From the Russian Revolution to the Fall of Communism.* New York: Routledge, 1993.

Bradley, John F. N. *Allied Intervention in Russia.* Lanham, Md.: University Press of America, 1984.

_____. *The Czechoslovak Legion in Russia, 1914–20.* Boulder, Colo.: Eastern Europe Monographs, 1991.

Brands, H. W., Jr. *Cold Warriors: Eisenhower's Generation and American Foreign Policy.* New York: Columbia University Press, 1988.

Brandt, Conrad. *Stalin's Failure in China.* Cambridge, Mass.: Harvard University Press, 1964.

Brecher, Michael, and Jonathan Wilkenfeld. *Crisis, Conflict and Instability.* Oxford: Pergamon Press, 1989.

_____. "International Crises and Global Instability: The Myth of the Long Peace," in Charles W. Kegley, Jr., ed.,*The Long Postwar Peace.* New York: HarperCollins, 1991: 85–104.

Brinkley, Douglas, and David R. Facey-Crowther, eds. *The Atlantic Charter.* New York: St. Martin's Press, 1994.

Brodie, Bernard. Book review, *Survival*, January, 1973: 32–34..

Brogan, Denis. "A Historian Questions Our Mood," *New York Times Magazine*, December 3, 1961: 17–20.

Brzezinski, Zbigniew. *The Soviet Bloc: Unity and Conflict*, rev. ed. Cambridge: Harvard University Press, 1967.

Buhite, Russell D. *Decisions at Yalta: An Appraisal of Summit Diplomacy.* Wilmington, Del.: Scholarly Resources, 1986.

Bullock, Alan. *Ernest Bevin: Foreign Secretary, 1945–1951.* London: Routledge, 1983.

Campbell, Angus, Gerald Gurin, and Warren E. Miller. *The Voter Decides.* Urbana: University of Illinois Press, 1954.

Caldwell, Dan. "Bureaucratic Foreign Policy Making," *American Behavioral Scientist*, September-October 1977: 87–110.

Campbell, David. *United States Foreign Policy and the Politics of Identity.* Minneapolis: University of Minnesota Press, 1992.

Campbell, John C. *Defense of the Middle East: Problems of American Foreign Policy*, rev. ed. New York: Macmillan, 1970.

Campbell, John Franklin. "An Interview with George F. Kennan," *Foreign*

Service Journal, August 1970: 15–24.

_____. *The Foreign Affairs Fudge Factory*. New York: Basic Books, 1971.

Campbell, Thomas M. *Masquerade Peace: America's UN Policy, 1944–1945*. Tallahasse: Florida State University Press, 1973.

Cantril, Hadley, and Mildred Strunk, eds. *Public Opinion, 1935–1946*. Princeton, N.J.: Princeton University Press, 1951.

Caridi, Ronald J. *The Korean War and American Politics: The Republican Party as a Case Study*. Philadelphia: Lippincott, 1968.

Carr, E. H. *The Limitations of Realism, The Twenty Years' Crisis, 1919–1939*. London: Macmillan, 1962.

Cattel, David. *Soviet Diplomacy and the Spanish Civil War*. Berkeley: University of California Press, 1955.

Chace, James. "Sharing the Atomic Bomb." *Foreign Affairs*, January-February 1996: 129–144.

Chamberlin, William Henry. "Russia: an American Problem," *Atlantic Monthly*, February 1942: 146–152.

Chen, Jian. *China's Road to the Korean War: The Making of the Sino-American Confrontation*. New York: Columbia University Press, 1994.

Churchill, Winston. *The Second World War*, Vol. V: *Closing the Ring*. Boston: Houghton Mifflin, 1951.

_____. Vol. IV: *The Hinge of Fate*. Boston: Houghton Mifflin, 1950.

_____. Vol. VI: *Triumph and Tragedy*. Boston: Houghton Mifflin, 1953.

Clark, Allen. *Barbarosa: The Russian-German Conflict, 1941–1945*. New York: William Morrow, 1965.

Claudin, Fernando. *The Communist Movement: From Comintern to Cominform*. New York: Monthly Review Press, 1975.

Clay, Lucius D. *Decision in Germany*. Garden City, N.Y.: Doubleday, 1950.

Clemens, Diane Shaver. *Yalta*. New York: Oxford University Press, 1970.

Cohen, Bernard. *The Public's Impact on Foreign Policy*. New York: Praeger, 1973.

Cohen, Stephen F. *Rethinking the Soviet Experience: Politics and History Since 1917*. New York: Oxford University Press, 1985.

Combs, Jerald D. *American Diplomatic History: Two Centuries of Changing Interpretations*. Berkeley: University of California Press, 1983.

Commager, Henry Steele. "A Historian Looks at Our Political Morality," *Saturday Review*, July 10, 1965: 15-18.

Condit, Kenneth W. *The History of the Joint Chiefs of Staff: The Joint Chiefs of Staff and National Policy, Vol. 2: 1947–1949*. Wilmington, Del.: Scholarly Resources, 1979.

Cook, Blance Wiessen. *The Declassified Eisenhower*. New York: Atheneum, 1981.

Cook, Fred J. "Juggernaut—the Welfare State," *The Nation*, October 28, 1961: 309-315.

Crankshaw, Edward. *Khrushchev*. London: Collins, 1966.

Crockatt, Richard. *The Fifty Years War: The United States and the Soviet Union in World Politics, 1941–1991*. New York: Routledge, 1995.

Cromwell, William C. "The Marshall Plan, Britain, and the Cold War," *Review of International Studies* 8 (October, 1982): 218–246.

Cummings, Bruce. *The Origins of the Korean War*. Vol. I: *Liberation and the Emergence of Separate Regimes, 1945–1947*. Princeton, N.J.: Princeton

University Press, 1981.

_____. *The Origins of the Korean War*. Vol. II: *The Roaring of the Cataract, 1947–1950*. Princeton, N.J.: Princeton University Press, 1990.

Dallek, Robert. *Franklin D. Roosevelt and American Foreign Policy, 1932–1945*. New York: Oxford University Press, 1979.

Dallin, Alexander. "Personality, Nationalism, and Commitment," Slavic Review, December 1977: 589–603.

Daniels, Robert. *Russia: Roots of Confrontation*. Cambridge, Mass.: Harvard University Press, 1985.

Davis, Lynn Etheridge. *The Cold War Begins: Soviet-American Conflict over Eastern Europe*. Princeton, N.J.: Princeton University Press, 1974.

Dawson, Raymond H. *The Decision to Aid Russia, 1941: Foreign Policy and Domestic Politics*. Chapel Hill: University of North Carolina Press, 1959.

de Tocqueville, Alexis. *Democracy in America*. ed., Phillips Bradley. New York: Vintage Books, 1958.

Deane, John R. *The Strange Alliance: The Story of Our Efforts at Wartime Cooperation with Russia*. New York: Norton, 1947.

Deibel, Terry L., and L. G. John. *Containing the Soviet Union: A Critique of U.S. Policy*. Washington, D.C.: Pergamon-Brasser's International Defense Publishers, 1987.

Deighton, Anne. "The 'Frozen Front': The Labour Government, the Division of Germany and the Origins of the Cold War, 1945–1947," *International Affairs* 65, 1987: 449–465.

De Santis, Hugh. *The Diplomacy of Silence*. New York: St. Martin's Press, 1980.

Destler, I. M., Leslie H. Gelb, and Anthony Lake. *Our Own Worst Enemy: The Unmasking of American Foreign Policy*. New York: Simon and Schuster, 1984.

Dinerstein, Herbert S. *Intervention Against Communism*. Baltimore: Johns Hopkins University Press, 1967.

Divine, Robert A. ed. *Blowing on the Wind: The Nuclear Test Ban Debate, 1954–1960*. New York: Norton, 1978.

_____. *Causes and Consequences of World War II*. Chicago: Quadrangle Books, 1969.

_____. *Eisenhower and the Cold War*. New York: Oxford University Press, 1981.

_____. *Foreign Policy and U.S. Presidential Elections, 1952–1960*. New York: Norton, 1974.

_____. *Roosevelt and World War II*. Baltimore: Johns Hopkins University Press, 1969.

_____. *Second Chance: The Triumph of Internationalism in America During World War II.*. New York: Oxford University Press, 1967.

Djilas, Milovan. *Conversations with Stalin*. London: Hart-Davis, 1962.

_____.*The New Class*. New York: Praeger, 1957.

Donovan, Robert J. *Conflict and Crisis*. New York: W. W. Norton, 1977.

_____. *Eisenhower: The Inside Story*. New York: Macmillan, 1956.

Dorn, Walter L. "The Debate Over American Occupation Policy in Germany in 1944–1945," *Political Science Quarterly*, December 1957: 481–501.

Draper, Theodore. *Castroism: Theory and Practice*. New York: Praeger, 1965.

Duiker, William J. *U.S. Containment Policy and the Conflict in Indochina*. Stanford, Calif.: Stanford University Press, 1994.

Dulles, Foster Rhea. *The Road to Teheran*. Princeton, N. J.: Princeton University Press, 1945.

Dulles, John Foster. "A Policy of Boldness," Life, May 14, 1952: 146–160.

_____. "Policy for Security and Peace," *Foreign Affairs*, April 1954: 349–361.

_____. "Thoughts on Soviet Foreign Policy and What to Do About It," *Life Magazine*, June 3 and 10, 1946: 113–26, 118–130.

Edelman, Murray. *Politics as Symbolic Action*. Chicago: Markham, 1971.

Eden, Anthony. *The Memoirs of Anthony Eden, Earl of Avon*. Vol. 2: *The Reckoning*. Boston: Little, Brown, 1965.

Edmonds, Robin. *Setting the Mould: The United States and Britain, 1945–1950*. New York: Norton, 1986.

Eisenhower, Dwight D. *The White House Years: Mandate for Change, 1953–1956*. Garden City, N.Y.: Doubleday, 1963.

_____. *The White House Years: Waging Peace, 1957-1961*. Garden City, N.Y.: Doubleday, 1965.

Emerson, Rupert, and Inis Claude, Jr. "The Soviet Union and the United Nations, An Essay in Interpretation," in Arthur E. Adams, ed. *Readings in Soviet Foreign Policy*. Boston: D. C. Heath, 1961: 268–286.

Emerson, William. "FDR (1941–1945)," in Ernest R. May, ed, *The Ultimate Decision: The President as Commander-in-Chief*. New York: Knopf, 1960: 135–177.

Engler, Robert. *The Politics of Oil: A Study of Private Power and Democratic Institutions*. New York: Macmillan, 1961.

Erickson, John. *The Road to Berlin*. London: Wiedenfeld & Nicholson, 1983.

Etheridge, Mark, and C. E. Black. "Negotiating on the Balkans, 1945-1947," in Raymond Dennett and Joseph E. Johnson, eds., *Negotiating with the Russians*. Boston: Houghton Mifflin, 1951.

Etzold, Thomas H., and John Lewis Gaddis, eds. *Containment: Documents on American Policy and Security, 1945–1950*. New York: Norton, 1978.

Eubank, Keith. *The Summit Conferences, 1919–1960*. Norman: University of Oklahoma Press, 1966.

Eudin, Xenia J., and Robert C. North. *Soviet Russia and the East, 1920–1927*. Stanford: Calif.: Stanford University Press, 1957.

Evangelista, Mathew A. "Stalin's Postwar Army Reappraised," *International Security, Winter, 1982–1983*: 111–128.

Fairbank, John K. *The U.S. and China*, 4th ed. Cambridge, Mass.: Harvard University Press, 1983.

Falk, Richard. "On Legal Tests of Aggressive War," *American Journal of International Law* 66, 1972: 560–571.

Farley, Philip J., Stephen S. Kaplan, and William H. Lewis. *Arms Across the Sea*. Washington, D.C.: Brookings Institution, 1978.

Feis, Herbert. *Between War and Peace: The Potsdam Conference*. Princeton, N. J.: Princeton University Press, 1960.

_____. *Churchill, Roosevelt, Stalin: The War They Waged and the Peace They Sought*. Princeton, N.J.: Princeton University Press, 1957.

Ferencz, Benjamin B. "Defining Aggression: Where It Stands and Where It's Going," *American Journal of International Law* 66, 1972: 491–508.

Filene, Peter J. *Americans and the Soviet Experiment, 1917–1933*. Cambridge, MA:

Harvard University Press, 1967.

Finer, Herman. *Dulles Over Suez.* New York: The Free Press, 1964.

Fireside, Harvey. "Analyzing Soviet Affairs: Methods and Myths," *Problems of Communism*, May-June 1972: 77–79.

Fischer, Louis. *The Road to Yalta: Soviet Foreign Relations, 1941–1945.* New York: Harper and Row, 1972.

Fish, M. Steven. "After Stalin's Death: The Anglo-American Debate Over a New Cold War," *Diplomatic History*, Fall, 1986: 343–353.

Flemming, D. F. *The Cold War and Its Origins, 1917–60.* Garden City, N. Y.: Doubleday, 1961.

Floyd, David. *Mao Against Khrushchev.* New York: Praeger, 1963.

Fontaine, Andre. *History of the Cold War from the October Revolution to the Korean War.* New York: Pantheon Books, 1968.

Foot, Rosemary. *The Wrong War: American Policy and the Dimensions of the Korean Conflict, 1950-53.* Ithaca, N.Y.: Cornell University Press, 1985.

Freeland, Richard M. *The Truman Doctrine and the Origins of McCarthyism: Foreign Policy, Domestic Politics, and Internal Security, 1946–1948.* New York: Knopf, 1972.

Gaddis, John Lewis. "Hanging Tough Paid Off," *Bulletin of the Atomic Scientists*, January/February 1989: 21–45.

_____. *Rethinking Cold War History.* Occasional Paper, Contemporary History Institute, Ohio University, March, 1955.

_____. *Russia, the Soviet Union and the United States: An Interpretive History.* New York: Wiley, 1978.

_____. *Strategies of Containment: A Critical Appraisal of Postwar American National Security Policy.* New York: Oxford University Press, 1982.

_____. "The Emerging Post-Revisionist Synthesis on the Origins of the Cold War," *Diplomatic History*, Summer 1983: 171–190.

_____. *The Long Peace: Inquiries into the History of the Cold War.* New York: Oxford University Press, 1987.

_____. "The Tragedy of Cold War History," *Foreign Affairs*, January/February 1994: 142–154.

_____. *The United States and the Origins of the Cold War, 1941–1947.* New York: Columbia University Press, 1972.

_____. *We Now Know: Rethinking Cold War History.* New York: Oxford University Press, 1997.

Gaitskell, Hugh. *The Challenge of Co-Existence.* Cambridge, Mass.: Harvard University Press, 1957.

Gamson, William, and Andre Modigliani. *Untangling the Cold War.* Boston: Little, Brown, 1971.

Gardner, Hall. *Surviving the Millennium: American Global Strategy, the Collapse of the Soviet Empire, and the Question of Peace.* Westport, Conn.: Praeger, 1994.

Gardner, Lloyd C. *A Covenant with Power: America and World Order from Wilson to Reagan.* New York: Knopf, 1984.

_____. *Architects of Illusion: Men and Ideas in American Foreign Policy, 1941—1949.* Chicago: University of Chicago Press, 1970.

_____. *Spheres of Influence: The Great Powers Partition Europe, from Munich to Yalta.* Chicago: Ivan R. Dee, 1993.

_____, Arthur Schlesinger, Jr., and Hans J. Morgenthau. *The Origins of the Cold War.* Waltham, Mass.: Ginn-Blaisdell, 1970.

Garrett, Stephen A. *From Potsdam to Poland: American Policy Toward Eastern Europe.* New York: Praeger, 1986.

Garson, Robert. "American Foreign Policy and the Limits of Power: Eastern Europe, 1946–1950," *Journal of Contemporary History,* July 1986: 73–91.

_____. "The Atlantic Alliance, Eastern Europe and the Origins of the Cold War," in H. C. Allen and Roger Thompson, eds., *Contrast and Connection: Bicentennial Essays in Anglo-American History.* New York: Macmillan, 1976.

Garthoff, Raymond L. "Sino-Soviet Military Relations," *Annals of the American Academy of Political and Social Science,* September 1963: 76–93.

Gati, Charles. "The Democratic Interlude in Postwar Hungary: Eastern Europe before Cominform," *Survey,* Summer 1984: 99–134.

Gillette, Philip. "Motivational-Ideational Analysis of Stalin's Foreign Policy," *Slavic Review,* December 1977: 574–578.

Gimbel, John. *The American Occupation of Germany: Politics and the Military, 1945–1949.* Stanford, Calif.: Stanford University Press, 1968.

Glennon, John P. "This Time Germany is a Defeated Nation, The Doctrine of Unconditional Surrender and Some Unsuccessful Attempts to Alter It, 1943–1944," in Gerald N. Grob, ed. *Statesmen and Statescraft of the Modern West.* Barre, Mass.: Barre Publishing Co., 1967: 109–151.

Goldhurst, Richard. *The Midnight War: The American Intervention in Russia, 1919–1920.* New York: McGraw-Hill, 1978.

Goncharov, Sergei N., John W. Lewis, and Xue Litai. *Uncertain Partners: Stalin, Mao and the Korean War.* Stanford, Calif.: Stanford University Press, 1993.

Gormly, James L. *The Collapse of the Grand Alliance, 1945–1948.* Baton Rouge and London: Louisiana State University Press, 1987.

Gowling, Margaret. *Britain and Atomic Energy, 1939–1945.* New York: Oxford University Press, 1964.

_____. *Science and Politics.* London: Birkbeck College, 1977.

Graebner, Norman A. "Cold War Origins and the Continuing Debate: A Review of the Literature," *Journal of Conflict Resolution,* March 1969: 123–132.

Grayson, Benson L. *Russian-American Relations in World War I.* New York: Unger, 1979.

_____, ed. *The American Image of Russia, 1917–1977.* New York: Unger, 1979.

Green, David. *The Containment of Latin America.* Chicago: Quadrangle Books, 1971.

Greenfield, Kent Roberts. *American Strategy in World War II: A Reconsideration.* Baltimore: Johns Hopkins University Press, 1963.

Griffith, William E. *Albania and the Sino-Soviet Rift.* Cambridge, Mass.: The MIT Press, 1963.

_____. *The Sino-Soviet Rift.* Cambridge, Mass.: Harvard University Press, 1964.

Gruber, Helmut. *Soviet Russia Masters the Comintern: International Communism in the Era of Stalin's Ascendency.* Garden City, N.Y.: Doubleday, 1974.

Gurtov, Melvin. *The First Vietnam Crisis: Chinese Communist Strategy and United States Involvement, 1953–1954.* New York: The Free Press, 1967.

Haas, Ernst. "Types of Collective Security," *American Political Science Review,* March 1955: 40–62.

Haffner, Sebastian. "Germany, Russia and the West," *Encounter*, October 1961: 14-21.

Hahn, Werner. *Postwar Soviet Politics: The Fall of Zhadanov and the Defeat of Moderation, 1946–1953*. Ithaca, N.Y.: Cornell University Press, 1982.

Halle, Louis. *The Cold War as History*. New York: Macmillan, 1967.

Halperin, Ernst. *The Triumphant Heretic*. London: Heinemann, 1958.

Hammett, Hugh B. "America's Non-Policy in Eastern Europe and the Origins of the Cold War," *Survey*, Autumn, 1973: 144–162.

Hammond, Paul Y. "Directives for the Occupation of Germany: The Washington Controversy," in Harold Stein, ed., *American Civil-Military Relations*. Birmingham: University of Alabama Press, 1963.

_____. "NSC-68: Prologue to Rearmament," in Warner P. Schilling et al., *Strategy, Politics and Defense Budgets*. New York: Macmillan, 1962: 303–317.

Hammond, Thomas T., ed. *Witnesses to the Origins of the Cold War*. Seattle: University of Washington Press, 1982.

Harbaugh, William Henry. *Power and Responsibility: The Life and Times of Theodore Roosevelt*. New York: Macmillan, 1961.

Hathaway, Robert M. *Ambiguous Partnership: Britain and America, 1944–1947*. Boston: Little, Brown, 1981.

Hartz, Louis. *The Liberal Tradition in America: An Interpretation of American Political Thought since the Revolution*. New York: Harcourt, Brace and World, 1955.

Hawkes, James R. "Stalin's Diplomatic Offensive: The Politics of the Second Front, 1941-1943". Ph.D. dissertation. Urbana: University of Illinois, 1966.

Herkin, Gregory. *The Winning Weapon: The Atomic Bomb and the Cold War, 1945–1950*. New York: William Morrow, 1980.

Hermann, Charles F. "Bureaucratic Constraints on Innovation in American Foreign Policy," in Charles W. Kegley, Jr., and Eugene R. Wittkopf, eds., *Perspectives on American Foreign Policy*. New York: St. Martin's Press, 1983: 390–409.

Herring, George C. "Lend Lease to Russia and the Origins of the Cold War, 1944–1945," *Journal of American History*, June 1969: 93–114.

Herz, Martin F. *Beginnings of the Cold War*. New York: McGraw-Hill, 1966.

Hewlett, Richard G., and Oscar E. Anderson, Jr. *A History of the United States Atomic Energy Commission: The New World, 1939–1946*. University Park: Pennsylvania State University Press, 1962.

Hewlett, Richard G., and Francis Duncan. *Atomic Shield: A History of the U.S. Atomic Energy Agency*, II, *1947–1952*. University Park: Pennsylvania State University Press, 1969.

Hoffman, George W., and Fred W. Neal. *Yugoslavia and the New Communism*. New York: Praeger, 1962.

Hoffmann, Stanley. *Gulliver's Troubles: Or the Setting of American Foreign Policy*. New York: McGraw-Hill, 1968.

Hogan, Michael J. *The Marshall Plan: America, Britain and the Reconstruction of Western Europe, 1947–1952*. New York: Cambridge University Press, 1987.

Holborn, Hajo. *American Military Government: Its Organization and Policies*. Washington, D.C.: Government Printing Office, 1947.

Holloway, David. *Stalin and the Bomb: The Soviet Union and Atomic Energy,*

1939–1956. New Haven, Conn.: Yale University Press, 1994.

_____. *The Soviet Union and the Arms Race*, 2d ed. New Haven, Conn.: Yale University Press, 1984.

Holsti, Ole. "Cognitive Dynamics and Images of the Enemy," in Samuel A. Kirkpatrick and Laurence K. Pettit, eds., *The Social Psychology of Political Life.* Belmont, Calif: Duxbury Press, 1972: 227–242.

_____. "The Belief System and National Images: A Case Study," *Journal of Conflict Resolution*, September, 1962: 245–271.

Hoopes, Townsend. *The Devil and John Foster Dulles.* Boston: Little, Brown, 1973.

Horowitz, Irving Louis. *Three Worlds of Development.* New York: Basic Books, 1966.

Houn, Franklin W. *To Change a Nation: Propaganda and Indoctrination in Communist China.* Glencoe, Ill.: Free Press, 1961.

Hughes, Emmet John. *The Ordeal of Power: A Political Memoir of the Eisenhower Years.* New York: Knopf, 1963.

Hull, Cordell. *Memoirs.* Vol. 2. New York: Macmillan, 1948.

Hunt, Michael H. *Ideology and U.S. Foreign Policy.* Boston: Little, Brown, 1987.

_____. "The Long Crisis in U.S. Diplomatic History," *Diplomacy*, Winter, 1992: 41–58.

Huntington, Samuel P. *The Common Defense: Strategic Programs in National Politics.* New York: Columbia University Press, 1961.

Immerman, Richard H. "Eisenhower and Dulles: Who Made the Decisions?" *Political Psychology*, Autumn 1979: 3–20.

_____. *The CIA in Guatemala: The Foreign Policy of Intervention.* Austin: University of Texas Press, 1982.

Ingram, Kenneth. *History of the Cold War.* London: Darwen Finlayson, 1955.

Isaacson, Walter, and Even Thomas. *The Wise Men: Six Friends and the World They Made. Acheson, Bohlen, Harriman, Kennan, Lovett, McCloy.* New York: W.W. Norton, 1986.

Jacobson, Harold K. *America's Foreign Policy.* New York: Random House, 1965.

Janis, Irving L. *Groupthink: Psychological Studies of Policy Decisions and Fiascoes.* Boston: Houghton Mifflin, 1983.

Jensen, Kenneth M., ed. *Origins of the Cold War: The Novikov, Kennan and Roberts "Long Telegrams" of 1946.* Washington, D.C.: United States Institute of Peace, 1991.

Jervis, Robert. "Impact of the Korean War on the Cold War," *Journal of Conflict Resolution,* December 1980: 47–61.

_____. *Perception and Misperception in International Politics.* Princeton, N.J.: Princeton University Press, 1976.

Jian, Chen. "The Sino-Soviet Alliance and China's Entry into the Korean War," *Cold War International History Project Working Paper No. 1*, Woodrow Wilson International Center. Princeton, N.J.: Princeton University Press, 1991.

Johnson, Robert H. "Exaggerating America's Stakes in Third World Conflicts," *International Security,* Winter, 1985–1986: 32–68.

Jones, Joseph M. *The Fifteen Weeks.* New York: Viking, 1955.

Kadushin, Charles. *The American Intellectual Elite.* Boston: Little, Brown, 1974.

Kahin, George McT. *Intervention: How America Became Involved in the War.* New

York: Knopf, 1986.

_____, and John W. Lewis. *The United States in Vietnam.* New York: Delta Books, 1967.

Kaplan, Fred. *Dubious Specter: A Skeptical Look at the Soviet Threat.* New York: Institute for Policy Studies,1980.

Katzenstein, Peter J., ed. *The Culture of National Security.* New York: Columbia University Press, 1996.

Kaufman, Burton I. *The Korean War: Challenges in Crisis, Credibility, and Command.* New York: Macmillan, 1986.

Keal, Paul. *Unspoken Rules and Superpower Dominance.* New York: Atherton Press, 1983.

Kegley, Chares W., Jr., and Eugene Witthopf. *American Foreign Policy: Pattern and Process.* New York: St. Martin's Press, 1987.

Kennan, George F. *Memoirs, 1925–1950.* Boston: Little, Brown, 1957.

_____. Russia and the West under Lenin and Stalin.

_____. *Russia, The Atom and the West.* London: Oxford University Press, 1958.

_____. *Soviet-American Relations, 1917–1920: The Decision to Intervene.* Princeton, N. J.: Princeton University Press, 1958.

_____. "The U.S. and the Soviet Union, 1917–1976," *Foreign Affairs,* July 1976: 670–690.

_____. "World War II: Thirty Years After," *Survey,* Winter-Spring 1975: 28–41.

Kertesz, Stephen D. *East Central Europe and the World: Development in the Post-Stalin Era.* East Bend, Ind.: University of Notre Dame Press, 1962.

_____. *The Last European Peace Conference. 1946.* Paris: University Press of America, 1985.

Kettle, Michael. *Churchill and the Archangel Fiasco, November 1918–July 1919.* New York: Routledge, 1992.

Kimball, Warren F. The Juggler: Franklin Roosevelt as Wartime Statesman. Princeton, N. J.: Princeton University Press, 1991.

Kistiakowsky, George B. *A Scientist at the White House.* Cambridge, Mass.: Harvard University Press, 1976.

Klare, Michael T. *American Arms Supermarket.* Austin: University of Texas Press, 1984.

_____. "The New World Order," *Progressive,* November, 1990: 13–22.

Kliuchnikov, I. V., and Andrei Sabanin, eds. Mezhdunarodnaia politika noveishego vremeni v dogovorakh, notakh i deklaratsiiakh. Moscow: Narkomindel, 1925–1928. II: 89–94.

Kolko, Gabriel. *The Politics of War: The World and United States Foreign Policy, 1943–1945.* New York: Random House, 1968.

Kovrig, Bennett. *Of Walls and Bridges: The United States and Eastern Europe.* New York: New York University Press, 1991.

_____. *Myth of Liberation: John Foster Dulles and the Diplomacy of the Cold War.* New York: Basic Books, 1973.

Krakau, Knud. "American Foreign Relations: A National Style?" *Diplomatic History,* Summer 1984: 253–272.

Krauthamer, Charles. "The Unipolar Moment," *Foreign Affairs,* November-December 1991: 18–29.

Krock, Arthur. *Memoirs: Sixty Years on the Firing Line.* New York: Macmillan,

1968.

Kunz, Diane B., ed. *The Diplomacy of the Crucial Decade*. New York: Columbia University Press, 1994.

Lacouture, Jean, and Philippe Devillers. *La Fin d'une Guerre, Indochine 1954*. Paris: Editions du Seuil, 1960.

LaFeber, Walter. *America, Russia and the Cold War, 1945–1992*, 7th ed. New York: Knopf, 1993.

_____. "American Policy-Makers, Public Opinion, and the Outbreak of the Cold War, 1945–1950," in Yonosuke Nagai and Akira Iriye, eds., *The Origins of the Cold War in Asia*. New York: Columbia University Press, 1977: 40–57.

_____. *Inevitable Revolutions*. New York: Norton, 1984.

_____. *The American Age*. New York: Norton, 1989.

_____. *The Origins of the Cold War, 1941–1947: A Historical Problem with Interpretations and Documents*. New York: Wiley, 1971.

Lancaster, Donald. *The Emancipation of French Indo-China*. London: Oxford University Press, 1961.

Lapp, Ralph. *The Weapons Culture*. Baltimore: Johns Hopkins University Press, 1969.

Laqueur, Walter Z., and Leopold Labedz, eds. *Polycentrism*. New York: Praeger, 1962.

_____. "Soviet Policy in the Middle East," *The World Today*, II, No. 12, December, 1955): 519–529.

Larsen, Deborah Welch. *Origins of Containment: A Psychological Explanation*. Princeton, N.J.: Princeton University Press, 1985.

Laserson, Max H. *The American Impact on Russia: Diplomatic and Ideological, 1784–1917*. New York: Macmillan, 1950.

Leffler, Melvyn P. *A Preponderance of Power: National Security, the Truman Administration, and the Cold War*. Stanford, Calif.: Stanford University Press, 1992.

_____. "The American Conception of National Security and the Beginnings of the Cold War, 1945-48," *The American Historical Review*, April 1984: 346–381.

_____. "The United States and the Strategic Dimensions of the Marshall Plan," *Diplomatic History* 12, 1988: 277–306.

_____, and David S. Painter, eds. *Origins of the Cold War: An International History*. New York: Routledge, 1994.

Leighton, Richard M., and Robert W. Coakley. *Global Logistics and Strategy, 1940–1943: United States Army in World War II: The War Department*. Washington, D.C.: Government Printing Office, 1968.

Lenczowski, John. *Soviet Perceptions of U.S. Foreign Policy: A Study of Ideology, Power and Consensus*. Ithaca, N.Y.: Cornell University Press, 1982.

Lerche, Charles O., Jr. *Foreign Policy of the American People*, 3rd ed. Englewood Cliffs, N.J.: Prentice-Hall, 1967.

_____. *Last Chance in Europe*. Chicago: Quadrangle Books, 1967.

Lerner, Daniel, and Raymond Aron, eds. *France Defeats the E.D.C*. New York: Praeger, 1957.

Lerski, Jerzy Jan. *A Polish Chapter in Jacksonian America: The United States and the Polish Exiles of 1831*. Madison: University of Wisconsin Press, 1958.

Levering, Ralph B. *American Opinion and the Russian Alliance, 1939–1945*.

Chapel Hill: University of North Carolina Press, 1976.

Levin, N. Gordon, Jr. *Woodrow Wilson and World Politics: America's Response to War and Revolution.* New York: Oxford University Press, 1968.

Lippmann, Walter. *The Cold War: A Study in United States Foreign Policy.* New York: Macmillan, 1947.

_____. *The New Republic,* March 22, 1919, Supplement.

_____. *The Communist World and Ours.* Boston: Little, Brown, 1959.

Lowenthal, Richard. *World Communism: The Disintegration of a Secular Faith.* New York: Oxford University Press, 1964.

Lundberg, Cary. "World Revolution, American Plan," *Harper's Magazine,* December, 1948: 23–28.

Lundestad, Geir. "Empire by Invitation: The United States and Western Europe, 1945–1952," *Journal of Peace Research* 23, 1986: 263–277.

_____. *The American Non-Policy towards Eastern Europe, 1943–1947: Universalism in an Area Not of Essential Interest to the United States.* New York: Basic Books, 1975.

Lyon, Peter. *Eisenhower: Portrait of the Hero.* Boston: Houghton Mifflin, 1974.

Lytle, Mark H. *The Origins of the American Alliance, 1941–1953.* New York: Holt Rinehart and Winston, 1987.

MacDonald, Douglas J. "Communist Bloc Expansion in the Early Cold War: Challenging realism, Refuting Revisionism," *International Security,* Winter, 1995/1996: 152–188.

Maclaurin, John. *The United Nations and Power Politics.* New York: Harper, 1951.

Maier, Charles. "Alliance and Autonomy: European Identity and U.S. Foreign Policy Objectives in the Truman Years" in Michael Lacey, ed., *The Truman Presidency.* New York: Woodrow Wilson International Center, and Cambridge University Press, 1989: 273–298.

Maisky, Ivan. *Memoirs of a Soviet Ambassador. The War: 1939–1943.* New York: Scribner & Sons, 1967.

Mark, Edward. "American Policy toward Eastern Europe and the Origins of the Cold War, 1941–1946: An Alternative Explanation," *Journal of American History* 68 (September, 1981): 313–336.

_____. "Charles E. Bohlen and the Acceptable Limits of Soviet Hegemony in Eastern Europe," *Diplomatic History,* 3 (Spring, 1979): 201–213.

Martin, Laurence W. "The American Decision to Rearm Germany," in Harold Stein, ed., *American Civil-Military Relations: A Book of Case Studies.* Birmingham: University of Alabama Press, 1963: 646–651.

Mastny, Voytech. *Russia's Road to the Cold War: Diplomacy, Warfare and the Politics of Communism, 1941–1945.* New York: Columbia University Press, 1979.

_____. "Stalin and the Prospects of a Separate Peace in World War II." *American Historical Review,* December 1971: 1365–1388.

_____. "The Cassandra in the Foreign Commissariat: Maxim Litvinov and the Cold War." *Foreign Affairs* 54, January 1976: 366-376.

Matloff, Maurice, and Edwin L. Snell. *Strategic Planning for Coalition Warfare: 1941–1942: United States Army in World War II. The War Department:* Washington, D.C.: Government Printing Office, 1953.

_____. *Strategic Planning for Coalition Warfare, 1943–1944: The U. S. Army in*

World War II. The War Department: Washington, D.C.: Government Printing Office, 1959.

May, Ernest R., ed. *American Cold War Strategy: Interpreting NSC-68.* Boston: St. Martin's Press, 1993.

_____. *"Lessons" of the Past: The Use and Misuse of History in American Foreign Policy.* New York: Oxford University Press, 1973.

_____. "The Cold War," in Joseph S. Nye, Jr. ed., *The Making of America's Soviet Policy.* New Haven, Conn.: Yale University Press, 1984.

_____. "The U.S., the Soviet Union and the Far Eastern War, 1941–1945," *Historical Review,* May 1955: 153–163.

Mayer, Arno J. *Politics and Diplomacy of Peacemaking: Containment and Counter-revolution at Versailles, 1918–1919.* New York: Knopf, 1968.

Mazour, Anatole G. *Finland Between East and West.* New York: Van Nostrand, 1956.

MccGwire, Michael. "The Genesis of Soviet Threat Perceptions," in Melvyn Leffler and David S. Painter, eds., *Origins of the Cold War: An International History.* New York: Routledge, 1994: 54–76.

McCagg, William O., Jr. *Stalin Embattled, 1943–1948.* Detroit, Mich.: Wayne State University Press, 1978.

McCormick, Thomas J. *America's Half-Century: U.S. Foreign Policy in the Cold War.* Baltimore: Johns Hopkins University Press, 1989.

McFadden, David W. *Alternative Paths: Soviets and Americans, 1917–1920.* New York: Oxford University Press, 1993.

McFarland, Stephen L. "The Iranian Crisis of 1946 and the Onset of the Cold War," pp. 239–256, in Melvyn P. Leffler, and David S. Painter, eds. *Origins of the Cold War: An International History.* New York: Routledge, 1994.

McLane, Charles B. *Soviet Policy and the Chinese Communists, 1931–1946.* New York: Columbia University Press, 1958.

McNeil, Robert H. "Roosevelt through Stalin's Spectacles," *International Journal of Politics,* Winter 1963: 194–206.

McSherry, James E. *Stalin, Hitler and Europe.* Vol. II. Cleveland, Ohio: World Publishing Co., 1968.

Mecham, J. Lloyd. *The United States and Inter-American Security, 1889–1960.* Austin: University of Texas Press, 1961.

Medvedev, Roy. *Khrushchev, A Biography.* Oxford: Blackwell, 1982.

Melanson, Richard A., and David Mayers, eds. *Reevaluating Eisenhower: American Foreign Policy in the 1950s.* Urbana: University of Illinois Press, 1987.

Messer, Robert L. *The End of Alliance: James F. Byrnes, Roosevelt, Truman and the Origins of the Cold War.* Chapel Hill: University of North Carolina Press, 1982.

_____. "World War II and the Coming of the Cold War," in John M. Carroll and George C. Herring, eds., *Modern American Diplomacy.* New York: Norton, 1986.

Mileykovsky, A. G., ed. *International Affairs After the Second World War.* Moscow: Progress Publishers, 1962.

Miller, Nicola. *Soviet Relations with Latin America, 1959–1987.* New York: Cambridge University Press, 1989.

Miner, Stephen Merrit. *Between Churchill and Stalin: The Soviet Union, Great Bri-

tain and the Origins of the Grand Alliance. Chapel Hill: University of North
        Carolina Press, 1988.

_____. "Revelations, Secrets, Gossip and Lies," *New York Times Book Review*,
        May 14, 1995: 19–21.

Miscamble, Wilson D. "Anthony Eden and the Truman-Molotov Conversations,
        April 1945," *Diplomatic History*, Spring 1978: 167–180.

_____. George F. Kennan and the Making of American Foreign Policy, 1947-1950.
        Princeton, N.J.: Princeton University Press, 1992.

Morgenthau, Hans. "Alliances in Theory and Practice," in Arnold Wolfers, ed.,
        Alliance Policy in the Cold War. Baltimore: Johns Hopkins University Press,
        1959: 202–221.

Morgenthau, Henry, Jr. *Germany Is Our Problem*. New York: Norton, 1945.

Morris, Bernard S. *Communism, Revolution and American Policy*. Durham, N.C.:
        Duke University Press, 1987.

_____. *International Communism and American Foreign Policy*. New York:
        Atherton Press, 1966.

Morris, Charles L. *Iron Destinies, Lost Opportunities: The Arms Race Between the
        U.S.A. and the U.S.S.R., 1945–1987*. New York: Harper and Row, 1988.

Morton, Louis. "Soviet Intervention in the War With Japan," *Foreign Affairs*, July
        1962: 653–657.

Mosely, Leonard. *Power Play: Oil in the Middle East*. New York: Atheneum, 1973.

Mosely, Philip E. "Some Techniques of Negotiation," in Raymond Dennett and
        Joseph E. Johnson, eds., *Negotiating with the Russians*. Boston: Little,
        Brown, 1951.

_____. "The Occupation of Germany: New Light on How the Zones Were
        Drawn," *Foreign Affairs*, July 1950: 580–604.

Moyle, Paul D. "A Policy of Percentages? British Policy and the Balkans after the
        Moscow Conference of October, 1944," *International History Review*, February
        1987: 47–63.

Murphy, Robert. *Diplomat Among Warriors*. Garden City, N.Y.: Doubleday, 1964.

Murray, Brian. "Stalin, the Cold War, and the Division of China: A Multi-Archival
        Mystery," *Cold War International History Project Working Paper No. 12*,
        Woodrow Wilson International Center. Princeton, N.J.: Princeton University
        Press, 1995.

Naimark, Norman. *The Russians in Germany: A History of the Soviet Zone of Oc-
        cupation, 1945–1949*. Cambridge, Mass.: Harvard University Press, 1995.

Narinsky, Mikhail M. "The Soviet Union and the Marshall Plan," *Cold War Interna-
        tional History Project Working Paper No. 11*, Woodrow Wilson International
        Center. Princeton, N. J.: Princeton University Press, 1994.

Neustadt, Richard E., and Ernest R. May. *Thinking in Time: The Uses of History for
        Decision-Makers*. New York: Free Press, 1986.

Noel-Baker, Philip. *The Arms Race*. London: Atlantic, 1958.

Nye, Joseph. *The Making of America's Soviet Policy*. New Haven, Conn.: Yale
        University Press, 1984.

O'Brien, Conor Cruise. *To Katanga and Back*. London: Hutchinson, 1962.

Okonogi, Masao. "The Domestic Roots of the Korean War," in Yonosuke Nagai and
        Akira Iriye, eds., *The Origins of the Cold War in Asia*. New York: Knopf, 1977:
        299–320.

Oneal, John. *Foreign Policy Making in Times of Crisis*. Columbus: Ohio State University Press, 1982.

Osgood, Robert E. *Limited War: The Challenge to American Strategy*. Chicago: University of Chicago Press, 1961.

Pach, Chester J., Jr. "The Containment of United States Military Aid to Latin America, 1944–1949," *Diplomatic History* 6, 1982: 232–234.

Parmet, Herbert S. *Eisenhower and the American Crusades*. New York: Macmillan, 1972.

Parrish, Scott D. "The Turn toward Confrontation: The Soviet Reaction to the Marshall Plan, 1948," *Cold War International History Project Working Paper No. 9*. Woodrow Wilson International Center. Princeton, N.J.: Princeton University Press, 1994.

Paterson, Thomas Graham, ed. *Cold War Critics: Alternatives to American Foreign Policy in the Truman Years*. Chicago: Quadrangle Books, 1971.

_____. *Meeting the Communist Threat: Truman to Reagan*. New York: Oxford University Press, 1988.

_____. *On Every Front: The Making of the Cold War*. New York: Norton, 1979.

_____. "Presidential Foreign Policy, Public Opinion, and Congress: The Truman Years," *Diplomatic History*, Winter 1979: 31–49.

_____. *Soviet-American Confrontation: Postwar Reconstruction and the Origins of the Cold War*. Baltimore: Johns Hopkins University Press, 1973.

_____. "The Abortive American Loan to Russia and the Origins of the Cold War, 1943-1946," *Journal of American History*, June 1969: 70–92.

Patterson, George W. *Peking Versus Delhi*. New York: Praeger, 1964.

Pechatnov, Vladimir O. "The Big Three After World War II: New Documents on Soviet Thinking about Post-War Relations with the United States and Great Britain" *Cold War International History Project Working Paper No. 13*. Woodrow Wilson International Center. Princeton, N.J.: Princeton University Press, 1995.

Perlmutter, Amos. *FDR and Stalin: A Not So Grand Alliance, 1943–1945*. Coumbia and London: University of Missouri Press, 1993.

Pickett, William B. "The Eisenhower Solarium Notes," *Society for Historians of American Foreign Relations Newsletter*, June 1985: 1–8.

Pollard, Robert A. *Economic Security and the Origins of the Cold War, 1945–1950*. New York: Columbia University Press, 1985.

Pogue, Forrest C. *George C. Marshall: Organizer of Victory*. New York: Holt, Rinehart and Winston, 1973.

_____. *The Supreme Command. United States Army in World War II: The European Theater of Operations*. Washington, D.C.: Government Printing Office, 1954.

Pollard, Robert A. *Economic Security and the Origins of the Cold War, 1945–1950*. New York: Columbia University Press, 1985.

Porter, K. H., and D. B. Johnson, *National Party Platforms, 1840–1956*. Urbana: University of Illinois Press, 1961.

Prados, John. *Presidents' Secret Wars: The CIA and Pentagon Covert Operations Since World War II*. New York: Morrow, 1986.

_____. *The Soviet Estimate: U.S. Intelligence Analysis and Russian Military Strength*. New York: Dial, 1982.

Pruesson, Ronald W. *John Foster Dulles: The Road to Power.* New York: Macmillan, 1982.

Rahe, Stephen H. *Eisenhower and Latin America: The Foreign Policy of Anticommunism.* Chapel Hill: University of North Carolina Press, 1988.

Range, Willard. *FDR's World Order.* Athens: University of Georgia Press, 1959.

Rapoport, Anatol. *The Big Two: Soviet-American Perceptions of Foreign Policy.* New York: Bobbs-Merrill, 1971.

Ravenal, Earl. *Never Again: Learning from America's Foreign Policy Failures.* Philadelphia: Temple University Press, 1978.

Rearden, Steven. *The Evolution of American Strategic Doctrine: Paul Nitze and the Soviet Challenge.* Boulder, Colo.: Westview Press, 1984.

Rees, David. *Korea, The Limited War.* New York: St. Martin's Press, 1964.

Resis, Albert. "The Stalin-Churchill Secret 'Percentages' Agreement on the Balkans, Moscow, October, 1944," *American Historical Review*, April 1978: 368–387.

Reyman, Karl, and Herman Singer. "The Origins and Significance of Eastern European Revisionism" in Leopold Labedz, ed., *Revisionism: Essays on the History of Marxist Ideas.* New York: Praeger, 1962: 215–222.

Reynolds, David. "The 'Big Three' and the Division of Europe, 1945–48: An Overview," *Diplomacy and Statecraft* 1, 1990: 117–136.

_____. *The Creation of the Anglo-American Alliance, 1937–1941: A Study in Competitive Co-operation.* London: Routledge, 1981.

Richter, James. "Reexamining Soviet Policy towards Germany during the Beria Interregnum," *Cold War International History Project Working Paper No. 3.* Woodrow Wilson International Center. Princeton, N.J.: Princeton University Press, 1993.

Ridgway, Matthew B. *Soldier: Memoirs of Matthew B. Ridgway.* New York: Harper, 1956.

Roberts, Chalmers. "The Day We Didn't Go To War," *The Reporter*, September 14, 1954: 31–35.

_____. "The Pious Truculence of John Foster Dulles," *The Reporter*, January 23, 1958: 220–223.

Robinson, James W. "Disengagement in Europe: An Evaluation of U.S. Policy," in Andrew W. Cordier, ed., *Columbia Essays in International Affairs*, New York: Columbia University Press, 1966: 31–58.

Roosevelt, Kermit. *Countercoup: The Struggle for the Control of Iran.* New York: Praeger, 1979.

Rosati, Jerel. *The Politics of United States Foreign Policy.* Fort Worth: Harcourt, Brace and Jovanovich, 1993.

Rosenberg, David Allen. "The Origins of Overkill: Nuclear Weapons and American Strategy, 1945–1960," *International Security,* Spring 1983: 11–27.

Rosenberg, William G., and Marilyn B. Young. *Transforming Russia and China: Revolutionary Struggle in the Twentieth Century.* New York: Oxford University Press, 1982.

Rosenfeldt, Niels Erik. *Knowledge and Power: The Role of Stalin's Secret Chancellery in the Soviet System of Government.* Copenhagen: Rosenkilde and Bagger, 1978.

Rosenthal, Joel H. *Righteous Realists: Political Realism, Responsible Power, and American Culture in the Nuclear Age.* Baton Rouge: Louisiana State University

Press, 1991.

Ross, Graham, ed. *The Foreign Office and the Kremlin: British Documents on Anglo-Soviet Relations, 1941–1945.* Cambridge: Routledge, 1985.

Rostow, W. W. *The United States in the World Arena.* New York: Harper, 1960.

Rothstein, Andrew, ed. *Soviet Foreign Policy During the Patriotic War*, Vol. 2. London: Oxford University Press, 1946.

Rotter, Andrew J. *The Path to Vietnam: Origins of the American Commitment to Southeast Asia.* Boulder, Colo.: Sage Publications, 1987.

Rovere, Richard. *Senator Joe McCarthy.* Cleveland, Ohio: Atheneum, 1959.

Rubenberg, Cheryl A. *Israel and the American National Interest.* Boston: St. Martin's Press, 1986.

Rush, Myron, ed. *The International Situation and Soviet Foreign Policy: Key Reports by Soviet Leaders from the Revolution to the Present.* Columbus: Ohio State University Press, 1970.

Russett, Bruce, and Elizabeth Hanson. *Interest and Ideology: The Foreign Policy Beliefs of American Businessmen.* San Francisco: Freeman, 1975.

Saiic, Liliana. *The Great Powers and Rumania, 1944–1946: A Study of the Early Cold War Era.* Boulder, Colo.: Eastern Europe Monographs, 1992.

Sainsbury, Keith. *The Turning Point.* New York: Norton, 1985.

Sander, Alfred D. "Truman and the National Security Council, 1945–1947," *Journal of American History*, 59, 1972–193: 369–388.

Schacter, Oscar. "The Lawful Resort to Unilateral Use of Force," *Yale Journal of International Law* 10, 1985: 271–293.

Schecter, Jerold, and Vyacheslav Luchkov, trans. and ed. *Khrushchev Remembers: The Glasnost Tapes.* Boston: Little, Brown, 1990.

Schelling, Thomas. *Arms and Influence.* New Haven, Conn.: Yale University Press, 1966.

Schick, Jack M. *The Berlin Crisis, 1958–1962.* Philadelphia: Lippincott, 1971.

Schlesinger, Arthur, Jr. "Origins of the Cold War," *Foreign Affairs*, October 1967: 22–52.

_____. *The Coming of the New Deal.* Boston: Houghton Mifflin, 1958.

Schlesinger, Stephen, and Steven Kinzer. *Bitter Fruit: The Untold Story of the American Coup in Guatemala.* New York: Anchor Books, 1981.

Schnabel, James F. *The History of the Joint Chiefs of Staff: The Joint Chiefs of Staff and National Policy*, Vol. 1: *1945–1947.* Wilmington, Del.: Scholarly Resources, 1979.

Schram, Stuart. *The Political Thought of Mao Tse-tung.* New York: Praeger, 1969.

Schuman, Frederick L. *American Policy Toward Russia Since 1917.* New York: Macmillan, 1928.

Seton-Watson, Hugh. *From Lenin to Khrushchev.* New York: Praeger, 1961.

Sherry, Michael. *Preparing for the Next War: American Plans for Postwar Defense, 1941–1945.* New Haven, Conn.: Yale University Press, 1977.

Sherwin, Martin J. "The Atomic Bomb and the Origins of the Cold War," *American Historical Review*, October 1973: 945–968.

Sherwood, Robert E. *Roosevelt and Hopkins: An Intimate History*, rev. ed. New York: Macmillan, 1950.

Shulman, Marshall D. *Stalin's Foreign Policy Reappraised.* Cambridge, Mass.: Harvard University Press, 1963.

Simmons, Robert R. *The Strained Alliance: Peking, P'yongyang, Moscow and the Politics of the Korean War*. New York: Knopf, 1975.

Sivard, Ruth Leger . *World Military and Social Expenditures*. Leesburg, Va.: World Priorities, 1993.

Smith, Howard K. *The State of Europe*. New York: Knopf, 1949.

Smith, Jean Edward. *The Defense of Berlin*. Baltimore: Johns Hopkins University Press, 1963.

Smith, M. Brewster. "The Personal Setting of Public Opinion: A Study of Attitudes Toward Russia," *Public Opinion Quarterly*, Winter 1947–1948: 507–523.

Smith, Robert F. *What Happpened in Cuba? A Documentary History*. New York: Praeger, 1963.

Smythe, D. W., and H. K. Wilson. "Cold War Mindedness and the Mass Media," in Neil D. Houghton, ed. *Struggle Against History: U.S. Foreign Policy in an Age of Revolution*. New York: Washington Square Press, 1968: 59–78.

Snell, John L. *Wartime Origins of the East-West Dilemma Over Germany*. New Orleans: Louisiana State University Press, 1959.

Soapes, Thomas F. "A Cold Warrior Seeks Peace: Eisenhower's Strategy for Nuclear Disarmament," *Diplomatic History*, Winter 1980: 51–64.

Starobin, Joseph. "Origins of the Cold War," *Foreign Affairs*, July 1969: 228–254.

Stavrakis, Peter J. *Moscow and Greek Communism, 1944–1949*. Ithaca, N.Y.: Cornell University Press, 1989.

Stebbins, Richard P. *The United States in World Affairs*. New York: Harper, 1961.

Stillman, Edmund, ed. *Bitter Harvest: The Intellectual Revolt Behind the Iron Curtain*. New York: Praeger, 1959.

Stimson, Henry, and McGeorge Bundy. *On Active Service in Peace and War*. New York: Norton, 1948.

Stoler, Mark A. *The Politics of the Second Front. American Military Planning and Diplomacy in Coalition Warfare, 1941–1942*. Westport, Conn.: Greenwood Press, 1977.

_____. "The 'Second Front' and the American Fear of Soviet Expansion, 1941–1943," *Military Affairs*, October 1975: 136–140.

Stookey, Robert W. *America and the Arab States: An Uneasy Encounter*. New York: Holt, Rinehard, and Winston, 1975.

Stuart, Douglas, and Harvey Starr. "The 'Inherent Bad Faith Model' Reconsidered: Dulles, Kennedy and Kissinger," *Political Psychology*, Fall/Winter 1981–1982: 1–33.

Stueck, William W., Jr. *The Road to Confrontation: American Policy toward China and Korea., 1947–1950*. Chapel Hill: University of North carolina Press, 1981.

_____ed. *The Soviet Takeover of the Polish Eastern Provinces, 1939–1941*. New York: St. Martin's, 1991.

Talbott, Strobe, trans. and ed. *Khrushchev Remembers*. Boston: Little, Brown, 1970.

_____. *The Master of the Game: Paul Nitze and the Nuclear Peace*. New York: Knopf, 1988.

Taubman, William. *Stalin's American Policy: From Entente to Detente to Cold War*. New York: Norton, 1982.

Taylor, A. J. P. "End of the Grand Alliance," *History of the Second World War*. London: BPC Publishing Co., 1966.

_____. *Bismark, The Man and the Statesman*. New York: Knopf, 1955.

Taylor, Maxwell D. *The Uncertain Trumpet*. New York: Harper & Row, 1959.

Theoharis, Athan. *The Yalta Myths*. Columbia: University of Missouri Press, 1970.

Thomas, Brian. "Ideology and the Cold War," in David Carlton and Herbert M. Levine, eds., *The Cold War Debated*. New York: McGraw-Hill, 1988: 172–179.

Thompson, Kenneth W. *Cold War Theories*. Vol. I: *World Polarization, 1943–1953*. Baton Rouge: Louisiana State University Press, 1981.

_____. *Interpreters and Critics of the Cold War*. Washington, D.C.: University Press of America, 1978.

Thornton, Richard C. *The Comintern and the Chinese Communists, 1928–1931*. Seattle: University of Washington Press, 1969.

Tivnan, Edward. *The Lobby: Jewish Political Power and American Foreign Policy*. New York: Free Press, 1987.

Toulouse, Mark G. *The Transformation of John Foster Dulles*. New York: Basic Books, 1985.

Trachtenberg, Marc. "A 'Wasting Asset': American Strategy and the Shifting Nuclear Balance, 1949–1954," *International Security* 13 (Winter, 1988/1989): 5–49.

_____. "The Berlin Crisis," *History and Strategy*. Princeton: Princeton University Press, 1991: 169–234.

Trask, Roger R. "The Impact of the Cold War on United States-Latin American Relations, 1945–1949," *Diplomatic History*, Summer 1977: 48–64.

Truman, Harry S. *Memoirs. I: Year of Decisions*. Garden City, N.Y.: Doubleday, 1955.

_____. *Memoirs. II: Years of Trial and Hope*. Garden City, N.Y.: Doubleday, 1956.

Truman, Margaret. *Harry S Truman*. New York: Morrow, 1973.

Tuchman, Barbara. "If Mao Had Come to Washington: An Essay in Alternatives," *Foreign Affairs*, October 1972: 44–64.

Tucker, Robert W. "The Emergence of Stalin's Foreign Policy," *Slavic Review*, December 1977: 579–588.

Tugwell, Rexford Guy. *Off Course: From Truman to Nixon*. New York: Praeger, 1971.

Ulam, Adam. *Expansion and Coexistence: Soviet Foreign Policy, 1917–1973*, 2d ed. New York: Praeger, 1974.

Uldricks, Teddy V. *Diplomacy and Ideology: The Origins of Soviet Foreign Relations, 1917–1930*. Beverly Hills, Calif.: Sage, 1979.

Unterberger, Betty. *America's Siberian Expedition, 1918–1920*. New York: Greenwood Press, 1969.

Varga, Evgenni. "Anglo-American Rivalry and Partnership: A Marxist View," *Foreign Affairs*, July 1947: 583–595.

_____. *Changes in the Economy of Capitalism as a Result of the Second World War*. Moscow: Gospolitizdat, 1946.

Vloyantes, John P. *Spheres of Influence: A Framework of Analysis*. Tuscon: University of Arizona Press, 1970.

Ward, Patricia Dawson. *The Threat of Peace*. New York: Oxford University Press, 1979.

Warth, Robert. *The Allies and the Russian Revolution*. Chapel Hill: University of North Carolina Press, 1954.

Weathersby, Kathryn. "Korea, 1945–1950: To Attack or Not to Attack? Stalin, Kim Il Sung, and the Prelude to War," *Cold War International History Project Bulletin 5*, Spring 1995: 1–9.

_____. "Soviet Aims in Korea and the Origins of the Korean War, 1945–1950," *Cold War International History Project Working Paper No. 8*. Woodrow Wilson International Center. Princeton, N.J.: Princeton University Press, 1994.

_____. "The Soviet Role in the Early Phase of the Korean War: New Documentary Evidence," *Journal of American-East Asian Relations*, Winter 1993: 425–458.

Welch, Richard E., Jr. *Response to Revolution: The United States and the Cuban Revolution, 1959–1961*. Chapel Hill: University of North Carolina Press, 1985.

Welch, William. *American Images of Soviet Foreign Policy*. New Haven, Conn.: Yale University Press, 1970.

Welch, William, and Jan F. Triska, "Soviet Foreign Policy Studies and Foreign Policy Models," *World Politics*, July, 1971: 704–717.

Welles, Sumner. *Seven Decisions that Shaped History*. New York: Random House, 1950.

Wells, Samuel F., Jr. "Sounding the Tocsin: NSC–68 and the Soviet Threat," *International Security*, Fall 1979: 116–158.

Wested, Odd Arne. *Cold War and Revolution*. New York: Columbia University Press, 1993.

_____. "Fighting for Friendship: Mao, Stalin, and the Sino-Soviet Treaty of 1950," *Cold War International History Project Bulletin 8–9*, Summer, 1995.

Westerfield, H. Bradford. *Foreign Policy and Party Politics: Pearl Harbor to Korea*. New Haven, Conn.: Yale University Press, 1955.

Wheeler-Bennett, John. *The Forgotten Peace: Brest-Litovsk, March, 1918*. New York: Norton, 1939.

_____, and Anthony Nicholls. *Semblance of Peace: The Political Settlement After the Second World War*. New York: Macmillan, 1972.

Whelen, Joseph G. *Soviet Diplomacy and Negotiating Behavior*. New York: Knopf, 1982.

Whelen, Richard. *Drawing the Line: The Korean War, 1950–1953*. Boston: Little, Brown & Co., 1990.

Whitcomb, Roger S. *An Uncertain Tradition: The American Approach to Foreign Affairs*. Westport, Conn.: Greenwood Press, 1998.

White, Ralph K. *Nobody Wanted War*. Garden City, N.Y.: Doubleday, 1970.

Williams, William Appleman. *American-Russian Relations, 1781–1947*. New York: Octagon, 1971.

Wilson, Joan Hoff. *Ideology and Economics: U.S. Relations with the Soviet Union, 1918–1933*. St. Louis: University of Missouri Press, 1974.

Wise, David, and Thomas B. Ross. *The U-2 Affair*. New York: Columbia University Press, 1962.

Wittner, Lawrence S. *American Intervention in Greece, 1943–1949*. New York: St. Martin's Press, 1982.

Wohlforth, William Curti. *The Elusive Balance: Power and Perceptions during the Cold War*. Ithaca, N.Y.: Cornell University Press, 1993.

Woodward, Llewellyn. *British Foreign Policy in the Second World War*. London:

Her Majesty's Stationery Office, 1971.

Yergin, Daniel. *Shattered Peace: The Origins of the Cold War and the National Security State*. Boston: Houghton Mifflin Co., 1977.

York, Herbert. *Race to Oblivion*. New York: Simon and Schuster, 1970.

Young, Roland. *Congressional Politics in the Second World War*. New York: Macmillan, 1956.

Zagoria, Donald. "Choices in the Postwar World: Containment and China," in Charles Gati, ed., *Caging the Bear: Containment and the Cold War*. New York: Bobbs-Merrill, 1974: 109–127.

_____. *The Sino-Soviet Conflict, 1956–1961*. Princeton, N.J.: Princeton University Press, 1962.

_____. *Vietnam Triangle: Moscow, Peking, Hanoi*. New York: Pegasus, 1967.

Zhadanov, Andrei. "The International Situation," in *The Strategy and Tactics of World Communism*, Supplement I. Washington, D.C.: Government Printing Office, 1948: 212–230.

Zhang, Shu Guang. *Deterrence and Strategic Culture: Chinese-American Confrontations, 1949–1958*. Ithaca, N.Y.: Cornell University Press, 1992.

Zimmerman, William. "Choices in the Postwar World: Containment and the Soviet Union," in Charles Gati, ed., *Caging the Bear: Containment and the Cold War*. New York: Bobbs-Merrill, 1974: 85–108.

_____. "Elite Perspectives and the Explanation of Soviet Foreign Policy," *Journal of International Affairs*, 1970: 84–98.

_____. "Russia and the International Order," *Survey*, January 1966: 209–223.

_____, and Robert Axelrod. "The Lessons' of Vietnam and Soviet Foreign Policy," *World Politics*, October 1981: 1–24.

Zinner, Paul. *Communist Strategy and Tactics in Czechoslovakia, 1918–1948*. New York: Praeger, 1963.

Zubok, Vladislav. "Khrushchev and the Berlin Crisis, 1958–1962," *Cold War International History Project Working Paper No. 6*. Woodrow Wilson International Center. Princeton, N.J.: Princeton University Press, 1994.

_____, and Constantine Pleshakov. *Inside the Kremlin's Cold War: From Stalin to Khrushchev*. Cambridge, Mass.: Harvard University Press, 1996.

Index

About the Author

ROGER S. WHITCOMB is Professor of International Relations/Foreign Policy Studies and Director of International Studies at Kutztown University. A widely published specialist in Russian-American relations, his latest book is *The American Approach to Foreign Affairs: An Uncertain Tradition* (Praeger, 1998).

ISBN 0-275-96253-9

90000>

HARDCOVER BAR CODE

**Sidney Silverman Library
and Learning Resource Center
Bergen Community College
400 Paramus Road
Paramus, NJ 07652-1595**